# Touring the

# California Wine Country

**Gulf Publishing Company**
Houston, Texas

# Touring the

# California

# Wine

# Country

Dennis Schaefer

# *Touring the California Wine Country*

Gulf Publishing Company
Book Division
P.O. Box 2608 □ Houston, Texas 77252-2608

10   9   8   7   6   5   4   3   2   1

**Library of Congress Cataloging-in-Publication Data**

Schaefer, Dennis
    Touring the California wine country / Dennis Schaefer.
       p.   cm.
    Includes bibliographical references and index.
    **ISBN 0-88415-159-X**
    1. Wine and wine making—California—Guidebooks.
  2. California—Guidebooks.   I. Title.
TP557.S268   1997
641.2′2′0974—dc21                      97-17680
                                                  CIP

# CONTENTS

# California Wine Country Regions

1. Mendocino/Lake Counties
2. Northern Sonoma
3. Sonoma Valley
4. Napa Valley
5. Sierra Foothills
6. Santa Cruz
7. Bay Area
8. Monterey
9. Central Coast
10. Santa Barbara County
11. Temecula

# INTRODUCTION

*A*t last count, California boasts more than 800 wineries, most of which are open to the public. The wine boom of the 1970s fueled the increase in wineries, as consumers began to develop a thirst not only for more wine but for better quality wine. For example, when the Robert Mondavi Winery opened in 1966, it was only the twenty-third winery in Napa Valley; now there are more than 200 wineries in that small region! In fact, Napa Valley attracts more visitors per year than Disneyland. Today, no matter which major metropolitan area of California you visit, within a ninety-minute drive you'll find vineyards and wineries. Every part of the state, from Mendocino to Temecula, has a familiarity with the grape.

Most wineries welcome visitors for obvious reasons. Once you taste how good the wines are (often for free), you'll no doubt want some to take home with you. But although that's encouraged, it's not the main purpose. The big picture is that each winery will treat you to its wines, history, and hospitality, hoping that you'll feel a connection with the winery once you get home and then regularly consume its wines. Conversely, fans of particular wines often visit the respective wineries when on vacation to see their favorite wines manufactured. They want to pay homage to the source.

No matter what reasons bring you to a winery tasting room, pure fun and enjoyment should rank high on your list. People should consume wine just like orange juice or milk—without fanfare or hoopla. Unfortunately, sometimes wine seems intelligible only to a secret society of wine geeks who communicate via enological technobabble ("fragrant floral proclivities of musk melon with overtones of $H_2S$ that shine like high-beam headlights in a fog"). Huh???

I once had a conversation about this misconception with the public relations director of a well-respected, medium-sized winery. In the summer, the winery would conduct concerts in its outdoor amphitheater, featuring the diverse sounds of Juice Newton, Steven Stills, the Count Basie Orchestra, and the Preservation Hall Jazz Band. I asked the director if any of these musical events produced a profit. Profitability was beside the point, she answered. The concerts occurred solely to attract people who normally would not come to a winery tasting room. Once there, these music lovers would discover that wine people did not have two heads or six arms. In short, concert goers would encounter wine in a fun, casual atmosphere rather than a stuffy, uptight one. And they didn't need any secret passwords. Wow, wine that fits into the rhythm of everyday life like the daily dining table: What a concept!

Still, the thought of visiting a tasting room intimidates many people. True, at a few wineries that have built cathedral monuments to "the art of wine," everyone whispers for fear of disturbing the wine muse. And yes, among tasting room employees you'll still find a few wine snobs who look askance at you when you ask what the difference is between Pinot Noir and Pinot Blanc.

But most tasting room hosts are everyday, hardworking people, just like you and I. Often, vintners, winemakers, or members of their extended families perform this duty, and most have a contagious enthusiasm for wine, which they delight in sharing with you. Hosts take pride in their wines and eagerly encourage you to taste and learn about them.

I know people who, when vacationing in wine country, will visit only one or two wineries instead of a dozen because they feel sheepish if they fail to purchase wine at every tasting room. They feel obligated to buy at least a bottle at every stop or, they mistakenly believe, hosts will view them as freeloaders or cheapskates. Nothing could be further from the truth. You, the consumer, are the winery's guest, and you keep the winery in business. Yes, you are a potential customer, but you don't make a purchase at every retail store you walk into either. View tasting rooms in the same way; if they don't sell a product that interests you, don't buy anything and continue on to the next store.

The real intangible in tasting rooms is the hospitality aspect. Wineries want you to feel comfortable and to sample their wines in a relaxing atmosphere. Even if you don't purchase during your visit, you'll probably think of them fondly later while shopping at your local supermarket or wine emporium. All that's demanded of you in a tasting room is common courtesy; winery employees appreciate nothing more than hearing you say, "I enjoyed tasting your wines; thank you very much."

## HOW TO USE THIS BOOK

This book will help you navigate the main highways and dusty backroads of California's wine country, from Mendocino in the north to Temecula in the south. Every effort has been made to identify the wineries that offer wine tastings to the public on a regular basis; I have omitted wineries that remain closed to the public and all but a handful of those that require special appointments. Visit the latter if at all possible, as I have included these treasures for a reason.

This guide groups wineries by region and lists them in the logical geographical order in which you likely will encounter them on your trip, rather than alphabetically or in some other arbitrary fashion. After a brief history of each region, specific travel directions will guide you easily along the right path.

A listing of each winery in the region follows and includes basics such as address, phone number, hours of operation, tours, whether tasting is free or not, and other attractions such as gift selection or picnic area. The guide provides a short history of each winery, including unusual features of the winery and vineyards, the types of wines offered, and specialties that you should not miss.

Following the wineries, I've provided a sampling of area restaurants with the same basic information, such as type of cuisine, atmosphere, and price range. The prices for a full dinner, not including wine, vary as follows:

Inexpensive: less than $10 per person
Moderate: $10–$25 per person
Expensive: over $25 per person

Remember, restaurants come and go with frequency in wine country, so when planning a romantic evening of dining, always check to make sure the restaurant still exists, the name hasn't changed, the food hasn't changed, the chef hasn't changed, etc. Call ahead for reservations, particularly if you plan to dine any weekend during summer or fall. During the wine country's off-season from November to April, you'll literally have the place to yourself on weekdays, and even the weekend crowds will be bearable.

Each region has a variety of seasonal wine events listed as well. Many wine country visitors find that patterning a vacation around a weekend wine festival, tasting, or harvest celebration increases their enjoyment of the entire visit.

Last, you can rely on resources listed at the end of each chapter to provide you with more information about the region, usually free of charge. In the interest of space, a listing of wine country accommodations numbering in the hundreds has been omitted. However, chambers of commerce routinely provide recommendations of area hotels and motels. Bed and breakfast referral services, also free, are noted for each region, where available. Contact the various regional vintners' associations for full-color touring maps and other useful information about the region and its wineries.

## WINE TASTING STRATEGY: THE FIVE S'S

While wine tasting should be casual and fun, it also educates by sharpening your sensory perceptions; the process will hone your ability to pinpoint the smells, flavors, and other characteristics of wines you prefer versus wines you dislike.

To that end, I'll share a tasting room strategy that, with a little attention to detail, will help you make the most of your wine-tasting experiences. Your host will pour a small amount of wine into your glass. From there you should use what I call the five S's: see, swirl, sniff, sip, and swallow or spit.

**SEE:** Wine appreciation begins with the sense of sight, as you size up the wine by its color. The hues alone will capture your interest: the light salmon blush of White Zinfandel, the golden straw color of Chardonnay, the deep purple of an intense Cabernet, and even the tiny effervescent bubbles of sparkling wine. Drink with your eyes first, noting the wine's attractiveness; it should appear clear, not cloudy, and free of sediment.

**SWIRL:** Grasping the stem of the glass, lift it from the tasting bar and gently swirl the wine around in the glass. Don't get too demonstrative; otherwise the wine might slosh out of the glass and onto your neighbor. Gently swirling the wine mixes it with air, allowing the wine to release its potential aromas. The tall, narrow design of the wine glass concentrates the aromas to facilitate the next step.

**SNIFF:** Now that you have jostled and released the aromatic compounds in the wine, stick your nose into the glass and inhale for the full effect. The wine's smell will give you an indication of the pleasure to follow. If you detect a lack of aroma, this may mean the wine has a subtle flavor or perhaps none at all. Swirl and sniff again, and if the aromas please you, try to notice the wine's more specific tones of flowers, fruits, vegetables, herbs, or spices.

**SIP:** Next, take a small sip roughly the size of a marble and swish it around in your mouth; allow the wine to come in contact with all parts of your tongue and its numerous taste receptors. Immediately you will detect various flavors within the wine. Then, as it crosses your midpalate, you will discern the wine's texture and balance. Some experienced tasters like to hold the wine in their mouths, purse their lips, and draw in air over the wine to distinguish the wine's subtleties. This process tends to make a funny gurgling noise and sometimes draws unwanted stares, so just do what you're comfortable with. Note the different flavor aspects of the wine and try to determine which flavors you find pleasing.

**SWALLOW OR SPIT:** Finally, swallow the wine to see if it leaves a pleasing taste in your mouth. Most likely, if it smells and tastes good, the wine will leave behind a nice finish. Many of the best wines have full, lasting finishes that continue long after you've swallowed. This final impression also may embed itself in your sensory memory banks as a benchmark of the meaning of good wine.

However, if you plan to visit several wineries in the same day, the wise alternative to swallowing is spitting. True, the idea of spittle in the context of fine wine and tasting rooms seems less than genteel. But frankly, sampling a half-dozen wines at each winery really can add up on the alcohol scale.

To counter the impracticality of spitting, wineries provide dump buckets on their tasting counters to pour out excess wine. In this scenario, take a sip to experience the wine, dump the remainder from your glass and proceed to the next wine. Because state laws prohibit spitting in the dump bucket, you may have the option to spit only at smaller wineries, where a sink is available. Of course, you can always step outside and expectorate with the wind.

When you find a wine you like, make a note of it. Most wineries provide a sheet listing the wines offered for tasting and/or purchasing that day. If you see no listing on the counter, ask for one and record your impressions of the wines. When you get home, this will answer the nagging question, "What was that great little Chardonnay we had on our trip?"

Last, designate a driver. Rotating driving responsibilities on a daily basis will ensure no one in your party feels excluded. Keep in mind that local authorities realize the potential for intoxicated driving is greater near wineries. Remember, a little planning may save the lives of people you love—including yourself.

## WINE-BUYING TIPS FOR TRAVELERS

When people visit wineries, the most irrepressible urge to purchase a bottle of wine or two routinely overcomes them (no surprise there!). Then they do the same at the next winery stop and the next until they suddenly realize they have dozens of bottles rolling around in their trunks. Don't let this encroaching wine bottle obsession take over your vacation!

Consider if you've traveled by plane to the wine country, you'll need to load the wine onto your returning flight. Assuming you check your other luggage, you legally and comfortably can tote two six-pack carriers on board. That case of wine will be all you can handle. Do not check full cases of wine in their original cartons through as luggage; these cartons, never meant for rough handling, will give way, causing the glass bottles to self-destruct long before they reach their destination. Resist the temptation to stuff a couple of bottles in your luggage, padded with T-shirts and underwear. If you do, you will find your clothing tie-dyed a deep purple by unknowing baggage handlers.

Airline travelers need not despair though; many wineries will ship wines to your home via a ground carrier (UPS, FedEx) for a fee. Local packaging stores will sell you Styrofoam inserts to protect wine during shipping, or they will package and ship your purchases home. Local wine stores that stock a wide variety of area wines usually will ship too.

Other tips apply to all wine country travelers. Look at your vehicle and calculate the amount of room currently occupied by passengers and luggage. Your wine purchases must fit in the leftover space—and remember you'll probably buy other gifts on the trip besides wine. A couple cases can take up a lot of room. Trust me, if your party of four squeezes into a subcompact, you won't be buying much wine. If renting, get at least a midsized car.

When deciding which wines to buy, consider availability first. In other words, if you taste a great wine at a large winery, don't slap down $10 on the spot if you probably can buy the same wine at your hometown grocery store for $7.99 (most wineries charge full retail price so they don't undercut and alienate stores selling their products). On the other hand, some special lots never hit the shelves of the retail shops and become available only at the winery. Maybe you'll come across a special bottling from a particular vineyard from which the winery made only fifty cases. Or maybe you'll find a special sweet Muscat Canelli or a single-vineyard Zinfandel that you won't see anywhere else.

Perhaps a certain winery's '90 Cabernet caught your interest years ago, but you can't find it in the stores anymore. Ask the winery staff about it; they often hold back a small portion of particularly ageworthy vintages for their visitors. You also may come across wineries having blowout sales of certain wines at incredibly reduced prices. Be sure you taste the wines first. If you like them, by all means stock up and congratulate yourself for being an astute shopper. In most cases, the wineries have shifted focus to the next vintage of releases and need to expediently move the older wines out the door. Only you can decide if you like the wine and if it's right for you. Remember, a $10 bottle of bad wine marked down to $2.99 is just cheap, bad wine.

Once you've made your purchases, protect your wine from one of its worst enemies: heat. An automobile trunk in the middle of a 100°F summer day in wine country is far from an ideal environment. Some people tote hand-carried coolers to keep the wine cool (though not necessarily chilled) during their travels. At your hotel, unload the wines and store them in a corner away from heat, vibration, or light. A little caution will reward you when you savor these wines at home.

# MENDOCINO AND LAKE COUNTIES

*M*endocino County, the northernmost wine-touring area in California, has two distinct grape-growing areas; ironically neither center around the coastal town of Mendocino. While cruising up U.S. 101 from Sonoma County, veering to the left at Highway 128 in Cloverdale will put you on the only interior thoroughfare, which passes through the cool climate of Anderson Valley, to the coast. On the other hand, if you continue north on U.S. 101, you'll find a number of inland wineries in a warmer area that stretches from Hopland to Redwood Valley. Lake County, which is often linked to Mendocino and sits just east of Hopland, is reached by Highway 175.

Grape growing and winemaking of any consequence, however, came late to the county compared with other regions. Immigrants planted grapes on the Anderson Valley ridges around the turn of the century, but they generally made the wine for their personal use. The Parduccis began making wine in Sonoma but moved up to Ukiah in 1932 in response to Prohibition. In the mid-1940s, Italian-Swiss Colony planted vineyards in Anderson Valley but deemed the area too cool to ripen grapes.

By 1966, when Robert Mondavi established his own winery in Oakville, two dozen wineries existed in Napa Valley, and the wine boom had begun. By contrast, Parducci remained the only winery in Mendocino County. Fetzer came a few years later to Hopland; then Edmeades and Husch began planting experimental vineyards

# Mendocino/Lake Counties

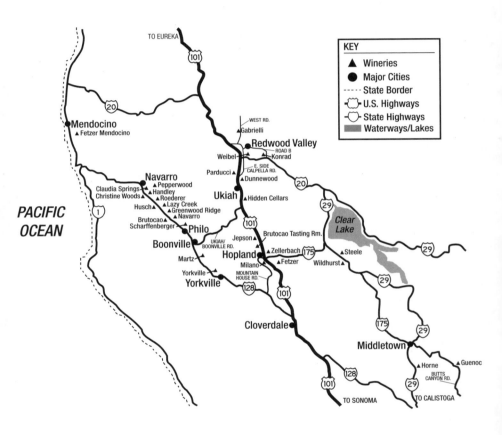

in Anderson Valley, and other pioneers of the region soon followed.

Lake County, on the other hand, has a long history of grape growing. In fact, at the turn of the century more than thirty-five wineries, reputedly far more than Napa Valley at the time, had planted thousands of acres to the vine. Today only a half-dozen wineries remain in Lake County.

As for climate, Anderson Valley feels the cooling influence of the nearby Pacific Ocean via its late evening and morning fogs. This long, cool growing season makes the area ideal for Riesling, Gewurztraminer, Chardonnay, and Pinot Noir; the latter two grapes also ripen appropriately for use in sparkling wines. The area straddling U.S. 101 from Hopland to Redwood Valley is warmer and gets little help from coastal fogs. Grapes that can take the heat, like Cabernet, Zinfandel, and Sauvignon Blanc, flourish here. Lake County does well with these same varietals.

## WINERIES

### ANDERSON VALLEY

*(listed from south to northwest)*

If time is a factor or you're headed to the Mendocino coast anyway, then focus on the Anderson Valley wineries. This bucolic, rural area is one of the prettiest wine valleys; it looks like the Napa Valley of thirty years ago. Its isolation probably has helped maintain its low profile among California winemaking regions. People go to Napa, then Sonoma, and figure they must have seen it all. They usually don't make it all the way north to Mendocino County, much less the Anderson Valley. But this natural, unspoiled treasure of an area provides normally uncrowded tasting rooms.

Touring the wineries doesn't require much brain power: They all sit on Highway 128, which diverges from U.S. 101 in Cloverdale. If you're in Hopland, take Mountain House Road, which will dump you onto Highway 128. If you're in Ukiah, the Ukiah-Boonville Road meets up with Highway 128 in Boonville, so you'll miss the two wineries in Yorkville. Both of these scenic roads have lots of twists and turns, so don't plan on setting any speed records. The first wineries, Yorkville and Martz, appear near Yorkville, but the big cluster begins on the other side of Boonville and continues until the even smaller hamlet of Navarro. Here, you'll find a dozen wineries, most easily spotted from the road. Take a short jog off the highway to visit Lazy Creek, Pepperwood Springs, and Claudia Springs; call ahead to make sure they're open and to get directions.

## Yorkville Cellars

**25701 Highway 128, Yorkville 95494 • 707-894-9177**
**Daily 11–6 • Most varieties poured, no fee**

The first winery on Highway 128 appears near the bend-in-the-road hamlet of Yorkville, appropriately called Yorkville Cellars. Owner/vintner Ed Wallo has been there nine years but only opened his doors to the public in 1994. Whites usually open for tasting include Sauvignon Blanc, Chardonnay, and Semillon, while the reds include Cabernet and Merlot. Prices are moderate in the $9–$15 range.

## Martz Winery

**20799 Highway 128, Yorkville 95494 • 707-895-2334**
**Fri.–Sun. 10–5:30 • All varieties poured, no fee.**

Larry Martz's winery stands a few winding turns off the highway. When you see an old, burned-out hulk of an antique car, you're at the right place: a homey, rural spot of land with goats and other animals wandering about. Like most small-production wineries, Martz is definitely a work in progress. Basically, a rarified tool shed with the insulation still showing serves as the winery.

You'll find the tasting room right inside the winery door, with no demarcation where one leaves off and the other begins. Tasting among the barrels and tanks amounts to an informal winery tour, with Martz's 1,500-case production looming large in front of your face. Slow but steady expansion plans will allow him to double his output. Right now, he gets half his grapes from his own vineyard, planted in 1989, and purchases the other half. Symphony, a hybrid grape developed by the University of California at Davis, makes an estate white wine of the same name, while a wine Martz calls Spring is an interesting blend of Symphony and Chardonnay. His lineup of reds includes Cabernet, Zinfandel, and Carignane, the latter an old workhorse grape normally used for blending but bottled separately by Martz. Prices are very reasonable, with all wines less than $10.

## Scharffenberger Cellars

**8501 Highway 128, Philo 95466 • 800-824-7754,**
**707-895-2065 • Daily 11–5 • Selected varieties poured, $3 fee**
**waived with bottle purchase**

John Scharffenberger looks young to have done all the things his resume says, including founding this premium sparkling producer in 1981. By 1989 the French Champagne house of Pommery made Scharffenberger a great financial offer that allowed him to retain a minority interest and remain president. The infusion of capital resulted in a 35,000-square-foot, state-of-the-art sparkling wine-making facility with an open balcony running through it, allowing visitors a bird's eye view of the winery.

The new buildings seem unpretentious, and the tasting room in front is an attractive white stucco residential-style building with a wraparound porch. You'll find randomly scattered tables and chairs for those who wish to sit and sip outside. Look for the whitewashed tasting bar at the far end of the building through an anteroom featuring hanging art. The Blanc de Blanc is one hundred percent Chardonnay, while the Brut Rose (tasty!) is one hundred percent Pinot Noir. The Brut and the Cremant sparklers offer blends of both grapes, although their majorities come from Pinot Noir. All are demonstrably flavored and well worth a taste.

## Brutocao Cellars

**7000 Highway 128, Philo 95466 • 707-895-2152**
**Daily: summer 10–6, winter 11–5 • Most varieties poured, no**
**fee • Good gift selection • Picnic tables**

Brutocao recently embarked on a building expansion program that will increase its physical size to accommodate 40,000 cases a year. So if you visit before the year 2000, you might encounter a little more sawdust and noise than usual. Right now the winery sits snugly on the highway in the Scharffenberger Cellars' previous location. The large, weathered wooden barn structure has flower beds in front with a thriving grape arbor at the side entrance. Inside, whitewashed stucco walls and a cathedral ceiling with wooden cross beams and ceiling fans provide quite a contrast from the rough-hewn exterior.

Sauvignon Blanc and Chardonnay are the whites, while Zinfandel, Merlot, and Cabernet are the reds. Every rustic but flavorful bottle can be purchased for less than $15. You can try special selections of Semillon, Merlot, Pinot Noir, and older Cabernet for $3 per pour, which can be applied to the purchase of that wine. Plenty of shaded picnic tables under the grapevine trellis await your visit as well.

## Navarro Vineyards
**5601 Highway 128, Philo 95466 • 707-895-3686 • Daily 10–5**
**Most varieties poured, no fee • Good gift selection • Picnic tables on outside deck**

The winemaking business in Mendocino attracted many early corporate refugees, among them owners Ted Bennett and Deborah Cahn. A high-powered partner in the original Pacific Stereo chain, Bennett became a bona fide millionaire when the company sold out to CBS. He then asked himself what he'd really like to do, and present-day Navarro Vineyards resulted. The couple thought the Anderson Valley a perfect climate to grow their favorite varietal: Gewurztraminer. They later planted Riesling, Pinot Noir, and Chardonnay on a 900-acre ranch they bought in 1974.

The redwood barn-style winery building has taken on a weathered patina of age; in fact, it looks like a romanticized version of a winery. Inside, burnished wood and a chandelier of empty wine bottles tower overhead. Unique to Navarro, tasting stations take the place of the usual long bar. Each station accommodates only four to six visitors at a time, which will help you get individual attention and learn about the wines. However, if the room gets busy, you'll have to wait for someone to acknowledge your presence. The wines, including Sauvignon Blanc, Chardonnay, Gewurztraminer, and Pinot Noir, will intrigue your taste buds for a fair price. If you want to enjoy these wines at home, sign up for the mailing list. Consumers buy seventy percent of Navarro's wines direct; the other thirty percent goes to fine restaurants.

## Greenwood Ridge Vineyards
**5501 Highway 128, Philo 95466 • 707-895-2002**
**Daily: summer 10–6, winter 10–5 • Most varieties poured, no fee • Good gift selection • Picnic tables on outside deck**

Down the road from Navarro, you'll find Greenwood Ridge housed in another beautiful redwood structure, complete with redwood shingles and a redwood walkway that leads to the spacious tasting room. Designed and built in 1986 by a Frank Lloyd Wright follower, the tasting room's twelve-sided ceiling rises to a dramatic point topped with a skylight. A tiled floor and an octagonal tasting bar add to the ambience. The room's backside opens up to a redwood deck studded with picnic tables that overlook the duck pond and vineyards. The actual winery and ridge vineyards sit further west on the other side of Highway 128.

Producing around 5,000 cases, Greenwood Ridge's tasting list may be smaller than Navarro's, but it's quality oriented. The winery has a short supply of current releases of Cabernet and Zinfandel, so you may purchase but not taste these selections. Surprisingly, this winery has poured an '85 Cabernet, as well as another oddity, a delicious late-harvest Chardonnay! Sauvignon Blanc and Riesling balance out the tasting menu. If you express an interest in visiting the smaller wineries, like Lazy Creek or Pepperwood Springs, your tasting room host will be glad to call ahead for you to make sure they're open (if she's not too busy). Kind neighbors make up the Anderson Valley lifestyle.

### Lazy Creek Vineyards

**4610 Highway 128 (unmarked; look for the mailbox marked Kobler on the right side of the road), Philo 95466 707-895-3623 • Usually open weekends, variable hours; call ahead**

You need to call ahead to visit Hans and Teresia Kobler because their home and winery exist on the same parcel they bought in 1972. The extra trouble will reward you; Hans makes one of the very best Gewurztraminers anywhere. Originally, the Koblers found a makeshift winery left over from Prohibition and a neglected vineyard on the property. Eventually, they planted twenty of the ninety acres to vines, and rebuilt and refurbished the house, winery, and series of buildings that encircle a central common area. It's both rustic and charming.

The Koblers call their winery Lazy Creek because visitors must drive slowly over several creek bridges before seeing the overgrown flower garden out front. Walking through the garden, the barn-style winery is on the right. Swiss-born Hans and Teresia are gracious in that Old World way rarely seen anymore. You seat yourself at picnic tables outside the winery, and they will bring you glasses of wine at a leisurely pace, telling you about the winery as you go. They offer a fruity Chardonnay that has guts and a light but very drinkable Pinot Noir. And don't forget the world-class Gewurztraminer. Expect limited production but extremely reasonable prices (less than $12) for this handcrafted quality.

## Husch Vineyards
**4400 Highway 128, Philo 95466 • 707-895-3216**
**Daily: summer 10–6, winter 10–5 • Most varieties poured,**
**no fee • Picnic area**

In 1971, Tony Husch, a vineyard pioneer in Anderson Valley, established the first winery in the valley since Prohibition. He since sold out to the grape-growing Oswald family, which gets grapes from the same vineyards as Husch but also plants new vines up north near Talmadge, where the Oswalds have another winemaking facility.

The tasting room itself hasn't changed a bit though; it still looks like a nearly falling down, small redwood cottage. Musty and cramped inside, the room's ancient window air conditioner in the wall opposite the tasting bar buzzes away during summer months, providing some relief when the place gets packed with tasters. Yellowing black-and-white pictures adorn the walls, giving the place a minor sense of history. White wines still rule here: Sauvignon Blanc and Chardonnay are good, while Gewurztraminer and the proprietary La Ribera Blanc (one hundred percent Sauvignon Blanc) are best buys. Pinot Noir and Cabernet, from the Oswalds' estate vineyards, sometimes rise to greatness.

## Roederer Estate
**4501 Highway 128, Philo 95466 • 707-895-2288 • Daily 11–5**
**Selected varieties poured, $3 fee applies to bottle purchase**

When the French Rouzaud family that produces the upscale, vintage-dated Cristal Champagne considered making a major land purchase and building a winery here in 1982, locals expressed concern about the ruination of Anderson Valley's beautiful, natural landscape. The 50,000-square-foot winery amazingly does not stick out, but instead its redwood and earth-toned exterior melds into the hillside. The owners continue to buy land and now have more than 500 acres throughout the valley, which helps control the consistency of the winery's sparkling wines from year to year.

The tasting room, like the winery's exterior, appears understated but with an Old World sense of luxury, all the way down to the restrooms. Art graces the walls, and hand-inlaid tile tables beckon you to sit and sip. The magnificent (though small) pewter tasting bar is more than 150 years old and hails from the Roederer facility in France. Although it's not posted, you can sample an array of sparklers that seem the opposite of Scharffenberger for $3. Here the flavors of Brut, Extra Dry, and Brut Rose are elegant, balanced, and subtle and invite another refreshing sip.

## Pepperwood Springs Vineyards

**1200 Holmes Ranch Rd., Philo 95466 • 707-895-2920**
**Usually open weekends, call ahead for appointment**
**Selected varieties poured, no fee**

Although it's one of the smallest producers in the Anderson Valley, Pepperwood Springs has been around awhile. You won't see any signs but stay on Highway 128 and make a right turn opposite Clark Road onto Holmes Ranch Road; follow it a little more than two miles. Pepperwood Springs is actually a residence, but part has been converted into a winery. First you'll notice the outdoor deck has one of the best views of the Anderson Valley. To the left you'll see a couple of portable barbecues and a small redwood deck along with the entrance to the tasting room.

Although a church pew is available for sitting, once eight people crowd inside, elbow room nearly vanishes. Case stacks of wine and pallets of the vintage just bottled border the small tasting bar. Consequently, you'll get a personal tasting and learn as much about the winery as you're willing to ask, since the owners usually pour. Chardonnay and Pinot Noir are the two varieties produced although the winery may offer different bottlings or vintages for tasting on a given day. You'll find it well worth your time to seek out these limited-production, hard-to-find wines.

## Christine Woods Vineyards

**3155 Highway 128, Philo 95466 • 707-895-2115 • Daily 11–6**
**All varieties poured, no fee**

Vernon and Jo Rose run this real mom and pop winery operation. Actually grape growers, the Roses sell to the likes of Greenwood Ridge, Brutocao, and Scharffenberger. But in 1989, they decided to make a small amount of wine under their own label from fifteen acres they dry-farm.

A Butler-style building, the winery has a dark-wood-paneled tasting room with large windows in the front. The view overlooks the pond and adjacent vineyards. Chardonnay and Pinot Noir (both rapidly becoming grapes of choice in the Anderson Valley) are the only varietals made here; a moderately priced, nonvintaged Pinot Noir is also tasty at an inexpensive price.

## Handley Cellars

**3151 Highway 128, Philo 95466 • 707-895-2190**
**Daily: summer 11–6, winter 11–5 • Most varieties poured,**
**no fee • Good gift selection • Picnic areas**

Winemaker Milla Handley, the great-granddaughter of brewer Henry Weinhard, may have fermentation science in her genes. If so, she fulfilled the prophecy when she started school at the University of California at Davis to study art but ended up with a degree in enology. She worked at both Sonoma and Mendocino wineries before she bonded her own winery in the garage beneath her home in Philo. Many successes and several years later, the winery moved to its present bucolic site and looks so comfortable you might think it's been there for decades. The redwood-sided (what else?) tasting room has huge-paned windows that overlook the vineyard. To the right, a large patio can be used for picnicking if it's not being used for the year's numerous winery events.

The whitewashed walls and the vaulted ceiling of the tasting room give a sense of openness to the space, but the ornate tasting bar provides the room's centerpiece, although the elephant-carved table and chairs will catch your eye too. The wines are extremely dependable every year; the whites include Sauvignon Blanc, Gewurztraminer, and Chardonnay, while the sole red is Pinot Noir. Sparkling wines—the Brut, Brut Rose, and Blanc de Blanc—fit squarely in the fruity tradition of California sparklers and themselves are worth the trip.

## Claudia Springs Winery

**2160 Guntly Rd. (off Highway 128), Philo 95466 • 707-895-3926**
**Usually open weekends, variable hours; call ahead**

Two couples from the Bay Area established this small 1,200-case winery in 1989 as a partnership. Both wives' first names are Claudia, and thus the winery had its moniker. Robert Klindt, winemaker/partner, hopes good fortune still lives on this property, the former home and winery of Milla Handley, who moved her Handley Cellars onto a much larger property down the road. The rambling, barn-style structure still houses a small winery on one level.

The primitive tasting room's decor includes tools of the wine trade and stacked barrels of wine all around. The tasting bar is likely to be an upturned, empty barrel. Chardonnay and Pinot Noir are among the selections, but the good Zinfandels deliver the knockout punch; in particular, the *Los Angeles Times* praised the '93 Pacini Vineyards bottling. If you like the wines, buy them here; you won't see them much elsewhere because of limited production.

## HOPLAND/UKIAH/REDWOOD VALLEY

*(listed from south to north)*

You'll find most Mendocino wineries on or adjacent to U.S. 101. Milano, Brutocao, and Zellerbach are in Hopland; just east of town on Highway 175 is Fetzer. Back on U.S. 101 to the north is Jepson, then right before Ukiah, take the Talmadge exit east and then go south on Ruddick-Cunningham Road to Hidden Cellars. Back on U.S. 101 north, exit at State Street north to Dunnewood. Follow State Street north to Parducci Road and make a left to Parducci. Back on State Street, continue north to Weibel. Again on U.S. 101, exit Highway 20 east; then take A and B streets to Konrad. Finally from U.S. 101, go north to West Road; turn right, heading east about three miles to Gabrielli.

### Milano Winery

**14594 S. Highway 101, Hopland 95449 • 707-744-1396**
**Daily 10–5 • Most wines poured, no fee • Good gift selection**
**Picnic area**

If you drive straight up U.S. 101 from Sonoma County, Milano is the first Mendocino winery you'll see. Housed in a distinctively shaped hop barn (the area used to supply hops to the beer industry), Frank Milone built the winery in 1947. The hop business died out in 1955, but twenty-two years lapsed before the Milone family converted the hop barn to a winemaking facility. An adventure begins when you climb the rickety, old stairs to the second-story tasting room. Once inside, a big leaded-glass bay window provides a view of continuous highway traffic.

The tasting bar is minute although you'll have plenty of room to move around and peruse the view and gift selection. White wine, particularly Chardonnay, has always been the ticket here, and recent vintages are no exception. One called Marguerite is a great value at $6. In the reds, Milano sometimes has Zinfandel, but it's usually sold out; a consolation is that some interesting older Cabernets are often poured for visitors who express interest.

### Fetzer Vineyards

**13601 Eastside Rd. (and Highway 175), Hopland 95449,**
**707-744-1250 or 800-846-8637 • Daily 9–5 • Most wines**
**poured, no fee • Excellent gift selection, deli foods, and soft**
**drinks • Picnic area**

Fetzer has become a major industry in tiny Hopland, a far cry from the small winery the Fetzers established when they came here in 1968. But even though the winery has grown to one of the state's largest by selling to Brown-Forman, quality has remained the cornerstone. The Fetzer Wine and Food Center, as it's called, attracts thousands of travelers a year. Wines, books, comestibles, and clothing cram the huge tasting and hospitality area. A full-service deli on the premises makes it convenient for visitors who want to picnic.

The most popular wines (and inexpensive too) include the Sundial Chardonnay, Valley Oaks Cabernet, and Eagle Peak Merlot. For a few dollars more a bottle, the wines labeled Barrel Select provide more flavor and complexity. Fetzer makes so many wines from almost every popular grape variety that you may find a dozen or so open on any given day; if you don't see your favorite on the bar, ask and the staff usually will open a bottle for you. Also ask to see the Fetzer garden, where more than 1,000 types of fruits, vegetables, herbs, and flowers grow organically without pesticides, herbicides, or synthetic fertilizers. The popularity of Fetzer's new organically certified wines under the Bonterra label affirm the winery's move toward the same with its grape growing.

## Fetzer Mendocino Tasting Room

**45070 Main St., Mendocino 95460 • 707-937-6191**
**Daily 10–6 • Four selected wines poured, $4 fee applies to purchase or logo glass • Good gift selection**
Realizing more than a million visitors come to Mendocino each year and many by the scenic Highway 1 coastal route, Fetzer decided to open a second tasting room. Centrally located next to the historic Mendocino Hotel on Main Street, the room offers selected wines for tasting and picturesque views of the Mendocino Headlands. A good selection of Mendocino specialty food products is available, as well as tons of Fetzer logo wear. A good place for an aperitif before lunch or dinner in town.

## Brutocao Tasting Room

**13500 South U.S. 101, Hopland 95449 • 707-744-1664**
**Daily 10–6 • Most varieties poured, no fee**
Brutocao recently opened a separate tasting room on Hopland's main drag in what was formerly part of Fetzer's old tasting room. See the Brutocao listing under "Anderson Valley" earlier in this chapter for information about the wines.

## Zellerbach/Estate William Baccala

**13420 South U.S. 101, Hopland 95449 • 707-774-1995**
**Daily 10–5 • Most varieties poured, no fee • Picnic area**

Zellerbach recently moved its tasting room from the old Tijsseling Estate property on bucolic McNab Ranch Road to the heart of downtown Hopland to attract more wine tourists. Zellerbach continues to produce large quantities of inexpensive but flavorful wines under three different labels: Zellerbach Estates, Robert Allison, and Estate Baccala.

The new visitors' center pours several different Chardonnays, as well as Merlot, Zinfandel, Cabernet, and White Zinfandel. Many of the winery's selections, especially the Chardonnays, are consistently rated best buys.

## Jepson Vineyards

**10400 South U.S. 101, Ukiah 95482 • 707-468-8936**
**Daily 10–5 • Most varieties poured, no fee • Small gift selection**
**Picnic tables**

From the highway, you'll see the Jepson landmark: a two-story, hundred-year-old farmhouse that now serves as the offices for the winery. The utilitarian winery actually sits just to the north with a small tasting room added on, seemingly as an afterthought. It's disappointing in the sense it would be marvelous to see the farmhouse's architecture and restoration. However, the wines at Jepson do not disappoint.

The tasting room is a modest affair, dominated by a wood bar, with every conceivable award-winning medal hanging on the back bar. White wines are the focus here, including Sauvignon Blanc, Chardonnay, and a sparkling Blanc de Blanc, all from estate-grown grapes. An unusual wine is the Chateau d'Alicia (named after one of the owners), made in the slightly sweet style, entirely from French Colombard grapes. Jepson also makes a traditional alambic-pot still Brandy, but due to archaic California laws it cannot be offered for tasting.

## Hidden Cellars

**1500 Ruddick-Cunningham Rd., Ukiah 95482**
**707-462-0301 • Call for appointment • Most varieties poured,**
**no fee • Picnic area**

Hidden Cellars is actually not so hidden, though it is a mile off the highway and about a half-mile down Ruddick-Cunningham Road. The name refers to vintner Dennis Patton's first winemaking classes at the University of California at Davis. The school asked for his winery affiliation and, since he had none at the time, he replied, "Hidden Cellars," a euphemism meaning he didn't own a winery . . . yet. He's come a long way since then, acquiring a partner in 1983, which allowed him to build the present winery.

Hidden Cellars is a barnlike structure with a tin roof; look for the tasting room entrance near the blue awning and windows on the east side of the building. It's a small, cozy room attached to the business end of the winery in the back. Always available are Chardonnay and Zinfandel, made from local grapes. An expensive-but-worth-it specialty is a Meritage-style blend of Sauvignon Blanc and Semillon called Alchemy, a stunning example of the vintner's blending skills. Depending on the vintage, sweet dessert wines might also be poured, including a Riesling and a late-harvest Semillon.

### Dunnewood Vineyards

**2399 N. State St., Ukiah 95482 • 707-462-2985**
**Daily 10–5 • Most varieties poured, no fee • Good gift selection**
**Picnic area**

Experienced wine travelers may recognize this as the old Cresta Blanca Winery, now renamed Dunnewood, with a new image and line of wines. Dunnewood is part of the larger corporate holdings of the Canandaigua Wine group. The facility looks pretty much the same though; if you drive to the end of the parking lot, Dunnewood seems more like a factory than a winery. While a winery located on one of Ukiah's main streets seems odd, the facility has been here since 1946, and much of Ukiah has grown up around it.

The tasting room, in front of the warehouse buildings, is a not-so-rustic, double-wide temporary trailer-type structure that seems to have become permanent. The wines here range from Chardonnay to Cabernet and just about everything in between; many of them, like the Barrel Select Merlot, are consistently cited as great values. An added attraction of visiting the winery is a large grape-arbor picnic area next to the tasting room.

### Parducci Wine Cellars

**501 Parducci Rd., Ukiah 95482 • 707-462-9463 • Daily 9–5**
**Most varieties poured, no fee • Good gift selection • Picnic area**

Parducci is one of those old-line Italian families that made its mark in winemaking before it was fashionable; a family of farmers, the Parduccis knew how to make wine, so that's what they did, starting back in 1932 at Prohibition's end. They started out making the typical Italian-style bulk table wines of the day and eventually upgraded their image with varietally labeled wines. In 1987, they finally modernized the fermentation cellar to compete with the latest wonders of the wine world. A recent change in family ownership is giving new life to this winery.

A huge, sprawling complex of disparate buildings among the vineyards makes up the winery. Out front, a mission-style, Spanish-revival stucco tasting room, complete with wood beams and mission bell, beckons to the visitor. Among the wines, the Cellarmaster selections are top-of-the-line, but the regular Cabernet, Zinfandel, and Petite Sirah are dependably tasty. The vast range of offerings will likely include Sauvignon Blanc, Chardonnay, and Merlot. In the back, burgeoning vines shield a large picnic area from the winery's concrete and steel.

## Weibel Vineyards

**7051 N. State St., Redwood Valley 95470 • 707-485-0321**
**Daily 9–5 • Most varieties poured, no fee • Good gift selection**
**Picnic area**

The Weibels took over the historic Stanford Winery in Mission San Jose in 1945. But foreshadowing of urban encroachment in the early 1960s caused them to move the bulk of their winemaking to this Mendocino site. With houses built up to the cellar door in Mission San Jose, that facility finally closed in the mid-1990s.

The Mendocino building will impress you; nothing else quite like it exists in this area. The circular brick building with huge redwood doors is surrounded by towering trees that disguise the stainless-steel industrial tanks of the winery. From the road, it looks like it might be the local upscale country club. Inside, a bubbling fountain reminds you of Weibel's heritage of sparkling wine, and a curved tasting bar lures you off to the side. The wines range from the ordinary bulk types to decently done Chardonnay. If you've ever tried sparkling wine at a hotel banquet, you've probably tasted one of Weibel's many private labels. For years, Weibel has been the largest producer of a slightly sweet white wine called Green Hungarian, certainly worth a taste for its oddity value. Recently a number of other wineries—many not open to the public—began pouring their wines here, including McDowell Valley, Duncan Peak, Domaine St. Gregory, MonteVolpe, Elizabeth, Frey, Claudia Springs, and Brauren Pauli.

## Konrad Estate Winery

**3620 Road B, Redwood Valley 95470 • 707-485-0323**
**Daily: summer 10–5, winter 10–4 • Most varieties poured,**
**no fee • Picnic area**

Off the beaten path, look for a wooden ridge-topped winery set back in the hills, with vista views both east and west. Founded with a partner in 1980, the winery's sole owner is now the Konrad family.

Main varietals include Chardonnay, Zinfandel, Riesling, and some Petite Sirah (Port), all of which show varietal distinctness. A house specialty—one you'll find nowhere else—is called Melange a Trois, a five-way blend of Barbera, Cabernet Franc, Cabernet Sauvignon, Charbono, and Merlot!

## Gabrielli Winery

**10950 West Rd., Redwood Valley 95470 • 707-485-1221**
**Daily 10–5 • Most varieties poured, no fee • Picnic area**

A relative newcomer to winemaking (1990), Gabrielli sits the farthest north of any winery in the area. The winery, about three miles east of U.S. 101, is located on a slight rise that can be seen from the road, and the entrance is well marked. Straightforwardness and practicality rule in the wooden winery and tasting room; the tasting bar might be an empty, upturned wine barrel.

Asanza is the name given to the proprietary red wine blend of five different varietals. Chardonnay, Pinot Noir, and Riesling are all made from local grapes. Perhaps Gabrielli's greatest success so far though has been its Zinfandel, which always has big, rich, chewy flavors.

## LAKE COUNTY

*(listed from west to southeast)*

Lake County, home to the largest natural freshwater lake in California, has miles of open space and lots of fresh country air. You'll find all the county's wineries along Highway 29, the same Highway 29 that runs through Napa Valley. In Hopland, Highway 175 runs east out of town until it hits Highway 29 near the lake. If you're in Redwood Valley, Highway 20 east eventually intersects Highway 29. From Hopland, proceed east on Highway 175 and turn right (south) on Highway 29 for the short drive to Steele Wines. A distance farther south on Highway 29 is Wildhurst. Continuing south on Highway 29, make a left on Butts Canyon Road just before Middletown to get to Guenoc Winery. After about six miles, you'll see a lake on the right; the winery turnoff is on the left. Back on Highway 29 south, you can't miss Horne, just the other side of Middletown. If you're coming from the Napa Valley and Highway 29 in Calistoga, reverse the order. Horne is only sixteen miles from Calistoga, so Lake County wineries offer an excellent and uncrowded day trip when staying in the upper Napa Valley.

## Steele Wines
**Highway 29 at Thomas Dr., Kelseyville 95451 • 707-279-9475**
**Daily 11–5 in summer and fall and on major holidays • All**
**varieties poured, $1 fee • Good gift selection • Picnic area**

Lake County grape growers who wanted one central location to vinify their wines founded Konocti Winery in 1974. Winery co-ops are relatively common in Europe but rare in the United States. But this arrangement seems to have worked out for the growers, who have to compete with Napa to the south and Mendocino to the west. The winery, with vineyards above the 1,000-foot elevation level, rests by Clear Lake in the shadow of dormant volcano Mount Konocti. A functional Butler building gets the job done, with the tasting at the other end of the winery complex. It's a homey sort of tasting room with a blonde wooden bar and a good selection of gifts, some produced by local artists.

The wines used to taste mediocre but have improved dramatically since 1992, when consulting winemaker Jed Steele joined the winery. Steele has since taken over the facility and changed the winery name to his own moniker. Chardonnay, Pinot Noir, and Zinfandel are of the highest quality. Excellent bargains can often be found here under Steele's Shooting Star label.

## Wildhurst Vineyards
**3855 Main St., Kelseyville 95451 • 800-595-9463 • Daily 10–5**
**All varieties poured, no fee • Small gift selection**

Wildhurst is a partnership of the Collin and Holdenried families, multigenerational farm families that have been in the fruit tree and grape-growing business for many years. Not content to merely grow, they decided to make their own wine. Formerly located just off the highway in Lower Lake, Wildhurst recently relocated to downtown Kelseyville.

These family farmers get their pick of 160 acres of grapes and produce about 17,000 cases. The Sauvignon Blanc, Fume Blanc, and Chardonnay are all fresh and tasty with some complexity, while the Cabernet, Merlot, and Pinot Noir are fruity and easily drinkable. Again, prices are low, while quality is high: The wines would sell for fifty percent more if the label read Napa Valley. Instead the wines bear the Lake County (and Sonoma and Mendocino) moniker, and nothing sells for more than $12.

## Guenoc Winery

**21000 Butts Canyon Rd., Middletown 95461 • 707-987-2385**
**Thurs.–Sun. 10–4:30 • Most varieties poured, no fee**
**Good gift selection • Excellent picnic area**

In the late nineteenth century, actress Lillie Langtry purchased property in Lake County to build a retreat and make world-class wine. Langtry never accomplished the latter, but in 1971 Orville Magoon bought the ranch and began planting what would eventually become 320 acres to vines. The Magoon family now maintains the ornate Victorian house Langtry built.

Six miles east of the highway, a lake comes into view on the right, with Guenoc on the left. A half-mile gravel road (to be paved soon) takes you up a hill to a plateau and the long redwood winery building. Look for the entrance around front (facing the road), halfway down the sidewalk. The room has a lot of character, with its well-worn bar and moody ambience created by the dappled light coming through the windows. Chardonnay and Sauvignon Blanc are good whites to start with, but don't miss the Langtry White, a nice Meritage-style wine. Cabernet and the Langtry Red are also fine, but the hosts are especially proud of their Petite Sirah. Since the winery is a drive from anywhere, pack a picnic lunch and enjoy the superb setting, with tables under the grape arbor overlooking the lake and Guenoc's new vineyards on the opposite hillside.

## Horne

**2200 Highway 29, Middletown 95461 • 707-987-3743**
**Thurs.–Mon. 11–5 • Most varieties poured, no fee**

Horne is primarily a grape grower with about twenty acres in Lake County. The blue ranch house with big, wooden double doors is nestled in a rustic setting on this residential property only sixteen miles out of Calistoga and Napa Valley.

Nothing but an old, broken-down van out front with a sign on its roof that reads Winery Open indicates someone makes wine here. Agricultural implements strewn all around the property will also tell you you're in the right place. Turn onto the country lane and park by the white fence. The wines—Sauvignon Blanc, Cabernet, and Petite Sirah among them—mimic the straightforward, rustic surroundings.

## Restaurants

### Bluebird Cafe
**13340 South U.S. 101, Hopland 95449 • 707-744-1633**
Breakfast and lunch daily, dinner Wed.–Sun. • No reservations
American • Inexpensive

One of the few independent places in town to get a substantial home-cooked breakfast that will fuel you up for a full day of wine touring. Lunches consist of soups, salads, sandwiches, and similar fare.

### Boonville Hotel Restaurant
**Highway 128 at Lambert Ln., Boonville 95415**
**707-895-2210 •** Dinner Wed.–Mon. only • Reservations
recommended • California cuisine • Moderate to expensive

Equally praised and damned in the 1980s, Boonville was considered the quintessence of California cuisine by some but known to others as the place with the worst service on the planet. Recent owners have committed to providing a completely pleasant dining experience. Once dark and brooding, the interior has been lightened. The kitchen focuses on the short menu that includes several grilled meat and fish selections as well as satisfying salads and pastas. Good local wine list too.

### Anderson Valley Brewing Company–Buckhorn Saloon
**14081 Highway 128, Boonville 95415 • 707-895-2337**
Lunch and dinner daily • No reservations • California-style
beer food • Inexpensive

This place looks ornate for a top-flight brew-pub located in a sparsely populated area. The brews, however, are widely known and exported to places like San Francisco and Los Angeles, where people appreciate the brews as a masterful expression of the brewer's art. The kitchen doesn't try anything fancy, just bountiful plates of hearty food, like burgers, sausages and deep-fried fish, that match up well with its full-bodied brews.

### Hopland Brewery
**13351 South U.S. 101, Hopland 95449 • 707-744-1015**
Lunch and dinner daily • No reservations • California-style
beer food • Inexpensive

This is the original, the real thing that every new brew-pub models itself after. On this spot in 1983, Mendocino Brewing Company opened the first brew-pub in California since Prohibition. The hundred-year-old building, known in the early 1900s as the Hopvine Saloon, has a long history in a town appropriately named Hopland. Red Tail Ale is the flagship bottling, but the brew-pub also offers Blue Heron Pale Ale and Black Hawk Stout as well as seasonal brews. Don't look for a fancy menu; the brew-pub serves down-home food like burgers, sausages, and cheese with some pastas, chicken, ribs, and salads thrown in for good measure.

## Cafe Beaujolais

**961 Ukiah Street, Mendocino 95460 • 707-937-5614 • Open daily • Reservations recommended • California cuisine Moderate to expensive**

Scarce dining opportunities in Anderson Valley force many travelers who make a day of tasting to lodge and dine in and around the seaside town of Mendocino. Locals and tourists alike flock to Cafe Beaujolais year after year. Owner Margaret Fox set a precedent by demanding the freshest and finest ingredients possible. The same care still transforms those ingredients into something typically American but with wonderfully creative twists. Roasted chicken, lamb, fresh shrimp, and seafood might show up on the menu along with salads and vegetable plates featuring produce picked only hours before. And don't miss the weekend breakfasts.

## 955 Ukiah Street

**955 Ukiah St., Mendocino 95460 • 707-937-1955 Dinner Thurs.–Sun • Reservations recommended California cuisine • Moderate to expensive**

Located in an old redwood water tower that once housed an artist's studio, 955 Ukiah Street combines funky Mendocino ambience and stylish, upscale food. The ground-level floor of this two-story restaurant looks out onto the garden, and the top level has a vaulted view of the Pacific. Mussels with garlic and white wine top the starters, while broiled swordfish and roasted chicken with wild mushrooms might be entree specials. Desserts are terrific, and the wine list spotlights Mendocino producers.

## Little River Inn Restaurant

**7751 N. Highway 1, Little River 95456 • 707-937-5942 Breakfast and dinner daily • American • Moderate to expensive**

Little River is an old-style dining room that somehow works because the mildly subdued look of the place leads you not to expect any fireworks with the food. On one side a glass wall looks out into the garden, where you might spy an occasional rabbit or cat. The menu is homey, but that doesn't mean it's not tasty and filling. The menu usually features meatloaf, mashed potatoes, fried chicken, and fresh fish along with daily specials.

### Albion River Inn Restaurant

**3790 N. Highway 1, Albion 95410 • 707-937-4044**
**Dinner daily • Reservations recommended • California cuisine**
**Moderate to expensive**

A perennial favorite, Albion River Inn's unobstructed view of the ocean draws crowds, particularly at sunset. And while people often assume great views mean mediocre food, Albion breaks that rule. Consistently presenting creatively prepared dishes, Albion's California cuisine has French, Italian, and Pacific Rim influences. Fresh fish, chicken, game, and pastas rotate seasonally on the menu. The wine list proudly showcases the best of the Mendocino County wineries.

### Park Place

**50 Third St., Lakeport 95453 • 707-263-0444 • Lunch and dinner daily • Reservations recommended • American/Italian Inexpensive to moderate**

With the possible exception of the nearby resorts, there is nothing like Park Place for many miles. A pasta and grilled meat style restaurant may be taken for granted in large, urban neighborhoods, but in the wilds of Lake County, it's the pleasant anomaly.

## ANNUAL EVENTS

---

### APRIL

**Lake County Spring Wine Adventure • 707-263-0911**
Annual celebration of Lake County wineries.

### JUNE

**Roll Out the Barrels and Pop the Corks • P.O. Box 63 • Philo 95466 • 707-895-2288, 707-895-3876**
Anderson Valley's annual group event; individual wineries all do something special that weekend, e.g., barrel tastings, offering older wines for tasting, pairing food and wine, etc.

## JULY

### California Wine-Tasting Championships • 707-895-2002

Blind varietal-identification contest open to novices, amateurs, and professionals in singles and doubles categories. Sponsored by Greenwood Ridge Vineyards.

## AUGUST

### Mendocino Bounty • P.O. Box 65 • Ukiah 95482
### 707-462-3306

Showcase of Mendocino County's wide variety of agricultural products, as well as those in the liquid form of wine and beer. The showcase presents the best from farmers, ranchers, fishermen, vintners, brewmasters, chefs, and food entrepreneurs.

## SEPTEMBER

### Winesong • 707-961-4688

Held at the beautiful Mendocino Coast Botanical Gardens, this wine and lifestyle auction is a premier fund-raising event. Related wine and food activities are scheduled for that weekend.

## RESOURCES

### Anderson Valley Winegrowers' Association
**P.O. Box 63 • Philo 95466**
Full-color winery touring map.

### Lake County Chamber of Commerce
**875 Lakeport Blvd. • Lakeport 95453 • 707-263-5092**
Accommodations, restaurants, and recreational activities.

### Lake County Grape Growers' Association
**65 Soda Bay Rd. • Lakeport 95453 • 707-263-0911**
Winery information.

### Mendocino County Convention and Visitors' Bureau
**P.O. Box 244 • Ukiah 95482 • 707-462-3091**
Accommodations, restaurants, and recreational activities.

### Mendocino County Vintners' Association
**P.O. Box 1409 • Ukiah 95482 • 707-468-1343**
Winery touring map and related winery information.

# SONOMA COUNTY

*O*f all the missions, the Franciscans built Sonoma last, establishing it in 1823. Of course, the good fathers brought with them, as they did to every mission along the trail, grape cuttings to plant for making sacramental wine. But within a decade, the Mexican government had secularized the Spanish missions, leaving little need for wine, at least for its original purpose.

But General Mariano Vallejo, who became the Mexican governor of California, had headquarters at Sonoma. He took over tending the original mission vineyard, and you can still see remnants across the street from Sebastiani Winery. He continued to make wine much the way the Franciscans had. Thus General Vallejo set the stage for Sonoma Valley to become the cradle of northern California winemaking. Several years later, George Yount would plant cuttings from General Vallejo's vineyard in what is now Yountville, and Napa would also be developing into a foremost grape-growing region.

But not until the arrival of Count Agoston Haraszthy, a wily raconteur and businessman, did the northern California wine industry begin to take shape. An immigrant from Hungary, Haraszthy came to Sonoma County in 1857 after stopping along the way in Wisconsin, San Diego, and San Francisco. He struck up a friendship with General Vallejo (Haraszthy's sons later married Vallejo's daughters in a double wedding ceremony) and planted several hundred acres of vines. With the help of Chinese laborers, Haraszthy carved caves in the hillsides on the east end of town for his winery, naming it Buena Vista or "good view." The oldest winery in California, Buena Vista's preserved grounds give visitors a sense of history.

23

Haraszthy's questionable reputation as the father of California viticulture came as a result of his trip to European vineyards in 1861. He sent back thousands of premier grape cuttings in hundreds of varieties for planting in vineyards throughout California. As a member of the state's agricultural commission, he thought the state would pay handsomely for his discoveries, but it gave him nothing. The cuttings were propagated anyhow. Haraszthy was apparently a better promoter than businessman, though he did bring recognition to northern California as a primary grape-growing region. He died broke and amid mysterious circumstances in South America in 1869.

By the turn of the century, a second wave of immigrants helped further establish Sonoma's grape-growing and winemaking roots. The families of Gundlach, Bundschu, Korbel, Simi, Sebastiani, Foppiano, Seghesio, Pastori, Nervo, Cambiaso, Martini, Prati, and Pedroncelli began to till the soil and make wine; many of their wineries still bear the family names and continue to prosper today. Those familiar names survived Prohibition in a variety of ways (prunes were a big alternate crop); many did not. By the time of repeal, only twenty-five wineries still existed. Those that survived emerged as bulk producers, not as the estate-bottled wineries we think of today.

The wine boom of the 1970s, initially fueled by the quest for quality in Napa Valley, caught Sonoma off guard. But Sonoma wineries caught up quickly by ripping out acres of orchards and planting new grapes until their acreage easily exceeded Napa's. Entrepreneurs and foreign investors also showed interest in the area, bringing capital and expertise.

For all the sophistication the term *wine country* conveys, Sonoma is markedly agricultural in nature and slower paced. Does a rivalry exist between Sonoma and Napa? Not really; more of a spirit of cooperation and sharing of grape-growing and winemaking ideas replaces a true rivalry. But as a wag remarked, Napa has Gucci loafers and Range Rovers, while Sonoma has cowboy hats and pickup trucks, though that type of facile distinction is fading now. But Sonoma vintners do seem to enjoy getting their hands dirty in the everyday winery business more than their Napa Valley counterparts. As comedian Tom Smothers, a vintner in Sonoma Valley, often says, "NAPA makes auto parts; Sonoma makes wine."

You'll find touring Sonoma completely different from touring Napa Valley because the wineries and vineyards cover a larger area. In Napa Valley, you can visit a half-dozen wineries in a row on

## Sonoma County
### (Includes insets for Northern Sonoma and Sonoma Valley)

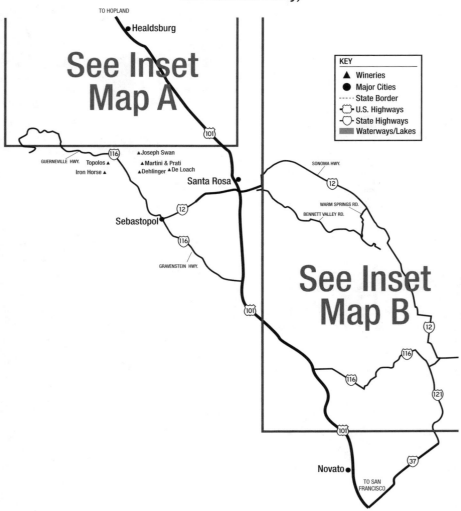

TO HOPLAND

● Healdsburg

See Inset Map A

101

KEY
▲ Wineries
● Major Cities
----- State Border
U.S. Highways
State Highways
Waterways/Lakes

116
GUERNEVILLE HWY.   Topolos ▲        ▲ Joseph Swan
                                    ▲ Martini & Prati
        Iron Horse ▲      ▲ Dehlinger ▲ De Loach    SONOMA HWY.
                              Santa Rosa ●           12

                                    WARM SPRINGS RD.
                                    BENNETT VALLEY RD.
    Sebastopol ●  12

116

GRAVENSTEIN HWY.

See Inset Map B

101                                                 12

                                                    116

                              116

                                                    121

101

                    Novato ●              37

                        TO SAN
                        FRANCISCO

# Northern Sonoma
## (Inset A from p. 25 map)

KEY
- ▲ Wineries
- ● Major Cities
- ---- State Border
- U.S. Highways
- State Highways
- Waterways/Lakes

▲ J. Fritz

DUTCHER CREEK RD.

▲ Silver Oak

▲ Pastori

▲ Geyser Peak

Canyon Road
▲ De Lorimier

CANYON RD.

▲ Lake Sonoma

Ferrari-Carano ▲
Meeker ▲

▲ Preston

CANYON RD.
J. Pedroncelli ▲

YOAKIM
BR. RD.

▲ Clos du Bois

128

101

**Geyserville**

Trentadue ▲
Chateau Souverain ▲

DRY CREEK RD.

▲ Quivira

A. Rafanelli ▲
Lambert Bridge ▲

Dry Creek

W. DRY CREEK RD.

Mazzocco ▲

Lytton
Springs

LYTTON SPRINGS RD.

▲ Bellerose

CANYON RD.

▲ Murphy-Goode

▲ Alexander Valley Fruit & Trading

▲ Sausal

White
Oak ▲

Jordan ▲

▲ Alexander Valley

Johnson's Alexander
Valley

▲ Hanna

▲ Field Stone

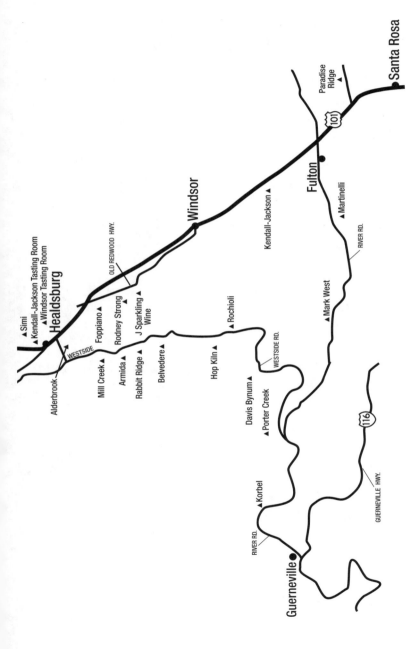

Simi ▲
Kendall-Jackson Tasting Room ▲
Windsor Tasting Room ▲
**Healdsburg** ●
Alderbrook ▲
WESTSIDE
Mill Creek ▲
Armida ▲
Rabbit Ridge ▲
Belvedere ▲
Foppiano ▲
Rodney Strong ▲
J Sparkling Wine ▲
OLD REDWOOD HWY.
Davis Bynum ▲
▲ Porter Creek
WESTSIDE RD.
Hop Kiln ▲
Rochioli ▲
**Windsor** ●
Kendall-Jackson ▲
Mark West ▲
Martinelli ▲
**Fulton** ●
RIVER RD.
Paradise Ridge ▲
**Santa Rosa** ●
101
RIVER RD.
▲ Korbel
116
GUERNEVILLE HWY.
**Guerneville** ●

*(See main map on p. 25 for additional wineries south of River Road.)*

# Sonoma Valley
## (Inset B from p. 25 map)

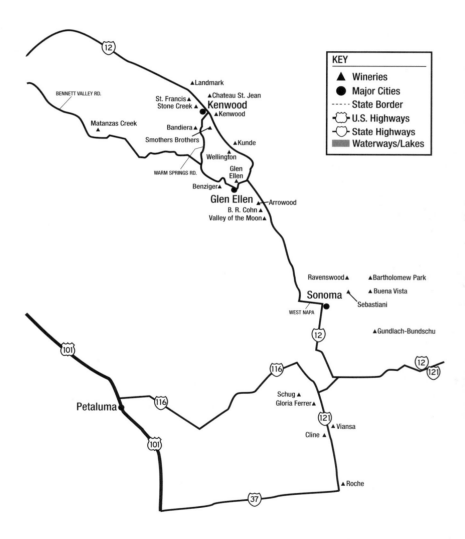

KEY
▲ Wineries
● Major Cities
----- State Border
-○- U.S. Highways
-○- State Highways
▨ Waterways/Lakes

BENNETT VALLEY RD.

▲Landmark

St. Francis▲    ▲Chateau St. Jean
Stone Creek ▲  Kenwood
▲Kenwood

Matanzas Creek
▲

Bandiera▲

Smothers Brothers    ▲Kunde

Wellington

WARM SPRINGS RD.    Glen
Ellen

Benziger▲

Glen Ellen  ▲—Arrowood
B. R. Cohn ▲
Valley of the Moon▲

Ravenswood▲    ▲Bartholomew Park

▲ Buena Vista
Sonoma
Sebastiani
WEST NAPA

▲Gundlach-Bundschu

101

116

Petaluma

116

Schug ▲
Gloria Ferrer▲

121
▲Viansa
Cline ▲

101

▲ Roche

37

Highway 29 just by turning into every driveway you come to. In Sonoma, you have to work more, but the odyssey and subsequent discovery make it equally rewarding, if not more so. Here you need to rid yourself of the notion of visiting as many wineries in one day as possible, like a gunslinger notching his belt. Downshift from the fast lane, and enjoy the dusty trails and back roads; it will take a bit more planning but will be worth it.

Carneros, the southernmost area in Sonoma, lies in an east-west direction bordering the cool San Pablo Bay and stretching into Napa Valley. The Sonoma Valley district—often called the Valley of the Moon after former resident and author Jack London's century-old description—encompasses the main city of Sonoma and the smaller towns that line Highway 12 into Santa Rosa. To the west of Santa Rosa, Russian River Valley stretches up to Healdsburg. North and northwest of Healdsburg is Dry Creek Valley, while to the southeast, Alexander Valley stretches almost back to Napa. Five regions: very distinct, each with its own wine specialties to be explored. And luckily, Sonoma County provides excellent signage on main highways and back roads to indicate the direction and mileage to nearby wineries.

## WINERIES

### SONOMA VALLEY

*(listed south to north, from Carneros to City of Sonoma)*

Traveling north from San Francisco on U.S. 101, exit east on Highway 37 and when the Sears Point Raceway comes into view, veer left on Highway 121, which will put you in the cool, grape-growing region of Carneros. From here you can see Roche, Viansa, Cline, and Gloria Ferrer. At the intersection of Highway 121 and 116, squint to see Bonneau Road, which heads west to Schug. Back on Highway 121, you'll soon connect with Highway 12, which will take you to the Sonoma town square. Make a right at the stop sign (Napa Street) and a left at Fourth Street; you'll find Sebastiani Winery within a few blocks.

Continue on Fourth Street, turn right on Spain Street, and then left on Gehricke Road and follow it around to Ravenswood. Back on Spain Street, it soon becomes Lovall Valley Road; turn onto Castle Road and then take Vineyard Lane to Bartholomew Park

Winery. Back on Lovall Valley Road, turn left on Old Winery Road to Buena Vista Winery. The last winery in the city limits is Gundlach-Bundschu: Go farther down Old Winery Road, turn right on Napa Street, left on Eighth Street, and then left on Denmark Street for about a mile.

## Roche Winery

**28700 Arnold Dr. (Highway 121), Sonoma 95476**
**707-935-7115 • Daily 10–6 (winter 10–5) • Most varieties**
**poured, no fee • Good gift selection • Picnic area**

Driving up from San Francisco, exit U.S. 101 onto Highway 37 and turn left onto Highway 121; the first winery you'll see is Roche. Conventional wisdom deemed this location too far south, and therefore too cold via its proximity to the bay, to fully ripen grapes. The Roches, both physicians, bought this 2,500-acre ranch and pasture land in 1977 primarily to get away from the city. By 1982 though, they had planted trial acreage of Pinot Noir and Chardonnay, both cool-climate grapes that enjoy long growing seasons.

In 1989, the winery bug bit; the Roches constructed a winery on the top of the hill and planted additional vines, including Merlot. The winery looks like a barn that might have sat on this ranch property in earlier times. The sizable tasting room is airy, with a high ceiling and a long bar; notice the great view south toward San Pablo Bay. Steve MacRostie, former winemaker at Hacienda, has a nice touch with Pinot Blanc and Chardonnay, both rich and racy. The reds, Pinot Noir and Merlot, have good flavor intensities.

## Viansa Winery

**25200 Arnold Dr., Sonoma 95476 • 707-935-4700,**
**800-995-4740 • Daily 10–5 • Four selected varieties poured,**
**no fee • Excellent gift selection and full-service deli on premises**
**Picnic grounds**

If the name Sebastiani sounds familiar, it's because the family has made wine in the city of Sonoma for decades. But oldest son, Sam, and his wife, Vicki, were ousted from control of the Sebastiani Winery in a widely publicized spat in 1986. So the couple set out to reclaim their Tuscan heritage by establishing their own place, Viansa Winery and Marketplace. Indeed this Cal-Italian villa would not look out of place in the hills of the Chianti region, though juxtaposing it to the Sears Point Raceway in southern Sonoma seems odd.

Walk around back to the main entrance, and you enter a veritable marketplace of all things Italian. Aromas of pungent cheese, garlic, and olive oil hang in the air. Against one wall a full-service deli provides everything you need for a sumptuous, wine-country picnic. In the middle of the room, samples of specialty products offered for sale—mustards, cheeses, crackers, olives, etc.—compete for your attention. Dual tasting bars stand at opposite ends of the room. Cabernet, Chardonnay, and Sauvignon Blanc are still big, but Viansa has obviously committed to Italian varietals, including Muscat, Nebbiolo, Sangiovese, and Barbera. An excellent picnic area overlooks the waterfowl preserve.

## Cline Cellars

**24737 Arnold Dr., Sonoma 95476 • 707-935-4310**
**Daily 10–6 • Four selected varieties poured, no fee • Small gift selection • Shaded picnic area**

Matt and Fred Cline inherited a vineyard in the town of Oakley in Contra Costa County, nowhere close to high-profile winemaking areas. Additionally, the vineyards were planted to old-time varieties like Mourvedre, Zinfandel, and Carignane. But by the mid-1980s, these heritage and Rhone varietals experienced a resurgence. After the Clines saw other winemakers' success with grapes they had bought from the Clines, the two decided to plunge into the winery business themselves.

The Clines purchased a 350-acre former horse ranch in Sonoma and planted additional acreage to their favorite Rhone varieties: Syrah, Viognier, Marsanne, and Roussanne. A two-story nineteeth-century white-clapboard farmhouse with green trim houses the tasting room and offices. Eternally curious, the Clines make more than a dozen different wines, four of which are poured daily and rotate on a monthly basis. The blended red wines, called Cotes d'Oakley and Oakley Cuvee, are de facto best buys: big, gutsy, and inexpensive. You'll also find varietally labeled Mourvedre, Zinfandel, and Syrah, all fine examples of their types. Rose bushes and shade trees abound on the property as do shaded picnic tables. Snapping turtles in the nearby pools may amuse children.

## Gloria Ferrer Champagne Caves

**23555 Highway 121, Sonoma 95476 • 707-996-7256**
**Daily 10:30–5:30 • Sparkling wines by the glass, $2.25-$3.75 fee; still wines, $2 fee • Tours hourly 11–4 • Small gift selection Picnic area for customers**

The Spanish influence abounds at Gloria Ferrer; the leading winemaking family of Spain, the Ferrers have made wine for hundreds of years. They produce the largest amount of *methode cham-penoise* (traditional, fermented-in-the-bottle sparkling wine) in the world under their flagship label, Freixenet. Additionally, they own wineries in France and Mexico, so it was only a matter of time before they found the right site in California in 1986.

You can see the whitewashed adobe walls, arched windows and doorways, and red tiled roof of the winery buildings from down the road. The cathedral-ceilinged tasting room features dark woods and wrought-iron fixtures; a green tiled fireplace stands opposite the tasting bar. Tours begin so often it seems a shame not to go on one, which will wind you through caves and riddling cellars, past thousands of sleeping bottles of sparkling wine. The civilized tasting room regime invites you to have a seat at one of the many tables in the tasting room or on the wraparound patio, and a host will take your order. Four sparklers are normally available for a fee, the best being the Brut. A Carneros Chardonnay and Pinot Noir, both tasty, are also offered. As another nice touch, a small plate of complimentary almonds comes with every glass of wine.

## Schug Winery
**602 Bonneau Rd., Sonoma 95476 • 707-939-9363**
**Daily 10–5 • Selected varieties poured, no fee**
Winemaker Walt Schug helped Joseph Phelps Winery in Napa Valley get off to a good start in its early years. Before leaving that winery in 1983, he already made wine under his own label, determined to discover the secrets of Pinot Noir. In 1990 he chose a site in the cooler Carneros region and built his winery close to the marine influence of the San Pablo Bay. There Schug planted forty acres, primarily to Pinot Noir and Chardonnay.

The actual location seems obscure, but Bonneau Road is right at the intersection of Highways 121 and 116; travel west down a country lane for a mile, and the winery will come into sight. Initially, it appears quite small, but once around back, you discover Schug recently finished digging wine caves into the hillside. Next he plans to complete a visitors' center, but presently the tasting room takes up the small quarters of the winery lab. Two different-style Chardonnays offer interesting contrasts. The Gamay Beaujolais is done in a lighter style, while the estate Pinot Noir features more serious flavors.

## Sebastiani Vineyards

**389 E. Fourth St., Sonoma 95476 • 707-938-5532,**
**800-888-5532 • Daily 10–5 • Most varieties poured, no fee**
**Tours every half-hour, 10:30–4 • Good gift selection**
**Picnic tables**

Visitors who stop at only one winery in Sonoma usually visit Sebastiani. The name is known worldwide, and the winery has a long history dating back to the turn of the century, when Italian immigrant Samuele Sebastiani came to Sonoma to haul quarry stones. He would later use those same types of stones to build a winery cellar, which today serves as the tasting room. Though Sebastiani started small, the empire covers several square blocks in this largely residential area. The original vineyard planted by the mission fathers, across the street from the parking lot, belongs to Sebastiani.

Perhaps the main reason folks travel to the winery is to see one of the largest collections of carved wine casks in the world. Earle Brown hand-carved all types of wine-related images into the heads of oak barrels and on the sides of large ovals and redwood casks. Sebastiani's tour also weaves through one of the biggest collections of mammoth redwood holding tanks still in use today. Many of them will easily hold 50,000 gallons of wine. Naturally the tour ends back at the tasting room, a dark, cool, spacious area. The wine menu runs the gamut from a sweet Rose style to Chardonnay to heavier reds like Cabernet and Merlot. A half-dozen picnic tables are next to the winery, but you'll find the best tables on the far side of the parking lot, where shade trees next to the road offer respite from the afternoon sun.

## Ravenswood

**18701 Gehricke Rd., Sonoma 95476 • 707-938-1960**
**Daily 10–4:30 • Selected varieties poured, no fee • Small gift**
**selection • Picnic area**

Winemaker Joel Peterson started out as a part-time winemaker after spending a few harvests helping out at Joe Swan Vineyards. Peterson went on to make wine out of the back end of a woodworking shop south of town until he could move into the former Haywood Winery in 1991. "No wimpy wines" is the Ravenswood motto, meaning the winery offers big, unapologetic wines, mostly red and mostly Zinfandel.

Although only about a mile from Sonoma Plaza, the winery sits in a quiet, secluded valley with rolling hills. Park in the lower lot and take a short hike up the hill to the cobblestone tasting room. Etched in the glass of the double doors, you'll see the famous ravens logo (by David Lance Goines), which appears on the Ravenswood label. Due for expansion, the tasting room is presently too small to handle the crush of Zin-fanatics on a summer weekend. However, on week-days in winter or spring, you can receive individual and friendly atten-tion. Zinfandels are the ticket, and Ravenswood has about a half-dozen different ones. But don't overlook the Cabernet, Chardonnay, Merlot, and late-harvest Gewurztraminer.

### Bartholomew Park Winery

**1000 Vineyard Ln., Sonoma 95476 • 707-935-9511**
**Daily 10:30–4:30 • Selected varieties poured, no fee • Small gift selection • Shaded picnic area**

Frank Bartholomew, former president of United Press International, resuscitated Buena Vista Winery after buying it in 1941. When he sold the winery in 1968, he retained the nearby vineyards; historically they are said to be among the first planted by Count Agoston Haraszthy in 1857. By 1973, Bartholomew had converted the adjacent old Sonoma hospital into a winery, naming it Hacienda after the mission style of the building, to process his grapes. Corporate winery interests purchased Hacienda in 1992 and renamed it Bartholomew Park.

The real attraction, though, is the modern reproduction of the Pompiean Villa, built by Haraszthy in 1857 and reputedly the site of the first California wine festival. You'll gape in awe at the sight before you ever see the winery, about a half-mile beyond. The style of that era is gracefully reconstructed through the furnishings of the time. The museum has limited hours but is usually open weekends. The winery itself serves up the usual suspects: Chardonnay, Cabernet, and Merlot, as well as an interesting photo exhibit about Sonoma grape growing. Pssst . . . the awareness of this winery is still so limited that you can practically have the beautiful, shaded picnic area, under the oak groves and overlooking the vineyards, all to yourself.

### Buena Vista Winery

**18000 Old Winery Rd., Sonoma 95476 • 707-938-1266,**
**800-926-1266 • Daily 10:30–4:30 • Four selected varieties poured, no fee • Excellent gift selection, including comestibles**
**Art gallery and reserve tasting bar upstairs, $3 fee**
**Picnic areas**

No winery is more steeped in history than the legendary Buena Vista. Count (a self-conferred title, no doubt) Agoston Haraszthy, the founder of Buena Vista in 1857, is sometimes called the father of California wine. Inspired by General Vallejo's vineyard adjacent to the Sonoma mission, Haraszthy began planting his own vineyard and soon had the largest acreage of wine grapes in the state. Needing to increase the quality of the wines, he traveled to Europe in 1861 and brought back a wide variety of grape cuttings to transplant in California. Over the years, the winery changed hands and is now owned by the German firm of A. Racke & Company, whose sole interest is the wine business.

Down a quaint country lane that passes through a forest of towering trees, you'll find the stone cellars of the original winery, now a state historical landmark. About a quarter-mile walk from the dirt parking lot takes you to the rough-hewn stone buildings covered with lichen and vines. In the courtyard surrounded by picnic tables, a Spanish-style fountain gurgles, and old photographs display the history of the winery. Through wrought-iron gates, you can see the winery tunnels and caves, dug by Chinese immigrants. The wines, however, are no longer made here; a modern production facility in Carneros, where most of the grapes grow, handles that chore. But you can taste the results here inside the original press room, which dates back to 1863. Chardonnay, Cabernet, and Merlot lead the tasting list; Sauvignon Blanc tastes especially good, and spicy varietals, like Gewurztraminer and Riesling, are popular.

## Gundlach-Bundschu Winery

**2000 Denmark St., Sonoma 95476 • 707-938-5277**
**Daily 11–4:30 • Selected varieties poured, no fee**
**Hilltop picnic area**

You may find Gundlach-Bundschu hard to pronounce, and finding the winery is none too easy either, nestled in a more rural section of the Sonoma Valley than the rest of the wineries. German immigrant Jacob Gundlach planted the Rhinefarm, as he called it, in 1855 and made his first wines three years later. Charles Bundschu became a partner in the venture and eventually married Gundlach's daughter. The winery survived phylloxera and the famous San Francisco earthquake but not Prohibition, though the grapes were still grown and sold to home-based winemakers. After Prohibition, larger wineries bought the grapes until fifth-generation Jim Bundschu decided to revive it in 1969. He took his time restoring the old, stone winery, and his first estate harvest occurred in 1973.

You can see the winery from the road through the trees; a short drive down the winery's country lane puts you at its doorsteps. In front of the ancient, stone winery, a few umbrella tables overlook the vineyards and the nearby pond. A colorful harvest-scene mural constructed in panels also graces the grounds. First, the tasting room most likely will offer Gewurztraminer, one of the best in the valley (and the subject of the winery's humorous sobriety test poster, available for purchase). Chardonnay, Zinfandel, Cabernet, and Merlot are also poured. Pinot Noir, which the winery is not noted for, can be quite impressive in good vintages.

## SONOMA VALLEY

*(listed south to north, from Glen Ellen to Santa Rosa)*

In front of Sonoma Plaza, head west on West Napa Street, which is Highway 12, and follow the highway as it winds through Glen Ellen and Kenwood. Almost all the wineries are within shouting distance of the highway, and directional signs abound. On the left, Valley of the Moon Winery comes up first, then B. R. Cohn Winery, and Arrowood Vineyards. A couple miles up the road, turn left onto Arnold Drive, and you'll find Glen Ellen Winery in town, while a right on London Ranch Road leads you into the hills to Benziger Winery. Back near Highway 12, Wellington Vineyards is on Dunbar Road. On Highway 12 again, to the right will be Kunde Winery, followed by Smothers Brothers, Kenwood Vineyards, Stone Creek Winery, Bandiera Winery, Chateau St. Jean Winery, St. Francis Winery, and Landmark Vineyards. Highway 12 then becomes increasingly commercial and takes you into Santa Rosa. Matanzas Creek Winery is isolated in the Bennett Valley; take Warm Springs Road in Kenwood or off Arnold Drive in Glen Ellen and then follow Enterprise Road to Bennett Valley Road.

### Valley of the Moon Winery
**777 Madrone Rd., Glen Ellen 95442 • 707-996-6941**
**Daily 10–5 • Most varieties poured, no fee • Good gift selection**
**Shaded picnic area**

Wine has been made on this property since the late nineteenth century. In fact, newspaper publisher and U.S. Senator George Hearst once owned the estate and built stone cellars for wine storage. The Parducci family took over the property in 1941 and has run the place ever since. Gradually the production of generic jug wines has given way to vintage-dated varietal wines.

Still, it looks like the winery time forgot, stuck in a 1950s time warp. Age has weathered the stone-and-wood front of the winery and tasting room; a bay laurel tree provides shade as does the front porch overhang, an important point on a hot summer day. The cast-iron grape motifs on the windows reflect the handiwork of an earlier time. Inside the tasting room, the original wood paneling remains, and the stone walls have stood the test of time. After a few minutes, your eyes will adjust to the dark, cool environment; find your way to an L-shaped bar. The varietals, including Sauvignon Blanc, Chardonnay, Cabernet, and Zinfandel, have a straightforward, no-nonsense style. The Private Stock red and white table wines are often good buys.

## B. R. Cohn Winery

**15140 Sonoma Hwy. 12, Glen Ellen 95442 • 707-938-4064**
**Daily 10–4:30 • Selected varieties poured, no fee • Small gift selection • Picnic area**

Rock 'n' roll may seem a long way from sedate country living and grape growing, but don't tell that to Bruce Cohn, former manager of the enormously successful Doobie Brothers band. Life in the fast lane can be stimulating, but spending half the year on the road with a touring band can be equally draining. A Sonoma County native, Cohn bought this property in 1974 as a home; he wanted to raise his kids in the kind of environment he grew up in. After selling his grapes to locals for several years, he converted an old dairy barn into a winery and began producing under his own label in 1984.

A winding path off the highway leads to an adobe-style tasting room with a cobblestone patio and a half-dozen tables out front. On the way in, you'll notice stately olive trees lining the driveway that continue past the winery to the private residence. Inside, a gorgeous burlwood bar and matching back bar claim the center of attention, while Cohn's gold records hang on the opposite wall. Cohn was one of the first in wine country to make and bottle an excellent extra virgin olive oil, made from the trees on the ranch.

The real reason you should make the pilgrimage, however, is to taste some very good Cabernets. Cohn offers several bottlings, ranging from intense to more intense; he often has different vintages open for comparison.

## Arrowood Vineyards

**14347 Sonoma Hwy. 12, Glen Ellen 95442 • 707-938-5170**
**Daily 10–4:30 • Two varieties poured, no fee.**

Arrowood's tasting room, modest by wine country standards, lets the wines, rather than a lavish visitor facility, do the talking.

Dick Arrowood and his wife, Alis, have long participated in the Sonoma County winemaking scene. Dick led Chateau St. Jean Winery to the forefront of California winemaking in the 1970s, but with a new corporate ownership and somewhat restricted conditions, he began to long for his own winery; he wanted to get back to hands-on basic winemaking and to produce exactly the wines he wanted in his own style. He started Arrowood in 1987 and began devoting his talents full time to his winery in 1990.

The simple, classic-style white barn winery sits on a sharp knoll, surrounded by the estate vineyards. Almost invisible from the highway, the winery hides amid a grove of oak trees. If you see more than a couple of visitors, park on the west side of the building and walk behind the winery, a walk nevertheless educational for its display of modern winemaking equipment. Wind your way around to a second-story veranda, and you'll discover the tiny tasting room, all blonde wood with windows looking out upon the vineyards below. Chardonnay, Viognier, Cabernet, and Merlot from the premium line are the heavy hitters here, though none is poured every day. Most likely, wines from the second label, Grand Archer, will be poured; these tasty wines didn't make the first team but usually offer a delicious bargain. If the room gets a little crowded, escape to the veranda, with its glass-topped tables and cushioned chairs, to sip and take in the view of the valley.

### Glen Ellen Winery

**14301 Arnold Dr., Glen Ellen 95442 • 707-939-6277**
**Daily 10–5 • Most varieties poured, no fee • History center with photographs and artifacts • Excellent gift selection**

Glen Ellen is one of those great American success stories. Bruno Benziger retired and brought his family to this area in 1980 to make wine. By the early 1990s, they were making more than three million cases of wine, and their "fighting varietals," made from premium grapes like Cabernet and Chardonnay, graced every grocery store shelf. In 1993, The Boys, as people called the five Benziger brothers, decided to sell the Glen Ellen and M.G. Vallejo labels to Heublein, while keeping the Benziger name and the London Ranch property.

Under corporate ownership, Glen Ellen opened a tasting room in the historic Jack London Village. Housed in the original Glen Ellen Winery built in 1881, the history center features black-and-white photos and collectibles from that era. In the rear, the bright, sunny tasting room has a blonde parquet wood floor and a long, blonde wooden bar, with wine barrels as a backdrop. Both the Glen Ellen and M.G. Vallejo labels are poured, and you can find just about every imaginable wine varietal available for tasting, including the ever-popular Chardonnay and Cabernet, but also Fume Blanc, White Zin, Pinot Noir, and an interesting blend of Semillon and Chardonnay. Look for some of the most exciting wines, however, under the Expressions label. These wines include exotic grapes like Viognier and Sangiovese, as well as old standards like Zinfandel.

## Benziger Family Winery

**1883 London Ranch Rd., Glen Ellen 95442 • 707-935-3000**
**Daily 10–4:30 • Selected varieties poured, no fee • Charge for**
**Imagery wine series • Vineyard tram tour three times daily**
**Self-guided tour • Art gallery • Picnic area**

When the Benzigers sold their interest in the huge Glen Ellen label (see previous listing), they retained the heart of the operation: the London Ranch and the surrounding vineyards, which allowed them to pursue quality winemaking on a smaller scale. Located a short back-road drive from town, the ranch provides an idyllic setting for immersing yourself in the total winery experience. First, you'll notice the viticultural discovery center; this display plot illustrates all manner of rootstocks, trellising systems, and clonal selections. An informational, electronic kiosk out front will direct you to other highlights of the hundred-acre property: a grove of redwoods, a charming rose garden, a peacock aviary, a shaded picnic area, and an art gallery.

A unique, fully narrated tram tour of the vineyards will take you to the different vineyard sites on the ranch. Perhaps it injects a little bit of Disneyland into rural Sonoma, but most people find the ride interesting. Inside the tasting room, a wide variety of wines are poured. Cabernet, Merlot, Zinfandel, Fume Blanc, and Chardonnay all provide very dependable choices. The special Imagery series features original artwork on the label and unusual varietals like Viognier, Aleatico, and Syrah. It's all folksy, down home, and an amazingly fun and educational experience for the whole family.

## Wellington Vineyards

**11600 Dunbar Rd., Glen Ellen 95442 • 707-939-0708**
**Daily 11–5 • Most varieties poured, no fee • Picnic area**

Father-son team John and Peter Wellington built this small winery in the late 1980s. The Wellingtons draw from a nearby vineyard with seventy-year-old to hundred-year-old vines. The white winery building with brown trim is strictly utilitarian; the Wellingtons would rather put their money into wine production. Out front, a small patio with shaded tables leads to a cozy tasting room, close to the vines.

Production is around 6,000 cases, with many of the wines made in such small lots that you'll only find them at the winery. The Wellingtons produce a Chardonnay, but skip over that; red wines are their forte. Cabernet and Merlot are good, but the Zinfandels, made from those old vines, taste big and hearty. A Cotes du Rhone blend, an amalgamation of different grapes, tastes pleasant, and the price is right. Unusual red varieties include Cab Franc, Dolcetto, and Cinsault; in addition, Wellington sometimes has Criolla, also known as the Mission grape, originally brought to California by the Franciscan fathers. Finish with the Old Vine Port which tastes sweet and easy on the way down.

## Kunde Estate Winery

**10155 Sonoma Hwy. 12, Kenwood 95452 • 707-833-5501**
**Daily 10–4:30 • Four varieties poured, no fee • Wine cave tours on weekends • Small gift selection • Picnic area**

The Kundes have grown grapes in Sonoma since the turn of the century, and they have primarily concentrated on farming and ranching. Their grapes have gone into quite a number of Sonoma wineries' award-winning wines. In 1990, a new generation decided to make wine under its own label. The Kundes built a new winery resembling the wood barn that once graced the property and burrowed 32,000 square feet of winery caves into the hillside. They added the magnificent tasting room onto the front of the winery in 1995.

A man-made pond with mini-geysers lies in front of the winery; shaded picnic tables line the patio. The gray, stone building that houses the tasting room has high ceilings and several glass-windowed walls for viewing the fermenting tanks and bottling line. On a recent visit, the host handed visitors samples as they wandered in and explained, "It's against the law to be in the tasting room without a glass of wine in your hand." Congeniality rules here, and the friendly staff conducts the balance of the tasting at the roomy, wood bar. The wines, as you would expect from someone who's spent a century understanding grape growing, are stellar. Sauvignon Blanc and Chardonnay offer fine examples of those varietals, while Cabernet, Merlot, Zinfandel, and the blended Claret are also good choices.

## Smothers Brothers Wines/Remick Ridge Vineyards
**9575 Sonoma Hwy. 12, Kenwood 95452 • 707-833-1010**
**Daily 10–4:30 • All varieties poured, no fee • Good gift selection**

People sometimes think it's just a bad joke upon discovering the Smothers Brothers tasting room on the corner of Highway 12 and Warm Springs Road, sandwiched between all those "serious" wineries. But in 1972, Tom Smothers bought a 110-acre ranch in Sonoma not far from here and planted vineyards. In recent years, Dick Arrowood, a neighbor from a winery down the road, has helped make the wines.

The store features plenty of Smothers Brothers memorabilia and clothing, along with all manner of novelties and souvenirs. The star-struck will find Smothers Brothers director chairs available, and you can even have your picture taken with cardboard cutouts of the Brothers. Reflecting typical retail strategy, you have to walk through the minefield of merchandise to get to the tasting bar. Several vintages of Chardonnay and Cabernet may be open, and it's interesting to taste the different bottlings side by side. Best buys include Mom's Favorite Red and Mom's Favorite White, the latter on the slightly sweet side.

## Kenwood Vineyards
**9592 Sonoma Hwy. 12, Kenwood 95452 • 707-833-5891**
**Daily 10–4:30 • Four selected varieties poured, no fee**
**Good gift selection**

The rustic, weathered barn of Kenwood Vineyards, surrounded by vines and shaded by oak trees, is one of the most inviting wineries in all of Sonoma. Wine was made here in the early 1900s, during the time Jack London lived nearby. But no one revived the property until 1970, and now the growth of Kenwood can be seen in the buildings that have grown up on both sides of the tasting room.

The folksy, woodsy interior sports wooden beams and whitewashed ceilings, as well as an L-shaped bar. Stacks of wine ready for purchase separate the tasting room from the gift shop. Behind the bar, many artists' labels the winery has commissioned over the years are on display; you can find many of those artists' shows on the surrounding walls. You must try Sauvignon Blanc; you'll either love it or hate it, but the wine has the typical weedy varietal flavors almost to a fault. Chardonnay, Zinfandel, and Cabernet are the main wines poured. Stand in line for the special edition Jack London Cabernet, as well as any of the limited edition wines from the artists series.

Amazingly, the winery usually opens more than a dozen different bottlings daily, many of them wonderfully aged red wines, real treats to taste.

## Stone Creek Winery

**9380 Sonoma Hwy. 12, Kenwood 95452 • 707-833-4455**
**Daily 10–4:30 • Most varieties poured, no fee; charge**
**for older vintages • Good gift selection**
A large outfit, Stone Creek produces around 250,000 cases of respectable, vintage-dated, varietal wine a year. Although the winery is located elsewhere, the tasting room lies on busy Highway 12 in Sonoma Valley to take advantage of the tourist traffic.

Situated in the historic Old Blue Schoolhouse that dates back to 1890, the Stone Creek tasting room's renovations allow plenty of sunlight to stream in from multiple window banks. A mammoth horseshoe bar dominates half the room. The bar offers a long list of varietals from the tasting menu. Chardonnay, Fume Blanc, Gewurztraminer, and White Zin lead the whites, while the requisite reds are Zinfandel, Merlot, and Cabernet. You can try the Chairman's reserve and higher-priced Valley Ridge wines for an additional fee. Most of the wines are modest in quality but value-priced for everyday drinking.

## Bandiera Winery

**8860 Sonoma Hwy. 12, Kenwood 95452 • 707-833-2448**
**Daily 10–4:30 • Most varieties poured, no fee**
The Bandiera Winery is actually located in Cloverdale, far up U.S. 101 from this well-traveled tourist location in the heart of wine country. They get a lot more visitors here on Highway 12 than they ever got at the winery. For four decades, the Bandiera family operated the winery. An investment group took over in 1980, hoping to capitalize on the growing need for inexpensive wines in the marketplace. The Bandieras' whole identity hinges on securing good grapes wherever they can to make good wines. The Bandiera strategy of offering value-priced varietals has worked well.

There's nothing fancy about their white, one-room tasting shack, but then there's nothing fancy about their prices either. White Zinfandel, Sauvignon Blanc, Chardonnay, and Cabernet all sell for less than $7; Merlot is the pricey selection at $12. Vintage Cabernets dating back to 1987 can taste quite dry and mellow.

## Chateau St. Jean

**8555 Sonoma Hwy. 12, Kenwood 95452 • 707-833-4134, 800-322-WINE • Daily 10–4:30 • Five selected varieties poured, no fee • Self-guided winery tour • Small gift selection**
**Picnic area**

This facility was one of the original must-see wineries of the county, built in the early 1970s wine boom. Hidden from Highway 12 by a grove of trees, you may feel a little startled to discover a Spanish-style estate, complete with fountains, arched doorways, red tiled roofs, and a bell tower. The winery developed an unrivaled reputation for Chardonnays, made by Dick Arrowood. The original owners sold out to the Japanese drink giant Suntory in 1984. Suntory stumbled at first but regained the quality momentum in the early 1990s. In 1995 the company that owns Beringer in the Napa Valley acquired Chateau St. Jean.

When the winery was built, it was one of the most modern facilities in the valley. The entire place, including the gardens and the grounds, which feature a great picnicking site, have been wonderfully maintained. The self-guided tour of the winery proper allows overhead views of stainless steel tanks and wines aging in oak barrels. Be sure to climb the circular staircase in the tower for a bird's eye view of the valley. The tasting room sits across the fountain from the winery in the corner of a former private residence. For all the grounds' expansiveness, the room looks undersized for more than a dozen visitors. The white wines are still very good, including Chardonnay and trio of blancs: Fume, Pinot, and Sauvignon. But the red wines come on strong too, including Merlot, Pinot Noir, and Cinq Cepages, the latter an excellent Bordeaux-style blend. Late-harvest dessert wines, a Muscat, and a Riesling have long been house specialties.

## St. Francis Winery

**8450 Sonoma Hwy. 12, Kenwood 95452 • 707-833-4666**
**Daily 10–4:30 • Selected varieties poured, no fee; reserve wines, $1 fee • Good gift selection and a variety of comestibles**
**Picnic area**

As late as 1971, this prime Sonoma property produced prunes and walnuts, but retiree Joe Martin uprooted the hundred acres and planted vines. After selling his grapes to larger wineries, he decided to take the plunge in 1979 by rehabilitating a nineteenth-century ranch home on the property and adding a brown, barn-style winery.

A bevy of flapping flags and a statue of Saint Francis (the patron saint of Martin's hometown, San Francisco) will catch your eye in front of the winery. A quick turn into the winery parking lot puts you directly across from the tasting room entrance, adjacent to the winery. The room features beamed ceilings, a stone fireplace, and an oak bar with a brass foot rail. Also look for historic photos on the walls, displaying the ranch's fruit-drying operation days. Out back, visitors picnic amid the flower gardens and olive trees that border the Merlot vineyard. And Merlot at St. Francis is among the best in California. More high-scorers include the Cabernet, Zinfandel, and Chardonnay.

## Landmark Vineyards
**101 Adobe Canyon Rd., Kenwood 95452 • 707-833-0053, 800–452-6365 • Daily 10–4:30 • Selected wines poured, no fee Excellent gift selection and comestibles • Pond-side picnic area**

Landmark began life in 1974 as a partnership based farther north in Windsor, but urban encroachment forced the winery to relocate. It found a home in the Sonoma Valley sans all partners except one: the present owner, Damaris Deere Ethridge, a descendent of agricultural-implement producer John Deere. Now nestled in the shadow of the Sugarloaf Mountains, the new winery, built in 1990, reflects the rustic grace and harmony of its surroundings, according to Ethridge. The Spanish, mission-style buildings with brown, thatched roofs encircle a central courtyard with tiled walkways, fountains, and manicured grounds.

Tastefully decorated, the tasting room conveys woodsy, Californian comfort. The whitewashed walls and beamed ceilings embrace a red tiled floor, a fireplace, a granite tasting bar, and an oversized wine-grape mural by Claudia Wagar. The wide variety of giftware includes ceramics and kitchenware, as well as comestibles and wine-themed logo items. Chardonnay reigns here, and the winery produces a number of different bottlings, though only one may be poured. A Chardonnay from the second label, Adobe Canyon, is often featured. Depending on availability, a Brut sparkler, Merlot, or Cabernet may round out the tasting.

## Matanzas Creek Winery
**6097 Bennett Valley Rd., Santa Rosa 95404 • 707-528-6464 Daily 10–4:30 • Selected varieties poured, no fee • Winery tours by appointment • Largest lavender garden in Sonoma; self-guided garden tours • Good gift selection from winery's lavender products line • Picnic area**

The only major winery located in the Bennett Valley, Matanzas Creek is a bit off the beaten path. But particularly during the summer, three acres of blooming lavender plants that give off a heady scent will reward you. Besides its ornamental function, the harvested lavender forms the basis for all kinds of decorative gift items available at the winery. But that's just an added attraction. The wines, made here since 1977, are of the highest quality. The MacIvers first planted vineyards here in 1974 and began making wine in an old dairy shed. Later they constructed a state-of-the-art winery on a hillside knoll.

Besides the lavender, many other wonders grace the property, including Bruce Johnson's redwood fountain out front. Brochures in the tasting room will guide you through the grounds; a winery tour is also available by appointment. The tasting room, in keeping with the mood at Matanzas Creek, is understated. The wines, Sauvignon Blanc, Chardonnay, and Merlot, are expensive but worth it. The MacIvers have limited themselves to these three varieties, with the ambition of producing world-class wine in each category. They are well on their way. A recent, limited-release Chardonnay called Journey is a selection of the best barrels in the winery. At $75, Journey is the most expensive Chardonnay in California, so don't expect them to pour it in the tasting room.

## NORTHERN SONOMA COUNTY

*(listed from Santa Rosa to Healdsburg; Russian River Valley listed from River Road to Westside Road)*

Santa Rosa is the industrial hub of the county and consequently the most cosmopolitan city, with a variety of activities and restaurants. While the city lacks the historical charm of Sonoma or Healdsburg, it lies close to Sonoma Valley wineries in the south county as well as Russian River/Dry Creek/Alexander valleys wineries in the north. You'll find Paradise Ridge, the only winery in Santa Rosa proper, off the Bicentennial exit east of U.S. 101 and then left on Thomas Lake Harris Drive. The Russian River Valley starts just up U.S. 101; exit River Road west and take a right on Fulton Road to Kendall-Jackson's new tasting facility. Drop back down to River Road, take a right, and head west to Martinelli. Farther down River Road, make a left at Olivet Lane to De Loach Vineyards; back on River Road, turn right on Trenton-Healdsburg Road to Mark West Vineyards. Now backtrack on River Road east, and make a right on Laguna Road to both Joseph Swan Vineyards and Martini and Prati Winery. Continue on Laguna Road to Guerneville Road and make a right, then another right on Vine Hill

Road to Dehlinger Winery. Back on Guerneville Road, go right on Highway 116 (Gravenstein Highway), then left on Ross Station Road to Iron Horse Vineyards. Farther down Highway 116 just before Forestville, is Topolos at Russian River.

For the next portion of the journey, continue on Highway 116, turn right on Martinelli Road, cross the Russian River, and go left on River Road several miles to Korbel. Backtrack on River Road and fork off left on Westside Road to Porter Creek Vineyards, Davis Bynum Winery, Rochioli Vineyards, Hop Kiln Winery, Belvedere Winery, Rabbit Ridge Vineyards, Armida Winery, and Mill Creek Vineyards. Then follow Westside Road into Healdsburg to dine or stay the night.

### Paradise Ridge Winery

**4545 Thomas Lake Harris Dr., Santa Rosa 95403**
**707-528-WINE • Daily 11–6 (winter 11–5) • All varieties**
**poured, no fee • Outdoor tables with hilltop view**

As you veer off U.S. 101 onto Bicentennial Drive and drive up the hill to Paradise Ridge Winery, you will certainly think you've lost your way. No agricultural enterprise like a winery could stand amid such tony, exclusive housing developments. But if you persevere, you'll find a winery building that matches its surrounding neighbors in fine style.

With beige walls, brown trim, and a red tiled roof, the imposing winery and visitors' center sits right on the edge of a hill. Your host, most likely a member of this family operation, says, "Welcome to Paradise," and indeed this layout looks pretty close to that. As long-time grape growers in the county who sold their grapes to other wineries, the Byck-Hoenselaars family finally decided to build their own palace to wine. The tasting bar stands in the corner of a large room that's reserved for hospitality events, wedding receptions, and the like. Presently you may taste two vintages of Sauvignon Blanc and three vintages of Chardonnay. Red wines will eventually join these on the list. The outdoor balcony provides a stunning view of Santa Rosa and vineyards to the west.

### Kendall-Jackson California Coast Wine Center

**5007 Fulton Rd., Fulton 95439 • 707-571-7500,**
**800-945-WINE • Daily 10–4 • Selected varieties poured, no fee**
**Good gift selection • Picnic area**

This incredible ersatz French chateau just off U.S. 101 provides a striking architectural contrast to other barn or hop-kiln style wineries in the Russian River. Ken and Grace De Baun acquired vineyard property in 1986 and decided in 1989 to build this show-piece, naming it Chateau De Baun. Their claim to fame revolved around the newly developed grape variety called Symphony, a cross between a White Grenache and a Muscat. Recently they had begun to place less emphasis on Symphony and also offered Chardonnay and Pinot Noir.

In 1996, however, Kendall-Jackson Winery bought the proper-ty and surrounding gardens to showcase the Artisan and Estates line of wines (e.g., Cambria, Stonestreet, Hartford Court), whose wineries are not open to the public, as well as the Kendall-Jackson wines. Definitely stop here to see the architecture, but a dozen different wines poured daily from the Kendall-Jackson properties will make your stop worth it. Expect everything, from main-stream Cabernet and Chardonnay to less familiar but equally interesting varietals like Semillon and Syrah, to appear on the tasting menu.

## Martinelli Vineyards

**3360 River Rd., Windsor 95492 • 707-525-0570,
800-346-1627 • Daily 10–5 • Selected varieties poured, no fee
Art gallery upstairs, open Thurs.–Sun. 11:30–4:30
Excellent gift selection • Picnic area**

The Martinellis have farmed in Sonoma County for several gen-erations, mainly concentrating on apples; in fact, the locals call the Martinelli place the Apple Barn. During apple harvest, hoards of people show up to get orchard-fresh apples; in the off-season, peo-ple clamor for the wide selection of dried fruits, apple juice, and other food-related items. The grape arbor on the front porch pro-vides shade for picnickers.

Wine almost seems an adjunct to the Martinellis' farming activ-ities, though they're also long-time grape growers who sold to other wineries. In fact, they only began making and bottling wine under their own label in 1987. You'll have to navigate your way through the sea of gifts to find the wine tasting bar in the back half of the barn. Chardonnay and Sauvignon Blanc are good starters, but the Zinfandels, some from nearly hundred-year-old vines, are particularly renowned. Gewurztraminer and Pinot Noir can be interesting too. Recently Martinelli brought in wine con-sultant Helen Turley to oversee the winemaking, and the quality has increased.

# De Loach Vineyards
**1791 Olivet Rd., Santa Rosa 95401 • 707-526-9111**
**Daily 10–4:30 • Selected varieties poured, no fee • Daily tours**
**Small gift selection • Picnic area**

In vintner Cecil De Loach, you'll find another one of wine country's retirees who burgeoned into a runaway success. A former San Francisco fireman who moved his family here in 1971, De Loach realized that in the move he had acquired sixty-year-old to eighty-year-old Zinfandel vines. Initially he sold the grapes, but De Loach made a few homemade batches of Zinfandel and thought they tasted as good as the big wineries'. He started constructing a winery in 1979. The public embraced his initial vintages, and he progressively expanded the winery in stages, reaching a production of about 130,000 cases per year.

For such a large winery, the grounds and the buildings look remarkably tasteful; the use of redwood and earth tones makes the winery seem like part of the land. A cobblestone courtyard with picnic tables leads to the tasting room, which sports whitewashed walls and wooden beams. With plenty of light streaming in the front windows, the tasting room provides a perfect spot for displaying art or a visual history of the winery.

The back wall of the tasting bar groans under the weight of hundreds of medals and ribbons. De Loach makes just about every varietal, including the much-maligned White Zinfandel (one of the best). Sauvignon Blanc, Fume Blanc, and Chardonnay are among the whites, while Pinot Noir and Cabernet are the reds. But Zinfandel is a real favorite; besides the good Sonoma County bottling, De Loach also makes intensely flavored (and very limited) Zins, named after the single vineyard (Barbieri, Papeta, Pelliti) from which the grapes come.

# Mark West Estate Winery
**7010 Trenton-Healdsburg Rd., Forestville 95436**
**707-544-4813 • Daily 10–5:30 • Selected varieties poured,**
**no fee • Good gift selection • Picnic area**

Mark West, a sailor, arrived here in 1820, privy to a 26,000-acre land grant. The creek running through this sixty-four acre vineyard property is named after him, as is the winery. Bob and Joan Ellis began making wine in the early 1970s, but after Bob retired from piloting for Pan Am in 1990, they sold the winery to the wine-savvy investors of the Marion Group.

The tasting room, a low-slung barnlike structure, looks cheerful and inviting, filled not only with gifts but meats, cheeses, sodas, and comestibles for picnicking at the numerous tables only steps away. An espresso machine stands ready should you need a caffeine jolt after lunch. A corrugated metal building houses the winery itself; a pond and a greenhouse of carnivorous plants form a scenic backdrop. Wisely, the winery has concentrated on cool-climate varietals (organically grown) that will ripen well here: Chardonnay, Gewurztraminer, Sauvignon Blanc, and Pinot Noir. Zinfandel, from one specific vineyard, is powerful though not often poured.

## Joseph Swan Vineyards
**2916 Laguna Rd., Forestville 95436 • 707-573-3747**
**Sat.–Sun. 11–4:30 • Selected varieties poured, no fee**
Joe Swan is one of the legendary cult figures of California wine-making; many now-fanatical Zinfandel winemakers apprenticed with him. Another retired airline pilot, Swan also practiced art, and he brought that mentality with him in 1969 when he came to this thir-teen-acre property in the coolest part of the Russian River Valley. Swan died in 1988, but fortunately for his friends and fans, son-in-law Rod Berglund took over the winemaking chores. Berglund was well-qualified, having been thoroughly indoctrinated in the Swan way of making wine and having worked as a winemaker elsewhere.

Swan usually made enough of the type of wines he liked to drink, and then he sold any excess. Even today the winery makes only about 4,000 cases of wine in small lots, much of it sold through the mailing list. Small production also limits the tasting room hours to weekends only. The winery proper is not much more than a glori-fied shack, but the wines do the talking here. You'll likely find Chardonnay, Pinot Noir, Cabernet, and a Semillon-Sauvignon Blanc blend available as well as Zinfandel, which accounts for half the production. Vintages may vary here, but the style and intensi-ty of Swan do not.

## Martini and Prati Winery
**2191 Laguna Rd., Santa Rosa 95401 • 707-575-8064**
**Daily 10–5:30 • Four selected varieties poured, no fee**
If you ever wondered how a post-Prohibition, country winery looked in the 1940s or 1950s long before the wine boom, Martini and Prati Winery will turn you into a time traveler. With a landmark water tower visible from a distance and low-slung, unpretentious

buildings, the place looks more like a forgotten West Texas ranch than a winery. Its history is even more ancient: Wine has been made on this property since 1881. Grandpa Rafaele Martini purchased the place around the turn of the century, and the current generation continues to run it, with help from partners of the last forty years, the Prati family.

The winery can ferment and store well into the millions of gallons; consequently a lot of the wine made here is for other wineries that don't have enough room. But Martini and Prati still makes a great deal of bulk wine, which the winery bottles or sells to others. The owners also reserve some lots for their Martini and Prati and Fountaingrove labels. As befits the operation, the tasting room at the far end of the complex is small and unadorned, with wines served in whiskey tumblers. You can sample from a dozen or so varieties, all rustic-style Italian country wines, including Vino Blanco, Vino Rosso, Riesling, Zinfandel, Cabernet, Sherry, and Vermouth.

## Dehlinger Winery

**6300 Guerneville Rd., Sebastopol 95472 • 707-823-2378**
**Fri.–Mon. 10–5; closed Sept. and Jan. • Most varieties poured,**
**no fee • Picnic area**

Tom Dehlinger established his winery twenty years ago in the far wilds of Sebastopol and Forestville, where apples were the cash crop and grapes were virtually unknown.

Through trial and error, he finally settled on making classic varietals solely from the fifty acres of estate grapes that surround the winery. A short drive off the highway down a one-lane gravel road, you'll find the long, narrow, weathered building that serves as the combination winery and tasting room. The vines, all color-coded to identify specific vineyard and flavor characteristics, grow nearly to the winery door.

A no-frills operation, in the tasting room you will sip amidst the barrel and case stacks on the concrete winery floor. About two thirds of the 8,000-case production consists of Chardonnay and Pinot, both generally excellent. The remainder is Cabernet, with small quantities of Cab Franc and Merlot either blended into the Cabernet or bottled separately in good vintages. Older red wines, like an '85 Cabernet often sit open on the back bar along with the current releases. Unfortunately most travelers don't journey to this distant winery. Dehlinger wines are very limited, rarely found at retail, made at the highest quality level, and reasonably priced (all less than $25).

# Iron Horse Vineyards

**9786 Ross Station Rd. (off Highway 116), Sebastopol 95472**
**707-887-1507 • Sat.–Sun. 10–4; weekdays by appointment only**
**Selected varieties poured, no fee • Daily tours by**
**appointment only**

Perhaps one of the loveliest wine estates in Sonoma County, Iron Horse Vineyards sits among the rolling hills of Green Valley. Audrey and Barry Sterling took over a stalled vineyard project in 1976 and hired Forrest Tancer (their future son-in-law) to plant equal amounts of Chardonnay and Pinot Noir in one of California's coolest vineyard sites. They initially concentrated on sparkling wines, but when Tancer joined the family (he married daughter Joy), they had access to his Cabernet vineyard in Alexander Valley. Iron Horse thus became a most pleasant oddity in the business: a winery that can make delicious sparkling wine as well as still wine.

Only twelve miles from the cooling breezes of the ocean, Iron Horse is worth the phone call to make an appointment. On Ross Station Road, off Highway 116, palm and olive trees flank the winery drive on both sides. At the top of the knoll, a series of understated red barns house the winemaking and cellaring operations. While not obligatory, on the tour you'll learn a lot about sparkling wines, including both hand and mechanical riddling of the bottles. The beautifully landscaped grounds include exquisite flower, herb, and vegetable gardens. The sparklers poured are many and varied: a Brut, Brut Rose, Blanc de Blanc, and the perennial favorite, Wedding Cuvee (Blanc de Noir). The lineup of still wines includes Sauvignon Blanc, Chardonnay, Cabernet, Pinot Noir, and a special blend called Cabernets.

## Topolos at Russian River Vineyards

**5700 Gravenstein Hwy. N., Forestville 95436 • 707-887-1575,**
**800-TOPOLOS • Daily 11–5:30 • Most varieties poured, no fee**
**Restaurant adjacent • No picnics**

Everything about Topolos—the setting, the buildings, and the wines—might aptly be described as rustic. The dark, weathered woods of the hop-kiln style winery building belie its youthful age. The winery's original owners, who wanted to pay tribute to the turn-of-the-century hop kilns in the area, constructed it in 1969. The Topolos family acquired the property in 1979, which included a restaurant on the former manor house's second floor that dates back to 1879.

The tasting room is downstairs in the stone cellar of the manor house. With a low ceiling and the perimeter stone walls jammed with wines and gifts, some visitors get a little claustrophobic. White wines like Riesling, Sauvignon Blanc, and Chardonnay aren't particularly distinguished. People come here to taste the red wines. Sure, they have Cabernet and Pinot Noir (both inexpensive), but their top wine is the massive Zinfandel from Rossi Ranch. Also worth a taste for the uniqueness, are the concentrated Petite Sirah and Alicante Bouschet. A pair of Muscats (black and orange) ice the dessert cake.

## Korbel Champagne Cellars

**13250 River Rd., Guerneville 95446 • 707-887-2294**
**Daily 9–5 (winter 9–4:30) • Most varieties poured, no fee**
**Winery tours on the hour; daily garden tours in spring and summer • Good gift selection • Shaded picnic area**
Korbel captures the quintessence of a classic, Old World style winery. The Korbels, Czech brothers, came to the north coast as redwood loggers; after clearing the land, they began to farm. By 1882, they settled on grapes as their primary crop and started making wine. Consequently, the stone-and-brick architecture of the grounds, including the turreted brandy tower, reflects their European heritage. However, the sprawling complex of vine-covered stone buildings and intricately landscaped grounds serve as a facade for the industrial winemaking that goes on behind the scenes.

The romanticism of a baronial winemaking estate beckons immediately to visitors by way of flowers, climbing ivy, and burgeoning bougainvillea. The tour, fascinating for the sense of history it imparts, winds through the cellar and past both the hand and machine riddling racks that facilitate movement of the yeast down to the neck of the sparkling wine bottle. In spring and summer, the winery conducts two tours per day of the lushly manicured grounds, including an antique rose garden that surrounds the Korbel brothers' original nineteenth-century home. The tasting room, a large, airy, red-brick affair, can handle tour groups by the busload. Sparklers poured include Blanc de Blanc, Blanc de Noir, Brut, Brut Rose, Extra Dry, and Natural, all moderate in both price and quality.

## Porter Creek Vineyards

**8735 Westside Rd., Healdsburg 95448 • 707-433-6321**
**Sat.–Sun. 10:30–4:30 • Most varieties poured, no fee**
The definition of home winemaking might loosely apply here. Proprietor George Davis happens to live on Westside Road, along

with neighboring giants like Rochioli and Davis Bynum. Actually, Davis is a professional winemaker whose rustic but efficient little winery sits on the same property as his residence. He doesn't advertise, and you won't see his wines in wide distribution, but discovering his Porter Creek wines is like stumbling across an unmined diamond.

Don't look for high-tech equipment like dejuicers and centrifuges; Davis makes wine the old-fashioned way: by hand. Drawing from twenty-one acres of estate vineyards, he makes less than 3,000 cases a year.

His Chardonnay tastes rich and full, and his two Pinot Noirs, especially the concentrated Hillside bottling, compare to his superstar neighbors'.

## Davis Bynum Winery

**8075 Westside Rd., Healdsburg 95448 • 707-433-5852, 800-826-1073 • Daily 10–5 • Most varieties poured, no fee Picnic area**

Davis Bynum, a former newspaperman, experimented with home winemaking and then began making wine commercially in a Berkeley warehouse near the University of California campus. In 1973 he made the big leap by purchasing the eighty-three acre River Bend Ranch in the heart of the Russian River Valley. Initially, he had great success in the marketplace with his inexpensive Barefoot Bynum line of wines (also known as Chateau La Feet), but that segment of the business became too competitive, and he sold that label in the late 1980s to concentrate on premium varietal wines.

The Bynum complex hosts a number of small buildings and houses, at the bottom of the hill off Westside Road. Traveling through the gate, wind your way up the hill until you see a massive, gray, stone-block cellar on the left side and, by the small parking area, the winery press and equipment in front of the other winery buildings. On busy days, there is so little space on the hill, one wonders how they get tons of grapes to the top or how the portable bottling line makes it up the one-horse lane. The utilitarian tasting room looks like a badly done, unfinished, suburban, recreational room. But the wines are generally top-drawer, including Chardonnay, Sauvignon Blanc, Gewurztraminer, Pinot Noir, Zinfandel, Cabernet, and Merlot. Considering Bynum's winemaking pedigree (award-winning winemaker, Gary Farrell) and the quality, the wines are very reasonably priced.

## Rochioli Vineyards and Winery
**6192 Westside Rd., Healdsburg 95448 • 707-433-2305**
**Daily 10–5 • Selected varieties poured, no fee • Picnic area**

The J. Rochioli family has owned and farmed this piece of real estate in the Russian River Valley since the 1930s, when hops (for beer production) still grew in the area. The Rochiolis were considered pioneers when they tore out the hops in 1959 and planted Cabernet and Sauvignon Blanc, grapes they then sold to other wineries. By the 1980s, they had added Chardonnay, Pinot Noir, and Zinfandel to their more than one hundred acres. After seeing award-winning wines made from their grapes by Dry Creek, Gary Farrell, and Williams-Selyem, the Rochiolis began producing a small amount of wine themselves in 1982. Three years later, with the third generation of Rochiolis involved, they built a full-fledged winemaking facility amid the vineyards.

The weathered exterior wood of the A-frame barn winery looks suitably rustic in its setting; from the road, it looks like it's been there for decades. After passing by some sheltering trees and vineyards growing right up to the parking lot, you'll find the tasting room at the back of the winery. Several directly adjacent picnic tables provide a perfect view of the vineyards. Rochioli's production hovers around 7,000 cases a year, and the cozy tasting room, while well-furnished, reflects the small size of the operation. Gewurztraminer is a good starter, as is the barrel-fermented Chardonnay. But the Sauvignon Blanc and Pinot Noir may be among the best in the county. Small quantities of Cabernet and Zinfandel are produced and may be available for tasting also.

## Hop Kiln Winery
**6050 Westside Rd., Healdsburg 95448 • 707-433-6491**
**Daily 10–5 • Most varieties poured, no fee • Good gift selection**
**Picnic areas**

Next door to Rochioli, you'll immediately notice the triple towers of a former hop kiln jutting into the sky. The building piques most travelers' curiosity whether they realize it now houses a winery or not. In 1977, California declared it a state historical landmark, one of the few remaining examples of a hop kiln from an earlier era. Constructed of stone and redwood timber in 1905, the building stood in a serious state of disrepair when Dr. Marty Griffin acquired it and the surrounding 240-acre ranch in 1960. By 1975, with the building refurbished, the winery produced its first wines, Petite Sirah and Riesling.

Today, walk up the steps to this landmark, open the wooden door, and you'll find it cool and dark inside. Your eyes soon adjust to drink in the woodsy rusticity of the tasting room. While Chardonnay and Riesling are among the white wine offerings, dry Gewurztraminer is the best choice. The winery really does well, however, with big, robust red wines like Zinfandel, Cabernet, and Petite Sirah. Perennial best buys include the proprietary A Thousand Flowers, which is a blend of Riesling and Gewurztraminer, and Marty Griffin's Big Red, which is a field blend that includes Zinfandel, Petite Sirah, and Gamay. Outside, picnic tables dot the perimeter of the pond, but during the summer look for the best tables just outside the front door, hidden under the cool cover of the creeping vine, bushes, and native plants.

## Belvedere Winery

**4035 Westside Rd., Healdsburg 95448 • 707-433-8236**
**Daily 10–4:30 • Four selected varieties poured, no fee**
**Good gift selection • Picnic area**

Bill Hambrecht, partner in the hugely successful venture-capital firm of Hambrecht and Quist in San Francisco, knows a thing or two about risk taking; he helped finance many Silicon Valley computer firms that are now household names. The unanswered question remains: Why would a venture capitalist want to become the sole proprietor in such a risky business as a winery? Hambrecht and his wife, Sally, did just that in 1989 when they bought out his former partner in Belvedere (named after the Marin County suburb where the Hambrechts live). But Hambrecht's secret to making good wine is controlling the vineyards, which at last count numbered more than 600 acres in Sonoma County.

You can barely see the country-style winery and tasting room from the road because of some towering, ancient oaks on the property. But a drive up the lane and a short walk on the flagstone steps reveals a building that marries dark woods with a judicious use of glass windows. Comfortable sofas and chairs beckon you to sit and taste a spell. Outside on the L-shaped deck, views of the Russian River inform the picnic area. Chardonnay is the focus, and the tasting room may pour any or all of the versions: Sonoma County, Russian River, Alexander Valley, and Preferred Stock. The list also includes Zinfandel, Cabernet, Merlot, and Muscat Canelli.

## Rabbit Ridge Vineyards

**3291 Westside Rd., Healdsburg 95448 • 707-431-7128**
**Daily 11–4:30 • Selected varieties poured, $2 fee applies to**
**purchase • Picnic area**

Named after the hill this modest winery sits on, Rabbit Ridge overlooks forty-five acres of vineyards and a duck pond. Winemaker Erich Russell, formerly at Belvedere next door, is a former track phenom who set a fast pace, evoking the moniker Rabbit. In 1979, during his summer hiatus from teaching, he worked at Chateau St. Jean and caught the winemaking bug. He soon bought this property and began making wine in 1985.

The tasting room features a half-moon tasting bar with a brass foot rail; on the opposite wall hang newspaper clippings about the winery and the Rabbit himself. Multiple bay windows stretch behind the bar and half the tasting room, providing a view of the pond below. Rabbit Ridge produces a long laundry list of eclectic wines, most of which your host will happily pour. Sure, they offer Chardonnay, Sauvignon Blanc, Zinfandel, Cabernet, and Merlot, but also notice the Viognier, Sangiovese, Syrah, and Carignane. Best buys include the white Mystique, which is a blend of Sauvignon Blanc, Semillon, and Riesling, and Allure, which is a blended Rhone-style red wine.

## Armida Winery

**2201 Westside Rd., Healdsburg 95448 • 707-433-2222**
**Daily 11–4 • Most varieties poured, no fee • Picnic area**

Another example of creative winery architecture, Armida consists of three large geodesic domes on a hilltop that house the tasting room, winery, and warehouse. In 1990, investment banker Bob Frugoli started the winery, which he named after his grandmother, who instilled in him a love of food and wine.

Coming up the drive, the beauty of the beige-walled, gray-roofed, octagonal buildings will strike you. The tasting room, in the first dome, has huge floor-to-ceiling, smoked windows; the room opens up to the patio deck, which has not only a view of the duck pond and bocce ball court below, but wonderful distant views of the Russian River, Dry Creek, and Alexander valleys. Armida sticks to what it knows best, producing only three wines: Chardonnay, Merlot, and Pinot Noir, all nicely done and moderately priced.

# Mill Creek Vineyards

**1401 Westside Rd., Healdsburg 95448 • 707-431-2121**
**Daily 10–5 (winter 10–4) • Most varieties poured, no fee**
**Picnic area**

The Kreck family has long grown grapes in Sonoma, though they originally settled here to raise cattle. With the vagaries of grape prices each year though, they decided to control their own destiny by also producing wine from their own grapes. The Krecks converted an old barn on this property and began the process. By 1982, they had grown and built the present redwood barn and waterwheel that's become a visual landmark on the Russian River/Dry Creek Valley border.

A low, stone wall lined with fruit trees marks the driveway to the parking lot. Inside the two-story barn, you'll see the Kreck brothers' handiwork all around you. They cut the beams, rafters, and tasting room bar top from one tree. The waterwheel outside came from trees felled on their property, too. Picnic tables set among the vineyards have a view of the hypnotic waterwheel. The white wines, Chardonnay, Sauvignon Blanc, and Gewurztraminer, are tasty, while Cabernet and Merlot are decent. The best buys are the blended wines: the Old Mill Red and Old Mill White.

## HEALDSBURG

Healdsburg puts the *country* in Sonoma wine country. Many people base their day trips here because of its plethora of bed-and-breakfast inns and its central access to the Russian River, Dry Creek, and Alexander valleys. To hit three wineries in a row, take the first Healdsburg exit off northbound U.S. 101 and travel south on Old Redwood Highway to Foppiano Vineyards, Rodney Strong Vineyards, and J Sparkling Wine Cellars. Back in Healdsburg proper, two tasting rooms stand within walking distance of the town square: Windsor Vineyards and the Kendall-Jackson tasting rooms. Drive to Simi Winery; it's on the northern edge of town on the main drag, Healdsburg Avenue. After visiting these close-to-Healdsburg wineries, two different and distinct winery routes beckon: Alexander Valley and Dry Creek Valley (see each individual section).

## Foppiano Vineyards

**12707 Old Redwood Hwy., Healdsburg 95448 • 707-433-7272**
**Daily 10–4:30 • Most varieties poured, no fee • Small gift**
**selection • Picnic area**

Look for the large, cream-colored, stone winery just south of Healdsburg's main shopping district on Old Redwood Highway. The Foppiano family, now in its fifth generation, began the winery in 1896 after gold fever didn't pan out for the immigrant patriarch John Foppiano. When Prohibition came, the Russian River ran red as the Foppianos opened their wine tanks, releasing 100,000 gallons onto the ground. They planted prune trees between the rows of the vines to survive; when Prohibition ended, they re-entered the wine business.

Buildings have been added to the winery complex over the years, and you'll have to navigate a narrow corridor through that phalanx of stone and mortar to find the tasting room, which sits hard by an ancient Northwestern Pacific Railroad caboose. What may look like grandmother's front porch leads to a moderately sized tasting room, with a back door that opens to a shaded picnic area and a view of the estate vineyards. Foppiano does make Chardonnay and a Sauvignon Blanc–Viognier blend under their Fox Mountain label, but their reputation does not lie on those. Red wines provided their early stock in trade and still do today through Cabernet, Merlot, and Zinfandel. They are also the largest producer and biggest fan of Petite Sirah in California. Bargains can be found among their Riverside Farms label bottlings.

## Rodney Strong Vineyards

**11455 Old Redwood Hwy., Healdsburg 95448 • 707-433-6511**
**Daily 10–5 • All varieties poured, no fee • Tours daily**
**Good gift selection • Picnic area**

Since establishment in 1961, the winery has gone through a number of name changes and identity crises; but through it all, Rod Strong has stayed at the helm, making the best of sometimes difficult situations. A former dancer and choreographer, the romantic side of winemaking no doubt attracted Strong. Starting at a tasting room called Tiburon Vintners, Strong moved the operation so the wines were actually made in Windsor. The direct mail wines, which could be ordered with personalized labels, sold under the Windsor label, while the retail wines carried the Sonoma Vineyards moniker. The winery changed hands a number of times and in 1982 was renamed Rodney Strong Vineyards to give the

place a human face amid the corporate turmoil. The present owners have brought financial stability to the winery, which produces
more than 500,000 cases a year, most under the Windsor label.
The magnificent cruciform winery was among the most modern
of facilities when built; its geometric design, with four areas of the
cellar positioned around a central work area, seems timeless today.
The pebbled exterior walls of the winery, with broad brown fram-
ing beams, blends in with the rural environment. A gurgling fountain in front borders the ramp to the front doors of the tasting
room. A domed skylight illuminates the square-sided tasting bar set
amid the redwood and glass of this octagonal second-floor perch.
Walk the perimeter of the room and you'll see the oak aging casks
and the stainless steel fermenters below. Don't miss the spiral staircase to the restrooms for a view from the crow's nest. The Rodney
Strong label once again features wines of real quality, many of them
vineyard designated. Chardonnay, Sauvignon Blanc, and Pinot
Noir are good, but Cabernet, Zinfandel, and particularly Merlot
are the real finds.

## J Sparkling Wine Cellars

**11477 Old Redwood Hwy., Healdsburg 95448 • 707-433-8843**
**Presently closed for remodeling; to reopen Spring 1998**
In 1980 the venerable Champagne firm, Piper-Heidsieck, was
only the second French company to establish a beachhead in
California for making sparkling wine. With no room to grow in
France, the firm obviously saw an opportunity to capitalize on the
growing American thirst for sparkling wines. All the wines followed
the traditional *methode champenoise* way, meaning the secondary
fermentation, which gives the wine its bubbles, occurs inside the
bottle. J, the sparkling wine branch of Jordan Winery, recently purchased this winery, formerly Piper-Sonoma Cellars.
The winery facility, built in 1982 next door to Rodney Strong,
sparkles like its wines. The contemporary, slab-sided-and-glass
building has almost a jewel box quality. A walking bridge crosses
over a small branch of the Russian River and a lily pond, and leads
to the double doors of the foyer. Directly upstairs, the self-guided
tour takes you through the Cool Rooms, detailing the various
stages of the sparkling winemaking process. Note the monstrous
mechanical riddling racks in the first room that automatically give
each bottle a quarter turn. Look to the right of the entrance for the
tasting salon; enjoy sipping here or outside on the umbrella-shaded patio overlooking the water. In addition to the J sparkling wines,

the new J still wines, including Pinot Noir, will be poured in the tasting salon.

## Windsor Vineyards Tasting Room

**239-A Center St., Healdsburg 95448 • 707-433-2822, 800-204-9463 • Mon.–Fri. 10–5, Sat.–Sun. 10–6**
**Most varieties poured, no fee • Good gift selection**

You'll find the Windsor Tasting Room located conveniently off the Plaza in Healdsburg. Windsor, once associated with what is now Rodney Strong Vineyards down the road, runs one of the country's largest mail-order businesses of premium wines, not available at retail stores. The winemaking, supervised by Windsor's own winemaker, occurs within the large Rodney Strong facility.

The bright and cheery tasting room mimics the wine-pouring hosts, who will treat you to tastes from a seemingly endless list of wine choices. Sauvignon Blanc, Riesling, Chardonnay, Merlot, Zinfandel, Cabernet, Pinot Noir, and Petite Sirah are almost always poured, as are some special lots. The wines have won many competition medals and are, on the whole, quaffable. Windsor specializes in personalized labels; if you'd like to order a case with labels reading, "Merry Christmas from the Johnsons, December 1997" (or just about anything else, for that matter), this is the place. For a nominal fee, Windsor will ship your order later to your home.

## Kendall-Jackson Tasting Room

**337 Healdsburg Ave., Healdsburg 95448 • 707-433-7102**
**Daily 10–4:30 • Selected varieties poured, no fee • Good gift selection**

Kendall-Jackson, one of the most successful wine-producing enterprises in the state, has San Francisco lawyer Jesse Jackson as sole proprietor. In addition to the amazingly successful Kendall-Jackson brand, Jackson has gone on an acquisition binge, acquiring many small- to medium-sized wineries throughout the state. He retains their independent identities but groups them under his Artisans and Estates banner. None of these wineries is open to the public, and until Jackson recently acquired the former Chateau De Baun in Windsor, visitors could only taste a wide variety of these wines in one place at Kendall-Jackson.

Look for the tasting room not far from the Plaza and right on Healdsburg's main drag. You'll recognize the Kendall-Jackson wines from the grape leaf on the label, as well as the many varietals, from Chardonnay to Cabernet but also from Viognier to Cabernet Franc. The number of quality-oriented wineries the company owns may surprise you, including Stonestreet, Robert Pepi, Cambria, Camelot, Edmeades, Kristone, Hartford Court, Bailey and Brock, La Crema, and Lakewood. Of course, not all the wines of all the wineries are poured every day, but you can certainly get an interesting cross section of Kendall-Jackson's repertoire.

### Simi Winery

**16275 Healdsburg Ave., Healdsburg 95448 • 707-433-6981
Daily 10–4:30 • Most varieties poured, no fee • Daily tours at
11, 1, 3 • Good gift selection • Shaded picnic area**

Although it's one of Sonoma County's largest wineries, Simi tries hard not to act like it. One of the oldest producers in the county, its historic grounds give a sense of solidness and security, achieved through 125 years of work. Giuseppe and Pietro Simi came from the Tuscan hills of Italy to discover gold in California. When that didn't pan out, they went into the produce business in San Francisco, eventually moving north to plant vines in an area of Healdsburg that reminded them of home. In 1890, a monumental stone winery was constructed by Chinese laborers, many of whom worked laying tracks on the Northwestern Pacific Railroad that ran by Simi's front door. After the tragic deaths of the brothers in 1904, Giuseppe's daughter, Isabelle (only fourteen at the time), took over the winery and ran it for almost seventy years.

Partially hidden by a grove of redwood trees planted by Isabelle to celebrate the end of Prohibition, the winery grounds and physical setting remain among the most attractive in California. As a bonus, the informative tours allow you to see the winery's innovative renovations juxtaposed with the core of the ancient winery and its three-foot-thick stone walls. After Prohibition, to better promote the Simi wines, Isabelle was one of the first to open a tasting room, which was carved out of a 25,000-gallon Champagne tank. Simi's modern tasting room is modeled after Isabelle's original. With present owners, the French firm of Moet and Hennesey, embarking on a modernization program, the wines taste better than ever, made under the guidance of former Mondavi enologist Zelma Long. Instead of making a laundry list of varietals, Simi concentrates on what it can do best: Sauvignon Blanc, Chardonnay, and Cabernet.

## ALEXANDER VALLEY

Based in Healdsburg, hop onto U.S. 101 north to start the day at Chateau Souverain, exiting at Independence Lane. Cross back under the highway and go left on Geyserville Avenue to find Trentadue Winery, Clos du Bois, and Canyon Road Cellars. A little farther north, Geyserville Avenue intersects with Highway 128; turn right and continue south on this road to visit all the remaining wineries in the Alexander Valley, including De Lorimier Vineyards, Murphy-Goode Winery, Alexander Valley Fruit and Trading Company, Jordan Vineyards and Winery (take a right on Alexander Valley Road), Sausal Winery, White Oak Vineyards, Johnson's Alexander Valley Winery, Alexander Valley Vineyards, Hanna Vineyards, and Field Stone Winery. If you make the journey via Highway 128 from Calistoga in the Napa Valley, enjoy the scenic drive and just reverse the order of the wineries.

### Chateau Souverain

**400 Souverain Rd., Geyserville 95441 • 707-433-8281**
**Daily 10–5 • Most varieties poured, no fee • Restaurant**
**adjacent, open for lunch and dinner on weekends only;**
**reservations recommended • Good gift selection**

Architecturally one of the most striking wineries in Sonoma, Chateau Souverain combines the stately French estate, baronial mansion style with the hop-kiln legacy of the region. An award-winning design by John Marsh Davis, the building incorporates the rising turrets of hop kilns as bookends to the elongated structure. The winery has not had a long and glorious history, but after Napa Valley Beringer Winery's corporate parent purchased it in 1986, much-needed funds helped acquire better equipment, new barrels, and a new winemaker, and also helped establish a destination restaurant on the premises. The quality of the wines has soared, while the prices have remained surprisingly reasonable.

The dual tendrils of an imposing staircase lead from the over-sized parking lot to the vast courtyard of the winery, embellished by a large, gurgling fountain. The tasting room is just to the left in the eastern hop-kiln style section of the building. With a long, dark wood bar and plush carpeting on the floor, the room's designer had visitor comfort in mind. A wraparound mural depicts the four seasons in the vineyards. If the bar seems busy, relax in cushy chairs and adjacent tables, and sit as you sip. Children amuse themselves while mom and dad taste by scribbling with crayons and paper. The second level of the room also provides excellent views of the

Alexander Valley. Many varietals are offered for tasting, and most can be considered best buys, including Sauvignon Blanc, Chardonnay, Pinot Noir, Cabernet, Merlot, and the perennial favorite, Zinfandel.

## Trentadue Winery

**19170 Geyserville Ave., Geyserville 95441 • 707-433-3104**
**Daily 10–5 • Most wines poured, no fee • Good gift selection**
**Picnic area**

This family-owned winery actually had its genesis when the Trentadues began growing fruit in the Santa Clara Valley in the early 1930s. But as the suburban residential expansion began to encroach on farmland in the Bay Area, the family moved to this northern Sonoma County ranch planted with prunes, apples, and grapes. At first they sold their grapes to other wineries, but by 1969 they decided to make a little wine and have now expanded to about 12,000 cases a year. *Trentadue*, the Italian word for *thirty-two*, comes from ancient times when thirty-two Egyptians settled in the Italian town of Bari on the Adriatic Coast. Since they mostly stayed with their own kind, the locals called them The Thirty-Two, and the name stuck.

A sandy, red-bricked warehouse covered with vines houses the winemaking operations; twenty-foot double doors open to the winery. The tasting room is to the right and up the stairs. The low-ceilinged, blonde wood tasting room gives way to a larger white stucco room in back, overflowing with glassware, pottery, jewelry, cookbooks, and related paraphernalia. You'll find it quaint and homey, just like the wines. Skip the white wines (not their forte) and go right to the big, robust red wines that pack a lot of flavor for the buck: Cabernet, Petite Sirah, Merlot, and a hearty Zin-fan-del. A tasty, old vines, red wine blend is sometimes available and can be the best buy in the house.

## Clos du Bois

**19410 Geyserville Ave., Geyserville 95441 • 707-857-3100,**
**800-222-3189 • Daily 10–4:30 • Most varieties poured, no fee**
**Small gift selection**

In 1974, Frank Woods and his partners based the Clos du Bois label on the premise that good grapes make good wine. They contracted the best possible grapes and made the wines at various sites around the valley. For years, the tasting room was located in a no-frills, corrugated metal building in a residential area of Healdsburg. In 1988 the Canadian whiskey firm Hiram Walker bought the Clos du Bois label since physically no winery existed. But the good name, well-established sales network, and control of more than 600 acres of prime vineyard land in Sonoma County, was the real prize. The mammoth winery, built in Geyserville in 1994, resembles a glorified warehouse. Follow the curve of the driveway though, and you'll find a separate and most inviting tasting room. The gray stucco and blonde wood building with a tin roof bears a passing but stylized resemblance to a regional hop kiln. With a cathedral ceiling, light streaming from second-story windows, and glass walls all around, you might feel as if you're in a large fishbowl. A sleek, modern, black-lacquer-topped bar accented with blonde wood has three sides and can easily handle summer crowds. The wines are appealing and well-made, with the emphasis on the barrel-fermented Chardonnay; you'll also find more intense versions, designated Calclaire, Flintwood, and Reserve. Don't overlook a nice Gewurztraminer and Sauvignon Blanc. The reds are well-regarded too, including Cabernet, the Bordeaux-style blend Marlstone, and everyone's current favorite, Merlot.

### Canyon Road Cellars

**19550 Geyserville Ave., Geyserville 95441 • 707-857-3417**
**Daily 10–5 • Most varieties poured, no fee • Small gift selection**
**Picnic area**

The old Nervo Winery, dating back to 1908, is really an extension of the much larger Geyser Peak Winery just up U.S. 101. The Trione family, now partners with the Penfolds of Australia in Geyser Peak, bought the winery a couple of decades ago, but in 1991 the Triones established the Canyon Road label and started pouring the Canyon Road wines out of the Nervo Winery. An attractive, rough-hewn, stone building and an adjoining concrete building with a tin roof house the old winery facility and tasting room.

Because Canyon Road Cellars' reputation has grown phenomenally across the country and more visitors show up at their door every day, the tasting room (at last visit) had been relocated to a corrugated, tin roof structure in front of the property's historic buildings. At some point, the new tasting room presumably will be finished and become a permanent fixture. Right now, a small bar at the east end of the room serves tasters, while clothing and comestibles cram the rest of the area. A bit of the Nervo Italian tradition still exists: You can taste the Nervo style of sparkling Spumante and nonalcoholic grape juice. But the real deals are the inexpensively priced Canyon Road wines. The winery offers

Chardonnay, Semillon, Cabernet, and Cabernet Franc, along with some blends from the latest vintage. Sauvignon Blanc is consistently a multiple medal winner and great buy.

## De Lorimier Vineyards

**2001 Highway 128, Geyserville 95441 • 707-857-2000, 800-546-7718 • Thurs.–Mon. 10–4:30 • All varieties poured, no fee • Self-guided tour**

This small, 4,000-case winery may seem an anomaly in the land of giant producers and large wine estates located on U.S. 101. But De Lorimier Vineyards sits at the top of the much more rural Highway 128 that meanders through the Alexander Valley grape-growing region and eventually connects with Calistoga at the northern tip of Napa Valley. Looking for a weekend retreat from his San Francisco surgery practice, Al de Lorimier bought a prune orchard. He ripped the prunes out and planted Chardonnay, basing the idea on a neighboring vineyard; the doctor also planted Sauvignon Blanc, Cabernet, and Cabernet-based varieties because he had a taste for Bordeaux wines. Presently one hundred planted acres surround the winery, though other wineries buy 80 percent of those grapes.

Down a gravel driveway, you'll find a parking area behind the only building. A jaunt up the stairs and through the door on the second floor thrusts you into the coolness of the actual winery. A walkway allows you a self-guided, eagle-eyed tour of the winery, with explanatory signs in front of you and the winery tanks, barrels, and presses below. The tastefully decorated tasting room rests at the end of the catwalk and is actually lorded over by a feline named Rorschach, after the black-and-white blotch down the front of her face. The wines, all made from traditional grapes, have proprietary names. The Chardonnay is called Prism; the Cabernet-based Bordeaux-style blend is Mosaic; and the Graves-style, white Bordeaux blend is Spectrum. Lace is the name of the late-harvest Sauvignon Blanc dessert wine. All the wines have interesting flavors and fair prices consistent with their high quality.

## Murphy-Goode Estate Winery

**4001 Highway 128, Geyserville 95441 • 707-431-7644 Daily 10:30–4:30 • Selected varieties poured, no fee**

Both Tim Murphy and Dale Goode began growing grapes in the Alexander Valley in the mid-1960s, selling their harvests to many of the most prestigious wineries in Sonoma County. By 1985 a wine grape glut had evolved, and their partnership, formed in 1980, couldn't sell all its grapes. They began making wine as a label only, without a winery, principally to make sure all their grapes had a home. The wines were made down the road at Rodney Strong, and with some marketing expertise from partner Dave Ready, their wines sold out. By 1988, with the partnership so successful, they built their own winery, which they subsequently outgrew by 1993. They've now expanded to 80,000 cases a year, nearly double their output just five years ago.

Climbing vines on the outside of the tasting room wall, however, make the winery seem it has been here for a while. The sloped wood ceiling and red brick walls of the tasting room make it a pleasant place to dawdle. Wood benches on the perimeter offer tired tasters a place to sit and sip if they would rather not stand at the blonde and dark wood bar. A large window looks out onto the barrel aging room below. Chardonnay, Fume Blanc, and Pinot Blanc, in both their regular and reserve versions, are usually top-flight. The Cabernet and Merlot taste good too. Don't forget to ask about their wines under the Goode and Ready label: Named after two of the partners, those bottlings provide exactly what the name describes.

## Alexander Valley Fruit and Trading Co.

**5110 Highway 128, Geyserville 95441 • 707-433-1944, 800-443-1944 • Daily 10–5 • Selected varieties poured, no fee Good gift selection • Picnic area**

Coming up the driveway of Alexander Valley Fruit and Trading Company, you might not know it had anything to do with wine. Sure, grapevines grace the front, but the faux fronts of their buildings resemble the set of a Western movie, with structures marked "Office," "Stage Express," and "Wine Merchants." Actually the proprietors, Steve and Candy Sommers, do make wine here (you can see the stainless steel tanks peeking over the fake walls), but they also run a thriving gourmet food mail-order business too.

The tasting room, ironically, does not have a facade. Instead, it sits just off the front wood deck and inside a cellar; the dark, wooden bar stands in one corner, while entire lines of comestibles are showcased in the country barn setting. You may purchase dozens of bottles of condiments, sauces, and marinades individually or in various gift packs. *People* magazine once featured Steve in an article because of the packing material he uses in his mail-order gift packs: popped popcorn. Amid all this commerce, the Sommers manage to make about 10,000 cases of wine a year, including White Zinfandel, Cabernet, Sauvignon Blanc, Chardonnay, and Carignane. You may sample a changing selection of condiments and dipping sauces each day with the wines. The late-harvest Zinfandel tastes even better after a shot of the chocolate sauce.

## Jordan Vineyard and Winery

**1474 Alexander Valley Rd., Healdsburg 95448 • 707-431-5250, 800-654-1213 • Daily by appointment only • Selected varieties poured, no fee • Tours daily by appointment only**

If you'd like to know how the other half lives, a visit to Jordan Winery will give you an idea. Stunning and beautiful in every way, the winery resembles a Bordeaux chateau. That's not surprising since Colorado-based oil man Tom Jordan has been a lifelong aficionado of Bordeaux wines. In fact, in the late 1960s Jordan scouted chateau properties in Bordeaux, hoping to make great wine there. It didn't work out though, and France's loss was California's gain. He settled on this 1,500-acre parcel, high on a knoll in Alexander Valley, of which 275 acres contain vineyards. The first vintage in 1976 received an over-hyped initial reception, but now the Jordan wines grace almost every tony restaurant's wine list in the nation.

Calling for an appointment is mandatory but worth it. As you negotiate the undulating drive off the main road, you'll gasp as a vine-covered, mustard-colored winery building comes into view in the middle of nowhere. On the grand tour, the winery casks seem to stand at attention; without a doubt this hygenic winery sparkles like no other in California. Style plays an important part in this presentation, and chandeliers light even the barrel room. You'll view the formal dining room, where folks in the wine trade often share a meal, emphasizing the marriage of food and wine. Finally you'll taste a high-toned Chardonnay and supple Cabernet, on which the Jordan reputation rests. J, the Jordan sparkling wine made in a separate facility on Eastside Road in the Russian River Valley, may be poured as well.

## Sausal Winery

**7370 Highway 128, Healdsburg 95448 • 707-433-2285**
**Daily 10–4 • Most varieties poured, no fee • Small gift selection**
**Picnic area**

Here's a winery that deserves more glory than it gets. Down a lane off Highway 128, you'll find Sausal inside a classic, redwood building that was once a prune dehydrator, with plenty of picnic tables under the shaded grape arbor. Patriarch Leo Demostene bought the property in

1955 when it still produced apples and prunes; he tore those out and began planting vines. No stranger to the vine, Demostene formerly was a winemaker at the old Soda Rock Winery down the road, like his father-in-law. The vineyards flourished, and Demostene sold the grapes to wineries both in and out of the county. He died in 1973, just as the family began converting the prune dehydrator buildings into a winery.

His sons and daughters took over and have made wine ever since, though at first they only sold the wine in bulk to other wineries for blending. After a while, they started making wines under their own label, drawing from their 125 acres of grapevines nearby. The tasting room of the redwood winery has large picture windows that look out on the well-manicured grounds, often with flowers in bloom. The long, burly bar looks like it came from an old-timey saloon; the back bar displays tons of medals and ribbons. Zinfandel is king here, and though only one may be open for tasting, you can purchase older vintages long gone from retailer's shelves. The Cabernet and even the White Zinfandel can also taste quite good; the Sausal Blanc is an interesting blend of white varietals.

## White Oak Vineyards

**7505 Highway 128, Healdsburg 95448 • 707-433-8429**
**Fri.–Sun. 10–4 (after Nov. 1997) • Most varieties poured, no fee**
Vintner Bill Myers, former successful contractor and fisherman in Alaska, relocated to the milder climate of Sonoma County, where he had relatives. Myers bought six acres planted to Cabernet and Chardonnay in the Alexander Valley and began making wine under his White Oak label in 1981. Additional tonnage from grower-partners in the county now augment those grapes, and production has grown to more than 13,000 cases.

The winery, formerly located within walking distance of downtown Healdsburg, is moving to a site in the Alexander Valley to be closer to its vineyards. The new winery and tasting room is expected to open November 1997. The wines, including Chenin Blanc, Sauvignon Blanc, Cabernet, and Zinfandel, have character. The top of the line is a special Myers limited reserve Chardonnay. Look for White Oak's new additions, Merlot and Pinot Noir from the surrounding thirty-acre vineyard.

## Johnson's Alexander Valley Winery

**8333 Highway 128, Healdsburg 95448 • 707-433-2319**
**Daily 10–5 • Most varieties poured, no fee**
If you want to discover the epitome of a small, family winery, visit Johnson's. They rarely advertise their presence or their wines;

in fact, they make only as much wine as the immediate family can produce (about 4,000 cases), so don't expect to find the wines back home. Proprietors Tom and Gail Johnson took over a fruit ranch from Tom's father. Some premium grapes planted on the property produced the first vintage in 1975. Daughter Ellen, a Fresno State enology grad, now handles the winemaking chores.

The rustic winery, with a small tasting room in the corner, comes by its rusticity naturally. This barn dates back to 1880, and the Johnsons spent quite a bit of time restoring it to its present, functional condition. An ancient farm tractor sits out front. But the big surprise is the vintage pipe organ in the middle of the winery. The Johnsons rescued it from a theater up north, and its billowing tones often form the centerpiece of the winery's events during the year. The wines seem admirably done and fairly priced, among them Cabernet, Chardonnay, Riesling, Pinot Noir, and Zinfandel.

## Alexander Valley Vineyards

**8644 Highway 128, Healdsburg 95448 • 707-433-7209**
**Daily 10–5 • Most varieties poured, no fee • Small gift selection**
**Picnic area**

Alexander Valley Vineyards' property overflows with history. Cyrus Alexander, for whom both the property and the valley are named, came here in 1840 to carve out a ranch from the Sotoyome land grant. In the next thirty years, he tamed the land, killing bears and coyotes, planting fruit and sowing wheat, all while building a mill, tannery, schoolhouse, and church. The land remained in the family for generations until the Wetzel family from Los Angeles bought several hundred acres that included a run-down Victorian house, an adobe, and the schoolhouse. They intended to make it a vacation retreat, but restoration of the property and winemaking soon became a full-time passion.

With the financial wherewithal, the family slowly restored the estate's buildings and in 1975 built a new winery among the vineyards. They furnished the tasting room esthetically, with a wooden bar, tiled floor, and antiques of the Victorian period. In the late afternoon, the veranda is a favored spot to sip, accompanied by views of the surrounding vineyards and hillsides. Cabernet and Merlot are the favorites, made in the typically supple, easily drinkable, Alexander Valley style. Chardonnay is also offered, along with limited quantities of Chenin Blanc, Riesling, Gewurztraminer, Zinfandel, and Pinot Noir.

## Hanna Winery
**9280 Highway 128, Healdsburg 95448 • 707-431-4310, 800-854-3987 • Daily 10–4 • Most varieties poured, no fee Small gift selection • Picnic area**

Cardiovascular surgeon Eli Hanna originally purchased property on Occidental Road in Santa Rosa, where he built a house and established his winery in 1985. But with various vineyard holdings not only in the Russian River Valley but also in Alexander Valley and the Mayacamas Mountains, he dreamed of building a more central hospitality center and winery. He chose his hundred-acre vineyard in Alexander Valley as the setting.

Hidden from the highway, wind your way through the vineyards to discover a modern Mediterranean-style building with Spanish roof tiles. Arched glass doorways and high windows on three sides accent the twenty-five-foot beamed ceiling of the tasting room. At the center of the tasting room is a mahogany and copper bar, along with a massive stone fireplace. Sauvignon Blanc has been their main varietal since the beginning, and the most recent vintage continues to be a winner. Drawing from extensive vineyard holdings, Hanna has put more emphasis on other varietals like Chardonnay, Cabernet, and Merlot, the latter two in the supple Alexander Valley style. You can sometimes find limited lots of Pinot Noir and Zinfandel at the tasting room only.

## Field Stone Winery
**10075 Highway 128, Healdsburg 95448 • 707-433-7266 Daily 10–5 • Most varieties poured, no fee • Picnic area**

In 1955 the late Wallace Johnson brought his cattle from Santa Cruz to this area; he later acquired adjacent land that included a cherry orchard and some gnarly, old Petite Sirah vines. In time, he planted more varieties and more vines, selling the grapes to local wineries. Johnson, a mechanical engineer, began constructing a unique winery to make his own wines in 1977. He cleared a hilly knoll surrounded by oaks and put up concrete walls and a roof, then buried the structure with the displaced earth. The fieldstone facade, the only part of the winery now visible, comprises stones unearthed during construction.

It's an energy-efficient design, although critics say the winery resembles a fallout shelter bunker. You will observe the utilitarian space while traversing a section of the winery to get to the tasting room. Field Stone started out making a lot of white wines but soon concentrated on the winery's strength, red wines like the old vine

Petite Sirah. Cabernet, including special vineyard-designated lots with names like Turkey Hill and Hoot Owl Creek, are also tops. For white wine lovers, Field Stone offers Chardonnay, Sauvignon Blanc, and Gewurztraminer. If still available, be sure to ask for a tasty, deeply colored Rose, made from Cabernet or Petite Sirah grapes.

## DRY CREEK VALLEY

Dry Creek Valley, northwest of Healdsburg, looks like one continuous carpet of grapevines, two miles wide and fifteen miles long. From Healdsburg, take Westside Road west out of town, turn left on Kinley Drive and right on Magnolia Drive to Alderbrook Winery. Take Westside Road farther west and turn right on slow, scenic West Dry Creek Road (not the fast, well-traveled Dry Creek Road nearby). Go several miles to Bellerose Vineyards and then Lambert Bridge Vineyards. Still traveling north, take a right at Lambert Bridge Road to Dry Creek Vineyard. Continuing on Lambert Bridge Road, turn right at Dry Creek Road, and then make a left onto Lytton Springs Road for Lytton Springs Winery and Mazzocco Vineyards. Now backtrack past Dry Creek Vineyard onto Lambert Bridge Road and turn right to get back on West Dry Creek Road for A. Rafanelli Winery, Quivira Vineyards, Preston Vineyards, and then Meeker Vineyards, where West Dry Creek Road dead-ends.

Drive back down West Dry Creek Road, and make a right on Yoakim Bridge Road and then a left at Dry Creek Road until the Ferrari-Carano Vineyards come into view. Several miles farther north you'll find one of the smallest producers, Lake Sonoma Winery. Backtrack down Dry Creek Road and turn left at Dutcher Creek Road; go several miles to J. Fritz Winery. Backtrack once again down Dutcher Creek Road, turn right on Dry Creek Road, pass Ferrari-Carano and turn left on Canyon Road; J. Pedroncelli will appear on the left. Continue up Canyon Road and right before U.S. 101, go left on Chianti Road to Geyser Peak Winery and Silver Oak Wine Cellars. Retrace your steps back to Canyon Road, go under the freeway, turn left on Geyserville Avenue and go about a mile to the quaint Pastori Winery. From this spot close to U.S. 101, you can easily explore the wineries in north Mendocino County, as well as the wineries of Alexander Valley, southeast on Highway 128.

*(listed from south to north)*

## Alderbrook Winery

**2306 Magnolia Dr., Healdsburg 95448 • 707-433-5987**
**Daily 10–5 • Most varieties poured, no fee • Good gift selection**
**Picnic area**

More people should know and appreciate Alderbrook, in the southernmost area of Dry Creek Valley just outside Healdsburg. Founded in 1981, the venture began as a partnership between a vineyard manager, a dentist-turned-winemaker, and a grape grower, the latter related to the Rafanelli family, who also has a winery nearby. The original idea was for the winery to be the permanent home for the fifty-five acres of grapes. The partners planned on a modest start, but they soon produced 30,000 cases a year. Then a couple years ago, the Gillemot family of Lake Tahoe purchased the winery.

A modern, ranch-style, gray building with white trim houses the tasting room and features a shady wraparound porch dotted with picnic tables. Inside, light-colored knotty pine walls and multiple glass doors give the room an open, airy feel. A white-tiled fireplace and an eclectic gift selection dominate one end of the room, with the spacious tasting bar at the other end. White wines were the original mainstay of the winery and still hold sway today. Chardonnay, Sauvignon Blanc, and an off-dry Gewurztraminer lead the list. Small lots of intense Semillon and dry, barrel-fermented Gewurztraminer, as well as a super late harvest Muscat, often appear only at the winery. Zinfandel and Syrah are the reds, soon to be joined by Cabernet and Merlot.

## Bellerose Vineyard

**435 W. Dry Creek Rd., Healdsburg 95448 • 707-433-1637**
**Daily 10–4 • Selected varieties poured, no fee • Picnic area**

Charles Richard came from a background of musical virtuosity, studying classical guitar and working toward becoming a professor of music at the University of San Francisco. But something about the artistry of the vineyard and winemaking appealed to him and eventually won him over when he purchased this vineyard in 1978. With twenty acres already planted to Cabernet and Merlot, Richard was among the first in California to work at making a Bordeaux-style blend from the classic varietals. Soon he made additional plantings of Malbec, Cabernet Franc, and Petit Verdot. On the white wine side, he planted the two symbiotic white Bordeaux grapes: Sauvignon Blanc and Semillon.

Off West Dry Creek Road, the paved driveway turns to gravel, then climbs a hilltop to find the rustic winery. Richard advocated organic farming before its popularity exploded, and he often personally plowed the rows between the vineyards with his Belgian horse team, Rowdy and Chucky. Don't look for manicured, picture-perfect vineyards or winery grounds at Bellerose; expect only a working farm that happens to produce some good wines. Walking past the old house on the property and some rusty agricultural implements, you'll find the winery building on the far side, with a bare-bones tasting room in front. Bending an elbow at the bar, the view of Dry Creek Valley below will add to the plain ambience of the place. The latest releases come from the 1994 vintage, a Malbec, which is usually reserved for blending. Merlot and the Bordeaux blend, now simply called Reserve Cuvee, are the rustic heavy hitters, available from several vintages. Tiring from the marketing grind rather than the agricultural one, Richard sold the 8,000-case capacity winery to Jack and Ann Air, who are replanting the vineyards and modernizing the facility.

## Lambert Bridge Vineyards
**4085 W. Dry Creek Rd., Healdsburg 95448 • 707-431-9600, 800-975-0555 • Daily 10–4:30 • Selected varieties poured, no fee • Picnic area**

When Jerry Lambert bought 119 acres to grow grapes in 1970, he found out the bridge leading to the property was named Lambert Bridge, after C. L. Lambert, an early settler in the valley but apparently no relation. Instead, Jerry Lambert was an heir to the family that started the giant pharmaceutical company Warner-Lambert. After five years of tending the vineyards, he built a redwood winery. The wine quality has gone up and down over the years, with a revolving door of winemakers providing little continuity of style. When Lambert finally started producing some really good wines, farming out the marketing and distribution to an outside party almost ruined him. Several years back, Lambert sold the winery to the Chambers family, who shares his enthusiasm for producing top-quality wine but could start anew.

Set against groves of firs and oaks, the redwood winery sits among the vineyards, with a view toward the Lambert Bridge. Once inside the front door, you'll need a few seconds to adjust not only to the darkness but also the coolness of the working winery. The only natural light filters in from a small, stained-glass window in front, and the overhead chandeliers hanging from the cathedral ceiling emit the dimmest light possible. All of this does make the winery seem like a church or monastery. The three-sided, blonde wood tasting bar sits near the entrance, with wine racks filled with bottles on both sides, accented by huge wreaths. The rest of the room, as far as you can see, contains six high stacks of barrels filled with aging wine. The Chardonnay and Fume Blanc form the base of the winery's reputation, though Lambert has started producing more exciting versions of Cabernet, Merlot, and Zinfandel.

## Lytton Springs Winery
**650 Lytton Springs Rd., Healdsburg 95448 • 707-433-7721
Daily 11–4 • Selected varieties poured, no fee**

Los Angeles publisher Dick Sherwin, along with a couple of friends, began producing wine under the Lytton Springs label in 1975. A few years earlier, Ridge Vineyards had discovered a fifty-acre patch of nearly hundred-year-old Zinfandel vines here and produced an intensely concentrated wine from those grapes. The folks at Lytton Springs Winery tried to duplicate that quality in the years that followed; they initially missed the mark but have improved in recent years. In 1991 the story came full circle when Ridge purchased both the winery and vineyards from the original proprietor. At first, some question existed as to whether Ridge would use just those grapes and abandon the Lytton Springs label, but wines are still made here.

The actual winery building, a low-slung, corrugated, metal-sided, brown-paneled structure, will never win any design awards, but most folks who make the pilgrimage here only care about one thing: old vine Zinfandel. The tasting bar looks equally unofficious, carved out of one end of the winery building. Typically the Lytton Springs Zinfandel sells out at retail, so the winery provides a good place to taste and buy the current vintage. Sometimes an older, reserve-style Zin may be open, as well as some extracted Zins and Cabs from Ridge Vineyards. During the summer tourist season, Lytton Springs keeps regular hours; the rest of the year, call ahead to make sure they're open before making the journey.

## Mazzocco Vineyards
**1400 Lytton Springs Rd., Healdsburg 95448 • 707-431-8159
Daily 10–4:30 • Most varieties poured, no fee • Small gift
selection • Picnic area for customers**

Los Angeles opthalmologist, eye surgeon, and inventor of a soft, intraocular lens, Tom Mazzocco loved wine so much he got involved in a partnership that owned a twenty-acre vineyard in Alexander Valley. Five years later in 1985, another vineyard property, near the Healdsburg airport, came up for sale. Mazzocco, a pilot, figured he could commute from Los Angeles in his private plane, touching down on a landing strip that was a five-minute walk from the vineyard. That sealed the deal. The next year he built a small but functional winery to use the twenty-five acres of classic Bordeaux grapes planted in the vineyards. But Mazzocco's busy schedule caused him to sell the winery in 1990 and then, in a complex series of financial dealings, later buy it back.

The wines seemed not to have suffered, and with the hiring of a new winemaker four years ago, the quality level has improved. The winery sits on a slight rise off Lytton Springs Road, with the winery tank farm gleaming in the sun on the left, and the spartan, prefab tasting room and offices on the right. With the tasting room so crammed with tchotchkes and gifts, the bar seems almost ancillary to the proceedings. Tasting the wines, however, proves otherwise. Chardonnay accounts for more than half the production; the reds, including Cabernet, Zinfandel, and Merlot, are uniformly good. The limited-edition Bordeaux blend called Matrix has real polish and charm. Also in the pipeline are small quantities of Viognier and Petite Sirah, available only at the winery. And if the tasting room gets too crowded, move out to the patio deck, where you can sit and sip in the shade while watching the planes take off and land at the airport.

## Dry Creek Vineyard

**3770 Lambert Bridge Rd., Healdsburg 95446 • 707-433-1000
Daily 10:30–4:30 • Most varieties poured, no fee • Small gift
selection • Picnic area**

Vintner Dave Stare, as much as anyone else in the area, can be credited with pioneering vineyards and winemaking in the Dry Creek Valley. A frustrated Massachusetts Institute of Technology-trained engineer from the East Coast, Stare finally acted on his instincts and bought this piece of property in 1972. Back then, some vineyards dotted the valley but not too many wineries. Now one of the larger producers in the county (more than 100,000 cases), Dry Creek owns more than one hundred acres of vineyards and buys from local grape growers as need dictates.

In the old days, the tasting room stood behind the winery, but after a makeover, it's now in front in the building closest to the parking lot, shaded by oak trees. The beautiful, gray-stoned block structure with arched windows and doorways beckons visitors; inside, a large, stone fireplace opposite a long, wooden bar leaves no doubt that this spot exists for lingering and enjoying the Dry Creek brand of hospitality. Stare's original varietal releases, Chenin Blanc and Fume Blanc, are still top-drawer today. Chardonnay, Cabernet, Zinfandel, and Merlot also make the grade. A number of varietals are made in more expensive (but worth it) reserve versions, Zinfandel always being a winner; likewise a red Bordeaux blend is sublime.

## A. Rafanelli Winery

**4685 W. Dry Creek Rd., Healdsburg 95448 • 707-433-1385
Daily 10–4, by appointment only • All varieties poured, no fee**

For years the Rafanelli family owned vineyards close to Healdsburg. But in 1954 the family sold that land to serve as a site for the new high school. They moved west of town and began planting one hundred acres to various varieties. Twenty years later, Americo Rafanelli decided to make wine commercially rather than sell all his grapes to others. Upon his death in 1987, his university-trained son, David, who had worked down the road at Lambert Bridge Winery, took over the winemaking reins and continues to hold production around 6,000 cases.

In practical terms, the best way to acquire the Rafanelli wines is to visit the winery; a cult following ensures that the wines disappear from retailers' shelves and restaurant wine lists in the blink of an eye.

The winery itself looks unpretentious inside a redwood barn that seems hardly worthy of all the attention. But as David Rafanelli says, "Wine is made in the vineyards," and thus you can hardly go wrong with good grapes. Only two wines are produced, Zinfandel and Cabernet, both ripe and intense with character and flavor.

## Quivira Vineyards

**4900 W. Dry Creek Rd., Healdsburg 95448 • 707-431-8333,
800-292-8339 • Daily 10–4:30 • Most varieties poured, no fee
Small gift selection • Picnic area**

As legend has it, European explorers of the New World sought out the Quivira region, roughly mapped as the area between Cape Mendocino and San Francisco. Today, you'll find Quivira Vineyards in the middle of that Sonoma County region. The winery is the retirement experiment of Henry Wendt, head of one of the largest pharmaceutical firms in the world, SmithKline Beecham. Wendt and his wife, Holly, chose not to spend their golden years playing golf; they selected this area because of its long history of grape growing. They also wanted a sense of challenge; from all reports, they have succeeded in growing the winery to the 20,000-case-a-year level, while maintaining quality in the bottle. The modern wood-paneled winery built in 1987 sports a barn-like, rectangular A-frame. Creeping vines and bougainvillea meander on the matching latticework and over the arbor out front; olive trees provide maximum shade for picnicking in the courtyard. Inside the tasting room, warm wood paneling continues the theme as pinpoint track lighting gives just the right effect. Windows provide a view of the winery from the tasting bar; down the hall to the restrooms you'll have an unobstructed view of the barrel room. Quivira strives to do a few wines well: Sauvignon Blanc and Zinfandel are their mainstays. A Dry Creek Cuvee, composed of Grenache, Mourvedre, Syrah, and Zinfandel, is also tasty. For the budget-minded, the Atlantis label features a blended red and white, as well as a vintage-dated Zinfandel, all less than $10.

## Preston Vineyards

**9282 W. Dry Creek Rd., Healdsburg 95448 • 707-433-3372 Daily 11–4:30 • Four varieties poured, no fee • Small gift selection • Picnic area**

Lou Preston came from a farming family, so it wasn't a surprise when he bought a ranch in Dry Creek Valley and converted the prune dehydrator into a small winery in 1975. By 1982, production had expanded so much that he built a full-scale winery from the ground up, modeled after Trefethen's classically designed, century-old winery in the Napa Valley. And while Lou still guides the progress, he's delegated much of the winery responsibility to other talented individuals on the Preston team. Ever the culinary Renaissance man, he's now exploring organic vegetable gardening (some of his vineyards are certified organic), making olive oil, and baking bread in his wood-fired, outdoor clay oven.

The winery indeed follows the classic barn style. You'll find the tasting room on the side, where a shaded front porch with comfortable chairs beckon to you. The double doors open onto an airy, roomy, high-ceilinged tasting room. A dozen or so wines are open for tasting at any one time, and you can munch on Lou's complimentary, delicious, crusty country bread between sips. Preston's mainstay was originally Sauvignon Blanc and Zinfandel, both still excellent. The Cuvee de Fume (a Sauvignon Blanc and Semillon blend) is always a best buy. But the most new and exciting things happening reflect Preston's commitment to producing Rhone-style wines, including Syrah, Viognier, and Marsanne. The inexpensive red blend, Faux, should not be overlooked either.

## Meeker Vineyards

**9711 W. Dry Creek Rd., Healdsburg 95448 • 707-431-2148**
**Mon.–Sat. 10–4:30 • All varieties poured, no fee**

You'll have to drive to find Meeker Vineyards, located at the dead-end of a long, dusty road. Yes, there is a sign on West Dry Creek Road, but that only points you in the right direction. Once you see dilapidated buildings that should have been torn down decades ago, you're almost there; just turn left and go up the hill past those structures, where you can park under an old oak tree that shades a Sioux tepee and an old, portable prune dehydrator. The brown, A-frame Meeker winery lies just steps away. A sign at the door, "Tourists treated the same as local home folks," should reassure you.

The Meeker tasting room is a narrow slit carved out of the winery; in fact, it properly serves as the winery lab when needed. Look for the entrance to the winery on the far side of the room, and examine their tidy arrangement of barrel stacks and concrete floor, if you wish. Since Meeker operates on such a small scale, the assistant winemaker or the winemaker himself may host you. In fact, you may have to interrupt some of his winery duties to get his attention, but don't be bashful. These friendly folks will make you feel at home and believe in giving you a generous taste of their handiwork. Meeker makes a Chardonnay, but skip over that and get straight into the heavy-duty reds, Cabernet, Merlot, and Zinfandel. If several vintages of each aren't open for tasting, express an interest, and they soon might be.

## Ferrari-Carano Vineyards and Winery

**8761 Dry Creek Rd., Healdsburg 95448 • 707-433-6700**
**Daily 10–5 • Selected varieties poured, $2.50 fee applies to purchase • Self-guided tour to underground aging cellars**
**Landscaped gardens and grounds • Good gift selection**
**No picnics**

Attorney Don Carano and his wife, Rhonda, bought, renovated, and expanded the El Dorado Hotel and Casino in Reno. In 1978 while looking for a weekend getaway, they found sixty vineyard acres with an old ranch house in Dry Creek Valley to their liking. Soon they purchased other vineyards and ultimately built a winery, a brown and beige modified warehouse, now partially obscured by the shrubbery and clinging vines. It's just as well because the centerpiece is the adjacent eye-popping, earth-toned estate (completed in 1994) that resembles a luxurious Italian villa, inexplicably plopped in the middle of rural Sonoma County.

The Caranos, both second-generation Italian-Americans, designed the building and the surrounding five acres of flowers and gardens as a tribute to their Italian heritage. Named Villa Fiore or *house of flowers,* this showpiece hospitality center fulfills the Caranos' dreams. Several paths lead through the multicolored flower gardens, punctuated by a man-made waterfall whose tributaries meander through the variegated landscape. The paths eventually lead to an open vineyard terrace, and the first-floor entrance to the tasting room of Villa Fiore. Inside, more soothing earth tones, a faux marble floor, and handmade, half-globe lighting sculptures suspended from the ceiling reinforce the sense of opulence. You'll find the tasting bar, mahogany with a black granite top, to your extreme left, past a sea of tastefully displayed gifts and comestibles. You must take a trip down the marble stairs to view the underground barrel room and also make use of the most lavish winery restrooms in Sonoma County. The wines have uniformly high quality and offer well-polished examples of each variety. The Fume Blanc is perhaps the benchmark of its type, while Chardonnay, Zinfandel, Cabernet, Sangiovese, and Merlot are big favorites too.

## Lake Sonoma Winery

**9990 Dry Creek Rd., Geyserville 95441 • 707-431-1550, 800-750-WINE • Daily 10–5 • Four varieties poured, no fee Small gift selection including comestibles • Picnic area**

This winery, the farthest north on Dry Creek Road, takes its name from the Lake Sonoma Recreation Area up the road. One of the smallest wineries in Sonoma (only about 3,000 cases a year), the Polsen family built Lake Sonoma Winery incrementally and finally finished in 1990. They previously had some vineyards in the Bay Area, though they also owned vineyard acreage in Dry Creek Valley. Once the Polsens completed the new winery, their winemaking efforts shifted to this site.

The winery sits off the road on a little ridge. The vines grow to the edge of the building, shaded by apple and peach trees. Wooden stairs lead to the second-story tasting room, where plenty of windows offer a view of the vineyards. An outdoor deck, encircling the tasting room, provides ample reason for dawdling while sampling. Again, it's no surprise these folks focus on what Dry Creek Valley does best: Zinfandel and Sauvignon Blanc. Late-harvest version dessert wines also come from these same varieties. An oddball Rhone variety, Cinsault, is rarely bottled separately but is tangy by itself here. Recently, after a number of buyout rumors surfaced (including an offer from actor Bill Cosby), the family announced the sale of the winery to Korbel Winery, whose Armstrong Ridge line of sparkling wines will also be featured in the tasting room.

## J. Fritz Winery

**24691 Dutcher Creek Rd., Cloverdale 95425 • 707-894-3389 Daily 10:30–4:30 • Selected varieties poured, no fee • Small gift selection • Picnic area**

Fritz is located in a nowhere-land, not quite on the Dry Creek Valley floor with the rest of the wineries, but not right off U.S. 101, where it would enjoy plenty of tourist traffic. San Francisco industrialist Jay Fritz meticulously planned the winery (with the help of a structural engineer) to fit inconspicuously into the hillside. And while you can't tell at first glance, Fritz designed the structure to work as a gravity-flow winery, with the crush pad on the top floor, the press and stainless steel holding tanks on the next floor, and the barrel aging cellar on the bottom. It's an old technique made new again, designed to minimize both the movement of the wine and the energy needed to make it happen.

Native grasses and trees surround the winery instead of vines, and due to the bunkerlike nature of the building, you wouldn't necessarily recognize it as a winery. Within a whitewashed, stucco wall with smoked glass, arched doorways lead to the tasting room on the second floor. An adjacent tiled patio with shaded tables makes an ideal spot for picnicking, bird watching, or entertaining the winery cat. Inside the tasting room, the atmosphere is subdued but not necessarily serious. A small, dark wooden bar doesn't entertain more than a half-dozen people at a time.

Zinfandel, usually a multiple award winner, is at the top of the list here, but the Merlot and Cabernet taste good too. Among the whites are a sleek, stylish Chardonnay, Sauvignon Blanc, and Melon (the more proper name for Pinot Blanc). The late-harvest Zin is as decadent as a dessert wine gets. And the prices are very reasonable for the quality.

## J. Pedroncelli Winery

**1220 Canyon Rd., Geyserville 95441 • 707-857-3531 Daily 10–5 • Most varieties poured, no fee • Picnic tables**

Pedroncelli is an old-timer in the county; in 1927, patriarch John Pedroncelli bought fifty acres of vineyards and an old winery used for a horse barn during Prohibition. He made bulk wine, mostly red, after Prohibition, but by the mid-1950s, grape prices had dropped, and an abundance of bulk wine saturated the market. At that point, the family decided to bottle the wine (the next crush rapidly approaching, they needed the tanks) and put their name on it just to stay in business. Pedroncelli grew from those modest beginnings to produce more than 100,000 cases a year.

The tasting room used to be in the old barrel storage cellar, where a wooden bar separated visitors from the casks. Now the winery has dedicated a building to tasting and visitor hospitality. In keeping with the Pedroncellis' low-key demeanor, it's nothing fancy, just a brown, wooden cottage with an L-shaped bar in front, but with an additional room to handle those perennial tour buses too. Zinfandel, a mainstay, can be tasted three different ways here: white, rose, or red. The Chardonnay and Sauvignon Blanc are dry, while the Riesling and Chenin Blanc show some sweetness. Cabernet and Merlot are straightforward, while a special reserve Cabernet, from the vineyard of late actor Raymond Burr, is a real mouthful.

## Geyser Peak Winery

**22281 Chianti Rd., Geyserville 95441 • 707-857-9400**
**Daily 10–5 • Most varieties poured, no fee • Good gift selection**
**Picnic area**

Geyser Peak Winery, one of the most visible wineries from U.S. 101, has had its share of wine peaks and valleys. Presently the winery has hit at the top of a boom cycle. The property's history as a winery dates back to 1880, but nothing notable ever came of it until modern times. Schlitz Brewing revived the ailing winery in 1972 and, for a while, successfully produced the jug-quality, bag-in-a-box wines seen on every grocery store shelf. That fad ran its course, and when Schlitz couldn't change gears, it sold out to the Trione family, who already owned more than 1,000 acres of vineyards. In 1989 the family brought in the Australian Penfolds Winery as a partner; with a new Aussie winemaker, both quality and quantity increased immediately.

The winery complex, which seems always under construction, is terraced on the hills to the west of the highway. It looks like some sort of Renaissance castle fortress. Up a series of steps, the tasting room offers a cool oasis, especially during summertime. In more temperate months, visitors favor the shaded outdoor tables a few steps away. The wide variety of wines produced here are available for tasting; the whites now taste fresher and fruitier: Chardonnay,

Sauvignon Blanc, Riesling, Gewurztraminer, and a peculiar but good Aussie-style blend of Semillon and Chardonnay called Sem-Chard. The reds are richer and more varietally intense: Cabernet, Pinot Noir, Gamay, Syrah, and a tasty but expensive Bordeaux blend called Reserve Alexandre. Prices generally haven't caught up with the increase in quality yet.

### Silver Oak Wine Cellars
**24625 Chianti Rd., Geyserville 95441 • 707-857-3562**
**Mon.–Fri. 9–4:30, Sat. 10–4:30 • Selected varieties poured, $5 fee applies to purchase**

Silver Oak has long been based in a former dairy barn off Oakville Cross Road in the Napa Valley. The winery produces Cabernets, considered among the finest in the state. The variety of Cabernet bottlings has always included one from Alexander Valley. So when this property, the former Lyeth Winery, became available in 1992, Silver Oak bought it for use as its Sonoma facility.

The winery and tasting room sit a mile or so down the road from Geyser Peak. Behind wrought-iron gates, the gray and white structure looks restrained and tasteful, like the tasting room itself. The Alexander Valley Cabernet is comparatively more supple and ready to drink earlier in life than Silver Oak's other offerings. You can usually try the Napa Valley Cab here for easy comparison, which is considerably more tannic. The bottles are expensive, but if you're a Cab fanatic and don't plan to stop at their place in Napa Valley, you'll happily pay to taste these fine examples.

### Pastori Winery
**23189 Geyserville Ave., Cloverdale 95426 • 707-857-3418**
**Daily 9–5 • Most varieties poured, no fee**

If you've visited all the big places on Geyserville Road, like Clos du Bois and Canyon Road, expect the antithesis at Frank Pastori's winery; it will give you an idea of what winemaking was like in northern Sonoma County a quarter century ago. Pastori has made wine for more years than he can count and has had his own place on the side of the highway since 1970.

Pastori doesn't buy into the fascination with modern technology; he still makes wine the old-fashioned way: by hand. The winery is a corrugated barn, a shed really, with a makeshift tasting area carved near the entrance. The words genteel and delicate do not describe his wines; inky and dark do. Zinfandel, the No. 1 seller, is appropriately rustic, as is a red blend he terms Burgundy. As a bow to modern times, he also offers a White Zinfandel. The wines are as inexpensive as they are rustic.

## RESTAURANTS

### SONOMA

#### Babette's Restaurant and Wine Bar

**464 First St. East, Sonoma 95476 • 707-939-8921**
**Dinner daily • Reservations recommended • California cuisine**
**Moderate to expensive**

Hidden down an alley off the Sonoma square, Babette's took over the space formerly occupied by L'Esperance. Chef Daniel Patterson, who spent time at the Eastside Oyster Bar and Grill, and his wife, Elizabeth Ramsey, wanted to put their spin on a menu and have succeeded well. In a short time, the food has become a favorite of local winemakers. The to-die-for starter is their Sonoma foie gras with carmelized pears and hazelnuts. They've matched duck, lamb, pork, tuna, and swordfish with creative sauces and accompanied them with fresh vegetables or polenta. For a bargain, try the ever-changing *prix fixe* menu, which really shows off the talent of the kitchen. For more casual dining, the wine bar in the front room serves steak and french fries until late hours. Babette's has a great wine selection, with many available by the glass.

#### Le Bistro

**110 West Spain St., Sonoma 95476 • 707-939-6955**
**Lunch and dinner daily • Reservations recommended**
**California cuisine • Moderate to expensive**

The 115-year-old Sonoma Hotel on the Plaza formerly housed Regina's and Bistro Lunel, but Zino Mezoni from Zino's across the square took it over and rechristened the restaurant Le Bistro. Zino wanted to do something different from his other restaurant, so he disdained Italian and instead looked to the Mediterranean for culinary inspiration. Dinner offers a wide variety of fresh fish, grilled meat, and poultry, all served in a casual setting. Expect a good wine list too, with many by-the-glass selections.

## Della Santina's
**133 Napa St., Sonoma 95476 • 707-935-0576 • Lunch and dinner daily • Reservations recommended • Italian • Moderate**

It's not a surprise to find another trattoria in wine country, but Della Santina's has a father-son team cooking up satisfying meals. You can get minestrone, antipasti, and caesar salad here (all good), as well as pappardelle pasta with a meaty rabbit sauce or the gnocchi of the day. Roasted chicken with Italian herbs is the best, but duck, pork loin, rabbit, and turkey taste pretty good too. A combo plate gives the undecided a choice of three different meats. For dessert, splurge on tiramisu, amaretto mousse, or white chocolate cheesecake. Good wine list too.

## Depot 1870 Restaurant
**241 First St. West., Sonoma 95476 • 707-938-2980**
**Lunch Wed.–Fri., dinner Wed.–Sun. • Reservations recommended**
**Northern Italian • Moderate**

This sometimes overlooked restaurant lies just north of the Plaza in a historic stone building that dates back to last century. If you use your imagination, you might even think you saw General Vallejo strutting past your table on his way back to the barracks. Vallejo would no doubt have approved of this genteel family-run Italian eatery, with tables dotting the poolside and patio. Start with carpaccio or an antipasto plate; maybe go on to a course of pasta, say linguine with garlic and black olives, or spaghetti bolognese. Or go directly to the meaty entrees like veal scallopine, chicken breast in white wine, or green peppercorn steak. Tiramisu, gelato, and New York style cheesecake lead the dessert list.

## The General's Daughter
**400 W. Spain St., Sonoma 95476 • 707-938-4004 • Lunch and dinner daily; Sun. brunch • Reservations recommended**
**California/eclectic cuisine • Moderate to expensive**

This renovated historic landmark built in 1864 is named after Natalia, General Vallejo's daughter. Her former residence provides a classic spot to dine, either in the pastel rooms or on the patio. The menu features hearty renditions of American favorites with a California twist. Fanny Bay oysters are barbecued and doused with red sauce, while applewood bacon informs the clam and grilled corn chowder. Pork carnitas show up with black beans and fresh salsa; mesquite-grilled pork tenderloin is glazed with barbecue sauce, and the mixed seafood grill might include tiger prawns, ahi tuna, and scallops with mango salsa and lemon rice. Chef J. J. Buchanan, architect of the menu, has since moved on, so it remains to be seen whether someone else will chart a new menu course.

## The Grille at the Sonoma Mission Inn

**18140 Sonoma Hwy. (Highway 12), Sonoma 95476**
**707-938-9000 • Lunch and dinner daily; Sun. brunch**
**Reservations recommended • California and spa cuisine**
**Expensive**

The Sonoma Mission Inn, with its Spanish mission architecture, takes you back in time to a kinder, more gracious California. The amenities at the Inn have been modernized for today's travelers, and The Grille is part of that fabric. Perhaps the priciest restaurant north of San Francisco, you'll find The Grille's seasonal menu nonetheless well executed, artfully presented, and gracefully served. Start with roasted red-pepper gazpacho, crab cakes with garlic aioli, or grilled portobello mushrooms. Salads, particularly for lunch, remain among the hotel guests' preferred items. Entrees include sauteed salmon with green lentils, filet of beef with portobello risotto, and grilled Sonoma lamb with couscous. Many dishes on the menu focus on attracting the Inn's clients, who have come for the spa treatment. But despite the dishes' low fat/calories/sodium, the food still tastes good. The wonderful wine list is for high rollers only.

## Ristorante Piatti

**405 First St. West, Sonoma 95476 • 707-996-2351**
**Lunch and dinner daily • Reservations recommended • Italian**
**Moderate to expensive**

Piatti, as locals call it, first began on the Napa side in Yountville; wildly successful, it spawned a number of branches that have maintained the quality of the regional Italian-style cuisine. Located in the historic El Dorado Hotel, Piatti has a wonderful country feel, with a warm interior and an outdoor courtyard. The wood-burning oven and rotisserie turn out fine pizzas and grilled meats, along with pastas and risottos. Fried calamari or sauteed sweetbreads with seasonal mushrooms are typical starters.

Rigatoni with meat-porcini mushroom sauce might be a good choice among the pastas, but it's also hard to resist an herb-crusted pork chop, Italian sausages with white beans and polenta, or roasted chicken with rosemary potatoes. Good, if semipricey, wine list too.

## Zino's

**420 First St. East, Sonoma 95476 • 707-996-4466 • Lunch and dinner daily • Reservations recommended • Italian • Moderate**
Yet another Sonoma Italian restaurant on the Plaza, Zino's is the no-frills, checker-tableclothed, Old World style Italian restaurant most of us grew up with. The regulars include locals who like the traditional dishes as prepared by chef Zino Mezoni. Bruschetta, caesar salad, and antipasto leads to heaping plates of pastas with a variety of sauces. Grilled lamb chops, pepper steaks, and osso bucco and scampi in lemon butter also grace the menu. Don't forget to investigate both the fish and risotto specials of the day.

## GLEN ELLEN/KENWOOD

### Cafe Citti

**19049 Sonoma Hwy. (Highway 12), Kenwood 95452
707-833-2690 • Lunch and dinner daily • Italian • Moderate**
Luca and Linda Citti, who gained experience at John Ash and Tra Vigne, struck out on their own with this little trattoria in Kenwood. Start with the salads, including calamari with roasted peppers and olives, and red peppers with basil and balsamic vinegar. You can mix and match the pastas and sauces, ranging from pesto to spicy clam to arrabbiata. Entrees include osso bucco, seafood or mushroom risotto, roasted pork loin, and leg of lamb in a chianti wine reduction sauce. You can order everything to go, so have them make up some pretty picnic baskets for lunching in the wine country.

### Kenwood Restaurant and Bar

**9900 Sonoma Hwy. (Highway 12), Kenwood 95452
707-833-6326 • Lunch and dinner Wed.–Sun. • Reservations recommended • California cuisine • Moderate to expensive**
A bright, contemporary restaurant, with polished wood floors and white stucco walls hung with art, Kenwood also offers shaded patio dining with views of the vineyards in every direction. Chef Max Schacher's preparations taste flavorful but fairly traditional, never going over the top with an amalgamation of ingredients. Escargots in garlic butter, though retro, can satisfy you, as do the portobellos with Sonoma goat cheese. Entrees on the seasonal menu include grilled rabbit with mushrooms and polenta, and

crispy duck in a subtle orange or cherry sauce. Fresh seafood sometimes ends up in a fragrant bouillabaisse or hearty clam chowder; when ordering grilled swordfish or salmon, you might find a surprising side of sauerkraut on your plate too. A nice, reasonably priced wine list of Sonoma Valley producers offers another plus.

## SANTA ROSA

### Cafe Lolo
**620 Fifth St., Santa Rosa 95404 • 707-576-7822**
**Lunch Mon.–Fri., dinner Mon.–Sat. • Reservations recommended**
**Regional California cuisine • Moderate to expensive**
The late, lamented Matisse restaurant, one of the best-kept dining secrets because of its great-value *prix fixe* offerings, is now Cafe Lolo. The husband and wife chef team of Michael Quigley and Lori Darling has revived the space and brought some fresh, sophisticated ideas to the dining table. Try lamb sausage with olives and peppers or rock shrimp and corn fritters to start. Entrees might include seared scallops with wild mushrooms, roasted duck breast with sherry vinegar and herb-roasted potatoes, or veal chops with carmelized onion vinaigrette. They've priced the small wine list attractively, and many selections come by the glass.

### John Ash & Company
**4330 Barnes Rd., Santa Rosa 95403 • 707-527-7687**
**Lunch and dinner daily except Mon.; Sun. brunch**
**Reservations recommended • Regional California cuisine**
**Expensive**
Chef John Ash, the original visionary in Sonoma County, planned to utilize the vast array of produce and meats right in his backyard. Ash, of course, left long ago to become winery chef and emissary of goodwill at Fetzer Vineyards in Mendocino and to appear in his own television show on the Food Network. Chef Jeff Madura, who trained with Ash, carries on the tradition, even though the restaurant is no longer the only game in town to use local ingredients matched with the wines. The ambience is elegant, perhaps as formal as Sonoma gets, though a look out the French windows reveals the ever present vineyards. Duck breast has the Oriental influence of ginger and orange; crab or shrimp cakes often team up with a chili mayo; aged strip sirloin is grilled and smothered with mushrooms in a Jack Daniel's sauce. You get the idea. An extensive but expensive (like the food) wine list.

## Lisa Hemenway's

**714 Village Court, Montgomery Village, Santa Rosa 95405**
**707-526-5111 • Lunch and dinner daily; Sun. brunch**
**Reservations recommended • California cuisine**
**Moderate to expensive**

The shopping center location in Montgomery Village belies the warm surroundings and creative cuisine at Lisa Hemenway's (you can even request sidewalk seating!). Hemenway trained under chef John Ash in those early heady days of wine country cuisine but now has established her own distinctive style. At lunch, fresh items from the grill include burgers and the catch of the day. In the evening, you'll usually find oysters, shrimp, salmon, duck, and lamb, all tweaked just enough to have surprisingly refreshing combinations of flavors. Tasty pastas also deserve commendation. You'll find a good selection of wines by the glass available here. Also, Hemenway can prepare imaginative wine country picnic baskets to go, with the likes of cold smoked chicken in chipotle sauce.

## Mixx

**135 Fourth St., Santa Rosa 95401 • 707-573-1344**
**Lunch and dinner daily • Reservations recommended**
**California cuisine • Moderate to expensive**

Bordering on Santa Rosa's historic Railroad Square, Mixx dubs itself an American bistro. In the evening the subdued lighting sparkles through the storefront windows, illuminating a long wooden bar and the art deco surroundings. Chefs/owners Dan and Kathleen Berman, graduates of the California Culinary Academy, offer an ever-changing menu of wine country cuisines, featuring local products. Carpaccio, brushcetta, and focaccia may lead the way, along with plenty of arugula, mesclun, local greens, and goat cheese on the salads. Specialties include duck, lamb, and variously stuffed raviolis, as well as the classic rendition of creme brulee. Good wine list with plenty of diverse selections by the glass.

## Willowside Cafe

**3535 Guerneville Rd., Santa Rosa 95401 • 707-523-4814**
**Dinner daily except Mon. and Tues. • Reservations**
**recommended • California cuisine • Moderate to expensive**

Chef Richard Allen, a San Franciscan who's cheffed at Chez Panisse and Domaine Chandon, brought a couple of other expatriates from the city to help him establish this roadhouse cafe. A most exciting recent addition to the northern Sonoma County dining scene, the cafe serves up rustic California style French-Italian cuisine that's direct in its flavors but not overembellished with distracting nuances.

The one-page menu changes with the seasons, but you might find grilled lamb chops, local goat cheese on salad greens, pork loin with lentils, and rabbit with mushroom polenta. Excellent desserts include knockout crisps and cobblers, among other delights.

## HEALDSBURG

### Bistro Ralph

**109 Plaza St., Healdsburg 95448 • 707-433-1380 • Lunch and dinner daily • Reservations recommended • California cuisine Moderate to expensive**

Chef Ralph Tingle took over a long, narrow space on the Plaza formerly home to the Plaza Grill. Renamed Bistro Ralph, the space has an energetic feel, which the chef brings to his work. At lunch, the locals go for dressed-up salads that are full meals, upscale burgers, or grilled fish. At night, Tingle gets serious, offering European-style bistro fare that sticks to your ribs. The complimentary bread, his trademark focaccia, can be downright addicting. The attractive appetizers might include crab cakes with horseradish sauce, steamed clams with garlic and white wine, or warm goat cheese salad. Lamb meatloaf is popular, as well as a grilled ribeye with onion rings, and grilled salmon, ahi, or sea bass. Save room for the creme brulee or the intense sorbets and sherbets.

### Southside Saloon

**106 Matheson St., Healdsburg 95448 • 707-433-4466 Lunch and dinner daily • Reservations recommended California cuisine • Moderate to expensive**

Charles Saunders, onetime chef at the Sonoma Mission Inn, opened this restaurant on the square in Healdsburg, though he no longer chefs there. Oysters are always the preferred starters here (how about a Red Eye Tequila oyster shooter?), though appetizer choices abound, including fried calamari, and artichokes with roasted garlic and herb aioli. Fresh fish, including salmon, swordfish, shrimp, and scallops, might be daily specials. Heartier fare like barbecued pork ribs, lamb shanks, and garlic-rosemary roasted chicken with mashed potatoes taste excellent as well. Southside offers a fine Sonoma wine list. The only drawback: Service can be problematic.

## SONOMA OUTLYING

### Catelli's The Rex

**21047 Geyserville Ave., Geyserville 95441 • 707-433-6000**
**Lunch Mon.–Fri., dinner daily • No reservations • Italian**
**Moderate**
    There is nothing special to recommend at Catelli's, but when caught in the no-restaurant area north of Healdsburg, you will welcome the repast. During the week, people probably come here only because there is no other lunch place around for miles. Local grape growers and vintners hang out here; so on any given day, you might see winemakers talking shop with each other. This Italian restaurant is the type that serves spaghetti and meatballs with red sauce, and it's not half-bad either. Filling and inexpensive, the food goes down well with a glass of hearty red wine.

### Chateau Souverain Cafe

**400 Souverain Rd., Geyserville 95441 • 707-433-3141**
**Lunch and dinner Fri.–Sun. • Reservations recommended**
**French • Moderate to expensive**
    Chef Gary Danko, who has since moved on to The Ritz Carlton-San Francisco, brought this moribund cafe to life years ago with imaginative California cuisine. His predecessors have followed in his footsteps. It's as formal (white tablecloths) as Catelli's is casual, while you can't beat the view of the Alexander Valley out the French windows. Local greens and country pate make great starters; lamb shanks with polenta, grilled squab, salmon, and sea bass appear as main courses. Definitely save room for dessert.

### Chez Peyo

**2295 Gravenstein Hwy. (Highway 116), Sebastopol 95472**
**707-823-1262 • Lunch and dinner daily except Mon.; Sun.**
**brunch • Reservations recommended • Country French**
**Moderate**
    Despite the changing fads of food in California, Chez Peyo has remained in its original French bistro mode, though it has updated the menu in recent years. From the highway, it looks like just another roadhouse, so the unpretentious French bistro menu sometimes shocks folks. Start with roasted brie and garlic, grilled marinated mushrooms, or a caesar salad. The entrees both charm and comfort: filet mignon wrapped in smoked bacon, lamb shank in Pinot Noir sauce, sea bass with dijon mustard, and chicken breast stuffed with pears and bleu cheese.

## Russian River Vineyards Restaurant

**5700 Gravenstein Hwy. N. (Highway 116), Forestville 95436
707-887-1562 • Lunch and dinner daily in summer (call for
off-season schedule); Sun. brunch • Reservations recommended
American/Greek cuisine • Moderate to expensive**

When the Topolos family bought this winery and vineyard, they
also acquired a working restaurant, quaintly ensconced in a manor
house dating back to 1879. Since Forestville is in the middle of
nowhere, the restaurant became a destination spot that also attracted people to the winery and vice versa. Because the Topolos family has Greek heritage, you'll find a meze appetizer plate, a Greek
salad, souvlaki, and spanakopita mixed among the more main-
stream menu entrees, like polenta with sun-dried tomatoes,
smoked trout, roasted duckling, rack of lamb, and broiled swordfish. A great wooden deck makes the restaurant a great lunch spot
by day and rustic, romantic retreat by night.

## ANNUAL EVENTS

### MARCH

**Russian River Wine Road Barrel Tasting • P.O. Box 127
Geyserville 95441 • 707-433-8236**

Buy an all-inclusive ticket and get your "passport" punched at
wineries all along the Russian River Wine Road. Every participating winery has an open house, often with special barrel tastings and
older vintages open too. Wineries even offer complimentary appetizers along the way, as each tries to outdo the next in hospitality.

### MAY

**Russian River Wine Tasting • 707-433-6935, 800-648-9922**

Usually the third Sunday in May, dozens of vintners from
Russian River Valley descend on Healdsburg Square for an entire
afternoon of wine tasting. The event features food and craft
booths, as well as continuous live music.

### JULY

**Sonoma County Showcase and Wine Auction • 800-939-7666**

Sonoma's down-home answer to the annual Napa Valley event is
a celebration in its own right. Vineyard tours, winery luncheons

and dinners, and seminars allow plenty of time (three days) to schmooze and preview the auction lots, which include new and old Sonoma wines and entire barrel lots of future wine.

## LATE AUGUST–SEPTEMBER

### Sonoma Valley Harvest Wine Auction • 707-935-0803

The Sonoma Valley Vintners (distinct from northern Sonoma County) put on this annual to-do as a fun affair. Rather than stuffy formal dinners, they plan more casual events, like lunches and dinners at the wineries or in the vineyards. Comedian Tommy Smothers, a local grower himself, sometimes hams up the auction proceedings, and even the vintners get into the fund-raising spirit by dressing up in goofy costumes or parachuting to the auction site to make a bid.

## SEPTEMBER

### Valley of the Moon Vintage Festival • 707-996-2109

Held at historic Sonoma Plaza, events feature historical reenactments, the blessing of the grapes, as well as wine and food tastings.

## OCTOBER

### Sonoma County Harvest Fair • 707-545-4203

More than just a wine fair, the Harvest Fair celebrates the agricultural bounty of the county in all its goodness. You can taste and purchase fresh breads, all manner of vegetables, and of course wines here.

## RESOURCES

### Bed and Breakfast Association of Sonoma Valley

**3250 Trinity Rd. • Glen Ellen 95442 • 800-969-4667**
Reservation service specializing in bed and breakfast accommodations.

### Better Bed and Breakfast Bookings

**P.O. Box 2888 • Santa Rosa 95405 • 800-510-2888**
Reservation service specializing in bed and breakfast accommodations.

### Healdsburg Area Chamber of Commerce

**217 Healdsburg Ave. • Healdsburg 95448 • 707-433-6935, 800-648-9922**
Winery touring maps, accommodations, seasonal events, and recreational and other activities.

## Russian River Chamber of Commerce

**16200 First St. • Guerneville 95446 • 707-869-9000, 800-253-8800**

Winery touring maps, accommodations, seasonal events, and other activities. Good listings of camping, hiking, and canoeing sites.

## Russian River Wine Road

**P.O. Box 46 • Healdsburg 95448 • 707-433-6782, 800-648-9922 (CA only)**

Excellent touring map that highlights wineries and accommodations in the Russian River, Dry Creek, and Alexander valleys. Also lists the annual Russian River Road wine events.

## Sonoma County Convention and Visitors' Bureau and Sonoma County Wine Center

**5000 Roberts Lake Rd. • Rohnert Park 94928 • 707-586-8100, 800-326-7666**

A one-stop wine touring, information, education, and buying center in Rohnert Park on U.S. 101, just south of Santa Rosa. A beautiful facility near the Red Lion Inn, sponsored by the county to help travelers discover Sonoma wines. Plenty of free winery touring maps and literature, as well as information about accommodations, recreation, and current events. Wine tasting of representative Sonoma wines available for a fee, while a good cross section of Sonoma County wines is also available for purchase.

## Sonoma County Farm Trails

**707-996-2154**

Full-blown, large, colorful map that geographically pinpoints many small farm producers who sell to the public. Spotlights everything from baby lettuce, goat cheese, honey, preserves, and all manner of fruits and vegetables.

## Sonoma Valley Visitors' Bureau

**453 First St. East • Sonoma 95476 • 707-996-1090**

Everything you need to know about the Sonoma Valley, the heart being the town of Sonoma itself. Winery touring maps, walking tour maps of historical downtown and the Plaza, visitors' guides, and current calendar of events.

## Wine Country Inns of Sonoma County

**P.O. Box 51 • Geyserville 95441 • 800-WINE-COUNTRY, 800-946-3268**

Reservation service sponsored by more than a dozen high-profile bed and breakfast inns from all parts of the county.

# NAPA VALLEY

*T*he name itself connotes wine. But if you look closer, Napa Valley makes only five percent of all the wine produced in California. Ironically, the region so closely allied with wine has a small output. But several reasons exist to explain why more people visit Napa Valley each year than go through the turnstiles at Disneyland. First, the wineries here only produce premium wine, that is, the best possible wine from the highest-quality grapes. Napa Valley leaves the big market of wine coolers, jug wines, bag-in-a-box wines, and bulk wines to other wine-producing regions.

Also, the wineries in this small valley, only thirty-five miles long and four miles wide, have grown phenomenally, further amplifying the area's notoriety. To put things in perspective, Robert Mondavi left the family business, Charles Krug, to start his own winery in 1966, and people called him a madman. At that time, Robert Mondavi Winery was only the twenty-third winery in Napa Valley and the first established since Prohibition. Old-timers thought Mondavi had clearly climbed out on a limb, but they did not foresee the changing consumer habits and wine boom of the 1970s and 1980s. Today, of more than 800 wineries in California, more than 200 exist in Napa Valley alone.

As the number of wineries grew, agricultural preserve laws were passed to protect the vineyard landscape from tract housing subdivisions. Now with more than 34,000 acres of vines, nearly every spot suitable for growing grapes on the valley floor has been planted.

And frankly, Napa Valley has done a great job selling not only its wines but also the Gucci loafer and Range Rover lifestyle of its gentleman farmers. Many people can't geographically describe exactly where to find Napa Valley within California, but they do immediately associate it with an idealized way of life, as depicted in the movie *A Walk in the Clouds.*

But Napa Valley does come by its history honestly. General Vallejo granted George Calvert Yount (after whom Yountville is named) land on the other side of the Mayacamas Mountains from Sonoma. Yount helped settle the area and planted vines near Yountville in 1838. After the gold rush though, the idea of vineyards and wineries in Napa Valley really started to take hold. Immigrants like Charles Krug, Jacob Schram, the Beringer brothers, and Gustav Niebaum came here to make wine in the New World. In its heyday during the late nineteenth century, the number of wineries swelled to nearly 150.

But phylloxera, a grapevine root disease, devastated the vineyards, and later Prohibition slammed the door shut on the remaining producers, except those who survived by producing sacramental wine. Entire vineyards were torn out and planted to fruit trees. After Congress repealed Prohibition, the long, slow journey back to making world-class wines culminated in the 1960s, when Joe Heitz began his own label and Robert Mondavi built a modern winery.

Now, once again the phylloxera pest plagues vineyards; throughout the length of the valley, large tracts of land stand vacant. The diseased vines have been torn out, and many vineyards await expensive replanting. A blessing in disguise perhaps? Vintners will now look seriously at which grape varieties to plant in various microclimates of the region. Napa Valley continues to produce great wine (and like every region, insipid ones too) and will weather the debacle in style, coming back stronger and better than ever. Meanwhile, with the explosion of restaurants, events, and activities, tourists continue to make the pilgrimage to what James Conway called "an American Eden" in his book *Napa.*

## WINERIES

### CARNEROS

*(listed from east to west on the Oakland side, from the intersection of Highway 12 and Highway 29 west to Highway 12/121, the Napa-Sonoma connector road)*

To explore the wineries of Carneros, you'll travel on an east-west highway on the southern extreme of the Napa Valley that connects it to Sonoma: Highway 12/121. Coming from the Oakland side,

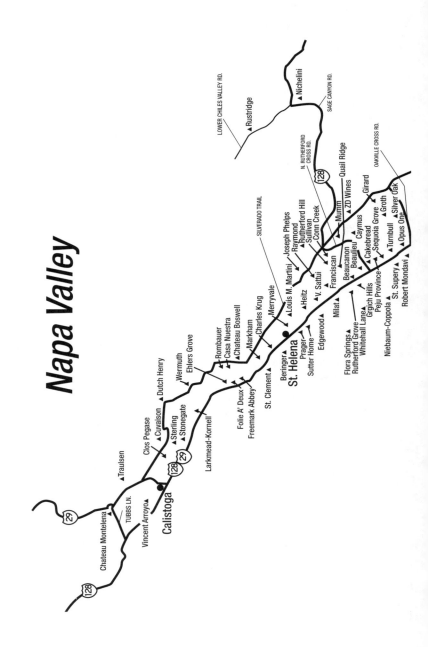

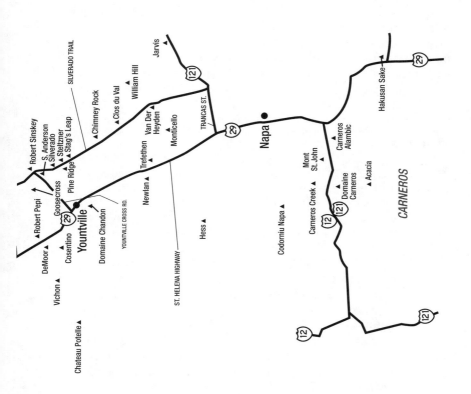

KEY

▲ Wineries
● Major Cities
----- State Border
⬡ U.S. Highways
◯ State Highways
▓ Waterways/Lakes

you'll stop at Hakusan Sake Gardens first; then when Highway 29 splits off into the heart of the valley, Highway 12/121 continues west. Carneros wineries cluster around this road, some like Mont St. John and Domaine Carneros are right on the highway, while the others sit off to the sides, within a few miles. Look for Carneros Alambic Distillery and Acacia to the south of Highway 12/121 and Carneros Creek and Codorniu to the north. Traveling from the San Francisco side, reverse the order, making Domaine Carneros the first winery and Hakusan Sake Gardens the last.

## Hakusan Sake Gardens

**1 Executive Way (Highway 29 at Highway 12), Napa 94558 707-258-6160, 800-HAKUSAN • Daily 9–6 • All varieties poured, no fee • Self-guided tour • Japanese rock garden adjacent • Small gift selection • No picnics**

Driving up from the Oakland side of the bay, the first place to taste and tour is, ironically, not a winery at all, but a sake producer. But perhaps it's not such an anomaly since sake means *rice wine*. Founder Toyokichi Hombo's dream of establishing a sake facility in America produced Hakusan. In 1989 he chose the Napa Valley, utilizing rice from the nearby Sacramento Delta to produce about 250,000 cases of sake a year.

The tasteful, low-slung buildings of Hakusan appear at the intersection of Highway 12 and Highway 29, although the entrance is around back, off Highway 12 at Kelly Road. Visitors are directed to large glass windows with informational signs that explain the process of sake making in sufficient detail to make you an instant expert. Stroll through a meditative Japanese rock garden on your way to the spacious, airy tasting room. Compared to the rest of Napa Valley, tasting is extremely civilized: Seat yourself at one of the many tables, and your host will serve you! Your host will bring four thimble-size cups of sake, both cold and warm, to your table, including a plum-flavored version. Hakusan offers one of the most relaxing ways to shake off the road dust and begin your Napa Valley trip.

## Carneros Alambic Distillery

**1250 Cuttings Wharf Rd., Napa 94559 • 707-253-9055 Daily 10–5 (winter 10–4:30) • No tasting of Brandies as prohibited by law; $2 fee includes multimedia presentation, tour of the distillery and aging cellars, and "nosing" various Brandy samples • Small gift selection**

There are Brandy makers in California but none open to the public and none built on the dramatic scale of Carneros Alambic

Distillery. The French pedigree (owned by the same family that controls Remy-Martin) is evident everywhere, including elegantly manicured grounds, the French salon-style visitors' center with comfortable chairs before the fireplace, and the actual Brandy production and aging facilities.

Tours begin at the visitors' center, where special effects and computerized motion control systems recreate the Brandy distilling process. A short walk leads to the still house, where eight large, hand-built copper pot stills line the perimeter. Obviously you'll see the most action here during harvest. Then onto the huge aging cellar, where 4,000 French barrels hold the sleeping Brandies; the fragrant smell in the barrel house, called the angel's share, is the evaporation of the Brandy into the air. Back at the visitors' center, the host ushers you into the smelling room, where you may savor the bouquets of the six different grape varieties that comprise the RMS special reserve Brandy. And while the law prohibits you from tasting, you may purchase Brandy right here at the source.

## Mont St. John Cellars

**5400 Old Sonoma Rd., Napa 94559 • 707-255-8864**
**Daily 10–5 • Most varieties poured, no fee • Shaded picnic area**

Mont St. John is a little-known winery outside the north coast area, where the Bartolucci family has grown grapes since 1922. During Prohibition they sold grapes in San Francisco to the many new home winemakers. After repeal, they began making wines under the Madonna label and later Mont St. John. Primarily they made bulk wines, which they sold to other wineries for blending. In 1978 the one remaining Bartolucci brother in Napa Valley built a winery in the then-new grape-growing region of Carneros.

A patina of wandering vines now covers the cement block building of a winery, and the peach adobe-style tasting room around front seems an afterthought. The medium-sized room with a wood inlaid bar is perfectly functional. Mont St. John pours a wide variety, including Sauvignon Blanc, Chardonnay, Riesling, and Gewurztraminer among the whites, and Pinot Noir and Cabernet among the reds. Finish with a sweet Muscat. The surprisingly good quality will cost you no more than $15, most less than $10. If a tour bus is parked outside though, you may want to come back later for a more personal and leisurely tasting.

## Domaine Carneros
**1240 Duhig Rd., Napa 94559 • 707-257-0101 • Daily 10:30–6**
**Most sparkling varieties poured, $4–$6 per glass • Daily tours**
**Small gift selection • No picnics or dogs**

You'll easily recognize Domaine Carneros, which was established on a Carneros hilltop in 1987. The word *palatial* will immediately come to mind. In fact the Louis XV style was inspired by the Chateau de la Marquetterie, the historic eighteenth-century Champagne residence owned by the founder of Domaine Carneros, Champagne Taittinger. Even if you don't wish to taste, it's worth the seventy-two steps from the parking lot to view the exquisite interior furnishings. In the foyer, a marble floor lies underfoot, and a magnificent chandelier hangs from a high-beamed ceiling.

To the right you'll find the tasting room, more properly called the tasting salon by the staff. A huge fireplace with a mantel imported from France dominates one wall, with the tasting bar opposite. Choose to sit in the salon, where classical music will serenade you, or on the garden terrace, where black wire chairs and tables allow you a sweeping view of Carneros and the surrounding vineyards. The sparkling wines here, Brut and Blanc de Blanc, are made with grapes only from the cool Carneros region but in the traditional French style. Finesse, delicacy, and balance are the hallmark of the wines as opposed to the mere fruitiness often found in California sparklers.

## Acacia Winery
**2750 Las Amigas Rd., Napa 94559 • 707-226-9991**
**Daily 10–4:30, by appointment (walk-ins generally accepted)**
**Most varieties poured, no fee.**

Established in 1979, Acacia is the Burgundian-style winery acquired in 1986 by Chalone, which also owns Carmenet in Sonoma, Edna Valley Winery on the central coast, and of course Chalone in Monterey County. Acacia remains among the first wineries to locate to Carneros and produce wines from the cool climate area that borders San Pablo Bay.

A barn of a building houses the winery, set atop one of many rolling vineyard hills. When remodeling the facility in 1990, builders carved a small, cozy tasting room out of the building. Signage is not visitor friendly, but a green awning marks the tasting area, paneled in blonde wood with a sloping whitewashed ceiling. Through the double glass doors at the rear, you can see a bevy of fermenting tanks. The Burgundian varieties, Chardonnay and Pinot Noir, are the ticket; even the reserve versions of these wines are often poured. The second label Caviste Zinfandel is anything but second rate and inexpensive to boot.

## Carneros Creek Winery

**1285 Dealy Ln., Napa 94559 • 707-253-9463 • Daily 9–4:30 Most varieties poured, $2.50 fee includes logo glass or applies to purchase • Shaded picnic area**

Francis Mahoney, winemaking proprietor of Carneros Creek, is considered one of the old-timers of the new generation who helped revive Napa Valley. He built the winery in 1973 next to the namesake creek and began making Zinfandel and Cabernet but soon decided the area more suited the Burgundian varieties of Chardonnay and Pinot Noir. The cool climate and well-drained soil of Carneros provided ideal conditions, so he began the search for the ultimate Pinot Noir clones, eventually planting six different types.

The tasting room, separate from the winery, is a whitewashed-walled former farmhouse with big windows that look out onto the winery and vineyards. The host pours Pinot Noir and Chardonnay in all their various label permutations. Carneros Creek is the top label, while Fleur de Carneros is the second wave, though Pinot Noir has an immediately appealing fresh and fruity style. The Mahoney Estate label, reserved for the best and smallest lots, generally appears only at the winery or at selected north coast restaurants. A fine shaded picnic area with a half-dozen tables is around back.

## Codorniu Napa

**1345 Henry Rd., Napa 94558 • 707-224-1668 • Mon.–Thurs. 10–5, Fri.–Sun. 10–3 • Most sparkling varieties poured, $4–$6 per glass • Daily tours**

Codorniu Napa is the sparkling wine outpost of the famous Spanish firm Codorniu, which has produced sparkling wines for more than a century. But don't look for some imposing super-structure winery like Domaine Carneros on the highway. Codorniu's less-traveled location (only two miles off the highway, a half-mile farther from Carneros Creek Winery) coupled with its earth-berm architecture, which resembles an Egyptian burial site, makes it one of the least visible wineries in the valley. But the con-temporary winery opened in 1991, planning to blend in with the surrounding countryside, with native California grasses camouflaging the modern technology of winemaking.

A cascading waterfall greets visitors at the entrance, where two sets of stairs lead to the hospitality center. If the idea of a winery set into an underground bunker seems a little funky, entering the winery will immediately change your mind. All black, chrome, and glass, Codorniu Napa presents as modern an architectural statement as you're likely to find in wine country. On the perimeter of the unique interior fountain courtyard, the winery displays nineteenth-century winemaking tools and an ever-changing art show, with the tasting room adjacent. The intimate and comprehensive tour will fascinate you with the engineering and architectural work, not to mention the winemaking aspect. You'll find no better way to decompress from city life than sitting out on the sunny patio at Codorniu, overlooking the vast expanse of Carneros vineyards, with a glass of sparkling Brut in hand.

## HIGHWAY 29

*(listed south to north, from Napa to Calistoga)*

This is perhaps the easiest route in California wine country. Start at the bottom of Highway 29 in the city of Napa and proceed north up the valley to Calistoga. This road is the most winery-intensive stretch of highway in the known world. In some spots, it will seem like a neverending parade, each winery only 500 yards from the last. Side roads intersecting with Highway 29 offer a wealth of other wineries, some barely a stone's throw from the main thoroughfare, others a few miles up in the hills.

A word of warning though: Highway 29 is the main artery in the valley and can get quite crowded on weekends, particularly during summertime. Even though turning lanes have been carved out, making a left turn into some wineries on the west side of the highway can be difficult and sometimes downright dangerous. So during these busy periods, stick to the wineries on the right (east) side of the road as you go north through the valley; then hit the wineries on the west side as you traverse back south down the valley. If you're only in the valley for a weekend or a few days, stick with this route; you'll visit all the wineries you can handle. (The east side of the valley is treated separately under "Silverado Trail," immediately following this section.)

## Hess Collection

**4411 Redwood Rd., Napa 94558 • 707-255-1144 • Daily 10–4**
**Most varieties poured, $2.50 fee • Self-guided tour of winery**
**and art gallery; continuous video presentation**
**Small gift selection**

This is a monument to the ego of one man, Swiss industrialist Donald Hess, who poured millions into revitalizing the old Christian Brothers Mont La Salle winery, high on the rugged slopes of Mount Veeder. But as monuments go, this winery and art museum, which opened to the public in 1989, is user friendly and free to boot. Because both art and wine are matters of taste, you may like or dislike what Hess has to offer on both subjects, but the visit will certainly stimulate your senses.

Six miles up the hill from Highway 29, you'll immediately recognize the landmark on the left side of Redwood Road. From the parking lot, walk back through the grassy sculpture garden and marvel at the old stone-block, vine-covered, renovated winery building that dates back to 1903. A congenial host often hands out brochures at the front door to make your self-guided tour more enlightening. The contemporary art includes works of Motherwell, Stella, and Bacon. Strategically placed windows allow various views of the winery. An excellent slide show, detailing the vineyard growing season and the winemaking, runs nearly continuously. Back on the first floor, a comfortable tasting room to the side offers both Cabernet and Chardonnay. You can tour the facility gratis, without tasting, but the generally excellent mountain-grown wines deserve your attention.

## Trefethen Vineyards

**1160 Oak Knoll Ave., Napa 94558 • 707-255-7700 • Daily**
**10–4:30 • Most varieties poured, no fee • Tours twice daily,**
**by appointment • Small gift selection**

Although Trefethen is the first winery as you drive north on Highway 29 from the city of Napa, some folks neglect visiting it because it's not right on the highway. And that's a shame because the Trefethen family bought the second oldest winery (1886) in the valley, Eschol Winery, and beautifully resuscitated it, as well as the six acres of contiguous vineyards. The pinkish-orange barn-style building was also one of the first gravity-flow wineries, wherein the grapes are pressed on the third floor, aged on the second floor, and bottled on the ground floor.

The tasting room sits on the far side of the winery; two giant oaks shade the parking lot and the interesting display of agricultural implements circa 1900. An archway and a cobblestone path lead to the tasteful redwood-beamed-and-paneled tasting room. The low-key staff offers as much or as little information about the wines as you wish. The wines usually include a dry Riesling, the inexpensive Eschol Cabernet and Chardonnay, and the estate Cabernet and Chardonnay.

### Newlan Vineyards and Winery

**5225 Solano Ave., Napa 94558 • 707-257-2399 • Daily 10–5**
**Most varieties poured, no fee • Small gift selection**
Former physicist Bruce Newlan started planting vineyards back in 1967, but not until 1977, after selling his grapes to Mondavi and Inglenook for a decade, did he hang out his own shingle as a winery. It's truly a family operation, with Bruce's wife, Jonette, in charge of hospitality and son Glen in charge of winemaking. Newlan doesn't advertise, doesn't have an impressive tour, and is unfashionably located in the southern part of the valley. The Newlans do, however, make a small quantity of very good wines.

Set back off Highway 29 (three miles south of Yountville), the winery is nothing more than a slab warehouse, elegantly disguised by large oak trees, a red tiled roof, and the Newlans' own vineyards. Once through the double doors, a long flight of stairs leads down to the concrete floor of the winery, where a makeshift table displays the wines open for tasting. The top-of-the-line reserve wines are Chardonnay and Pinot Noir. The Newlan estate wines include Cabernet, Chardonnay, Zinfandel, and Pinot Noir. Wines bottled under Newlan's Napa-Villages label—Chardonnay, Pinot Noir, and Pinot Blanc—represent exceptional quality at around $10 a bottle.

### Domaine Chandon

**1 California Dr., Yountville 94599 • 707-944-2280**
**Daily 11–6 (Nov.–Apr.: closed Mon.–Tues.) • Most sparkling**
**wines poured, $3–$5 per glass • Frequent daily tours**
**Award-winning restaurant adjacent, 707-944-2892**
**Good gift selection • No picnics**
Domaine Chandon led the French new wave in California. And while it may seem like ancient history now, Chandon's parent (Moet & Chandon) was the first French Champagne company to make a major vineyard purchase in 1973 with the intent of making New World sparkling wines. A dozen French and Spanish companies followed their lead. From the day the winery opened to the

public in 1977, it has been an attractive showpiece and an unstuffy ambassador for the French. Elegant and civilized, it looks decidedly French with an American flair.

Located in the heart of Yountville, by the Veterans' Home, the low-slung stone winery built into the hillside deceptively masks the much larger buildings housing the fermenting and aging facilities. A walking bridge from the parking lot leads across the pond to a spacious contemporary hospitality center. Inside, various displays highlight barrel and bottle making. The tour, well worth taking, departs every half-hour or so. Knowledgeable guides walk you through the facility, stopping at the massive, modern-mechanical "riddlers," which automatically turn the bottles so the yeast will end up in the neck. If they are bottling that day, you can observe the proceedings from an overhead walkway. At the end, you will have come full circle, and the guides will deposit you at the salon, where you can purchase sparkling Brut, Blanc de Noir, Etoile, reserve, and other small lots by the glass.

## Cosentino Winery

**7415 St. Helena Hwy., Yountville 94599 • 707-944-1220**
**Daily 10–5 • Six varieties poured, $2 fee includes logo glass or applies to purchase • Small gift selection • Picnic area**

Mitch Cosentino started making wine in Modesto as Crystal Valley Cellars in 1980. The standing joke is Modesto just wasn't big enough for both Cosentino and the Gallos, so Cosentino moved to Napa Valley in 1990. In reality, no matter how many award-winning wines Cosentino made in Modesto, he was the Rodney Dangerfield of the wine world; so he came to Napa Valley to get some respect and, coincidentally, a wider market for his wines.

The winery, just north of Mustard's Grill, resembles a white-washed faux French chateau; redwood beams frame the double doors that lead directly into the tasting room. A spacious L-shaped wooden bar accommodates plenty of visitors at one time, and a blackboard overhead displays what wines you may taste that day. Chardonnay, Sauvignon Blanc, Semillon, and Gewurztraminer are usually among the whites, while Cabernet, Cabernet Franc, Merlot, Zinfandel, and Pinot Noir are the reds. Ideally, you can try his Meritage white wine blend called The Novelist and its red wine counterpart The Poet. Don't overlook Cosentino's latest creative endeavor: Italian-style wines, like Sangiovese and Nebbiolo.

## DeMoor Winery

**7481 St. Helena Hwy., Oakville 94562 • 707-944-2565, 800-535-6400 • Daily 10–5 • Two complimentary tastes poured; $2 fee for all varieties, includes logo glass • Small gift selection • Shaded picnic area**

DeMoor is perhaps more famous for its geodesic dome architecture than its wines. The hexagon-shaped building houses the tasting room, with the vine-covered winery in a separate utilitarian building. DeMoor began life as Napa Cellars in 1976 and went through several ownership changes. Now a Japanese corporation owns it.

Winery production has increased to 15,000–20,000 cases a year, and you can generally taste all the varietals. Chardonnay, Sauvignon Blanc, and the little-seen Chenin Blanc are the whites, while reds include Cabernet, Merlot, and Zinfandel. Often a sweet dessert Sauvignon Blanc is poured. Look for the excellent picnic facilities set among the vines.

## Robert Pepi Winery

**7585 St. Helena Hwy., Oakville 94562 • 707-944-2807 Daily 10:30–4:30 • All varieties poured, $2 fee includes logo glass**

San Franciscan Robert Pepi originally bought a vineyard in 1966 with the idea of selling his grapes to others. But fifteen years later, he took the plunge and opened his own winery, constructing a stone building on a hill just east of Highway 29. In 1994, Pepi sold the winery to Kendall-Jackson, where it became one of the wineries in its Artisans and Estates portfolio.

Perhaps Pepi is most widely known for Two Heart Canopy Sauvignon Blanc, a reference to the unique vine-trellising system that produces riper grapes and thus a more flavorful wine. Reserve Sauvignon Blanc, Chardonnay, and Cabernet are routinely available, but the Italian varietals like Sangiovese are promising. The initial vintages of Sangiovese tasted more like a young, sappy Zinfandel, but now a richer, fuller-bodied wine is offered, with the moniker Colline di Sassi.

## Vichon Winery

**1595 Oakville Grade, Oakville 94562 • 707-944-2811 Daily 10–5 (winter 10–4:30) • Four selected varieties poured, no fee • Shaded hilltop picnic area by reservation, for Vichon customers only**

Only a mile and a quarter west of Highway 29, Vichon sits up on the Oakville Grade, but the steep ascent gives you a little bit of God's heavenly view of the valley floor below. Take a left into the parking lot, and you'll feel like you've discovered a mountain aerie. The dusty rose warehouse building, covered with vines, houses both the winery and tasting room. The Mondavi kids bought the place in 1985 and have refined the wines as well as fine tuned the marketing.

The tasting room, with peach-colored walls and a cement floor, tries to minimize its industrial surroundings with a well-displayed selection of gifts and wine. Vichon's Napa Valley wines are being phased out, and by the end of 1997, the Mondavi La Famiglia line will be featured for tasting. Expect many of the new Italian-style varietal wines to be poured, including Tocai, Moscato Amabile, Nebbiolo, and Sangiovese. Without question, the landscaped, tree-shaded picnic area, overlooking a patchwork of vineyards, oak-covered knolls, and Vichon's own four-acre hillside vineyard, is truly idyllic. During the summer months, make reservations. Oh, did I mention the bocce ball court?

## Chateau Potelle

**3875 Mount Veeder Rd., Napa 94558 • 707-255-9440**
**Thurs.–Mon. 12-5; call in advance to verify • Most varieties poured, no fee • Picnic tables**

A young French couple with experience in the Bordeaux wine trade came to the Napa Valley in the early 1980s. Then a funny thing happened: Jean Noel and Marketta Fourmeaux decided to stay and start their own winery called Chateau Potelle. They planted vineyards and eventually acquired the former Vose Vineyards, high on Mount Veeder. The remoteness of the property attracts visitors, as the bucolic setting in the woods seems light years away from the sometimes frenetic Highway 29. Even so, it's only four miles up Oakville Grade, then left on Mount Veeder Road for a mile and a quarter to the entrance.

Rugged, steeply terraced mountain vineyards greet you as you proceed the last mile on the paved, winding private road that eventually deposits you at the tasting room door. The surrounding winery buildings down the hill as well as the imposing natural scenery dwarf the little clapboard, country-style farmhouse that serves as the tasting room. The small bar rarely gets crowded, but if it does, a sliding glass door leads to a patio with perimeter benches and tables for dallying. The fresh air and view of the vineyards will invigorate you. The wines too, Chardonnay and Cabernet, are pretty special: Californian in style, inspired by a French sensibility that values finesse and balance. You also must try a mountain-grown Zinfandel. Be sure to call in advance before driving out; tasting room hours can be sporadic, especially during winter.

## Opus One

**7900 St. Helena Hwy., Oakville 94562 • 707-944-9442**
**Daily by appointment only • Tour precedes tasting; no charge**
**for tour, $10 fee for tasting the latest release**

The Franco-American friendship of Robert Mondavi and Baron Phillipe Rothschild of Chateau Mouton Rothschild of Bordeaux culminated in this magnum opus. The goal of the partnership, formed in 1979, was to produce the finest Bordeaux-style red wine possible in California. At the time, it conferred considerable cachet to California wines; the idea that a renowned French vintner would deem a California vintner his equal broke new ground. Initially the wine, called Opus One, was made at the Mondavi winery across the road, while elaborate plans were made for the Opus One winery. The same architectural firm that designed the Transamerica Building in San Francisco planned this temple to wine, and construction commenced in 1989.

The winery gives a structured thirty to forty-five minute tour several times daily at no charge, but make reservations in advance, preferably the previous day or early the same morning. The building itself would be worth seeing, whether or not wine happened to be made in its confines. Walking in the front door and lounging in the drawing room while waiting for the tour to begin, you'll feel pure luxury. The neoclassical interior utilizes literally tons of Texas limestone throughout. The center latticework top that sticks out above the building may remind you of a flying saucer.

The quite informative tour proceeds through all levels of this gravity-flow winery, ending in the *chai*, French for "cellar." An impressive 180-degree half circle of French barrels laid out in perfect symmetry stretches as far as the eye can see. The tour concludes back in the foyer, where you may leave. If however, the tour piqued your interest, the small tasting room is down the outdoor walkway to the right. For $10, your host will pour you exactly four ounces (glasses are marked with a line) of the latest edition of Opus One, $75 a bottle. While certainly an elegant and interesting winery tour, it's perhaps not for everyone.

## Turnbull Wine Cellars

**8210 St. Helena Hwy., Oakville 94562 • 707-963-5839,**
**800-TURNBUL • Daily 10–4, by appointment (walk-ins**
**generally accepted) • All varieties poured, no fee**

When local lawyer Reverdy Johnson and architect Bill Turnbull purchased this run-down vineyard in 1977, they intended to use the property as a weekend getaway and sell the grapes to other wineries. However, being smack in the middle of Oakville, they realized they had outstanding Cabernet grapes and built an award-winning barn of a winery on the property, appropriately named Johnson-Turnbull Vineyards. The wines met with success, but the root louse disease, phylloxera, intervened, and all the vineyards were completely replanted by 1992. The next year, Bay Area businessman Patrick O'Dell purchased the property and renamed it Turnbull Wine Cellars.

On a recent visit, the weathered barn-style building that houses the winery was being expanded, starting with the grape arbor and walkway that will eventually lead to a new tasting room. Cabernet is the main thing here, but Turnbull also pours a variety of older vintages, up to 1992, when the vineyards were replanted. All this will interest Cab fans since several of the wines have that minty/eucalyptus flavor that gave Heitz Wine Cellars its fame. Depending on the time of year, your host may pour small amounts of Sauvignon Blanc, Chardonnay, and Sangiovese. Appointments are encouraged, but you will generally be welcome without one.

## Robert Mondavi Winery

**7801 St. Helena Hwy., Oakville 94562 • 707-259-9663, 800-MONDAVI • Daily 9:30–5:30 (winter 9:30–4:30)**
**Daily one-hour tours precede tasting, no fee but reservations recommended; tasting without tour, $1–$3 fee**
**Good gift selection • No picnics**

Mondavi is the granddaddy of the winemaking revolution in California. When Robert Mondavi broke away from his family at Charles Krug Winery in 1966 and established his own eponymous winery, it was only the twenty-third winery in Napa Valley and the first new winery since Prohibition; today more than 200 wineries inhabit the valley. *Crazy* was one of the less pejorative terms used to describe Mondavi. From the modern mission-architecture winery design by Cliff May to the expensive French barrels and all the high-tech equipment money could buy, Mondavi let people know he intended to set standards for those who came after him. He was the first to back up beliefs on such a large scale. Time, along with the wine boom of the 1970s, has proven him right.

Mondavi places a high priority on wine education and provides a wide variety of options to visitors. The basic tour, about one hour, starts out front at the arched entryway, then proceeds to the vineyard bordering the parking lot, the crush pad, the fermentation room, and the aging cellar, and concludes with a tasting in one of the small adobe rooms. During the summer, Mondavi offers an in-depth tour, lasting three to four hours, as well as a wine and food seminar that includes lunch ($45 for the latter). For the really gung ho, a two-day tour of all Mondavi's facilities and several vineyards, including lunch and dinner along with in-depth tastings, is offered quarterly ($195). However, most folks find the regular tour enough to suit their needs. Mondavi usually pours several current releases (they make just about every variety), sometimes an older vintage, and if you're lucky, the sweet Moscato. The gift shop does a brisk business with the Mondavi wines and is a great source for wine books.

### Cakebread Cellars

**8300 St. Helena Hwy., Rutherford 94573 • 707-963-5221**
**Daily 10–4 • Selected varieties poured, no fee**
**Tours by appointment**

Architect Bill Turnbull, who owned and designed Turnbull Cellars just down the road, also drew up the plans for Cakebread Cellars' simple but classic barn. Recently another building was con-structed alongside it, in the same style, because the winery has expanded from a few thousand cases when it began in 1973 to more than 50,000 cases today. Despite the size, Cakebread keeps a fairly low profile; you may even drive right past it before you real-ize what it is. The small mailbox on the highway is the only telltale sign beckoning visitors to the undersized parking lot.

The cozy redwood tasting room also belies the size of the win-ery. Cases of wine are stacked to the ceiling on the opposite side of the tasting bar, which can get crowded in a hurry. You'll find plen-ty of room outside to mingle and admire the flower gardens. Sauvignon Blanc is the signature wine poured at Cakebread, done in the classic melony/lemony style. Chardonnay fares well without too much new oak, so you can really taste the wine. Big and tannic Cabernet takes a few years to mellow out. Occasionally, Merlot and Zinfandel might be offered.

### Sequoia Grove Vineyards

**8338 St. Helena Hwy., Rutherford 94573 • 707-944-2945,**
**800-851-7841 • Daily 11–5 • Selected varieties poured, $3 fee**
**includes logo glass • Small gift selection**

The signage at the Allen Brothers' Sequoia Grove Vineyards isn't much of an improvement over Cakebread, but a piece of burlwood displaying the winery name really is a necessity. Tall sequoias surrounding the tasting room and winery nearly obscure both; it's one of the last remaining groves in the valley. Thus came the name of the winery established in 1980. With the purchase of the twenty-five-acre vineyard, the Allens acquired the amazing trees and a hundred-year-old barn. They worked around the trees and preserved the barn although the foundation had to be redone to accommodate the technical aspects of a functioning winery.

On a hot summer's day, trees keep the tasting room cool and dark. Large German oval casks dominate one wall; they hold the Cabernet for six months before it comes to rest in smaller oak barrels. Chardonnay and Cabernet are the only games here, though a couple different versions are available. An estate Chardonnay is top-of-the-line, followed by a Carneros Chardonnay and an inexpensive Allen Family Chardonnay, available only at the winery. But Sequoia's strength lies in robust Cabernets, which come in both Napa Valley and estate versions, the latter so limited that you can only buy two bottles.

## St. Supery Vineyards and Winery

**8440 St. Helena Hwy., Rutherford 94573 • 707-963-4507, 800-942-0809 • Daily 10–6 • Most varieties poured, $2.50 fee Self-guided wine discovery center • Excellent gift selection**

The St. Supery complex looks more like an office building—two stories and low slung—but you'll get a homey feeling when the well-preserved Victorian house from the 1880s greets you first thing down the driveway. Inside the glassed entrance, you may be welcomed by a host, who can advise you of touring and tasting options. If you have neither the time nor inclination for a formal tour, go upstairs for the self-guided one.

Catwalks above the winery floor allow views of the holding tanks and the wine production area. Look for an entire vine and its eight-foot roots, all visually showcased, as well as interesting displays of soil and grape types. By far the most popular feature of the tour is the "smellotron," a device that expels aromatic smells often identified in the bouquet of a wine. Black pepper, cherry, cedar, and bell pepper aromas abound in red wine, while green olive, hay, grapefruit, and wildflower scents are associated with white wine. Choose your aroma, press a button, and get a whiff! The entire presentation tries hard to be a fun, interactive, learning experience.

Look for the tasting room downstairs amid the well-stocked gift shop. Sauvignon Blanc and Chardonnay can be very tasty here, as can Merlot and Cabernet; Moscato is the charming dessert wine. If you've opted for the formal tour, you may be led to tasting tables near the exhibit area, where you can browse further and also enjoy the periodically changing art exhibit.

## Peju Province Winery

**8466 St. Helena Hwy., Rutherford 94573 • 707-963-3600, 800-446-7358 • Daily 10–6 • Most varieties poured, $2 fee applies to purchase • Good gift selection • Picnic area**

People know Peju Province perhaps more as a lush sculpture and rose garden that happens to have a winery attached. Former nurseryman Tony Peju bought the property almost ten years before the county allowed him to finally build and open a winery in 1991. With that struggle behind him, he implemented his plans for a total hospitality center and winery.

The Weldon Rotz marble sculptures catch your eye first, even from the parking lot. The marble pieces, scattered throughout an incredible cascade of manicured flowers and roses, are powerful renditions of the sculptor's art. The winery tasting room also looks impressive, with a ceiling thirty-five feet high and a huge multi-paned front window that lets in the natural light. Fashioned in a French contemporary style, the rough-hewn walls feature stones from a local quarry. A few steps up from the tasting room floor, an indoor bridge over the barrel room provides a glimpse into the production area. Karma and Carnival are the two inexpensive proprietary wines, the former a Rose and the latter a Colombard. The host will usually pour two Chardonnays and two Cabernets, the HB Vineyard wines being the most flamboyant.

## Niebaum-Coppola Estate Winery

**1991 St. Helena Hwy., Rutherford 94574 • 707-967-3450 Daily 10–5 • Most varieties poured, $5 fee • Good gift selection**

In 1975, film director Francis Ford Coppola purchased the house of Gustave Niebaum, Inglenook Winery founder, and some adjoining vineyards. Like some of his film projects, it took a while to get things going, and wine was made in 1978 but not released until 1985. He made only one wine, Rubicon, and in the traditional Bordeaux style, he thought it the finest and longest-lived blend of Cabernet, Cabernet Franc, and Merlot he could produce. He succeeded, and the wine, while very limited in quantity, received wide praise.

In 1995, Coppola bought the former Inglenook Winery, across the gravel path from his property, and plans to reunite the parcels. The first order of business has been to renovate the original

Inglenook building and turn it into a multimedia center, featuring both the long history of the winery and Coppola's film career. The Italian Neo-Renaissance building will house plenty of movie artifacts, including the car from *Tucker*, the costumes from *Dracula*, and four academy awards. But the best news for wine buffs is the winery has expanded but with emphasis on quality bottlings under the Coppola Family Winery label or the recently revived Gustave Niebaum label. On any given day, hosts may pour Merlot, Cabernet Franc, Chardonnay, and a wine they call Claret, which could easily pass for Cabernet. In addition, the enthusiastic staff is not stingy in pouring the top-of-the-line, expensive Rubicon.

### Beaulieu Vineyard

**1960 St. Helena Hwy., Rutherford 94573 • 707-963-2411**
**Daily 10–5 • Five selected varieties poured, no fee; older wines**
**poured in adjacent Private Reserve Room, $2–$5 • Daily tours**
**Good gift selection**

Located in the heart of the valley, called the Rutherford Bench, Beaulieu Vineyard has a long, fabled history dating back almost a century, when Frenchman Georges de Latour bought four acres here. The winery expanded and survived Prohibition, providing the archdiocese of San Francisco with sacramental wine. He later hired French-trained winemaker, Andre Tchelistcheff, who made the Beaulieu wines legendary during his fifty years at the helm. Even though the winery is now owned by liquor giant Heublein, in turn owned by the even larger British Grand Met PLC, the quality still seems to make it into the bottle.

Its visitors' facility, once considered state-of-the-art, has now been surpassed by those of its richer, flashier competitors. Still, its two-story, octagon-shaped hospitality center (ironically hidden from view by the newcomer Rutherford Grill) seems timeless. Almost as soon as you walk in the door, a host greets you verbally but also immediately proffers a glass of Beaulieu Sauvignon Blanc or Chardonnay. Now that's hospitality! As you sip, you can peruse the various historical and informative displays about the evolution of the winery. Return to the long tasting bar for additional tastes of Chardonnay, Cabernet, Pinot Noir, and Muscat.

Eventually you will find yourself downstairs in the gift shop and wine store; off to one side, a multimedia show gives you a visual history of the winery, vineyards, and winemaking. For serious fans of the famous Georges de Latour Cabernets or other older vintages, the reserve tasting room lies just a few steps across the parking lot; $10 will get you five more tastes of Beaulieu's marvelous history.

## Grgich Hills Cellars

**1829 St. Helena Hwy., Rutherford 94573 • 707-963-2784**
**Daily 9:30–4:30 • Six selected varieties poured; no fee on**
**weekdays, $2 fee on weekends includes logo glass**
**Tours twice daily, by reservation • Good gift selection**

Born into a Croatian winemaking family, Miljenko "Mike" Grgich got a degree in enology from the University of Zagreb. He came to California wine country in 1958 and put in many years at Souverain Cellars, Beaulieu, and Mondavi before becoming the chief winemaker at Chateau Montelena. His reputation was assured when his 1973 Chateau Montelena Chardonnay beat out the top French white Burgundies in the famous 1976 Paris tasting. In 1977, he coupled his talent with the capital of Austin Hills, heir to the Hills Brothers coffee fortune, producing Grgich Hills.

The exterior of the winery looks typically Napa Valley rustic, with an ivy-covered grape arbor and the walls of the building surrounded by vines and flower beds. Inside, the small, dimly lit tasting room seems like an afterthought. Its wood-paneled walls and concrete floor basically extend from the winery, visible in the background. But as they say, you don't drink the ambience; you come for what's in the bottle. Grgich still makes the Chardonnay in the old, minerally style that forgoes a secondary fermentation in the barrel. The Fume Blanc exhibits a nice toastiness from the oak aging, while the Cabernet and Zinfandel tend to be big and rich. Try the late-harvest Johannisberg Riesling as a sweet dessert treat. If you happen to spy a guy in a beret walking around—that'd be Mike—be sure to say hi because he loves to talk about his wines.

## Quail Ridge Cellars

**1155 Mee Ln., St. Helena 94574 • 707-963-9783,**
**800-706-9463 • Daily 11–6 (winter 10–5) • Most varieties**
**poured, $3 fee includes logo glass • Small gift selection**

The former French-owned Domaine Napa winery, established on this ten-acre site, recently became Quail Ridge Cellars. Located in the Atlas Peak area for a number of years, Elaine Wellesley and her late husband ran the winery in its early years. But it ended up in liquor giant Heublein's portfolio until winemaker Anthony Bell and his partner bought out the corporate interest in 1994; they settled on the Domaine Napa property the next year.

Expect the property to undergo some positive changes, but expect the winemaking style to remain the same. Presently the small tasting room, jammed with wine and gift items, can get crowded easily; they plan to triple the size of the tasting room. Other visitor-friendly touches will include a latticework grape arbor, a gazebo, and a gurgling fountain in the pond. Quail Ridge has a reputation for Chardonnay, and the winery's version continues to be rich and buttery. Sauvignon Blanc is also tasty, but the real deals here may be the moderately priced Merlot and Cabernet, already bottle-aged for a couple of years at the winery.

## Beaucanon Winery

**1695 St. Helena Hwy., St. Helena 94574 • 707-967-3529, 800-660-3520 • Daily 10–5 • Five varieties poured, no fee Small gift selection**

The Jacques de Coninck family, which has a long history of winemaking in Bordeaux, established Beaucanon in 1987, drawing on several hundred acres of vineyards throughout the valley. They aspired to intertwine the French sensibility of winemaking with Napa Valley's fine grapes. Their design aptitude, however, is less than stellar. The winery's state-of-the-art interior contrasts with the exterior, which leaves something to be desired: A massive slab-sided building resembling a dreary warehouse sticks out in this environment.

Inside however, the tasting room looks bright and airy, with a roomy U-shaped bar; behind it, large bay windows look into the barrel aging room. The Lacross line, the second label, includes a Cabernet and Chardonnay at around $8. The first line, Beaucanon, includes those varietals as well as a Merlot. The late-harvest (dessert) Chardonnay, which has some sweet baked apple and cream flavors wins the prize for most unusual wine. Prices are moderate for the quality, and the winery offers generous case discounts.

## Rutherford Grove Winery

**1673 St. Helena Hwy., St. Helena 94574 • 707-963-0544 Daily 10–4:30 • Most varieties poured, $3 fee includes logo glass • Good gift selection • Picnic area**

Old-timers will remember that the couple who owned Rutherford Vintners used to pour their wines out of a tasting room that extended from their house at the corner of Galleron Road and Highway 29. That's part of valley history now, but set a bit further back from the road, you'll find a winery appropriately called

Rutherford Grove. Longtime winemaker Ray Coursen set up shop in a beautiful new winery surrounded by hundred-year-old eucalyptus trees that tower over the building.

A 180°F stone fountain gurgles right up to the front door of the tasting room, which has soaring ceilings with plenty of windows to let in the light. One wall utilizes recycled wood from a seventy-five-year-old barn, while opposite sits a massive stone fireplace. The wines are all top-drawer, starting with a slightly sweet Johannisberg Riesling and a dry, barrel-fermented Chardonnay, and continuing with Cabernet and Sangiovese. Under Coursen's personal label, Elyse (named for his daughter), you'll find a concentrated Zinfandel. The winery houses the Napa Valley Grapeseed Oil Company, its product akin to olive oil, and complimentary tastes are set out on the bar. On the south side of the winery, the grove hides a quiet picnic area.

## Franciscan Vineyards

**1178 Galleron Rd., Rutherford 94573 • 707-963-7111**
**Daily 10–5 • Four selected varieties poured, $2 fee includes**
**logo glass • Good gift selection**

No Franciscans live at Franciscan Vineyards, so don't look for friars in robes making the wine. In the early 1970s, the association with monks was probably considered instrumental in the promotion of brand image. After all, the Christian Brothers winery, just down the road, produced among the largest volume in the state. A group of Bay Area investors actually started the winery, though it went through a number of hands before a German outfit, Peter Eckes Company, bought the winery in 1979. Today, Franciscan is quite prosperous, owning such labels as Mount Veeder Winery and Estancia.

The Galleron Road address belies the fact that the winery fronts Highway 29. Pull into the parking lot, and you'll find a double-tiered fountain in the courtyard along with the oversized piece of furniture dubbed the Rutherford Bench. The low-slung, A-frame barn of a building has two huge tasting bars at either end of the room and an extensive selection of gifts. Chardonnay and Gewurztraminer are among the whites usually poured; Merlot and Cabernet are the popular reds. Experienced tasters should ask for the Cuvee Sauvage Chardonnay and the Magnificat Red. Don't overlook the Estancia line of wines: big flavors for small change.

## Sullivan Vineyards

**1090 Galleron Rd., Rutherford 94573 • 707-963-9646**
**Daily 11–5, by appointment only • Selected varieties poured,**
**no fee**

Down the road from Franciscan, the Sullivan family makes about one-fiftieth the amount of wine as its giant neighbor. The burnished two-story office and Sullivan residence sits across the courtyard from the winery. Tasting is by appointment, so it's courteous to call first, but if you arrive unannounced, someone from the office might pour these handmade wines for you. Tasting is pretty rudimentary here: a couple of open bottles on top of some empty barrels in the winery, with Shawn or Jim Sullivan pouring.

The white wines, Chenin Blanc and Chardonnay, ferment in stainless steel to retain the freshness of the fruit flavors. However, the two reds, Cabernet and Merlot, are the usual favorites. Big, bold, and full of flavor, these two wines are aged in heavily toasted American oak barrels from Minnesota. Located a bit off Highway 29, you'll get personal attention at Sullivan and learn about their way of winemaking. Here, you'll notice a true feeling of family spirit and hospitality that seems more and more uncommon in Napa Valley these days.

## Whitehall Lane Winery

**1563 St. Helena Hwy., St. Helena 94574 • 707-963-9454,**
**800-963-9454 • Daily 11–5 • Selected varieties poured, $3 fee**
**includes logo glass or applies to purchase • Daily tour**
**Small gift selection**

Two brothers, Alan Steen and Art Finkelstein, decided to turn their amateur interest in winemaking into the real thing when they bought a prime twenty-six-acre vineyard site in 1979. Finkelstein, a Los Angeles area architect and builder, designed this odd geometric building to be strictly energy and cost efficient. Solar panels heat the water, and the sunny side of the winery has an earthen berm to dissipate the effects of the heat. Massive insulation and a night air-exchange cooling system lessen the wine's evaporation from the barrels. But the tasting room manager still describes the building as ugly.

In the 1990s, the winery has changed hands several times. Now it's owned by a San Francisco industrialist who plans to maintain the winery's reputation for outstanding red wines but also wants to bring its whites up to the same quality level. And while Whitehall Lane looks large, it emphasizes its small production of around

15,000 cases a year as the key to quality. The small tasting bar, just inside the door, pours Chardonnay and Sauvignon Blanc for starters. Then on to the big guns, Cabernet and Merlot. Particularly fine are the reserve Cab and the intense Morisoli Vineyard Cab, both real teeth stainers.

### Raymond Vineyard and Cellar

**849 Zinfandel Ln., St. Helena 94574 • 707-963-3141, 800-525-2659 • Daily 10–4 • Four varieties poured, no fee Good gift selection • No picnics**

You'll barely notice the Raymond family's ranch-style winery from Highway 29 (half-mile down Zinfandel Lane) because its weathered gray facade blends into the surrounding environment of flora, fauna, and vines. The family history of winemaking stretches back to just after Prohibition when Roy and Walt Raymond's dad, Roy Sr., came north to work at Beringer Winery and ended up marrying the boss's daughter. When Nestle bought Beringer in 1970, the Raymonds bought these ninety acres and have since expanded both the winery and vineyard with help from their recent financial partner, Kirin Brewing.

After a quick drive down the private paved parkway, you'll find the multiwindowed tasting room on the north side of the complex, closest to the large parking lot. The Raymonds have devoted the bulk of their production to Chardonnay, which is very serviceable, as Napa Valley Chards go; a Sauvignon Blanc is the second white usually poured. But the red wines are the bell ringers: Pinot Noir, Merlot, and especially Cabernet all taste quite good. Their Private Reserve label showcases the top-of-the-line, while the Amberhill brand appeals to the budget-conscious who seek varietally correct Cabernet and Chardonnay.

### Flora Springs Winery

**1978 W. Zinfandel Ln., St. Helena 94574 • 707-963-5711 Mon.–Thurs. 10–4, Fri.–Sat. 10–3; by appointment only Selected varieties poured, no fee**

In 1977, Jerry and Flora Komes wanted to retire to the Napa Valley, sit on their front porch, and just watch the grapes grow. They stumbled upon a completely abandoned, decrepit ghost winery from the 1880s, and they were on their way. So much for sitting in that front porch rocking chair: The extended family now owns and farms more than 450 acres of vines in all parts of the valley and has beautifully renovated the old stone buildings on the property.

On the west side of Highway 29 all the way down Zinfandel Lane, the winery complex and the 110-acre home vineyard hug the foothills of the Mayacamas Mountains. The old, vine-covered stone buildings look like something from a postcard; in the center, three arches open up to a courtyard with shaded tables. Steps lead to a topiary garden bordered by a stand of old trees. The tasting room sits to the right of the courtyard, through a set of double-windowed, paneled doors. Flora Springs takes only the best grapes from the vineyards for bottling under its label; tasting the Chardonnay, Cabernet, and Sangiovese provides the proof. The red wine blend, Trilogy, and the Sauvignon Blanc–based Soliloquy just add the exclamation point. You're encouraged to drive through the vineyards on your way out and view an interesting display of the various vine trellising systems.

## Milat Vineyards

**1091 South St. Helena Hwy., St. Helena 94574**
**707-963-0758, 800-54MILAT • Daily 10–6 • All six varieties poured, $2 fee includes logo glass • Small gift selection**
You've probably not heard of Milat Vineyards because they only make a few thousand cases of wine a year and figure they can sell it all out of this beige clapboard building right on the highway. Longtime grape growers in the valley, the Milat brothers eventually decided to get into the winery business themselves in 1986.

The tasting room is a simple affair: tile floors, a bar of mixed woods, and lots of windows that make the space seem airy. A sweet Chenin Blanc poured here is something unusual; it may remind you of fruit cocktail. Even the "dry" Chenin Blanc tastes a bit on the sweet side, as does Zivio, a light pink, blush wine made from Zinfandel and Cabernet. However, the Chardonnay, as well as Zinfandel and Cabernet, taste completely dry and have pleasant varietal flavors. Prices are reasonable.

## V. Sattui Winery

**1111 White Ln., St. Helena 94574 • 707-963-7774,**
**800-799-8888 • Daily 9–6 (winter 9–5) • Most varieties poured,**
**no fee • Self-guided winery tour • Full-range deli with**
**sandwiches made to order and extensive selection of other**
**comestibles • Excellent gift selection • Large picnic grounds**
V. Sattui provides one of the most convenient places in the valley for a winery picnic, with a wealth of tables scattered about the tree-shaded grounds. Unfortunately, just about everybody else

knows that too, so it's often crowded, especially during summer. But V. Sattui also is the Wal-Mart of wine in the Napa Valley. Located in a vine-covered barn-building, the huge tasting room holds mounds of items that might appeal to anyone with even the most casual interest in wine and food. It's one of the few wineries in California with a full-service, made-to-order deli right on the premises. In fact, in its first year, the winery sold more food than wine. Oh yes, they also sell wine: The tasting bar runs the entire length of the back wall.

What looks like a historic stone building in back houses a dining area, aging cellars, the winery, and a wine museum. The Sattui family only built this stone structure in 1985, though it could easily pass as a century older. Arrows point the way to a self-guided tour through parts of the winery. Most folks, however, don't venture out of the veritable shopping center of the tasting room. Sattui makes just about every type of wine, and most are open for tasting. You name it, they pour it: Cabernet, Chardonnay, Riesling, Sauvignon Blanc, White Zinfandel, Gamay Rouge, and Zinfandel. But if you like it, buy it here because you won't find it elsewhere.

### Heitz Wine Cellars
**436 South St. Helena Hwy., St. Helena 94574 • 707-963-3542**
**Daily 11–4:30 • Selected varieties poured, no fee**

Vintner Joe Heitz has become a legend in these parts as a crusty old winemaker who, after apprenticing at Beaulieu, opened his own Napa Valley winery in 1961, long before the wine boom. Acting as the personality behind the wines, Heitz gave them distinction, but he went on to make his mark with Cabernet, notably from the nearby Martha's and Bella Oaks Vineyards. Even today, faithful wine bozos line up every January to purchase their limited quotas of the newly released vintage, paying up to $75 a bottle.

The Heitz shingle hangs out on Highway 29, though you may blink twice and think you're in the wrong place when you pull up to the tasting room: It's the quintessential little, old redwood wine-maker's shack that looks like it barely survived the ravages of time. Step inside though and discover a surprisingly understated elegance, with carpeting on the floor and a wall-length wooden wine rack holding rare vintages of Heitz Cabernet. A carved oblong walnut tasting table occupies center stage in the room. For obvious reasons, Heitz doesn't pour the expensive Cabernets, so be content with some lesser but moderately priced wines. Chardonnay is usually followed by Ryan's Red, a sound table wine blend of Cabernet and Zinfandel. The most interesting varietal, however, is the rarely seen Grignolino, which is made three different ways: as a Rose, a varietal red table wine, and as a smooth Port.

## Edgewood Estate Winery

**401 South St. Helena Hwy., St. Helena 94574 • 707-963-7280, 800-755-2374 • Daily 10–6 • Four selected varieties poured, $2 fee • Small gift selection • Picnic area**

This winery, owned by the Golden State Vintners co-op, has gone by a variety of names, including J. Wile and Bergfeld. The winery traces its history back to 1885, and part of the original building has been engulfed by the much larger, modern winemaking facilities. The wine boom and increase in Napa Valley tourism gave rise to a separate hospitality center and tasting room on the property.

The tasting room, off to the right, has a huge ceiling with arched windows, making the room seem light and airy, especially when the sun streams in. Partially hidden in the back sits a secluded patio and picnic area that only locals seem to know about. Edgewood has the usual lineup of Napa-Valley-style wines, including Cabernet, Chardonnay, and Sauvignon Blanc. But the most intriguing ones are usually mixed into Bordeaux-style blends and rarely bottled separately: Cabernet Franc and Malbec.

## Sutter Home Winery

**277 South St. Helena Hwy., St. Helena 94574 • 707-963-3104 Daily 9–5 (winter 10–5) • Four selected varieties poured, no fee Daily tour of adjacent gardens • Extensive gift selection**

In 1972 Sutter Home virtually invented White Zinfandel, a new wine category that propelled this long-standing, family-owned winery to one of the largest producers in the state. At last report, Sutter Home sells more than three million cases of White Zin a year. This came from a winery that started out making robust red Zinfandels (and still does) that go well with hearty tomato-based Italian fare.

The actual winery production is down the road in a large industrial complex on, appropriately enough, Zinfandel Lane, so don't expect any winery ambience. The tasting room, however, got a complete makeover in recent years. Murals line the walls, and a large horseshoe bar stands ready to handle the seemingly perpetual crowds, with the gift annex just a step down. Go north down a walkway and through the glass doors of the tasting room to the family's elegantly restored Victorian mansion, complete with a cottage and water tower. The real tour to take is of Sutter Home's gardens, featuring hundreds of roses and other perennials; it's usually con-ducted on the hour Wednesday through Sunday. The wines include the ubiquitous White Zinfandel, red Zinfandel and a reserve, Chenin Blanc, Sauvignon Blanc, Chardonnay, and Cabernet.

## Prager Winery and Port Works

**1281 Lewelling Ave., St. Helena 94574 • 707-963-PORT**
**Daily 10:30–4:30 • Five selected varieties poured, $3 fee**

Sutter Home's massive Victorian house dwarfs Prager, and con-sequently most visitors miss the small sign just to the north on the same side of Highway 29, which is a real shame. A quarter mile down the lane, an amazingly dense vineyard surrounds the historic wooden barn that dates back to 1865. The Prager brothers started making wine here in 1979 and then expanded in 1982, preserving the same style and spirit of the original building.

The winery cats, Corky and Useless, may greet you, but the real character is Jim Prager himself, a dead ringer for Kris Kringle with his white beard. He will tell you Prager is the only serious Port (six-teen to twenty percent alcohol fortified with Brandy) producer in Napa, all the while charming you with his gentlemanly stories and humorous asides. The interior of the tasting room looks like a Hollywood set, with cobwebs on the windows and every form of foreign paper money tacked to the walls. A clock with all the hours showing nine o'clock declares, "We will drink no wine before nine." You get the idea that they don't stand for much formality at Prager. Chardonnay and Cabernet are poured first to warm up your taste buds. Then on to a White Port, a late-bottled vintage Port, and a late-harvest wine. You'll smile as you walk away from this personal-ized experience, usually with an esoteric Port purchase in hand.

## Louis M. Martini Winery

**254 South St. Helena Hwy., St. Helena 94574 • 707-963-2736**
**Daily 10–4:30 • Four selected varieties poured, no fee; reserve wines, $5 fee • Daily tours • Good gift selection • Picnic area**

The Martini Winery and tasting room has not changed much over the years, Louis M. being one of the most respected patriarchs of an old-line (1933) Napa Valley wine family. Son Michael, though, has updated some of the wines, particularly the whites, and brought them into the modern age. The reds remain as hearty and robust as ever.

Directly across from Sutter Home, the Martini tasting room entrance is halfway back in a low-slung, cinder block building. Once inside, a left turn puts you in the tasting area, with a weathered wooden bar running the entire length of the room. In the middle against the wall, browse displays of the current and vintage wines along with a good assortment of gift items. The red wines of note are Cabernet, Merlot, Zinfandel, and Pinot Noir, and among the whites, Chardonnay and Sauvignon Blanc. A delicious dessert wine, Moscato Amabile, is only available at the winery. You can find an underutilized picnic area, away from the frenetic activity of Highway 29, in the back under the shade of sycamore trees.

### Merryvale Vineyards
**1000 Main St., St. Helena 94574 • 707-963-7777**
**Daily 10–5:30 • Five selected varieties poured, $3 fee**
**Good gift selection**

This old building, formerly housing Sunny St. Helena Winery, was the first winery built in Napa Valley after the repeal of Prohibition. It has also housed Charles Krug Winery, a grape growers' cooperative, and Christian Brothers' wine storage. A group of partners took over the place in 1985, gutting it to move in modern winemaking machinery but retaining the massive stone walls, as well as a great piece of history.

The winery's barrel aging rooms flank the tasting room. A U-shaped blonde wooden bar is in the center, while subdued lighting from overhead redwood beams creates an intimate atmosphere. On the northwest side, you'll see a dramatic display of double-decked, century-old, 2,000-gallon oval wine barrels, while the northeast view offers rows of gleaming stainless steel tanks. Cabernet and Merlot are reliable if pricey; the Chardonnay tastes buttery, while a white Meritage called Vignette, a blend of Sauvignon Blanc and Semillon, is tasty. The wine in the funny, square bottle tastes unusual as its package: It's Muscat de Frontignan, which has a nutty, slightly sweet taste that grows on you. Don't miss the oversized painting on the south wall that features the who's who in Napa Valley lounging on the patio of what is now Tra Vigne restaurant next door.

### Beringer Vineyards
**2000 Main St., St. Helena 94574 • 707-963-7115**
**Daily 9:30–5 • Selected varieties poured, no fee; reserve tasting 10–4:30 in Founder's Room, $2–$4 fee • Daily tours on the half-hour • Excellent gift selection**

Certainly Beringer, with its imposing Rhine House built by German immigrants the Beringer brothers in 1883, needs no introduction to tourists. Almost everyone stops at this winery, if only to admire the century-old handiwork of the mansion. But there are other engaging reasons to visit: It offers one of the best historical tours in the valley, along with some of the best wines. The oldest continuously operating winery in Napa Valley, Beringer began production in 1876. The next year, Chinese laborers carved 1,000 feet of aging tunnels out of the hillside property; the caves highlight the tours, which end back in the Rhine House tasting room.

The house was a marvel for its time and is even more so today, when the material costs alone would be prohibitive. California redwood frames the native stone foundation; staircases and mantelpieces have intricate carvings, while builders custom cut the floors from a variety of expensive woods. The stained-glass windows alone are worthy of a cathedral. The current corporate owners have maintained all the beauty and antiquity of that bygone era, and one feels a little privileged to taste wine in a building that's a historical landmark. As for the wines, Beringer makes just about every kind of varietal, from a winsome Gamay Beaujolais to a heavy-duty reserve Cabernet. But you really can't miss with anything on the tasting menu. Wine aficionados who like to taste older, rarer vintages can take the stairs to the second-floor Founder's Room, where an interesting array of goodies are poured for a fee.

### Charles Krug Winery

**2800 Main St., St. Helena 94574 • 707-963-5057**
**Mon.–Thurs. 10:30–5 (winter 10:30–4:30), Fri.–Sun. 10–6 (winter 10–5) • Most varieties poured, $3–$6 fee • Daily tours, $1 fee, followed by tasting, no fee; Wed. only: free tasting, no tours • Excellent gift selection • Picnic area for customers**

Just past Beringer, the historic Charles Krug Winery sits through the tunnel of elm trees and on the other side of the road. Here Jacob Beringer worked in 1867 before starting his own winery. Karl Krug, another German immigrant, helped pioneer grape growing and winemaking in the valley beginning in 1860. Upon his death, though, the winery went through hard times before the Cesare Mondavi family acquired it in 1943. Son Robert later split from the family to start his own eponymous winery, while son Peter and his children remained in charge of Krug. While Robert went on to experiment with different grapes and production methods, his brother Peter stuck mostly to the more traditional way of doing things.

The tour is a good one, by the way, winding through the massive stone winery building, into the vineyards, and ending at the tasting room, where those who took the tour taste for free. Krug makes all manner of modestly priced varietals—nothing really fancy. First bottled here as a varietal in the early 1950s, Chenin Blanc remains one of Krug's best white sipping wines. Cabernets, particularly the Vintage Selection releases, have earned Krug a reputation over the years. With the new line of Family reserve wines (Chardonnay, Sangiovese, and Merlot), Krug attempts to bring its wines up to date. In the same vein, Generations is the winery's Bordeaux-style blend.

## Markham Winery

**2812 North St. Helena Hwy., St. Helena 94574**
**707-963-5292 • Daily 10:30–5:30 (winter 10–5) • Four selected varieties poured, $3 fee includes logo glass • Good gift selection**

When founder Bruce Markham sold his winery in 1988 to Mercian, the largest wine producer in Japan, production was small and the wines were not widely known. After an infusion of capital for winery improvements, production boomed to more than 100,000 cases, quality remained high, and wine consumers took notice.

The winery's imposing, rough-hewn stone walls are softened by dual water fountains out front that lead through the double glass doors to the visitor-friendly tasting room. The stone theme continues inside, where an Ahwanee-style two-story fireplace of black granite bordered by small boulders dominates the room. A five-sided wooden bar at the rear, dappled by light from the front windows, beckons tasters. Markham doesn't offer an entire list of wines to taste; instead the winery does the best it can with its specific vineyards. Chardonnay and Sauvignon Blanc are the whites; Cabernet and Merlot, the reds. A special Muscat Blanc is sometimes available also. Quality is uniformly excellent, with moderate prices.

## St. Clement Vineyards

**2867 North St. Helena Hwy., St. Helena 94574**
**707-967-7221 • Daily 10–4 • Four selected varieties poured, $2 fee applies to purchase • Daily tours by appointment**
**Shaded picnic area**

Tourists slow down and gawk when passing this magnificent Victorian on the hill just north of St. Helena. But St. Clement didn't open its doors to the public for tasting until Japanese brewing giant Sapporo bought the winery about ten years ago. In 1876 a San Francisco businessman who made wine in the cellar built the house. Over the years, the building deteriorated. In the mid-1960s

Mike Robbins established his first Spring Mountain Winery there; during his tenure, the Victorian was lovingly restored in detail. Robbins later moved on, and the new owner renamed the winery St. Clement after his home island in Chesapeake Bay and in honor of the patron saint of mariners.

To get up close and personal to this Victorian piece of history, you'll have to make the steep walk up the hill from the parking lot, bordered by terraced vines. On the front porch, you have a commanding view of the surrounding vineyards to the other side of the valley. You'll also notice shaded picnic tables underneath the sheltering fir trees. Once inside, take a look at the handcrafted interior that includes two antique glass-etched chandeliers. St. Clement makes only a few different varieties: Chardonnay (a particularly fine sunny and lemon tart version), Sauvignon Blanc, Cabernet, and Merlot, all uniformly excellent and priced commensurately. A tasty Rose is sometimes poured, as well as older vintages.

### Freemark Abbey Winery

**3022 North St. Helena Hwy., St. Helena 94574**
**707-963-9694 • Daily 10–4:30 (winter Thurs.–Sun.)**
**Five selected varieties poured, $5 fee includes logo glass**
**Daily tour at 2 • Small gift selection**

Freemark Abbey has a long, tangled history, and like its Napa Valley neighbor Franciscan, bears no relation to a religious order of monks. The name comes from the nickname of a previous owner, Abbey Ahern, and his friends, Freeman and Mark. The amazing rough stone buildings, which now constitute a shopping center, were built around the turn of the century. Today the Hurd candle factory and retail store occupy the upper level; the partners of Freemark Abbey took over the lower level in 1967 for winemaking. Most of the wines are made from vineyards the partnership either owns or controls, thus ensuring a consistent supply of grapes.

A sign directs visitors back through the French doors into a genteel and civilized tasting room, with a large stone fireplace, baby grand piano, and chairs for weary travelers. A Riesling may be offered first, followed by two different styles of Chardonnay, one that has gone through secondary (malolactic) fermentation and one that hasn't. A juicy Merlot is usually available, as well as several Cabernets; you're in luck if they're pouring the Cabernet Bosche, a benchmark of the varietal in Napa Valley. A super dessert wine called Edelwein, which tastes like liquid nectar of honeysuckle, is rare and often only available for purchase at the winery.

# Folie A' Deux Winery

**3070 North St. Helena Hwy., St. Helena 94574**
**707-963-1160, 800-473-4454 • Daily 11–5 • Selected varieties**
**poured, no fee; sparkling wine, $5 fee • Small gift selection**
**Picnic area**

*Folie a' deux* is a French phrase that refers to a fantasy or delusion shared by two people; literally, it means "folly for two." The founders, a pair of psychiatrists, aptly applied this diagnosis to themselves when entering the winery business in 1981. Their flashy gray, silver, and black label even has a Rorschach blot that resembles a pair of dancers as its centerpiece.

In the early years, the proprietors lived in the turn-of-the-century farmhouse on this former goat and sheep ranch. It eventually became the tasting room, which explains the huge fireplace in the front and the spiral staircase to the second floor in the back. The tasting room/winery buildings are hidden from the highway, which may explain why few people use their pleasant shaded picnic area. Share the fantasy is the motto, and the staff will eagerly share the winery's style of the little-seen Chenin Blanc, along with Cabernet, Pinot Noir, and two different Chardonnays. For an extra fee, they also pour a Muscat-infused sparkling wine, limited-production Sangiovese, and reserve wines.

# Larkmead-Kornell Cellars

**1091 Larkmead Ln., St. Helena 94574 • 707-942-0859,**
**800-574-WINE • Daily 10–4:30 • Selected varieties poured,**
**no fee • Picnic area**

A German immigrant, Hans Kornell escaped the Nazi regime during World War II. Through a series of mishaps, he ended up in California working at various wineries until he established his own winery on the old Larkmead property in 1958. Kornell came from a long line of German sparkling-wine makers, so he knew something about the production end of the business. He made sparklers in the *sekt* tradition, meaning he used primarily Riesling for his wines. As tastes shifted toward drier sparklers, Kornell's style fell out of favor, and the winery went into bankruptcy. Then Koerner Rombauer, who has an eponymous winery on the Silverado Trail, purchased it several years ago.

Nothing much has changed in the interim. You still have to walk by the 1906 rough stone Larkmead winery building, now listed on the National Register of Historic Places, to get to the modest tasting room. The Brut and Extra Dry sparklers are now made with traditional Champagne grapes: Chardonnay, Pinot Noir, and Pinot Blanc. Often vintage-dated Blanc de Blanc and Blanc de Noirs will be open for tasting also. All are tasty, and the quality is back in the bottle. You can only buy these wines at the winery, although Larkmead-Kornell will ship direct to your home. In addition, hosts pour the Rombauer wines in a connected tasting room, so you can taste two different producers in one stop.

### Ehlers Grove Winery
**3222 Ehlers Ln., St. Helena 94574 • 707-963-3200**
**Daily 10–5 • Selected varieties poured, no fee • Picnic area**
Bernard Ehlers constructed this rustic fieldstone winery in 1886, and it fell into disuse over the years, until the modern wine boom, when different winemakers rented out the space for fermenting and barrel aging. A partnership headed by Tony Cartlidge and Glenn Browne began revamping the property in 1993, and the tasting room opened to the public late that year. However, *tasting room* seems an odd term for the L-shaped bar barely squeezed into one corner of the historic winery building and surrounded by hundreds of aging barrels.

The emphasis, under both the Ehlers Grove and the Cartlidge & Browne labels, is on moderately priced wines ($15 and less) that deliver flavor. Sauvignon Blanc and three different-style Chardonnays lead the parade of whites, with Cabernet, Merlot, Pinot Noir, and Zinfandel the highlighted reds. While the winery is relatively new and unknown, do stop and taste the wines. Shaded tables stand ready for picnicking under the olive trees.

### Stonegate Winery
**1183 Dunaweal Ln., Calistoga 94515 • 707-942-6500**
**Daily 10:30–4:30 • Selected varieties poured; no fee on weekdays, $1.50 fee on weekends includes logo glass**
**Small gift selection • Picnic area**
A stone archway marks the entry and leads to the modest A-frame tasting room of Stonegate Winery, on the corner of Highway 29 and Dunaweal Lane. The winery's name was a spur-of-the-moment choice for the winery, which the Spaulding family established in 1973. Although their label depicted a stone gate from the beginning, they didn't build the actual stone gate out front until many years later. The tasting room abuts their home vineyard, and the stainless steel tanks stick out of the winery around back.

Over the years, they've kept the production small and prices moderate, concentrating on just a few wines. Sauvignon Blanc tastes crisp, and the Chardonnay can be good. Vintage-dated Merlot and Cabernet often age in bottles before being poured in the tasting room, allowing the wines to mellow their tannins a bit. In years when the right conditions exist, Stonegate produces a late-harvest dessert wine, made from a blend of Sauvignon Blanc and Semillon.

### Sterling Vineyards

**1111 Dunaweal Ln., Calistoga 94515 • 707-942-3344**
**Daily 10:30–4:30 • Accessible only by sky tram, $6 fee ($2**
**applies to wine purchase) • Selected varieties poured, no fee**
**Self-guided winery tour • Good gift selection**
**Picnic area for customers**

A real showpiece of the valley, a whitewashed, vaguely Mediterranean series of buildings sits high up on a hill. Seen from the highway, it resembles something out of a fairy tale. Sterling Vineyards winery, constructed in 1973, still seems monumental and contemporary today, but its design, starting with the aerial tram ride from the parking lot to the hilltop, is intended to be visitor friendly. On top, the self-guided tour so clearly explains what's before your eyes that it sets the standard for other tours of its type. In addition, the panoramic view of the valley from the bell tower patio will take your breath away.

The tour eventually winds back toward the tasting room; you can proceed there directly from the sky tram, but then you'd miss half the fun of exploring this architectural phenomenon. The tasting room also provides a good view, through a forest of trees toward Calistoga. On a nice day, you'll covet outside spots on the patio, while during the summer heat, the air-conditioned tasting room provides a cool respite. Tasting is civilized here, with alert hospitality servers bringing the latest releases of Sauvignon Blanc, Chardonnay, Merlot, and Cabernet to your table. If you express further interest or ask what special wines are open that day, they might bring around anything from the limited-production Sangiovese, Pinot Noir, and Pinot Grigio to the older reserve wines.

### Clos Pegase

**1060 Dunaweal Ln., Calistoga 94515 • 707-942-4981**
**Daily 10:30–5 • Selected varieties poured, $3 fee includes**
**logo glass • Guided tours twice daily, by appointment**

Once thought an eyesore that didn't fit in with its rural, grape-growing surroundings, people have slowly accepted Clos Pegase, with its renowned architectural design by Michael Graves. You'll see owner Jan Shrem's monument to both art and wine at every turn on the property, beginning with the sculptures at the edge of the parking lot. The building itself, done in peach and tan earth tones, features a huge colonnade-style entryway that leads you down a tiled path, giving you a close-up view of the architectural details, while at the same time pointing the way to the tasting room. Making your way through the complex, you can look up on the hill and see Shrem's residence, rendered in the same style but even more ornate.

The tasting room is a dark, hushed affair, with almost a reverent cathedral atmosphere prevailing. A huge medieval-style tapestry fills one wall, as dappled light filters in from the opposite window. Hosts usually pour a melonlike Sauvignon Blanc first, followed by Chardonnay. Cabernet and Merlot are the reds, along with Hommage, a proprietary Bordeaux-style blend. Students of both art and architecture should call ahead for the guided winery tour, which examines samples of the owner's extensive collection of sculptures, paintings, and historical artifacts, and also shows off one of the largest underground wine caves ever built.

## THE SILVERADO TRAIL

*(listed south to north, from Napa to Calistoga)*

Poet Robert Frost might have called the Silverado Trail "the road less traveled" for good reason. The locals would rather keep this secret for getting up and down the valley quickly to themselves. Yes, fewer wineries reside here than on Highway 29, but it's bucolicly agricultural and much less developed too. Traffic never backs up, and the touring pace slows down, but many quality wineries are located here as well. Particularly on summer weekends, traveling the Silverado Trail beats the Highway 29 crowds. To get to the Silverado Trail from Highway 29, turn right on Trancas Avenue in the city of Napa, proceed east, and turn left onto the Silverado Trail. It runs north to Calistoga.

### Jarvis Winery

**2970 Monticello Rd., Napa 94558 • 800-255-5280**
**Daily by appointment only • Selected varieties poured, $10 fee**
**One-hour tour of winery caves followed by tasting**

Bill Jarvis and his wife, Leticia, bought 1,500 acres along Monticello Road, just north of the Silverado Country Club, as a weekend retreat from the pressures of Palo Alto business life. They started planting a vineyard, and Jarvis decided to construct a winery—but not just any old winery. After ten years of planning, he bored a huge hole into his mountainside property to locate the entire winery facility in underground caves.

If you make an appointment, you'll find Jarvis four and one-half miles east of the Silverado Trail from Trancas Avenue. Press the security keypad, and the gates open; keep to your right on the blacktop until you see the big golden double doors set back in a parabolic archway. Stepping into the caves, your host will greet you and lead you on an hour-long tour of the structure, followed by a sit-down tasting.

The caves stay at 55°–58°F and eighty percent humidity, which is a perfect aging environment for wine but also decreases wine evaporation from the barrels. The wine in barrels is laid out in the circular cave so that, from any point, the winemaker never stands more than 200 feet away from any barrel. You'll see the most splendiferous private ladies' room ever, along with the private entertaining room (1,000 person capacity) which features gigantic amethyst and quartz crystals. The waterfall in the middle of the caves, which provides the humidity, looks straight out of *Raiders of the Lost Ark*. And the wines? The Chardonnay, Cabernet, and Cabernet Franc are all tasty but expensive, as you might imagine after observing the physical plant. For those who think they've seen and done it all in Napa Valley, this just might be worth $10.

### William Hill Winery

**1761 Atlas Peak Rd., Napa 94558 • 707-224-4477**
**Daily 10–4:30 • Selected varieties poured, no fee**
**Daily tours by appointment • Small gift selection**

Take Hardman Avenue off the Silverado Trail for about a mile and then make a left onto Atlas Peak Road; the large beige structure up the hill is William Hill Winery. Established in 1976, the winery was known as a producer of quality wines from mountain-grown grapes. In 1990 Hill sold out to The Wine Alliance, which also owns Callaway and Clos du Bois, so he could concentrate on his next winery project on the cutting edge in Oregon.

Look for the tasting room around the backside, where the top notched exterior beige walls with teal trim give way to a series of glass doors (the view is lovely). The long blonde wooden tasting bar overlooks the winery production area and barrel room. Without Hill, the winery continues to turn out full-flavored Cabernet and Chardonnay, both done in two different versions; Merlot and Sauvignon Blanc are relatively new. Hill hired talented winemaker Jill Davis, formerly at Buena Vista, and her first hands-on vintages are now available.

## Van Der Heyden Vineyards
**4057 Silverado Trail, Napa 94558 • 707-257-0130**
**Daily 10–6 • Four varieties poured, $2.50 fee**
**Small gift selection • No picnics**

People probably don't know Van Der Heyden because you can only get their wine at the winery. But about five years ago, they put their shingle up on the road and opened to visitors. You may do a double take at first when you pull up the driveway and find a parking spot. The ramshackle grounds are strewn with empty wine barrels, pallets, motor homes, and assorted tools of the agricultural trade; it looks like Sears blew up!

The tasting room sits a couple hundred feet down the lane on the right, past a private residence. The small shack, crammed with mementos and gift items, has a small bar at the back by the cash register. No doubt a family member will pour from their selection of four wines. On this particular day, the winery offered a full-on, barrel-fermented buttery Chardonnay at $72 a case ($6 a bottle). Also poured were the much more expensive Cabernet and Zinfandel. As a finale, a seven-year-old late-harvest dessert Semillon iced the cake. The entire experience leans a bit toward the funky side, but it's refreshing for its lack of pretense. Cat lovers take note: More than twenty felines patrol the premises, and you're likely to make a new friend immediately.

## Monticello Cellars
**4242 Big Ranch Rd., Napa 94558 • 707-253-2802,**
**800-743-6668 • Daily 10–4:30 • Selected varieties poured,**
**$2.50 fee includes logo glass • Daily tours • Small gift selection**
**Shaded picnic area**

When Jay Corley thinks, he thinks big. Monticello Cellars' hospitality center replicates Thomas Jefferson's Monticello home. Content in 1970 just to sell his grapes to other wineries, in 1980 he built his own Virginia-style mansion as a tribute to Jefferson, a devoted wine lover in his time.

The tasting room, done in the same tasteful style, is directly across from the Monticello replica. Woodsy and comfortable, it's packed with gift items and plenty of Monticello wines, artfully displayed. The not-to-miss wine here is the elegant and rich Cabernet, issued as the moderately priced Jefferson Cuvee or the pricey Corley Reserve. The Chardonnays might include several selections, including the one fermented solely with wild yeast. Pinot Noir is rapidly improving, but consider this fickle varietal a work in progress. Absolutely smashing (and expensive but worth it) is the late-harvest dessert wine, designated as Chateau M.

### Clos du Val

**5330 Silverado Trail, Napa 94558 • 707-252-6711**
**Daily 10–5 • Four varieties poured, $3 fee applies to purchase**
**Daily tour • Good gift selection • Shaded picnic tables**

Perhaps the most French-styled wines in the Napa Valley appear at Clos du Val. This is not surprising because winemaker Bernard Portet graduated from a French enology school and is son of the director of the famous first growth, Chateau Lafite-Rothschild. When he started making wine here in 1972, Portet was one of the first to make really Bordeaux-style Cabernets in California.

The winery and surrounding vineyards have grown over the years to larger capacity. Ivy and vines completely cover the exterior stone walls of the winery as if to suggest a century of age rather than a couple of decades. The massive double wooden doors of the tasting room open to a comfortable space, with orange hexagonal brick tiles beneath your feet and a massive cathedral ceiling overhead. A long L-shaped bar is up to the tasting task, even on a crowded summer's day; glass doors on the opposite wall give visitors a peek into the barrel aging room. Cabernet is the top call here, along with a very good Zinfandel. The top white is Fume Blanc or a waxy Semillon. As a treat, an older vintage of Cabernet may also be poured; you can purchase many past vintages only at the winery. While sipping, amuse yourself with Ronald Searle's witty wine posters, which have become collector's items.

### Chimney Rock Winery

**5350 Silverado Trail, Napa 94558 • 707-257-2641**
**Weekdays 10–5, weekends 10–4 • Four varieties poured, $3 fee includes logo glass or applies to purchase • Daily tours by appointment • Small gift selection.**

Natives of South Africa, Hack and Stella Wilson transplanted the regal Cape Dutch architecture to their winery, clearly visible from the Silverado Trail. They originally bought the Chimney Rock Golf Course in 1980, then plowed over nine of the holes to plant seventy-five acres of vineyards. The Huguenot-style winery buildings and hospitality center, with graceful curves, were not completed until nearly a decade later. A well-tended flower garden borders the cobblestone walkway to the visitors' center.

Inside, whitewashed walls, dark woods, and an exquisite brass chandelier set a mood of understated elegance. As do most wineries in the Stag's Leap area, Chimney Rock specializes in Cabernet; hosts pour the current release and often an older vintage for comparison. Chardonnay and Fume Blanc are not as outstanding, but serviceable enough.

## Stag's Leap Wine Cellars

**5766 Silverado Trail, Napa 94558 • 707-944-2020**
**Daily 10–4 • Selected varieties poured, $3 fee includes**
**logo glass • Daily tours • Small gift selection • Patio picnic area**

What first looks like a series of low-slung office buildings in a high-tech Silicon Valley suburb turns out to be Stag's Leap Wine Cellars. Over the thirty years or so the winery has been here, it's continued to expand, although the ancient oak trees on the property tend to disguise the growth. Still owned and operated by the Winiarski family, it was one of the original quality-oriented wineries of the valley. It still holds to that course today, and consequently constantly bustles with visitors, many longtime customers.

For a winery with such a regal reputation—the '73 Cabernet bested French counterparts in the famous 1976 tasting in Paris—they don't put on airs here, though that's not to say the staff can't handle any winemaking questions you might have. Ditto for the tasting room; it's unpretentious as well: merely a large wooden table in the corner of the cellar. Massive oak casks and stainless steel tanks flank you as you walk through. Cabernet is the real thing here, but don't expect them to pour their Cask 23 reserve ($75). Riesling, Chardonnay, and Sauvignon Blanc are all well made. The Hawk Crest label offers good everyday Cabernet and Chardonnay values for less than $10.

## Pine Ridge Winery

**5901 Silverado Trail, Napa 94558 • 707-253-7500**
**Daily 10–5 • Selected varieties poured, $3 fee includes logo glass**
**Daily tours • Small gift selection • Excellent hillside picnic area**
**with tables and barbecue grills**

Pine Ridge looks like a modest, unassuming building from the road. But once inside the tasting room, you'll see the beginning of the hidden wine caves, laboriously built into the hillsides. Indeed

Pine Ridge now produces in excess of 70,000 cases annually, not to say it is so large that quality isn't a factor here. In fact, after a fallow period, it seems to have increased its quality control vigilance.

Certainly Pine Ridge, which takes its name from a stand of pines on the property, is as consumer friendly as they come. The tasting room is done in warm woods, and the personnel has enthusiasm, something that can be quite contagious, even if this is your first tasting stop of the day. The front terrace is a real gem for travelers, especially those with families. A dozen picnic tables sit scattered under the shady pines, along with a barbecue pit, gazebo, and even swings for the kids. As for the wines, start with the dry Chenin Blanc, one of the best versions made in California. Chardonnay and Merlot also have good fruit underpinnings. Save the best for last: Cabernet comes in a variety of versions, indicating the specific vineyards from which the grapes came. Perhaps the Rutherford Cuvee tastes the best, but the others are equally gutsy.

### Steltzner Winery
**5998 Silverado Trail, Napa 94558 • 707-252-7272**
**Wed.–Sun. 10–5 • Selected varieties poured, no fee**
A longtime Napa Valley viticulturalist, Dick Steltzner planted and managed plenty of other people's vineyards before planting his. Even then, he sold his grapes to others before starting to make his own wine in rented facilities; then finally he began making wine on his vineyard property in 1983.

Presently the wine tasting at Steltzner takes place among the fairly rudimentary but romantic atmosphere of the winery lab, at the head of the underground wine caves that reach far back into the hillside. A new winery under construction, delayed by weather and other factors, may be open by the time you read this. The nouveau mission-style building looks both utilitarian and attractive, with a red tiled roof and clock tower. If you're a Cabernet grape nut, definitely add this stop to your list because that's what Steltzner does best. They may pour a few other wines, but several different vintages of Cabernet will typically be open; depending on the vintage, they can range from average to fabulous.

### Silverado Vineyards
**6121 Silverado Trail, Napa 94558 • 707-257-1770**
**Daily 11–4:30 • Selected varieties poured, no fee**
This house that Disney built is not a Mickey Mouse operation. Walt's widow, Lillian Disney, purchased a few acres in the Stag's

Leap district in 1977. With the help of her daughter and son-in-law, she made plans for a winery, constructed in 1981. With little fanfare and no Disneyland-style hype, the winery makes fine wines. Built on a hill above the Silverado Trail, you can't see the winery from the road.

If you make your way up the private blacktop road to the winery, you will discover a tasteful hacienda-style building, set in stone from local quarries. In the main courtyard, a beautiful fountain gurgles and weathered wooden benches line the perimeter of the building. The tasting room aspect seems mildly overlooked in this setting, as the area just inside the doors resembles something more along the lines of a receptionist's desk. But get a splash of Sauvignon Blanc in your glass and walk down the long corridor, admiring the Spanish tiles underneath your feet, the fine furnishings, and the beautiful hillside view from the windows. The wines are something special too. In addition to the Sauvignon Blanc, there is a mouth-filling Chardonnay, as well as a supple Merlot. The Cabernet is still the big thing though, and it's one of the best, made in an elegant, balanced style. Sangiovese, with a lot of vanilla from the oak, is also coming into its own and is only available at the tasting room.

### Robert Sinskey Vineyards
**6320 Silverado Trail, Napa 94558 • 707-944-9090**
**Daily 10–4:30 • Selected varieties poured, $3 fee includes**
**logo glass • Small gift selection • No picnics**

Dr. Robert Sinskey, a renowned eye surgeon, helped pioneer the invention and use of the artificial lens. He is also a longtime wine lover and one of the original investors in Acacia Winery, later sold to the Chalone Group. Sinskey had purchased vineyards next door to Acacia in the Carneros region and added even more prime vineyard land after the sale. Looking for a site for his own winery, he looked north to a parcel on the Silverado Trail, rather than near his own vineyards. He wanted the room to build a first-class winery, and the results bear him out.

Construction began in 1987 on this beautiful, rough-hewn stone structure. Outside, a ten-foot-high grape arbor trellis borders the parking area, while a fully stocked koi pond sits off to one side. The wooden deck, with terraced vines creeping to the perimeter, faces the valley floor. Inside, the high-beamed wood ceiling and natural rock wall facings convey a sense of permanence and strength; opposite the blonde wooden tasting bar, floor-to-ceiling glass panels offer a view of the barrel aging room. Architecturally, it's a visual feast for the eye, but since the winery and its caves are integrated into the hillside, they never seem ostentatious. The wines, too, are very balanced, including Chardonnay, Merlot, Pinot Noir, and an expensive but very good Bordeaux blend simply called Claret. The reasonably priced second label, Aries, is consistently rated a best buy for Chardonnay and Pinot Noir.

## S. Anderson Vineyards

**1473 Yountville Cross Rd. (quarter-mile west of Silverado Trail), Yountville 94599 • 707-944-8642, 800-4-BUBBLY Daily 10–5 • Most varieties poured, $3 fee • Twice daily tour of winery aging caves, 10:30 and 2:30 • No picnics**

The Anderson family came to the Napa Valley in the early 1970s, intrigued with the idea of starting a winery and thinking they would produce still wines, like their friends and neighbors. While they still produce Chardonnay and Cabernet, the primary focus has become sparkling wines. Rose bushes surround the two-story hospitality center; go down the stone walkway past the white gazebo, where you'll find an old, stone nineteenth-century pumphouse that has been converted to the tasting room.

Anderson was one of the first to build caves in the valley, the main focus of the twice daily tours. A marvelous engineering masterpiece built into a nearby hillside, the caves boast eighteen-foot cathedral ceilings, cobbled floors, and 500,000 bottles of sparkling wine resting at angles in traditional racks. Cabernet is so limited, it is rarely available for tasting, though several Chardonnays are often poured. But the sparklers are really what everyone comes here for: the vintage-dated Brut, Rose, and Blanc de Noirs. To get the full effect, take your glass and sit out back on the shaded cobblestone patio to view the home vineyards.

## Goosecross Cellars

**1119 State Ln., Yountville 94599 • 707-944-1986, 800-276-9210 • Daily 10–5 • All varieties poured, $1 per taste; Cabernet if available, $3 • Small gift selection**

One of the smaller family operations (5,500 cases) open to the public, Goosecross initially sold the grapes from its vineyard, but in 1985 the father-son team of Ray and Geoff Gorusch figured they could make good wine on their own. They located the winery building on their property, with the stainless steel tanks out front.

The tasting room, carved out of a small corner of the warehouse-style winery, has oak barrels stacked to the ceiling. In a mom and pop winery like this, you're likely to be greeted by a member of the family, who will invite you to taste their two Chardonnays, one from their own vineyard and the other from a blend of Napa Valley grapes. A special limited-release Cabernet, called Aeros, is poured for an extra fee. Goosecross is certainly off the beaten path down a vineyard country lane, but this far from the crowds, you'll get individual attention. Every Saturday morning, they have a crash course in wine tasting/appreciation; call for details.

## Groth Vineyards and Winery
**750 Oakville Cross Rd., Oakville 94562 • 707-944-0290**
**Mon.–Sat. 10–4, by appointment (walk-ins generally accepted)**
**All varieties poured, $3 fee applies to purchase • Daily tours**
**by appointment**

Dennis Groth, a former highly paid Atari executive in Silicon Valley, switched valleys in 1981 and moved to Napa to start a winery. He purchased vineyards and made wine at leased facilities until 1990, when he was able to fund his dream winery, built in the middle of his 121-acre home vineyard on Oakville Cross Road. The peach nouveau mission-style building with a red tiled roof has vaguely Moorish overtones and a sculptured entrance that looks like icing on a cake.

Depending on the winery activities that day, tastings may be upstairs in a huge room with windows that look out on the vineyards, or downstairs in the dark, more intimate bottle cellar room. No matter where you taste the wines, however, you'll find they are elegant and well-balanced examples of their types. Sauvignon Blanc is a perennial winner, and the Chardonnay tastes lush. But the rich, full-bodied Cabernet is the real reason wine buffs make pilgrimages to this site.

## Silver Oak Cellars
**915 Oakville Cross Rd., Oakville 94562 • 707-944-8808**
**Mon.–Fri. 9-4:30, Sat. 10–4:30 • Selected varieties poured, $5**
**fee includes logo glass or applies to purchase • Small gift**
**selection**

Just a short jaunt from Groth, down a one-lane paved country road, sits the home of Cabernet. The massive white and gray stone front of the building reminds one of an abbey, and in fact, winemaker Justin Meyer is a former Christian Brother. The wooden water tower out front is represented on the Silver Oak label.

The two large wooden doors open to a massive two-story tasting room, with red tiles on the floor and flanked on both sides by the winery proper. On the north side, a barrel aging room has been cleverly laid out on black steel racks, while on the south side, a spiral staircase allows access to same. Straight ahead, an Ahwanee-style stone fireplace is the focus of the beige-walled room with dark wood trim. Off to the side, and seemingly an afterthought, rests the small tasting bar. Cabernet is the only wine made here, and rabid fans of the label say it's the best in the state. They offer several versions though, and current releases include a Napa version and an Alexander Valley version. The winery always has older vintages of these wines for sale, many of them collector's items, although expensive ones.

### Girard Winery

**7717 Silverado Trail, Oakville 94562 • 707-944-8577**
**Daily 11–4:30 • Four varieties poured, no fee**
**Small gift selection**

Steve Girard's father, Stephen Sr., was a Kaiser Steel executive who bought Napa Valley land in the early 1970s and planted a vineyard. Like many others when they first came to the valley, the Girards did not start a winery but sold their grapes to Robert Mondavi Winery, among others. But by 1980, the winery bug had bitten them, and the Girard family constructed gray stone and brick winery buildings in an oak grove on the vineyard property. The oak cluster was the basis for the Girard label. The Girards recently sold the winery, and the new owners are remodeling the winery and tasting room to make them more visitor friendly.

The winery stands directly north of the parking lot, while the tasting room is just west, directly down a flight of stairs. The small and cozy room has dozens of wine medals and awards displayed on the back bar. Chenin Blanc has been a mainstay, and Girard continues to produce a dependable one, along with Chardonnay. The Cabernet comes from local vineyards, while the reserve tends to be from their own special vineyard on the slopes of Mount Veeder. The best buy, though, is the nonvintaged Ol Blue Jay, a blend that has a lot of Zinfandel in it.

### ZD Wines

**8383 Silverado Trail, Napa 94558 • 707-963-5188,**
**800-487-7757 • Daily 10–4:30 • Selected varieties poured, $3**
**fee includes logo glass or applies to purchase**
**Small gift selection**

Aerospace engineers Gino Zepponi and Norman de Leuze, the ZD of the label, started out making a small amount of wine in a rented Sonoma County shed in 1969. They soon outgrew that space and built a model winery on the Silverado Trail in 1979, which has recently been expanded. Now entirely in the hands of the De Leuze family, everyone is involved in the winery's day-to-day operations.

The parking lot is on the south side of the earthy, peach-colored hacienda-style complex. The production end of the winery is nearest, with a courtyard and flower gardens separating it from the tasting room on the far end. A long wooden bar runs the entire length of the room, and glass windows look out on the six-acre home vineyard. Behind the bar, you can get a glimpse of the barrel room.

Chardonnay has long been the mainstay, and it makes up eighty percent of production at ZD; it carries a California appellation because it draws not only from vineyards in Napa, but also Sonoma and Santa Barbara. Amazingly consistent over the years, the Chardonnay shows big, rich, tropical flavors, along with new American oak. A Cabernet is tasty, and two different Pinot Noirs are flavorful as well.

## Mumm Napa Valley

**8445 Silverado Trail, Rutherford 94573 • 707-942-3434**
**Daily 10:30–6 (winter 10–5) • Sparkling wine purchased**
**by the glass, $3–$6 fee • Hourly tours • Art gallery**
**Good gift selection • No picnics**

One of the many French Champagne houses that decided to set up shop in Napa Valley, Mumm is a joint venture with Seagrams, which also owns Sterling Vineyards just down the road. The beautifully weathered redwood barn-style winery with a green shingled roof fits right into the environment because most of it is actually underground. The visitors' center, adjacent to the parking lot, opened to the public in 1990 and has been a popular stop ever since. The tour, one of the best, leaves from the center hourly. It traverses a path to a demonstration vineyard, then into the winery, where an overhead walkway allows visitors to view the entire operation on one level.

The tour ends back at the sun-drenched tasting room, around back of the gift shop, but you don't have to tour in order to taste. Mumm offers several varieties of sparkling wine for a fee, along with some mini-appetizers to clear the palate. The floor-to-ceiling glass doors of the tasting salon, as they call it, afford a view of the vineyards. The Brut and Blanc de Noir are the most popular and, as with all the sparklers, are made in the traditional French method, in which the wine undergoes the secondary fermentation right in the bottle. They also offer an excellent vintage-dated reserve and a single-vineyard Winery Lake Cuvee. A very limited DVX Cuvee, the richest of them all, is usually available for purchase. The outdoor patio is the perfect place to enjoy the day's last glass of wine as the sun sinks behind the Mayacamas Mountains.

## Conn Creek/Villa Mount Eden Winery

**8711 Silverado Trail, St. Helena 94574 • 707-963-5133**
**Daily 10–4 • Five selected varieties poured, no fee**
**Good gift selection**

It's a long, complicated story, but both these successful wineries started out as separate entities in the 1970s. Through a series of events, the corporation that owns Chateau St. Michelle Winery in Washington State acquired both, giving them a winery presence in California. Operations have been consolidated at the former Conn Creek Winery on the Silverado Trail.

The beige Mediterranean ranch-style building with a burnished, red earth-tile roof looks bright on the inside, sunlight streaming from the floor-to-ceiling windows. Peach walls and brick-orange tiles on the floor provide more warmth to the tasting area on the right. Through an archway, you'll find the gift shop in a separate room. The tasting bar features the Villa Mount Eden wines, including Chardonnay, Merlot, and Cabernet. Not often poured but worth purchasing are the Bien Nacido designated Pinot Noir and Pinot Blanc. A Conn Creek Cabernet is also offered, and many older vintages are for sale, often at a discount.

## Caymus Vineyards

**8700 Conn Creek Rd., Rutherford 94573 • 707-967-3010**
**Daily 10–4:30 • Three selected varieties poured, $2 fee includes logo glass • Picnic area**

In the midst of the valley's floor of vineyards, Caymus sits about equidistant from Highway 29 and the Silverado Trail. At the intersection of Conn Creek Road and Highway 128 (one and one-half miles off Silverado Trail), you'll find a beautiful rough-hewn stone building with a grape arbor overhang and a lush flower garden out front. After years of making wine in a small barn adjacent to their home, the Wagner family finally built this functional winery in 1990. The Wagners' lineage goes back to near the turn of the century in Napa Valley, but they didn't establish Caymus until 1972.

Inside, the tasting room is much like family patriarch Charlie Wagner: plain, simple, and direct. A long, narrow adobe-style room with minimal art on the walls, the tasting bar consists of regular wood planks serving as a tabletop. In a way, the simplicity is refreshing as an antidote to some of the valley's more glorified wine palaces. Cabernet is the strong suit here, but don't expect to taste either of their fine Cabs because they're almost always either sold out or on allocation. But the Sauvignon Blanc is a fine example of that grape, while their proprietary white wine blend, called Conundrum, will refresh you on a hot day. The Zinfandel will give you an inkling of what kind of hot hand they have with red wines.

### Nichelini Winery
**2950 Sage Canyon Rd., St. Helena 94574 • 707-963-0717**
**Sat.–Sun. 10–6 (summer), 10–5 (winter) • All varieties poured,**
**no fee • Woodsy picnic area**

If you view life, and travel in particular, as an adventure, then you'll want to veer off Silverado Trail and motor eight miles up the east side of the mountains to the historic Nichelini Winery. You won't believe the incredibly well-preserved home with basement winery, built in 1890 by Anton Nichelini. Many modern fieldstone wineries on the valley floor imitate this structure. It's said to be the oldest winery in the county operated by the same family, now in the third generation.

In good weather (most of the time), you'll enjoy being served in the outdoor tasting room. The large, lacquered wooden bar rests just outside the old winery building and overlooks the hillside picnic area and groves of walnut trees. Overhead look for a Rube Goldberg type of contraption, called a Roman press, used until the late 1950s to make wine. Anton's grandchildren now run the winery and wisely called in Greg Boeger from Boeger Winery in the Sierra Foothills to help with the winemaking. One of the family members usually pours and will regale you with stories as you sip the many different varietals, including Chardonnay, Sauvignon Vert, Riesling, Cabernet, Zinfandel, Merlot, Barbara, and Petite Sirah. Nichelini is an ideal spot for a quiet, unhurried picnic.

### Rustridge Winery
**2910 Lower Chiles Valley Rd., St. Helena 94574**
**707-965-2871 • Daily 10–5 • All varieties poured, no fee**

If you're adventuresome enough to make it to Nichelini, you'll no doubt be in the spirit to check out Rustridge Winery by continuing up Highway 128 and making a left on Lower Chiles Valley Road. Just when you think you're lost, you'll see a winery sign. The large Rustridge property includes a southwestern ranch-style bed and breakfast inn and large track for thoroughbred horse training. Confused yet? Look for the stainless steel fermenting tanks way at the back of the property, and you'll find the horse barn cum winery. Due to its seemingly remote location, Rustridge doesn't get a steady stream of visitors; honking your horn will usually get someone's attention. Inside the winery barn, the tasting area is in one corner, past the aging barrels of wine. The first vines were planted in 1977, and the grapes were sold to other vintners. By 1985 Rustridge made its own wine; in 1991 superstar winemaker Merry Edwards joined the team as a consultant. The wines, showing Merry's steady winemaking hand, taste quite good. Chardonnay, Cabernet, and Zinfandel (with twenty percent Cab) are flavorful.

## Rutherford Hill Winery

**200 Rutherford Hill Rd., Rutherford 94573 • 707-963-7194 Most varieties poured, $3 fee includes logo glass • Wine cave tours several times daily • Good gift selection including picnic supplies • Woodsy picnic area reserved for customers**

The Rutherford Hill property began life as Pillsbury's Souverain Winery of Rutherford. In 1976, Pillsbury decided the wine business was not for them and sold to a partnership of investors from the Freemark Abbey Winery, headed by the Jaeger family. It's somewhat surprising to drive past the tony Auberge du Soleil resort complex and find one of the most handsome wineries in the valley.

The A-frame, barn-style structure is actually a cement shell covered in cedar, weathered with age. The massive double wooden doors lead to the tasting room, where tours of the wine caves begin. And Rutherford Hill's wine caves may be the mother of all wine caves: They consist of nearly a mile of tunnels and passageways. Back in the tasting room, the Chardonnay is OK, but Merlot is really the focus, particularly the reserve. Cabernet is also a good bet. You can purchase Lila Jaeger's special extra virgin olive oils, produced from century-old trees on the grounds, in the gift shop. A superb picnic area in a wooded glen not far from the parking lot has a view of the vineyards of the Rutherford Bench below.

## Joseph Phelps Vineyards

**200 Taplin Rd., St. Helena 94574 • 707-963-2745, 800-707-5789 • Mon.–Fri. 9–5; Sat.–Sun. 10–5, by appointment only • Selected varieties poured preceded by winery tour, no fee**

Railroad timbers provide the gated entrance to Joseph Phelps Vineyards, east of the Silverado Trail on Taplin Road. A Colorado contractor, Phelps came west to build wineries for others in the valley but liked the area so much he ended up buying a 670-acre ranch for himself. He planted vineyards and built a large, barn-style winery on the knoll above in 1973. A small courtyard in the middle leads to a reception area.

If you make an appointment and arrive on time, you'll be given a short tour through the barrel and tank rooms of the winery, followed by an informal tasting on the vine-trellis-shaded back patio that overlooks the vineyards. The redwood hospitality room directly behind the patio holds huge German oval casks along one wall. Your tour host will rejoin you after making a selection of Phelps wines to be poured that day, normally about six different varieties. The host usually leads with a Chardonnay from Carneros vineyards followed by a Syrah or Le Mistral, from the Phelps Vin du Mistral line of Rhone-style wines. Cabernet is also prominent, but two vintages of the top-of-the-line Bordeaux blend, called Insignia, have also been offered (terrific!). A late-harvest Riesling dessert wine may end the session. It's worth the phone call to taste world-class wines in an unhurried, small-group atmosphere. Allow one hour total for the experience.

## Casa Nuestra

**3473 Silverado Trail, St. Helena 94574 • 707-963-5783**
**Fri.–Sun. 11–5 • Most varieties poured, $2 fee applies**
**to purchase • Picnic area**

Casa Nuestra represents the way the wine business was when Napa was a sleepy, little valley. The Kirkhams bought this old vineyard in 1980 and decided to make a little wine. They still do; they don't want to get any bigger or work any harder. They still make wine the old-fashioned way, with an ancient wooden basket press that would be relegated to the historical artifacts display at most other wineries. They sell pretty much all they make out the cellar door anyhow.

The winery is a little, gray concrete block affair, but the tasting occurs in the quaint yellow farmhouse. *Casa Nuestra* means "our house," so the homey atmosphere seems quite appropriate. The underrated Chenin Blanc grape comes off very nicely here, but they usually have Chardonnay too. Among the reds is Tinto, a catch-all red wine destined for everyday drinking. Quixote, an interesting Bordeaux-style blend, has a high percentage of Cabernet Franc, augmented by Merlot and Cabernet.

## Chateau Boswell

**3468 Silverado Trail, St. Helena 94574 • 707-963-5472**
**Fri.–Sun. 10–5 • Selected varieties poured, $4 fee includes logo glass**

Here lies a unique situation: a winery that never seems to be open. To the curious passerby, the monumental castle behind the closed wrought-iron gates seems intriguing. At one time, Chauteau Boswell did produce wine, but apparently not lately. Word was they were pouring a six-year-old Chardonnay and a twelve-year-old Cabernet, not necessarily a good sign. But who knows? Be forewarned: If the winery is open when you drive by, if you put your money down, you take your chances.

## Rombauer Vineyards

**3522 Silverado Trail, St. Helena 94574 • 707-963-5170**
**Daily 10–5 • Most varieties poured, no fee • Small gift selection Picnic area**

Koerner Rombauer is well known in the valley for custom-crushing grapes for others who have grapes and a label but who don't physically have a winery. In other words, he rents out space and equipment to other winemakers to work on their projects here. Perhaps his eponymous label has suffered less notoriety because of that. Of the 75,000 cases of wine made here annually, only about 15,000 bear the Rombauer label. But let's keep that our little secret, because Rombauer is making some of the best wines in its history.

Coming up the driveway, the gray stone block winery building looks a little deceiving because it burrows three stories down into the hillside, which is not apparent. Two huge fir trees provide shade in the parking area, and a short walk around the corner on the wooden deck, which provides a great view of the valley below, leads to the combination office and tasting room. The Rombauer wines are spread out on the two small wooden bars, and staff members know their stuff. The current release of Carneros Chardonnay is fine, while the Merlot tastes supple, and even the Cabernet Franc is snappy. Best of the bunch, though, includes the Cabernet and the red Bordeaux-style blend, labeled Le Meilleur du Chai ("best of the cellar"). No matter what you call it, the latter is a great bottle of red wine. Prices range from moderate to expensive, but you get what you pay for.

## Wermuth Winery

**3942 Silverado Trail, Calistoga 94515 • 707-942-5924**
**Daily 11–5 • Most varieties poured, $1 fee**

Practically a one-man band, Ralph Wermuth has done everything necessary to make wine here since 1981. If the winery sign out front reads Closed, then Ralph is probably out pruning the vines, racking or topping the barrels, or bottling the wine. If the sign reads Open, you'll want to stop in just to meet Ralph, who might remind you of your eccentric high school chemistry teacher. He doesn't put a lot of stock in the prevailing wine trends; he just makes wine out of the grapes, like Gamay and French Colombard, that grow in his front yard.

The winemaking occurs in corrugated pink sheds, while the tasting occurs in what looks like a gutted dining car. It's all a bit ramshackled and disoriented, like in *The Nutty Professor*, but Ralph knows where everything is and will lead you through the tasting. Along the way, feel free to discuss censorship, *The New York Times,* and the World Wide Web if the feeling comes over you, because Ralph will offer a considered opinion on just about anything if you solicit it. Meanwhile, the French Colombard (a variety rarely seen) is not bad, the Zinfandel zippy, and the Gamay quite interesting. Ralph usually offers a Cheez-It cracker and a chocolate chip as matching food accompaniments to his wines. A unique tasting experince, to say the least.

## Dutch Henry Winery

**4300 Silverado Trail, Calistoga 94515 • 707-942-5771**
**Daily 10–4 • All varieties poured, no fee**

Forget about Dutch Henry; he doesn't exist. The winery's name comes from a canyon that stretches back into the eastern hills. Kendall Phelps, who couldn't use either of his names on the label (both were already taken), inspired this defunct winery, which he and a partner resuscitated in 1991. The two-story pinkish stucco winery building sits on a private lane, past a private residence and a tool shed. Two winery watchdogs, intimidating but harmless, may greet you on arrival.

The winery itself is strictly a utilitarian concrete slab building, filled with plenty of oak barrels. A folding table set up in a corner of the winery against case stacks of bottled wine is the designated tasting area. For such a small winery, Dutch Henry makes a lot of different wines fairly well. The Cabernet and Merlot are perennial sellouts; an inexpensive blended Claret tastes good, though the fun quaffer of the reds is the juicy Gamay Beaujolais. Sauvignon Blanc and Chardonnay are also well made. On a slow day, if you express an interest, Phelps might invite you to taste some wines aging in nearby barrels.

## Cuvaison Winery

**4550 Silverado Trail, Calistoga 94515 • 707-942-6266, 800-253-9463 • Daily 10–5 • Most varieties poured, $2.50 fee includes logo glass • Good gift selection • Shaded picnic area**

In its early days, Cuvaison Winery, founded in 1970, was awfully lonely in this location, being one of the few wineries on the "wrong" side of the valley, along the Silverado Trail. But in time, many other wineries set up shop here away from the crowds, and Cuvaison's decision proved a presaging of things to come. Ironically, the majority of Cuvaison's grapes come from its Carneros vineyards in the extreme southern end of the valley and from the Oakville and Rutherford areas as well.

You'll easily spot the California mission-style winery with the red tiled roof and multiple curved archways just south of Calistoga. The tasting room sits closer to the road in a separate A-frame stucco building, whose interior sports whitewashed adobe walls and a wood-beamed ceiling. When things get really busy on weekends, the original tasting bar inside the front door is augmented by another one in a side room.

The Cuvaison style over the years has been to strive for elegant, well-balanced wines with every element in harmony. The Carneros Chardonnay certainly shows that, as does the supple Merlot. They have made progress with Pinot Noir, but the Cabernet is unimpressive for the price. Quite a few shaded picnic tables dot the property, both in front of the tasting room and in back on the terraced hillside.

## Traulsen Vineyards

**2250 Lake County Hwy., Calistoga 94515 • 707-942-0283 Thurs.–Mon. 10–5 • All varieties poured, no fee**

If you favor mom and pop wineries to the larger corporate winery meccas, you'll want to visit Traulsen, only a half-mile off Silverado Trail on Lake County Highway. Actually, when you pull into the driveway, the Traulsen's stone-block ranch house sits to the right; the winery lies just beyond in a small shed. A beautiful rose garden (almost as large as the vineyard) is off to the left, with the vineyards on the opposite side, up the hill. The massive double wooden doors to the winery belie the modesty of the operation.

One stainless steel tank and one oak fermenter stand upright in the middle of the room, while French oak barrels line the perimeter. A wooden table at the front of the shed serves as the tasting bar. More often than not, co-owner Patty Traulsen will pour and tell you a bit about the operation. It's purposely kept small, 300-500 cases annually, so the family can keep track of everything. Zinfandel is all they produce, but often several vintages are open for sampling; all of the wines are intense and flavorful in the traditional red Zinfandel style. Express an interest, and Patty might thieve a shot of the current vintage from the barrels.

### Vincent Arroyo Winery

**2361 Greenwood Ave., Calistoga 94515 • 707-942-6995**
**Weekdays 9–4:30, weekends 10–4:30 • Most varieties poured,**
**no fee**

Vince Arroyo is almost a one-man operation at his small winery, housed in a two-story clapboard farm-style building, down the lane from his house. Constructed in 1989, the winery is purely functional, with a concrete floor and high ceiling so barrels can stack on top of each other. Stainless steel fermenting tanks dominate the back wall; a spiral staircase that leads to the winery office provides the only embellishment.

Joy, the winery's black Labrador, officially greets visitors; she'll show you to the tasting area, just inside the winery doors. Vince is likely to be on hand, working in the winery or the office, and prides himself on giving visitors a personal tasting experience. The relatively small operation produces only around 3,000 cases a year, so Vince handcrafts each lot and will happily tell you about each wine. Chardonnay always sells out, though Vince says his favorite is the concentrated Petite Sirah. Cabernet is made in a more expensive reserve style, as well as a light, less pricey one. The Melange, a blend of red grapes including Gamay and Merlot, is an inexpensive quaffer.

### Chateau Montelena Winery

**1429 Tubbs Ln., Calistoga 94515 • 707-942-5105 • Daily 10–4**
**Selected varieties poured, $5 fee applies to purchase**
**Daily tours • Picnic area by reservation**

Montelena is truly a landmark of wine country. Built by Albert Tubbs in 1882, it was certainly a stellar example of the "A man's home is his castle" philosophy. Tubbs wanted something in the French chateau tradition but got what appears more like a medieval fortress, complete with turrets and towers. The estate fell into disuse, and in the late 1950s a new owner put in a man-made lake out back, with a red footbridge leading to a small island that houses a gazebo. In 1972 a partnership headed by the Barrett family renovated the location and began to make wine there for the first time since Prohibition.

A recent modernization, completed in 1995, maintains and enhances the historic feel of the place. Now stone columns with a redwood trellis overhead visually lead you to the tasting room entrance. On the left, a three-tiered fountain gurgles away. Inside, the tasting room has been enlarged and brightened with blonde parquet wood flooring and a series of high windows that let the natural light in. As always, the wines are of the highest quality and, with the exception of the Riesling, expensive. Chardonnay, made from purchased grapes, is done in the steely, high-toned style. Two Cabernets, one in a more accessible style and one for aging, are fine. Don't leave without walking down the stone steps to see the lake; the surrounding benches provide a great place for a momentary break from the rigors of wine tasting.

## RESTAURANTS

*(listed from Napa to Calistoga)*

### Napa Valley Wine Train

**1275 McKinstry St., Napa 94558 • 707-253-2111,
800-427-4124 • Lunch, brunch, and dinner daily
Reservations recommended • California cuisine • Expensive**
If you're a train buff, then this is your ticket; if you're a food and wine buff, well, the results are mixed. Born amid controversy, the Wine Train had many locals opposed to it before it even got on track. But after a decade of leaving the depot in the city of Napa, running parallel to Highway 29, and up to St. Helena and back, people have pretty much accepted it. The vintage Pullman cars have been well refurbished, and your fine dining experience will include linens, bone china, silver flatware, and etched crystal appointments. The meals in the dining car, featuring the likes of pasta, chicken, and rack of lamb, all come at a fixed price: $61 for lunch, $75 for dinner. You can, however, tag along and sample the fare in the deli car or the wine tasting car—without getting the entire red carpet treatment—for $24. Allow three hours for the slow-moving round trip (thirty-plus miles at ten to fifteen miles per hour).

## Bistro Don Giovanni

**4110 St. Helena Hwy. (Highway 29), Napa 94558**
**707-224-3300 • Lunch and dinner daily**
**Reservations recommended • Italian • Moderate**

Over the years, quite a number of restaurants have occupied this space on Napa's northern city limits, but it looks as though proprietors Donna and Giovanni Scala have a crowd pleaser on their hands. *Bistro* is probably a misnomer; *trattoria* is more like it because the restaurant is Italian to the core, though in bistro fashion, they serve continuously from 11:30 a.m. on. They offer plenty of pastas, including ravioli and a risotto of the day. Main courses might include braised lamb shanks, grilled duck breast, cured pork tenderloin, or salmon. A lively crowd congregates here, particularly on the great outdoor patio.

## Domaine Chandon

**1 California Dr., Yountville 94559 • 707-944-2892**
**Lunch daily, May–Oct.; lunch Wed.-Sun., Nov.–Apr.; dinner year-round Wed.–Sun. • Reservations recommended • French Expensive**

Domaine Chandon was the first restaurant to bring real French cooking to the valley. Chef Phillipe Jeanty, who trained in France and has cooked here for almost two decades, constantly reinvents the menu as the seasons change. Compared with other places in the valley, dress fairly formal at dinner, but a little more casual at lunch. The menu takes advantage of California's bounty, while informed by the chef's French sensibilities. Caramelized scallops in a Chardonnay sauce, grilled salmon in pancetta, grilled rabbit with rosemary, and calf's liver with onion and parsnip puree lead the list of entrees. Leave room for dessert: The gooey chocolate cake and creme brulee are killers.

## The Diner

**6476 Washington St., Yountville 94599 • 707-944-2626**
**Breakfast, lunch, and dinner daily except Mon.**
**American/Mexican • Inexpensive to moderate • No credit cards**

Aptly named, The Diner has front counter seating and cozy booths that might make you nostalgic for the 1950s. While overnighting in Yountville, it's the most obvious place in town for breakfast, with all the usual breakfast fill-ups. Lunch stays along the line of salads and sandwiches, all freshly prepared and well turned out. In the evening, chicken, burgers, and a few Mexican specialties add to the short order menu. Unlike most other "serious" restaurants in town, The Diner has a casual, child-friendly quality.

## Piatti

**6480 Washington St., Yountville 94599 • 707-944-2070**
**Lunch and dinner daily • Reservations recommended • Italian**
**Moderate**

This is the original Piatti (another is in Sonoma) that pioneered the idea of regional Italian cooking in a relaxed country atmosphere. The wood-burning oven and rotisserie turn out great pizzas—you'll see one on almost every table—and roasted chicken. From the grill, homemade sausages with peppers, onion, and soft polenta is a treat, as is the marinated veal chop with black olive butter and a ragout of artichokes, potatoes, and spinach. Of course, pasta is a winner, in a dozen variations.

## The French Laundry

**6640 Washington St., Yountville 94599 • 707-944-2380**
**Lunch Fri.–Sun.; dinner daily • Reservations essential**
**(call weeks before you arrive) • California/French • Expensive**

The French Laundry (yes, it was a laundry once) occupies a hundred-year-old cottage on Washington Street with no discernible signage. That's part of its mystique. Sally Schmidt cooked here until 1994, when Thomas Keller came from Los Angeles and started giving the food his world-class spin. Expect a leisurely dining experience in which every dish is a production number but also tastes as good as it looks. The restaurant offers only one *prix fixe* menu nightly (five courses $57 or nine for $70), but with several choices for each course. Items on the seasonally changing menu include caviar with onion creme, sea bass with mustard sauce and cabbage, and foie gras on sweet braised onions. Good but overpriced wine list. Make reservations well in advance of your visit; it's the hot ticket.

## Napa Valley Grille

**6795 Washington St. (Washington Square), Yountville 94599**
**707-944-8686 • Lunch and dinner daily; Sun. brunch**
**Reservations recommended • California cuisine • Moderate**

Napa Valley Grille faces Highway 29 and the adjacent vineyards. The restaurant started life as the California Cafe, clearly a knock-off of the wildly successful Mustards Grill up the highway. But Chef Bob Hurley has worked hard to distinguish the menu by showcasing the bounty of the region. Dungeness crab cakes, smoked salmon with sun-dried-tomato crostini, and chicken spring rolls lead off the menu. Main courses include pepper-crusted rack of pork with potato, leek, and goat cheese gratin; smoked duck breast with portabello mushrooms and cranberry chutney; and grilled mahimahi with pineapple-jalapeno salsa. The sometimes neurotic service can be frustrating though. Great wine list.

### Brix

**7377 St. Helena Hwy., Yountville 94599 • 707-944-2749**
**Lunch and dinner daily • Reservations recommended**
**California/Pacific Rim cuisine • Moderate**

*Brix,* a term of measurement, refers to the degree of ripeness (i.e., sugar concentration) of grapes. What better name for a new restaurant in the heart of wine country? Brix, the restaurant, attempts to show off the bold flavors of fusion cuisine in a wine-friendly context. Chef Tod Kawachi puts a Pacific Rim spin on just about everything, including jumbo scallops in lime sauce and ginger-honey infused chicken with roasted shallots. The growing wine list emphasizes the locals.

### Mustards Grill

**7399 St. Helena Hwy., Yountville 94599 • 707-944-2424**
**Lunch and dinner daily • Reservations recommended**
**California cuisine • Moderate**

Mustards Grill is still *the* place to go, particularly at lunchtime, when it's difficult to get a seat edgewise at the counter. It's hard to believe that only fourteen years ago this landmark grill set up shop and, in effect, started the restaurant stampede to Napa Valley. Now the valley has dozens of dining choices, instead of only a couple. Mustards has the best of California cuisine, including great burgers with the best onion rings, baby back ribs with cole slaw, grilled chicken in hoisin sauce, and grilled ahi tuna with basil mayo. The dishes may sound fairly mundane, but Mustards helped originate the idea of utilizing the best possible ingredients in a unique way. It still does today; that's why it's still on top. There's also "way too many wines," as the sign outside says.

### Stars Oakville Cafe

**7848 St. Helena Hwy., Oakville 94562 • 707-944-8905**
**Lunch and dinner daily; closed Tues.–Wed. in winter**
**Reservations recommended • California cuisine**
**Moderate to expensive**

Stars Oakville Cafe spun off from chef Jeremiah Tower's fabulously successful Stars restaurant in San Francisco. Next door to the

Oakville Grocery in a store front, the restaurant is seriously casual with linens and flowers on the tables. Tower has been called the father of California cuisine, and that philosophy carried over to this wine country incarnation with varying degrees of success. Warm local chevre is served with eggplant caponata and herb croutons. Typical entrees include pan-roasted salmon with basil sauce and orzo or roasted duck breast with garlic-roasted potatoes and blue lake beans. The menu changes frequently to take advantage of the seasonal bounty.

## Rutherford Grill

**1180 Rutherford Crossroad (at Highway 29), Rutherford 94573 • Lunch and dinner daily • No reservations American/California cuisine • Moderate**

The Rutherford Grill has adapted to the needs of its clientele in wine country so well that few people even comment or care that it's part of a chain (Houston's). You'd never know it by the quality of the food; someone obviously keeps a close eye on this kitchen. Starters might be a grilled chicken salad or a sashimi salad with tuna and cilantro. Well turned out portions of barbecue ribs and New York strip steak are quite popular. The house specialty, spit-roasted chicken with garlic mashed potatoes, sells for less than $10! The wine list is ninety-nine percent Napa Valley, with dozens of by-the-glass selections, all big seven-ounce pours. Big portions and moderate prices make Rutherford Grill a place where people are willing to wait in line.

## Auberge du Soleil

**180 Rutherford Hill Rd., Rutherford 94573 • 707-963-1211 Breakfast, lunch, and dinner daily • Reservations recommended California cuisine • Expensive**

Perhaps the most expensive restaurant in the valley is located in the most expensive resort. Originally, the chef from Masa's in San Francisco set the innovative style of the restaurant, but these days the menu is a bit more conservative and stylized. You'll find the setting at the Inn of the Sun exquisite, with soothing colors, high-backed chairs, and bouquets of flowers. Expect thoroughly competent preparations of Sonoma duck liver with wild mushrooms, Peking duck with red cabbage and green onion pancakes, and roasted rack of lamb with a white bean casserole. Your best bet here though, unless you want to splurge, is to go for lunch, snag one of the fifteen outdoor tables on the patio, and enjoy the great valley view.

## Pinot Blanc
**641 Main St., St. Helena 94574 • 707-963-6191**
**Lunch and dinner daily • Reservations recommended**
**California/French cuisine • Moderate**

Chef Joachim Splichal, renowned for his famous Patina restaurant in Los Angeles, lately has opened spin-offs, and this is the furthest away from home he's ventured so far. If he can maintain the same quality of food and service that he does at his original restaurant, it'll be a great addition to the valley dining scene. So far, that's been the case. Splichal is the king of the potato, so expect to find all manner of potato permutations on the menu, including the lowly but comforting potato pancake. Lots of rustic, French bistro fare, like roasted chicken and crispy duck breast with balsamic vinegar, appear on the menu, as well other rotisserie/grill fare. Splichal loves wine, so the eclectic list gives a big bow to the local producers.

## Tra Vigne
**1050 Charter Oak Ave., St. Helena 94574 • 707-963-4444**
**Lunch and dinner daily • Reservations recommended • Italian**
**Moderate to expensive**

No one ever seems to tire of Tra Vigne. The building looks like some sort of monument, the place always buzzes with activity, and it even has a great patio for alfresco dining. Chef Michael Chiarello has done a fantastic job of highlighting the natural flavors in his Italian dishes. Servers bring fresh Italian country bread flecked with herbs to your table for dipping in extra virgin olive oil while you peruse the menu. Start with fresh shrimp, brushed with olives and herbs, then grilled. The calamari are quickly deep fried to a light golden color but perfectly crunchy. The permutations of pastas and sauces seem endless, but each matchup is well thought out. A quick tip: You can bet whatever the chef chooses as the risotto of the day and fish of the day will taste great. The service may be the most professional but unobtrusive in the valley. Good wine list too.

## Trilogy
**1234 Main St., St. Helena 94574 • 707-963-5507**
**Lunch Tues.–Fri.; dinner Tues.–Sun. • Reservations**
**recommended • California/French cuisine**
**Moderate to expensive**

A quirky little restaurant, Trilogy occupies a plain store front on Main Street. Chef Diane Pariseau is usually in the kitchen, and she uses herbs and spices to accent the food. Rabbit charcuterie, grilled shrimp, or smoked salmon might serve as an appetizer. Follow the appetizer with roasted rack of lamb with a whole-grain mustard sauce; steamed halibut with black beans, garlic, and ginger; or medallions of veal with shiitake mushrooms and Sherry, all informed by the chef's interpretation and appropriate fresh side accompaniments that day. Best bet is the seasonally changing *prix fixe* menu, $32, or with matching wines, $48. Ask to sit on the private back patio. Terrific wine list; this is the place the locals keep to themselves.

### Showley's at Miramonte

**1327 Railroad Ave., St. Helena 94574 • 707-963-1200**
**Lunch and dinner daily except Mon. • Reservations recommended**
**California cuisine • Expensive**

Chef Grant Showley has quietly held down the fort here for years, and quietly he's built a clientele that transcends fads and fashions by offering what he does best. He gives a California twist to dishes grounded in the French tradition. Starters might include a sampling of house-made pate and local goat cheese. Then on to wild mushrooms, duck breast, sweetbreads, and cassoulet, all flavorful and filling. The patio is particularly romantic in the evening. Good wine list too.

### Terra

**1345 Railroad Ave., St. Helena 94574 • 707-963-8931**
**Dinner daily except Tues. • Reservations recommended**
**California/Pacific Rim cuisine • Expensive**

Down the block from Showley's, Terra is located in a foundry building listed in the National Register of Historic Places. Its ancient fieldstone walls and pin-point track light lend a sense of quiet intimacy to this dining experience. Chefs Hiro Sone and Lisa Doumani, "graduates" of Wolfgang Puck's Spago in Los Angeles, didn't want their style of cooking to get categorized, so they called the restaurant *terra,* meaning "from the earth." Still, Sone's Asian roots inform the food. Quickly fried shrimp with local greens are about as fresh as it gets, while foie gras with endive is right on the money. The signature dish is sake-marinated sea bass with shrimp dumplings in a ginger broth. Wow! The wine list is expensive, but you can find super Napa Valley Smith Madrone Riesling for $18. Desserts are up to the task.

### Pairs Parkside Cafe

**1420 Main St., St. Helena 94574 • 707-963-7566**
**Lunch and dinner daily • Reservations recommended**
**California cuisine • Moderate**

Pairs has a double meaning. Craig and Keith Schauffel, a pair of brothers, chef the restaurant, but *pairs* also refers to the two dozen or so wines offered nightly by the glass to pair with the menu. Winemakers dine here, so the word is getting around. Fine starters include the roasted garlic and onion soup, as well as lemon-fried calamari with lemon and fennel chips dressed with a citrus aioli. Grilled French pears with crumbled bleu cheese and a walnut dressing offer diners a classic match. On the entree side, sage-roasted salmon with porcini and white bean stew tastes excellent as does the grilled sirloin with shoestring sweet potato puree and browned brussel sprouts. A wine varietal match is suggested for each offering on the menu. Discover this place before it really becomes crowded.

### Wine Spectator Restaurant at Greystone
**2555 Main St., St. Helena 94574 • 707-967-1010**
**Lunch and dinner daily except Tues. • Reservations recommended**
**Mediterranean • Moderate**
The marvelous old Greystone Cellars of the Christian Brothers has been preserved and updated by the Culinary Institute of America, which located its West Coast teaching branch here. The *Wine Spectator* magazine funded the restaurant, located on the top of the stone cellars, which opened in late 1995. Regardless of what you've heard, the students do not prepare the meals here; a professional cooking-teaching staff does, with help from some interns. It's a great place to stop by and sit at the bar, which faces the open kitchen. Spanish tapas and a glass of wine hit the spot if you're on your way to or from somewhere, or just taking a break from winery touring. The sit-down menu features Mediterranean-style food that might include Spanish onion and potato tortilla or grilled oyster mushroom bruschetta for starters. Tasty choices include the grilled rosemary skewered swordfish with warm potato salad; spit-roasted Sonoma lamb with white beans and truffle oil; and paella with shrimp, mussels, chicken, chorizo, and saffron rice. The wine list has improved, with many selections by the glass. Save room for the Valrhona chocolate cake with espresso sauce.

### Brava Terrace
**3010 St. Helena Hwy., St. Helena 94574 • 707-963-9300**
**Lunch and dinner daily; closed Wed., Nov.–Apr. • Reservations recommended • California cuisine • Moderate to expensive**
Chef Fred Halpert apprenticed in France before opening his restaurant in St. Helena, so look for California cooking with a French bistro flair. The dining room is airy, with a patio overlooking its namesake terrace. For starters, the portabella mushrooms are huge and meaty; at lunch, they're served as a sandwich with red

peppers and rosemary aioli. House-cured salmon with mixed greens and juniper berry oil also wins the prize. Salmon shows up on the entree side, perfectly done with red wine sauce and cabbage slaw. A white bean, corn, and onion relish accompanies the grilled pork tenderloin. Try cassoulet, with pork, turkey, chicken, and lentils, on a cool winter evening. Good wine list too.

### Calistoga Inn
**1250 Lincoln Ave., Calistoga 94515 • 707-942-4101**
**Lunch and dinner daily • Reservations recommended**
**California cuisine • Moderate**
Located inside the Calistoga Inn, the Napa Valley Brewing Company is the first brew-pub in the area, hence the No. 1 reason to go here. Dinner in the adjacent cutesy country dining room always seems a little over-ambitious and overpriced. But lunch on the patio, with buffalo chicken wings, hamburgers, or grilled sausages *and* a fresh cool draft are the way to go. Or, if wine tasting wears out your palate, stop off in the evening and grab a brew at the bar.

### Las Brasas
**1350 Lincoln Ave., Calistoga 94515 • 707-942-5790**
**Lunch and dinner daily • Mexican • Inexpensive to moderate**
A number of Mexican restaurants have made their way to the Napa Valley, though most really offer ersatz Mexican food with an upscale clientele slant. Decorator-designed and soothing to the eye, the food often tastes bland. Las Brasas is just a hole-in-the-wall Mexican joint, clean and well lit, that's survived on this downtown block for a decade. The food will not shake the earth; you could probably recite the menu in your sleep: carnitas, fajitas, chile rellenos, red snapper vera cruz, all with the accompanying beans, rice, and flour tortillas. But Las Brasas does offer an inexpensive break from the California, French, and Italian cycle of dining in the valley. Don't worry about reservations; don't worry about how you're dressed; the biggest worry you'll have is whether to drink Bohemia or Dos Equis with your meal. Las Brasas has a very casual, child-friendly atmosphere.

### Wappo Bar and Bistro
**1226 B Washington St., Calistoga 94515 • 707-942-4712**
**Lunch and dinner daily except Tues. • Reservations**
**recommended • California/Pacific Rim/whatever • Moderate**
World cuisine might best describe what locals Aaron Bauman and Michelle Mutrux cook up at the Wappo Bar and Bistro.

Whatever name it goes by, their informed style is rapidly gaining a following. The interior of the place gleams with polished wood and copper-topped tables; the vine-covered patio is the place to be at lunchtime. Curried squash soup or gazpacho might lead the menu listings, alongside Asian noodle chicken salad with a hoisin dressing. Anything from chile rellenos to lamb tagine to cassoulet (the best!) might appear on this daily changing menu. You never know what the chefs will come up with, but that's the thrill of eating at Wappo. For the less adventurous, the menu is posted daily on the door, so you can stroll by and be forewarned. For dessert, the sorbets have intense flavor. The short wine list has some interesting choices.

## All Seasons Cafe

**1400 Lincoln Ave., Calistoga 94515 • 707-942-9111**
**Lunch and dinner daily except Wed.**
**Reservations recommended • California cuisine • Moderate**
    All Seasons embodies everything a cafe should be in wine country. Unpretentious and casual in design, the restaurant's ambience comes from being housed in one of the older buildings in Calistoga. In the tradition of the bistro, the menu changes seasonally. Start with warm spinach salad with smoked chicken, pancetta, and feta cheese or a ragout of fresh wild mushrooms. Several forms of pizza and pasta always grace the menu too. Entrees may include pan-roasted chicken with African spices on a bed of couscous; ahi tuna with orange, mint, and basil salsa; grilled duck breast with cherry and cranberry sauce; and grilled salmon on a bed of lentils. The incredible wine list has many older selections not found elsewhere, all modestly priced.

## Boskos

**1364 Lincoln Ave., Calistoga 94515 • 707-942-9088**
**Lunch and dinner daily • No reservations • Italian • Moderate**
    If you're looking for someplace quick and easy, where you don't have to dress up, and where the whole family is welcome, stop at Boskos. With a checkerboard-tiled floor and bistro tables and chairs, here you can relax and enjoy some good, old Italian-style food, like spaghetti and meatballs. A number of pasta variations dot the menu, as do Italian sausage and meatball sandwiches. Pizzas come piping hot, direct from the wood-burning oven.

## Catahoula Restaurant and Saloon

**1457 Lincoln Ave. (in the Mount View Hotel), Calistoga 94515**
**707-942-BARK • Lunch and dinner daily; Sun. blues brunch**
**Reservations recommended • California/Louisiana/Cajun**
**Moderate to expensive**

Jan Birnbaum came to Napa Valley from Campton Place in San Francisco, but his cooking roots are in the Deep South. He named Catahoula after the state dog of Louisiana and located it in the historic Mount View Hotel. Jan usually mans the helm nightly, in front of the wood-burning ovens in this open kitchen. Gazpacho or spicy corn and poblano soup may start off the parade of spices from the kitchen. Here's just a few of the spicy, flavorful entrees: andouille sausage, onion marmalade, and fontina pizza pie; seafood jambalaya with tasso; spiced country chicken with roasted garlic potatoes; and pan-fried catfish with a pecan crust. Desserts are of the down-home variety: strawberry shortcake, pecan pie, fresh berries, and the like. The wine list needs work; more Roses, Rieslings, and Gewurztraminers would be welcome, along with a wider selection of beers.

## ANNUAL EVENTS

### FEBRUARY–MARCH

**Napa Valley Mustard Festival • 707-938-1133**

In late winter, the mustard sprouts in between the rows of dormant vines; a perfect opportunity to celebrate the food and wine of the valley! All manner of events are scheduled over six weeks, including food and wine tastings, a celebration of fine art, caviar tastings, a golf benefit, and special winery events.

### JUNE

**Napa Valley Wine Auction • 707-963-5246**

Perhaps the single most exciting event and pull-out-all-the-stops wingding Napa Valley puts on all year. The most recent auction raised more than two million dollars for community health providers. While the auction is exciting, the veritable flood of peripheral events will amaze you. Every winery has an open house, with special lunches, dinners, barrel tastings, concerts, and other extravaganzas. The four-day event is a one-of-a-kind Napa Valley experience. Spectacle doesn't come cheap though; tickets now cost $1,500 per couple, but you'll probably remember it for a lifetime.

## RESOURCES

### Accommodations Referral
**P.O. Box 59 • St. Helena 94574 • 800-240-VINO**
Free hotline referral service specializing in accommodations in the Napa Valley.

### B & B Style Reservations
**800-955-8884**
Referral service specializing in bed and breakfast inns.

### Calistoga Chamber of Commerce
**1458 Lincoln Ave. • Calistoga 94515 • 707-942-6333**
Accommodations, restaurants, spas, recreations, and other activities.

### Napa Valley Conference and Visitors' Bureau
**1310 Town Center • Napa 94559 • 707-963-7395**
Valley-wide accommodations, restaurants, recreations and other activities.

### Napa Valley Tourist Bureau Reservations
**6488 Washington St. • Yountville 94599 • 800-523-4353.**
Free reservation service for lodging, balloon flights, and group tours.

### Napa Valley Vintners Association
**P.O. Box 141 • St. Helena 94574 • 707-963-0148, 800-982-1371**
Excellent free winery touring map and other winery-related information.

### Silverado Trail Wineries Association
**P.O. Box 453 • Deer Park 94576 • 800-624-WINE**
A map and guide to the Silverado Trail, "the quiet side of Napa Valley." Listing of wineries, tours, tastings, and current hours.

## St. Helena Chamber of Commerce
**1080 Main St. • St. Helena 94574 • 707-963-4456**
Accommodations including bed and breakfast inns, restaurants, winery maps, recreations, and seasonal events.

## Wine Country Reservations
**P.O. Box 5059 • Napa 94581 • 707-257-7757**
No fee reservation referral service specializing in accommodations, particularly bed and breakfast inns.

## Yountville Chamber of Commerce
**6515 Yount St. • Yountville 94599 • 707-944-0904**
Accommodations, restaurants, recreations, and other activities.

# SIERRA FOOTHILLS

*T*he Sierra Foothills is perhaps the least explored winery region in California . . . and for no good reason. The wine-growing area, just east of Sacramento and bounded by Placerville to the north and Angels Camp to the south, is steeped in history.

In 1849 gold was discovered at Sutter's Mill, just north of Placerville, and suddenly the gold rush ensued, attracting Americans and foreigners alike to seek out their fortunes. *Rush* is the appropriate word. In the next four years, California's population increased by a power of ten; at the height of the craze, Nevada City had more residents than San Francisco.

As the area grew, so did the demand for goods and services, among them wine. People planted vines almost immediately following this inbound exodus. Many unsuccessful miners, in fact, turned to farming and planted all manner of crops, including grapes. Even John Sutter himself, after losing most of his property and fortune in the tumultuous years that followed the gold craze, turned his efforts to grape growing in a vineyard planted in 1851 south of Yuba City.

Thirty years after the rush to the mother lode, the foothills boasted more than one hundred wineries, far outnumbering those in Napa or Sonoma. But as the mining era subsided, so too did the wineries; at the turn of the century, their number had vastly diminished. Later, the effects of Prohibition really did the wineries in; many of the vineyards were planted over to pears and apples.

In the late 1960s, the University of California at Davis, the premier viticultural school in the state, established an experimental grape-growing station in El Dorado County to determine what

# *Sierra Foothills*

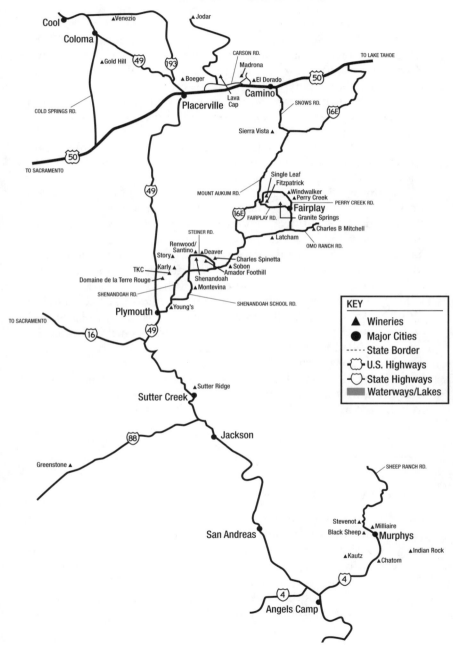

Cool

Coloma

▲Venezio

▲Jodar

▲Gold Hill (49) (193)

CARSON RD.

Madrona

TO LAKE TAHOE

▲Boeger

▲El Dorado

Camino

(50)

Lava

Placerville Cap

SNOWS RD.

COLD SPRINGS RD.

(16E)

Sierra Vista ▲

(50)

TO SACRAMENTO

Single Leaf

Fitzpatrick

MOUNT AUKUM RD.

▲Windwalker

▲Perry Creek

PERRY CREEK RD.

(49)

Fairplay

(16E)

FAIRPLAY RD.

Granite Springs

FAIRPLAY RD.

▲Charles B Mitchell

STEINER RD.

▲Latcham

OMO RANCH RD.

Renwood/

Santino ▲ ▲Deaver

Story ▲

Charles Spinetta

TKC Karly ▲

▲Sobon

▲Amador Foothill

Domaine de la Terre Rouge

Shenandoah

SHENANDOAH RD.

▲Montevina

Plymouth ▲Young's

SHENANDOAH SCHOOL RD.

TO SACRAMENTO

(16) (49)

▲Sutter Ridge

Sutter Creek

(88)

Jackson

Greenstone ▲

SHEEP RANCH RD.

Stevenot ▲

▲Milliaire

Black Sheep ▲

San Andreas

Murphys

▲Indian Rock

▲Kautz

▲Chatom

(4)

(4)

Angels Camp

### KEY

▲ Wineries
● Major Cities
----- State Border
◯ U.S. Highways
◯ State Highways
▬ Waterways/Lakes

types of grapes would grow to full ripeness and maturity in the area. By the early 1970s, new wineries, like Boeger, Story, and Montevina, had begun the gradual resuscitation of the foothills as a distinct grape-growing region.

Today, Zinfandel is the most widely planted variety and still the wine of choice in almost every tasting room; and that's red Zinfandel, not White Zin, though many still make that as a good cash flow wine. Sauvignon Blanc is most popular among the whites, making a far better wine with full flavors than Chardonnay does here. Once beyond those two wines, it's a shoot-out among the various producers. You'll certainly find Cabernet, Merlot, and Chardonnay, but the most interesting trend leans toward the Rhone and Italian varietals like Syrah, Viognier, Barbera, and Sangiovese.

The most diverse region in terms of geography, the Sierra Foothills has vineyards at the floor of the Sierra Nevada range all the way up to 3,200 feet. The wineries spread across three counties, El Dorado, Amador, and Calaveras, each with its geographic and scenic diversity. And each perhaps worthy of a couple of days of winery touring, not to mention all the historic museums and artifacts preserved in many of the gold rush towns.

Don't look for direct routes or straight-line highways, like Highway 29 in Napa; instead you'll find lots of backroads, country lanes, and switchbacks. And oh, yes, the stunning natural scenery provided by the Sierra Nevada Mountain range itself. No need to be in a hurry here; if you go with the flow, your pulse rate will probably drop by ten beats. Relax, downshift from the fast lane, enjoy the trip, and sip some interesting wines. Quite a few wineries here open only on weekends, so keep that in mind when planning a traveling schedule.

## WINERIES

### EL DORADO COUNTY

About three hours from the Bay Area and only an hour east of Sacramento, the El Dorado County wineries are among the most easily accessible, bordering both sides of U.S. 50, the main route between Sacramento and Lake Tahoe. Two distinct winery regions exist: wineries north of U.S. 50 near Placerville and an entire cluster of wineries south of U.S. 50, via Mount Aukum Road (Highway 16 east) in the hamlet of Fairplay.

Coming from Sacramento east on U.S. 50, exit north on Highway 49 at Placerville. Proceed to Sutter's Mill in Coloma, and go about a mile on Cold Springs Road to Vineyard Lane and Gold Hill Vineyard. Backtrack to Highway 49, but continue north to Cool. Turn right on Highway 193, right on Cherry Acres Road, and right again on Overton Road to Venezio Vineyards. Backtrack down the highway to U.S. 50 east again, exit at Schnell School Road north, and then go east on Carson Road (which parallels U.S. 50) about a half-mile to Boeger.

The small Jodar Vineyards (open weekends only) sits high up in the hills, about twenty minutes from Boeger; if you have the time, take Carson Road east beyond Boeger and go left on Union Ridge Road, then right on Mosquito Road, crossing the famous suspension bridge, then veer left on La Paz Road, left on Mosquito Cutoff Road, left on Rock Creek Road, and finally right on Gravel Road (whew!) to the winery. Retrace your route back down to Union Ridge Road, and go left on Hassler Road, just before Carson Road. Then make a left at Fruitridge Road to Lava Cap Winery. If you don't want to make the longer trip to Jodar, Lava Cap is only a few minutes from Boeger. Continue back down to the intersection of Fruitridge and Hassler roads and stay on Fruitridge, taking a right on North Canyon Road, and then a left back onto Carson Road, going east. Turn left on High Hill Road to Madrona Vineyards. Make your way back to Carson Road, going left (east) a few miles farther to El Dorado Winery. That's the eastern end of the wineries north of U.S. 50.

You may need to undertake another entire journey to visit the wineries south of U.S. 50, scattered throughout the communities of Pleasant Valley, Somerset, and Fairplay. If you want to proceed from El Dorado Winery, go east on Carson Road to the town of Camino and then right on Snows Road under the freeway. (If you're coming east on U.S. 50 from Placerville, you'll exit at the first Camino off-ramp and then go north to Carson Road, because there is no exit at Snows Road.) Go left when you hit Newtown Road and then left again at Pleasant Valley Road, then right on Leisure Lane and follow it up to Sierra Vista Winery (the view will reward you). Backtrack and go a short distance further down Pleasant Valley Road, then go right on Mount Aukum Road, which puts you on your way to the half-dozen wineries of Fairplay.

Quite a few scenic miles later, take a left on Fairplay Road and another quick left on Perry Creek Road, which leads to Windwalker Vineyards and then Perry Creek Vineyards right next door. When Perry Creek Road hits Fairplay Road, turn right and you'll find Fitzpatrick Winery, Single Leaf Vineyards, and Granite Springs Winery in rapid succession. Retrace your route on Fairplay, following it to the not-very-well-marked Stoney Creek Road. Make a left and drive through a rural residential compound to Charles B Mitchell Vineyards. Return to Fairplay Road and go left, traveling a short distance to Omo Ranch Road, where you'll turn right. Follow it to the well-marked Latcham Vineyards, the last winery in El Dorado County.

A few miles down the highway, Omo Ranch Road turns into Mount Aukum Road (Highway 16 east), which leads you into the Amador County winery tour through the back door. If you choose that option, just reverse the directions given below for Amador County touring. However most folks, coming from Sacramento on Highway 16 or Placerville on Highway 49, tend to begin touring Amador County at its most natural starting point: the town of Plymouth.

## Gold Hill Vineyard

**5660 Vineyard Ln., Placerville 95667 • 916-626-6522**
**Weekends 10–5 • Most varieties poured, no fee • Picnic area**
Not too far from historic Sutter's Mill, Hank Battjes resuscitated an old vineyard in 1980 and began making wine under the Gold Hill label in 1985. The University of California at Davis had planted an experimental plot of vines there in the mid-1960s. Battjes expanded and nurtured thirty-five acres of vines planted in sandy, well-drained soil to produce Bordeaux-style reds and Chardonnays, starting in 1985.

The winery itself is built into the hillside to take advantage of the cooling temperature consistency of earthen insulation. The tasting room overlooks the vineyards and the nearby American Canyon. Chenin Blanc, Riesling, and Chardonnay are among the whites that might be offered; but the bread-and-butter of Gold Hill are the reds: Cabernet, Cabernet Franc, and Merlot. In good years, Gold Hill produces a wonderful Bordeaux-style red Meritage blend.

## Venezio Vineyards

**3520 Overton Rd., Cool 95614 • 916-885-6815**
**Call for appointment, weekends only 11–4**
**Most varieties poured, no fee**
Not far from the intersection of Highways 49 and 193, Venezio Vineyards sits just six miles south of Auburn, among the rolling hills and groves of pine trees.

This family-owned winery and vineyard is so small and off the beaten path, you will need to call ahead to see if someone will pour that particular weekend. The handcrafted wines include Chardonnay, Sauvignon Blanc, Zinfandel, and Cabernet.

## Boeger Winery

**1709 Carson Rd., Placerville 95667 • 916-622-8094**
**Daily 10–5 • Most varieties poured, no fee • Picnic area**

Winemaker Greg Boeger had winemaking in his blood so to speak, having helped out at his grandpa's winery, Nichelini Vineyards, high up in the Chiles Valley in Napa. After graduating with a master's in agricultural science from the University of California at Davis, he and his wife began to look for a vineyard property.

They settled on the old Fossati Winery and Distillery near Placerville, founded in 1857 after the gold rush. A fire destroyed the original winery in 1872, but the Fossatis rebuilt it from stones gathered from the vineyards. Steeped in history, it's on the National Register of Historic Places and now serves as the Boeger tasting room. After rehabilitating the old stone buildings, the Boegers built a winery in the same rustic style but with all the latest modern winemaking technology. They cleared out the brush, timber, and fruit trees and planted their estate vineyard. The drive down a country lane to the estate will take you back to last century. Step down into the low-ceilinged, historic tasting room (where gravity helped make the wine in the nineteenth century), and sample the likes of Chardonnay, Sauvignon Blanc, Riesling, Cabernet, Merlot, and Zinfandel. Boeger also experiments with small lots of Italian, Spanish, and Rhone varietals, bottling them as proprietary blends, primarily available at the winery.

## Jodar Vineyards

**2393 Gravel Rd., Placerville 95667 • 916-626-4582**
**Weekends 12–5 • Most varieties poured, no fee • Picnic area**

One of the newcomers to the region, Jodar pushes the grape-growing envelope to the northernmost area of the county. This family operation opened in 1992, high up in the hills, with breathtaking views of the surrounding ridges. The Jodars acquired this forty-acre property a dozen miles north of Apple Hill and began planting vineyards as time and money permitted.

The winery building is of the functional variety—a bare bones type that houses a minimum amount of winemaking paraphernalia to get a quality winemaking job done. A small area carved out of the winery is designated for tasters who make the scenic trip through American Canyon to the winery. The focus is on Cabernet and Chardonnay, though a rose-colored Cabernet Blanc along with their blended American Canyon Red and White are the bargains, at around $5 a bottle.

## Lava Cap Winery

**2221 Fruitridge Rd., Placerville 95667 • 916-621-0175**
**Daily 11–5 • Most varieties poured, no fee • Shaded picnic area**
    You'd have to go a ways to keep up with the Joneses here because the Jones family owns and operates this winery and vineyard, established by professor David Jones in 1986. Son Tom makes the wines, and son Charles manages the vineyard at Lava Cap, which takes its name from the local geology. Millions of years ago it seems, volcanic ash and lava were deposited on the Sierra Nevadas. The volcanic deposits covered the veins of gold; the gold rush '49ers who came west seeking their fortune soon learned the richest gold deposits occurred underneath a thick layer of volcanic ash. Thus a lava cap signified an area where gold was most likely to be found.
    Today, the analogy extends to the twenty-five acres of vineyards planted in the rich, volcanic soil at an elevation of more than 2,500 feet. Hundreds of gold medal ribbons line the back wall of the tasting room, housed in a brown barn-style winery structure perched on a hilltop. At this elevation, the vines get plenty of daytime heat but cool down at night, which bodes well for their roster of white wines: Chardonnay, Sauvignon Blanc, and a terrificly refreshing Muscat Canelli. Cabernet and Zinfandel are rich and well concentrated. A beaut of a location for a picnic, the outdoor wooden sundeck juts from the tasting room, overlooking the uphill-sloped vines.

## Madrona Vineyards

**High Hill Rd. (P.O. Box 454), Camino 95709 • 916-644-5948**
**Daily 11–5 • Most varieties poured, no fee**
    The highest vineyard in El Dorado County, or perhaps anywhere in California, is Madrona Vineyards, located on a scenic ridge at the 3,000-foot elevation mark. Dick Bush purchased fifty-two acres about five miles east of Placerville in 1972; convinced that the warm days and cool nights could produce a wide array of grape varieties, he planted the vineyards with the same type of grapes grown in Napa. Madrona sold its harvest to other wineries until 1980, when the winery was hand-built amid the conifers and madrone trees.

The winery and tasting room require some effort to find, even though they stand only about a mile off Interstate 50. Circle around an orchard/fruit processing facility (follow the signs), then get off onto gravel and wind around until you see a low-slung wooden building, nearly obscured by the namesake madrones. Inside, the wood-paneled tasting room is warm and cozy with a small bar; the winery is actually a floor below, burrowed into part of the hillside. The cool climate helps produce fresh and fruity whites, like Riesling, Chardonnay, and Gewurztraminer. Zinfandel, Merlot, Cabernet, and Cabernet Franc are tasty as well.

### El Dorado Winery

**3550 Carson Rd., Camino 95709 • 916-644-2854 • Daily 11–5**
**Most varieties poured, no fee • Picnic area**

Located right on Carson Road, parallel to the freeway, El Dorado Winery produces small lots of premium wines, using traditional Old World techniques and minimal handling to retain true varietal character. Foothill-grown grapes are carefully selected from the proper soil and climate for each type.

Chardonnay, Cabernet, Merlot, and Zinfandel are among the usual suspects poured at the tasting room. But El Dorado also experiments with limited quantities of Italian and Rhone grapes, including a Barbera and a red Rhone-style blend.

### Sierra Vista Winery

**4650 Cabernet Way (end of Leisure Ln.), Placerville 95667,**
**916-622-7221, 800-WINE-916 • Daily 11–4 • Most varieties**
**poured, no fee • Picnic area**

John McCready started out as a home winemaker in his native Ohio and, in spite of his Ph.D. in electrical engineering, ended up buying seventy acres next door to his sister's ranch in El Dorado County in 1973. Prior to Prohibition, there had been a number of vineyards in the Pleasant Valley area. McCready wanted to plant Cabernet among other things, but the university types told him the 2,800-foot level was too cold to ripen. He outsmarted conventional wisdom though, planting Cabernet and Syrah in the warmest microclimate on the property and the remaining grape varieties in the cooler sites. He began making wine in 1977 in a garage-type building, which has been expanded over the years.

It's a climb over the backroads, south of Interstate 50 toward the Fairplay area wineries, to find Sierra Vista, but the impressive view is worth it. Only in 1995 did they finally finish their official tasting room; the knotty wood building can now comfortably hold a small crowd. A well-used picnic area lies just steps away, featuring the spectacular view of the Sierra Nevadas, which the winery is named for. Cabernet, Zinfandel, Chardonnay, and Sauvignon Blanc are among the original mainstays of the winery, and they are still very good. But recently they have gotten serious about Syrah and Viognier, as well as some red Rhone-style blends, the latter quite inexpensive.

### Windwalker Vineyards

**7360 Perry Creek Rd., Somerset 95684 • 916-620-4054**
**Weekends 11–5 • All varieties poured, no fee**
**Shaded picnic area**

This winery is exactly what you might expect from a small family winery tucked away in the country. You might think the proprietors, the Gilpin family, have a love of horses; all their labels and glassware feature a stallion. However the inspiration for the label came from the previous owners, who trained Arabian horses at the ranch as well as made wine. When the owners put the property up for sale in 1992, the Gilpins thought it would be a perfect family opportunity: Son Rich had worked for other wineries since graduating from the University of California at Davis with a degree in enology.

Travel up the country driveway and park below the *barn moderne* building that houses the winery. On the way in, a wooden deck patio sits under an old shade tree, which makes for a relatively secluded picnic site. The tasting room itself is strictly utilitarian, with a small bar directly across from the entrance and wine barrels sticking out on both sides. The Chardonnay is most pleasant and the Chenin Blanc is one of the few in the state that is finished dry. Aged in the bottle, Cabernet and Zinfandel will also intrigue you. The prices, all under $10, certainly feel right.

### Perry Creek Vineyards

**7400 Perry Creek Rd., Somerset 95684 • 916-620-5175,**
**800-880-4026 • Weekends 11–5; November and December,**
**Wed.–Sun. 11–5 • Most varieties poured • Classic car collection**
**adjacent • Western dude ranch lodging in log cabins available at**
**Seven-Up Bar Guest ranch (owned by Perry Creek), 916-620-**
**5450 • Excellent gift selection, deli items, cigar humidor**
**Picnic area**

In direct contrast to Windwalker, Perry Creek is exactly the kind of place you do not expect to find in the backwoods of El Dorado County. A good road leads up to an expansive black-topped parking lot as well as a spacious stucco mission-style winery building and hospitality center. Proprietor Mike Chazen was prospering in the rag trade in Los Angeles when he stumbled across this property while on vacation. Within a year he bought the 155 acres, which came with an old vines Chenin Blanc vineyard. At the time, there was no road, no parking lot, and no winery. He cleared out a wooded area and not only built the winery and residence but also a small warehouse for his collection of vintage autos.

Perry Creek is the showpiece winery in the county. Its white-washed stucco walls and red tiled roof visually invite visitors; in addition, a gurgling fountain graces the front entrance with stylish picnic tables and high-backed chairs scattered on both sides. The tasting room and adjacent gift shop have high wood-beamed ceilings with lazily turning ceiling fans. The Chenin Blanc, vinified dry, is a good place to start tasting, as is the White Zin or the tutti-frutti Zinfandel Nouveau. Merlot, Zinfandel, Riesling, Chardonnay, and Sauvignon Blanc may also be on the tasting menu. Look for recent plantings on the property to bear fruit, including Syrah, Viognier, Sangiovese, Nebbiolo, and Cabernet. Chazen hired Nancy Steele away from a Sonoma County winery to work her magic at Perry Creek, so expect these good wines to become even better.

### Fitzpatrick Winery

7740 Fairplay Rd., Somerset 95684 • 916-620-3248,
800-245-9166 • Weekends 11–5 • All varieties poured, no fee
Wooden deck with view, lunch served on weekends
Adjoining bed and breakfast accommodations in the lodge,
916-620-3248 • Good gift selection

In the Irish sense of hospitality, Fitzpatrick endeavors to be all things to all people: a winery, a restaurant, and a lodge. Originally Brian Fitzpatrick came west to California in 1972, ostensibly to further his education, but he became involved in the organic food movement. Several years later he settled on a property in El Dorado County, where he cleared the land of pine and oak trees and began to plant apple trees. But the grape siren called to him, and by 1980 he was making wine. Achieving some measure of success, in 1986 he moved the operation high on a hill (2,500-foot elevation) that overlooks the vineyards of Fairplay and the surrounding Sierra Foothills.

A handcrafted A-frame log lodge was constructed to house the visitors' center on the main floor, while the winery is situated underground. The bed and breakfast, four cozy rooms with private baths, has its own entrance, although it shares the foyer with the tasting room. If you're not staying at the bed and breakfast, you'll find the tasting room entrance on the near side, with a large wooden deck that takes advantage of the spectacular view. Almost all the wines come from organically grown grapes, including Cabernet and Zinfandel. Their flagship white, a Sauvignon Blanc called Eire Ban, is tasty, as is their Celtic Cider. Their proprietary blends, Sierra Dreams and King's Red, have attractive prices.

## Single Leaf Vineyards

**7480 Fairplay Rd., Somerset 95684 • 916-620-3545**
**Fri.–Sun. 11–5 • All varieties poured, no fee • Picnic tables**

When you look down from the deck at Fitzpatrick Winery, you see one of the oldest Zinfandel vineyards in the county, and if you squint hard enough, you might be able to pick out Single Leaf Vineyards' winery building, set among the sheltering pines. The Miller family set up shop here in 1988 and began making wine and expanding the Zinfandel acreage. The winery takes its name from the pinion, or single-leaf pine tree, native to the area and recognizable by its unique single needle cluster. A single leaf now graces the otherwise black winery label.

The winery is redwood plank on the outside and a glorified warehouse on the inside, with barrels and wine cases stacked everywhere. Near the front door, a small table is set up for tasting the wines, though some new concrete was being poured out front in preparation for an expansion of the facility. Zinfandel is still in the forefront, though Cabernet and Chardonnay are good too. The bargains are the red and white table wine blends; tasty without busting the budget. Don't overlook the Port, a real mouthful and available in half bottles.

## Granite Springs Winery

**5050 Granite Springs Winery Rd., Somerset 95684**
**916-620-9365, 800-638-6041 • Daily 11–5**
**Most varieties poured, no fee • Good gift selection • Picnic area**

Les and Lynne Russell left the city life behind in 1979 when they bought this forty-acre plot in the Sierra Foothills with the intention of starting a vineyard and winery. Les was at a career crossroad and, having helped at David Bruce Winery in the Santa Cruz Mountains years before, opted for a change in lifestyle. Part of the land was already cleared and could be planted to vines immediately, but the Russells had to jackhammer through a lot of granite in order to construct the winery into the side of a small mountain. The first crush occurred in 1981, and the winery has grown to 10,000 cases in the 1990s. Lynne passed away several years ago, and Les decided to sell the winery to the Latchams, whose eponymous winery is only a few miles down the road.

About a mile off Fairplay Road, go up and over a hill, then veer to the right, and you'll find the winery down in a hollow. The first impression, from the parking lot, is the gorgeous view of the vineyards nearby and the carpet of green on the neighboring hillsides. Picnickers often use the tables around the duck pond. The winery building is a simple barn-type structure, with a long wooden bar that spans the back wall. Granite Springs produces about a dozen different wines, among them the bargain Sierra Red and Sierra White reserves. Cabernet and Zinfandel are typically gutsy and, for dessert, a tasty Black Muscat and Petite Sirah Port round out the list.

## Charles B Mitchell Vineyards

**8221 Stoney Creek Rd., Somerset 95684 • 916-620-3467, 800-704-WINE • Wed.–Sun. 11–5 • Most varieties poured, no fee • Good gift selection • Shaded picnic area**

In the late 1960s and early 1970s, the University of California at Davis planted experimental vineyards at this site; those vineyards, on south-facing slopes, were later farmed and expanded to twenty acres by the Gerwer family, which sold the winery to raconteur Charles Mitchell in 1994. The winery is located back off the road, through a rural enclave of chicken farmers and apparent junk collectors. An A-frame building houses both the tasting room and winery, set back among the oaks. The wood-paneled tasting room with a back bar looks appropriately homey, and Charles Mitchell sometimes removes himself from the winery down the hallway to gauge tasters' reactions to his handiwork. Mitchell has focused on upgrading the rustic quality of the wines to a more rounded and palatable style; his efforts have born fruit with Chardonnay, Chenin Blanc, Fume Blanc, and Semillon. Cabernet and Zinfandel are soft and fruity, and his Red Sunshine, a light-styled red similar to a quaffing Beaujolais, is perfect for picnicking in the adjacent shady grove.

## Latcham Vineyards

**2860 Omo Ranch Rd., Mount Aukum 95656 • 916-620-6834, 800-750-5591 • Daily 11–5 • All varieties poured, no fee Picnic area**

This winery lies a bit out of the winery loop on Fairplay Road, but it's a short and scenic drive to the vineyard property, located at the foot of Mount Aukum. The twenty-five-acre vineyard was planted in 1981, but Bay Area tax attorney Frank Latcham and his wife, Patty, didn't start making wines from the estate until 1990. And lacking a proper facility, they crushed the grapes down the road at Granite Springs Winery.

Their gray California barn-style tasting room sits at the end of the driveway, surrounded by the vineyard, shade trees, and a pond. Inside, expect the no-frills approach: a bare bones utilitarian wooden structure with a cement floor, while the tasting bar consists of wood planks on top of empty wine barrels. But it's what's in the bottle that really counts here. Chardonnay and Sauvignon Blanc are done well, but the reds are the real powerhouses: Zinfandel, Cabernet, Cabernet Franc, and Petite Sirah. The nonvintaged El Dorado White and Gold Rush Red can be good bargains. In fact, most of the bottles cost less than $10.

## AMADOR COUNTY

Coming east from Sacramento (less than an hour's drive) on Highway 16, you'll run right into Shenandoah Road in Plymouth. Coming south from Placerville on Highway 49, follow the signage—Amador County has very good winery signposts— directing you also to Shenandoah Road. The first winery, Young's Vineyards, comes up immediately on the right; in fact most folks drive by it, not realizing how quickly they arrive in the wine country of Amador. A couple miles further on Shenandoah Road brings you to Domaine de la Terre Rouge, to the left on Dickson Road. Continue further on Shenandoah Road to Ball Road, and go left to find TKC Vineyards, Karly Winery, and Story Winery in that order, down their respective country lanes. Backtrack to and continue on Shenandoah Road, turning left on Steiner Road, where a number of wineries are clustered: Renwood/Santino, Shenandoah Vineyards, Amador Foothill Winery, Deaver Vineyards, and Charles Spinetta Winery. Continue on Steiner Road in the same direction (east) until it intersects with Shenandoah Road; follow Shenandoah Road about a mile further east to Sobon Estate Winery. Now backtrack on Shenandoah Road west until it hits Shenandoah School Road. Make a left to climb up to Montevina Winery.

All the wineries above lie within what I call the Shenandoah-Steiner roads loop, virtually within spitting distance of each other. With this many wineries concentrated in one area, you could spend an entire extended weekend just picking up the fine points of Amador County wines. A couple other wineries await in the south part of the county, a short, leisurely drive away. From Plymouth, take Highway 49 south to Sutter Creek, and then go west on Highway 88 about eleven miles to Greenstone Winery, outside Ione near Jackson Valley Road. For the last winery regularly open to the public in Amador County, retrace your route into Sutter Creek. Then go east on Ridge Road to Sutter Ridge Winery. If you want to continue to explore the wineries in neighboring Calaveras County, get back on Highway 49 and head south.

## Young's Vineyards

**10120 Shenandoah Rd., Plymouth 95669 • 209-245-3198**
**Weekends 10:30–5 • Most varieties poured, no fee • Picnic area**
This property, located at the beginning of the Shenandoah-Steiner roads loop of Amador County wineries, has changed hands a number of times in its short history. The Kenworthy family, with John Kenworthy at the helm, planted vineyards in 1979. The winery closed, and then for a short time it was known as Sonny Grace Vineyards. In 1995 the Young family took over and reopened the winery to the public.

The Youngs began to remodel and refurbish the property, and a new tasting room opened in 1996. The vineyards are adjacent, and a short stroll takes you to the duck pond for a quiet picnic. The Youngs are intent on improving the quality of the wines from what has been offered in the past. Reds reign here, including Cabernet and Zinfandel and sometimes Ruby Cabernet.

## Domaine de la Terre Rouge

**10801 Dickson Rd., Plymouth 95669 • 209-245-4277**
**Fri.–Sun. 11–4 • Most varieties poured, no fee**
Winemaker Bill Easton, a longtime fixture in the Amador County wine scene, has an established reputation for Rhone-style varietals that are among the best wines of the Sierra Foothills area. But only recently did he establish his own physical winery. The Baldinellis, who had acquired the old (1923) Dixon Zinfandel vineyard and then planted Sauvignon Blanc and Cabernet, built this winery in 1980.

Easton acquired the facility in 1994 as his permanent winemaking home; he says, "Terre Rouge is where the Rhone Valley meets the Sierra Nevada." To that end, he cultivates or has access to the traditional Rhone grapes: Syrah, Grenache, Mourvedre, and Cinsault, which are blended into a Chateauneuf-du-Pape style wine he calls Terre Rouge reserve. The Syrah, bottled by itself, is also extracted and flavorful. Additional but non-Rhone-style offerings might include an old vine Zinfandel, Riesling, a dry pink Vin Gris, and his blended Bordeaux-style Terre Rouge Blanc (Sauvignon Blanc and Semillon).

### TKC Vineyards

**11001 Valley Dr., Plymouth 95669 • 209-245-6428**
**Sat. 11–4, Sun. 1–4 • Most varieties poured, no fee**

This winery is one of the smallest family enterprises in Amador. Established in 1981 by aerospace engineer dropout Harold Nuffert and his wife, Monica, TKC recently planted its own vineyards to help secure its future.

From the beginning the emphasis was on big red wines, mostly tannic and mostly Zinfandel, though Cabernet is part of the regimen too. The tasting room has been carved out of one end of the winery. Production is limited to what the Nufferts can handle themselves, but you're likely to be poured a couple different Zins, along with a Cabernet if it hasn't sold out already. Some people term these highly extracted high-alcohol reds "monster wines" (as in huge), but they do provide an intense tasting experience.

### Karly Winery

**11076 Bell Rd., Plymouth 95669 • 209-245-3922 • Daily 12–4**
**Most varieties poured, no fee • Small gift selection • Picnic area**

Probably the last thing Buck and Karly Cobb contemplated when they moved here from the Bay Area in 1976 was starting a winery. At that time, only a few wineries existed in the area. Buck had been an Air Force fighter pilot in Korea before returning home to pursue a career as a research engineer. A new job with the California Energy Commission relocated him to Amador County. Soon enough, the winemaker bug bit him, first as a hobby, then full time in 1980. Buck's now on his fourth career!

About a mile off the main road, you'll churn up a little gravel to find Karly, but you'll recognize it by its simple Butler-building structure dug into the hillside, surrounded by twenty acres of estate vineyards. The small tasting room sits in the middle of the winery's working kitchen, but on weekends that kitchen usually provides tasters with warm, fresh sourdough bread and bits of cheese to wash down the vino. The Chardonnay, normally from Edna Valley grapes, can be tasty, and the Sauvignon Blanc has varietal fruit. Karly's real strength is Zinfandel and Petite Sirah: big, dark, highly extracted red wines that have good balance despite their high alcohol. Up and comers to taste include Sangiovese and Syrah. And last but not least, the sweet Orange Muscat is a terrific dessert wine.

## Story Winery

**10525 Bell Rd., Plymouth 95669 • 209-245-6208, 800-713-6390 • Sat.–Sun. 11–5 • Most varieties poured, no fee Good gift selection • Quiet shaded picnic area with a view**

Just when you think you can't go any further on Bell Road, you'll see Story around the bend on your left. Eugene Story helped pioneer this area when he established this vineyard in the early 1970s. He originally called it Cosumnes River Vineyards, but since no one could remember that name much less pronounce it, he changed it to his own moniker. When Story died, the Tichenor family acquired the property, though not much has changed (thankfully) at the winery since the early days.

In those days, Story had the good foresight to own one of the older, mature Zinfandel vineyards in the area. To this day, the winery concentrates on making classic estate Zinfandel. Don't be put off by the aging structure you first see where the road ends; that's part of the winery proper. Pull around to the side and park, then take a short walk up a hill, where a weathered cottage serves as the tasting room. The reward upon reaching it includes the magnanimous views of the forested Cosumnes River Canyon below. White Zinfandel and/or Chenin Blanc might be poured to start things off, but the burly, gnarly Zins (several vintages are apt to be open) are the reason to make the trip—that and the picnic tables on the adjacent deck or under the trees closer to the canyon. This secluded, quiet picnic spot (reserved for Story's customers) is a local secret, so don't breathe a word about it to anyone else.

## Renwood/Santino Winery

**12225 Steiner Rd., Plymouth 95669 • 209-245-6979 Daily 11–4:30 • Most varieties poured, no fee • Picnic area**

Without question, Renwood/Santino is one of the leaders in developing and producing the best possible high quality wines from Amador County grapes. The ownership of the winery, established in 1979, is a long and involved story. Suffice it to say that the Santinos are no longer involved in the winery, having sold it to then winemaker Scott Harvey and a third party. In 1995 Harvey, who was certainly responsible for the winery's high reputation, left, and an outside investor is now the proprietor. Still, if you visit the tasting room today, you can taste the results of Harvey's handiwork as it ages in the bottle.

Steiner Road in Plymouth more or less constitutes Winery Row in these parts, and you'll find Renwood/Santino at the beginning, easily recognizable with the parking area just a stone's throw from the road, on this side of the tasting room. Cool, dark, and comfortable, the tasting room has an old tiled floor, a cobbled-together bar, and a beautifully framed back bar mirror that was probably rescued from an old Victorian house. The simpler and more modest wines are bottled under the Santino label, while more interesting and expensive (though worth it) wines carry the Renwood name. The White Zin is as good as you'll find, but the red Zins are super, especially the Grandpere Vineyard bottling from century-old vines across the street. Both the Rhone-style and Italian-style wines are among the best, including Viognier, Syrah, Barbera, Nebbiolo, and Sangiovese. Two things you should ask to see: the label on the red Rhone blend Satyricon and the "hidden" restroom.

### Shenandoah Vineyards

**12300 Steiner Rd., Plymouth 95669 • 209-245-4455**
**Daily 10–5 • Most varieties poured, no fee • Art gallery**
**Small gift selection • Picnic area**

Despite being part of a research team at Lockheed that helped improve color television and X-ray machines, Leon Sobon knew his research career had ended when his garage was so completely consumed with his home winemaking hobby that he had to build a new addition to house the aging wine. So the Sobons left the Bay Area in 1977, purchasing seventy-four acres of land with a stone house (but no winery or vineyards) overlooking the Shenandoah Valley. That first year, Leon purchased grapes, made wine, and drove around California selling wine out of the back of his station wagon.

From those humble beginnings, Shenandoah now makes about 40,000 cases a year. The fieldstone home still exists, and the winery was built in the same style next to it. Two whimsical Sheila Ganz sculptures flank the tasting room entrance, and on slow days, you might need to ring the bell to get someone's attention. Inside, the multilevel winery looks cheerfully funky, with a log beam ceiling and a tasting bar that runs the entire back wall. Downstairs, among the aging casks of wine, the seasonally changing art show features paintings, ceramics, and quilts. The Sauvignon Blanc is a good start, then on to the full-bodied reds like Zinfandel, Cabernet, and Zingiovese (an interesting blend of Zinfandel and Sangiovese). Shenandoah is also one of the few places you'll find a full menu of dessert wines, including late-harvest Zinfandel, Vintage Port, Orange Muscat, and Old Cream Muscat.

## Amador Foothill Winery

**12500 Steiner Rd., Plymouth 95669 • 209-245-6307**
**Sat.–Sun. 12–5 • Most varieties poured, no fee • Picnic area**
Leon Sobon, from Shenandoah Vineyards (above), sold twenty acres of his property in 1979 to Ben Zeitman, who ironically was also looking for a lifestyle change after his first career as a NASA chemist. And voila, Amador Foothill Winery was born. Zeitman had the good sense and opportunity to purchase grapes from some of the great old Zinfandel vineyards in the county, which he still does to this day. He planted non-Zinfandel vineyards on his own property and married Katie Quinn, a University of California at Davis enology graduate and assistant winemaker for Gundlach Bundschu in Sonoma County. Today, Quinn is a passionate spokesperson for Amador County wines wherever she goes, and together they have increased production to around 30,000 cases while maintaining quality.

Enter Amador Foothill from Steiner Road; just turn in on your right and follow the lane to the hilltop. The winery itself, partially solar energized, is designed to minimize undue handling of the wines. From the tasting room, you can actually glimpse the intriguing setup of the winery. White Zin, obligatory in this county, is offered, though the Sauvignon Blanc is more interesting, while the White Meritage (a blend of Sauvignon Blanc and Semillon) is more interesting yet. Again, Zinfandel is king here, and you'll do yourself a disservice unless you taste through all their vineyard-specific offerings, including Grandpere, Ferrero, and Fiddletown.

## Deaver Vineyards

**12455 Steiner Rd., Plymouth 95669 • 209-245-4099**
**Thurs.–Mon. 11–5 • Most varieties poured, no fee**
**Amador Harvest Inn bed and breakfast adjacent, 800-217-2304**
**Excellent gift selection of jewelry, glassware, and comestibles**
**Picnic area**
The Deaver clan can trace its ancestry in this valley back to the gold rush days. The Deaver complex of buildings, on the same side

of the road as Renwood/Santino and just a stone's throw away, looks spic-and-span because most its history is recent, even though the Deavers are longtime grape growers and farm some of the oldest Zinfandel vines in the area.

By Amador County standards, the facility is large; you'll have to go around the short half-circle drive to see all the components of the little village. On one side, a small barnlike structure houses the winery production, around 500 cases, begun in 1990. On the other end, the beautiful Amador Harvest Inn, a reconstructed farmhouse with four rooms (and private baths), appears quaint with Victorian touches and looks out onto the vineyards. You'll find the tasting room cum gift shop in the middle of things. You can taste at the blonde wooden bar with a convenient old-time foot railing or peruse the large gift selection with glass in hand. Skip the Chardonnay; the red table wine is passable for the price. The Zinfandels are the real stuff here, and Deaver will likely have several vintages open for tasting and comparison, some even from the late 1980s.

### Charles Spinetta Winery

**12557 Steiner Rd., Plymouth 95669 • 209-245-3384**
**Daily except Mon. 10–4:30 • Most varieties poured, no fee**
**Wildlife art gallery and frame shop • Picnic area**

Practically next door to the Deaver Vineyards farm village sits the Charles Spinetta Winery; its white rectangular-block building, in direct antithesis to the Deaver's, looks more like some kind of small factory. Spinetta, a wildlife conservationist, bought vineyards here in the late 1970s; his family goes back four generations in Amador County.

Once inside, you'll find the high-ceilinged building does serve a purpose, more than meets the eye outside. The tasting area is open and spacious, and artwork surrounds you. Upstairs on the second floor, an art gallery is filled with wildlife paintings and prints, all for sale. White Zinfandel might be the first offering, but the Chenin Blanc is the preferable choice, even over the Chardonnay. On the red side, Cabernet and Merlot are available, but several old vine Zinfandels are likely to be open too. The sweet Muscat Canelli, almost a dessert in itself, rounds things out.

### Sobon Estate

**14430 Shenandoah Rd., Plymouth 95669 • 209-245-6554**
**Daily 10–5 • Most varieties poured, no fee • Shenandoah Valley**
**Museum adjacent, free • Good gift selection • Picnic area**

Leon Sobon and family got so successful at Shenandoah Vineyards, they bought the old D'Agostini Winery, just a couple miles up the road from their original facility. While Shenandoah Vineyards concentrates on the traditional Amador varietals, Sobon Estate explores the Rhone-style varietals that have become so popular. The original fieldstone building, with hand-hewn wooden beams, dates back to 1856, when it was Adam Uhlinger's winery; it's still in use today, though the Sobons have added on a whitewashed stucco tasting room with a big, wooden barn-door entrance.

Directly across the courtyard from the tasting room, the Sobons have preserved Uhlinger's handiwork, along with many great winemaking tools, barrels, and artifacts of the gold rush era. It's a fascinating trip back in time and well worth the time and effort, having been designated a state historic landmark. The wines are as new and refreshing as the building is old. Look for a pleasant Fume Blanc and a finely aromatic Viognier. On the red side, the Rhone Rouge and Syrah lead the way, but the Cabernet, Cabernet Franc, and Zinfandel are equally interesting. A highly extracted and dense Zinfandel Port is often open and poured for the stout hearted.

## Montevina Winery

**20680 Shenandoah School Rd., Plymouth 95669**
**209-245-6942 • Daily 11–4 • Most varieties poured, no fee**
**Large shaded picnic patio area**

This winery was one of the early proponents in the Amador County winemaking revival. Vineyards were planted and a winery was built in 1973; production concentrated on Zinfandel. That varietal's reputation was already well-known, because Napa Valley's Sutter Home, in the days before White Zinfandel, bought grapes here to make red Zinfandel. After a family ownership dispute, Montevina's focus drifted, and Sutter Home bought it in 1988. So while Sutter Home now has access to more great grapes for its label, it keeps Montevina a totally separate operation and is getting back to the basics of making Zinfandel, while also exploring Italian-style varietals.

A little more than two miles off Shenandoah Road, the white stucco and dark wood winemaking and hospitality complex looks impressive. Inside, the huge tasting room, done in dark woods and with twin tasting bars, looks like a dignified Teutonic dining hall. Again, Montevina has white wines, like White Zinfandel, Chardonnay, and Fume Blanc, which are passable. However, all the new Italian-style varieties and blends seem much more interesting: Barbera, Sangiovese, Montonaro (Barbera and Zinfandel), and Matrimonio (a five-variety blend). Don't forget the original

Zinfandel and the reserve version, which still carry on the Amador tradition. Just off the tasting room, a large outdoor trellis-covered patio sports dozens of picnic tables overlooking the vineyards.

### Greenstone Winery

**Highway 88 at Jackson Valley Rd., Ione 95640 • 209-274-2238**
**Wed.–Sun. 10–4 • Most varieties poured, no fee**
**Shaded picnic area**

Located in the foothills near Ione, this winery sits a ways out of the Steiner Road loop, where a dozen Amador County wineries are centered. A ride out in the country, so to speak, will present a little different vista of the Sierra Foothills. In 1980 the Van Spanje and Fowler families carved forty acres of vineyards out of this eighty-acre ranch.

This French country-style winery places an emphasis on lighter-styled and sweet white wines, like French Colombard, White Zinfandel, and Chenin Blanc. A big Cabernet is usually offered, but Greenstone's proudest product is its jammy, old vines Zinfandel. The Zinfandel Port is so big it nearly stands up without a glass.

### Sutter Ridge Vineyards

**14110 Ridge Rd., Sutter Creek 95685 • 209-267-1316**
**Thurs.–Sun. 11–4 • Most varieties poured, no fee**

Located at a 2,000-foot-high ridge in the Foothills overlooking the historic gold rush towns of Sutter Creek and Jackson, the winery still belongs to and functions under a fourth generation of the family in Amador County.

Sutter Ridge makes a wide variety of wines, including White Zinfandel, Chardonnay, Cabernet, Cabernet Franc, and Zinfandel. They are experimenting with Italian varietals to see which ones work the best in this area. They have the only commercial planting in California of Pinotage, a hybrid of the French Pinot Noir and Hermitage grapes, which is widely cultivated in South Africa but little known here. Finish with a powerful Port.

### CALAVERAS COUNTY

Highway 49 is the north-south route that cuts through the heart of the Sierra Foothills. From a starting point in either Placerville, Plymouth, Sutter Creek, or Jackson, you can traverse the highway's length into Calaveras County, past the town of San Andreas and into Angels Camp. Here you'll go left (east) onto Highway 4 toward the Murphys, known as the Queen of the Sierras. About two miles up the road, you'll spot the spiffy-looking Chatom Vineyards on your right. Continue on Highway 4 and, nearly into town, turn right on Pennsylvania Gulch Road to find Indian Rock Vineyard about a mile beyond. Back on Highway 4, continue on a short distance, then make a quick left on Jones Street and a right on Main Street, where you'll see Milliaire in an old gas station. Backtrack on Main Street, going west to its end at Murphys Grade Road, and discover Black Sheep Vintners. Backtrack on Main Street, go left at Sheep Ranch Road, then take another left at San Domingo Road to Stevenot Winery. And last but certainly not least, don't miss the modern showpiece winery of Calaveras County, Kautz Ironstone Vineyards. From Stevenot, take a left back onto Main Street, then a right on Algiers Road at the historic Murphys Hotel. Then turn right on Six Mile Road and drive a little over a mile to Kautz's impressive venue.

### Chatom Vineyards

**1969 E. Highway 4, Douglas Flat 95229 • 209-736-6500, 800-435-8852 • Daily 11–5 • Most varieties poured, no fee Good gift selection • Shaded picnic area**

This is the first winery you'll encounter after the infamous earthquake town of San Andreas. Proprietor Gay Callan descended from Mark Hopkins, one of the scions of early San Francisco society. After a successful career in the Bay Area broadcast business, she retired to the quiet country life in Calaveras County in 1980. Vineyards were planted, and by 1985 Chatom was making wine from its own grapes.

While Chatom may be a back-road winery, its winemaking facility and tasting room provide an oasis for visitors. The L-shaped rammed-earth building, with redwood siding and verdigris roof, is quaint but thoroughly modern. The tasting room, with a tiled floor, large windows, and a long oak bar, appears particularly warm and inviting. From Callan's sixty-five acres of vines, you can sample Semillon, Fume Blanc, and Chardonnay among the whites; the reds include Cabernet, Merlot, Zinfandel, and sometimes Sangiovese. A trellised picnic area makes this winery a perfect lunchtime destination.

### Indian Rock Vineyard

**1154 Pennsylvania Gulch Rd., Murphys 95247 • 209-728-2266 Sat.–Sun. 11–5 • Most varieties poured, no fee • Picnic area**

Fifty acres of vines just east of Murphys are farmed by this former grape grower that is gradually evolving into an estate-grown winery.

The Thompson family purchased the former dairy ranch and started planting the vineyards in 1985; a couple years later they began making wines and finally opened their rustic tasting room in 1991. The Indian Rock property lies in a beautiful spring-fed meadow, with ancient oak trees and abundant wildlife. The tasting room is the old milking barn, minimally embellished. An oaky Chardonnay was the first release, but Cabernet and Merlot have since joined the list. An unusual varietal, Charbono, is thought to be Italian in origin. One of the few made in California, Charbono will prove worth a sip. The secluded picnic tables, under the shade trees by the pond, look about as bucolic as wine country gets.

### Milliaire

**276 Main St., Murphys 95247 • 209-728-1658**
**Fri.–Mon. 11–5 • Most varieties poured, no fee**
**Small gift selection**

This building, right on Main Street in downtown Murphys, is home to The Little Winery That Could. Steve Millier, proprietor along with his wife, Liz, has made wine for a couple decades. He's particularly well-known in mother lode country, having worked as winemaker at Stevenot and Kautz, in addition to consulting at other wineries. The Milliers established their own winery, named Milliaire as a take on their own name, in an improbable space that was formerly an old country gas station. A long flower trough replaced the gas pumps in front. The service bays, where oil ran in the gutter, are now stacked high with oak barrels full of wine.

The modest tasting room is the revamped office area of the service station. Though Milliaire owns no vineyards, it has enough longtime connections in the area to secure good grapes from a variety of Sierra Foothills vineyards. For such a small-production winery, Milliaire makes a surprising number of different wines, albeit in limited quantities. Chardonnay, Sauvignon Blanc, and Gewurztraminer can be found at the tasting bar (if they haven't yet sold out), as well as Cabernet, Zinfandel, and Merlot. Save room for the dessert wines, a real specialty at Milliaire; they can include late-harvest Zinfandel, Zinfandel Port, late-harvest Sauvignon Blanc, and Orange Muscat.

### Black Sheep Winery

**Main St. at Murphys Grade Rd., Murphys 94247**
**209-728-2157 • Sat.–Sun. 12–5 • Most varieties poured, no fee**

Down at the end of Main Street, you'll find a little bit of wine history at Black Sheep Vintners. In the early 1970s, pioneer Bob

Bliss used this faded barn to establish Chispa Cellars, the first bonded winery in Calaveras County. David and Janis Olson, locals and home winemakers, bought the place and began making wine in 1987 as Black Sheep Vintners. Their label, showing a shepherd and his flock, includes a lone black sheep, which signifies the Olsons' desire to do something a little different at their winery. The winery owns no vineyards, but each year the Olsons travel throughout the foothills, searching for the best possible grapes, which are handmade in small lots. They produce only around 1,000 cases total.

The winery appears as rustic as they come. The wooden barn, constructed in the 1920s, certainly looks it, with its weathered exterior and rusted, corrugated roof. The tasting room lies just inside, hard by the aging wine barrels. Black Sheep specializes in only a few wines, including Sauvignon Blanc, Cabernet, and a rich Zinfandel. In honor of the annual Calaveras County frog jumping contest, they produce an inexpensive white blend called Lily Pad White.

### Stevenot Winery
**2690 San Domingo Rd., Murphys 95247 • 209-728-3436**
**Daily 10–5 • Most varieties poured, no fee • Good gift selection**
**Picnic area**

The Stevenot clan has a long history in this area. Proprietor Barden Stevenot's great-great-grandfather originally came from France in the frenzied search for gold. For decades, his ancestors owned and mined one of the most profitable mines in the area. In 1969 Barden Stevenot purchased the old Shaw ranch, where he had spent some time as a child. On the advice of his friends and Sonoma vintners Dave Stare and Lou Preston, he began planting vines on the former cattle ranch in 1974. Fours years later he made 2,000 cases of wine; now he's approaching 50,000 cases and is one of the largest producers in the area.

There are a number of rustic buildings on the ranch, though a modern addition was needed to handle the volume of wine. Tasting, though, still occurs in the historic Alaska House, which a previous owner built at the turn of the century to resemble the types of structures he had seen on a visit to Alaska. The small log cabin, which originally had a dirt floor, is topped by a sod roof for the cooling effect. Stevenot makes a wide variety of wines; the winery was among the first to produce White Zinfandel, but also offers Chardonnay, Merlot, Zinfandel, and Cabernet. The best wines are the reserves, made from grapes grown on the twenty-seven-acre estate vineyard and given special treatment in the cellar.

## Kautz Ironstone Vineyards

**1894 Six Mile Rd., Murphys 95247 • 209-728-1251**
**Daily 11–5 • Most varieties poured, no fee • Excellent gift**
**selection • Art gallery, full service deli, and picnic area**

Rising like a phoenix out of a forest of trees, the red roof of Kautz Ironstone Vineyards winery building in the distance warns you you're in for something big. To find a compound this sprawling in the middle of the country is impressive. To give you an idea, the winery facility and hospitality center stands seven stories high, built as a modern replica of a historic 1859 Gold Stamp Mill. On the 1,150-acre ranch, Lodi farming titan John Kautz chose sixty acres for the site of the winery; then he blasted 10,000 feet of aging tunnels fifty feet below the surface of a solid rock mountain to provide a perfect aging environment for the wines.

A tiled entryway gives way to a huge multilevel hospitality area, with a high ceiling and skylights. The centerpiece is a massive forty-two-foot rough-hewn stone fireplace that rivals the classic one at the Ahwahnee Hotel in Yosemite. It's a great spot for a picnic, even if you're unprepared; a full-service deli and bakery is adjacent to the tasting bar, and you can dine on the wooden deck or under shaded oaks. Antique farm tools line the walls, and a western art gallery lives on the second floor. Tours of the caves, offered several times a day, highlight any visit here. Meanwhile, back at the tasting bar, several different Chardonnays may be open for tasting, as well as Merlot, Cabernet, and Cabernet Franc. Symphony, a hybrid grape, makes for a slightly sweet wine called Obsession. For something different, a mellow apple wine is made, as is a potent apple Brandy. Older vintages are occasionally open and available for purchase.

# RESTAURANTS

## EL DORADO COUNTY

### Zachary Jacques

**1821 Pleasant Valley Rd., Placerville 95667 • 916-626-8045**
**Dinner daily except Mon.–Tues. • Reservations recommended**
**Country French • Moderate to expensive**

A longtime bastion of country French cuisine in the Sierra Foothills, Zachary Jacques serves up sizeable portions of Gallic comfort food. Start with escargot, sweetbreads, and warm goat cheese salad, followed by dishes like rabbit in mustard sauce or pepper steak in Cognac sauce. The Provencal side of the menu offers loin of venison in a red wine sauce, roast duck with shallots, and lamb medallions with ratatouille and tapenade. Good wine list.

## Cafe Sarah's & Pub

301 Main St., Placerville 95667 • 916-621-4680 • Lunch daily American/California cuisine • Moderate

This casual cafe is a particularly good spot for lunch, with its soups, salads, and sandwiches. At dinner, the menu is a bit more elaborate, including beef, chicken, and seafood.

## Mama D'Carlos

482 Main St., Placerville 95667 • 916-626-1612 • Dinner daily except Mon. • Reservations recommended • Italian • Moderate

It's hard to go wrong with a big plate of pasta and red sauce, which is what they do best here, although Mama D'Carlos offers a multitude of other pasta-sauce selections. Good local wine list.

## Powell Brothers Steamer Company

425 Main St., Placerville 95667 • 916-626-1091 • Lunch and dinner daily • Reservations accepted • Seafood/American Moderate to expensive

A little bit of San Francisco's old Barbary Coast is transported to the foothills at this old-timey seafood emporium. The seafood bar features fresh oysters and steamed clams; the main menu is chockablock with fresh fish selections, including the catch of the day, shrimp, and cioppino. For die-hard beef eaters, surf and turf combos are highlighted. Excellent local wine list.

## AMADOR COUNTY

## Bellotti Inn

53 Main St., Sutter Creek 95685 • 209-267-5211 Lunch and dinner daily • Reservations recommended Italian • Moderate

The restaurant at the Bellotti Inn, which dates back to the gold rush days, serves up good-sized portions of Italian specialties. Pastas, with appropriate sauces, come in all shapes and sizes. Fried calamari, veal, prime steaks, and chicken, all done in the Italian style, are mainstays, augmented by the specials of the day.

## Imperial Hotel Restaurant

14202 Highway 49, Amador City 95601 • 209-267-9172
Dinner daily; Sun. brunch • Reservations recommended
California cuisine • Moderate to expensive

This hotel dates back to 1879 and has been lovingly restored throughout. The dining room features exposed brick walls decorated with mirrors and prints from the Victorian era. White tablecloths and comfy high-back chairs establish an air of casual elegance. The menu is equal to its surroundings, with roast lamb loin with mint and rosemary, and smoked salmon with golden California caviar and potato pancakes. Wonderful desserts also and a good wine list.

## Ron and Nancy's Palace

76 Main St., Sutter Creek 95685 • 209-267-1355
Lunch and dinner daily • Reservations recommended
American • Moderate to expensive

This turn-of-the-century Victorian that was originally a country restaurant and saloon has been tastefully gussied up and restored—now it's more tasteful and refined than any time in its history (dress accordingly). You'll treasure the comfortable and relaxing ambience after a long day of wine touring. Fresh fish may often grace the menu: trout, snapper, calamari, and shrimp. Oven-roasted prime rib is also a favorite. Good local wine list.

## CALAVERAS COUNTY

## City Hotel Restaurant

Main St., Jackson 95642 • 209-532-1479 • Dinner daily except Mon.; Sun. brunch • Reservations recommended
California/French cuisine • Expensive

One of the most adventurous restaurants in gold country, City Hotel retains much of the nineteenth-century feel, with its red velvet drapes and dark wood interiors. The thoroughly modern menu, though, changes seasonally and has plenty of pleasant surprises, like baked catfish stuffed with shrimp, poached salmon in white wine sauce, and oven-roasted rack of lamb. Expect to dress up for the elegant surroundings. Excellent desserts; go with the souffles. Good wine list.

## Murphys Hotel Restaurant

457 Main St., Murphys 95247 • 209-728-3444 • Breakfast, lunch, and dinner daily • Reservations recommended
American • Moderate to expensive

This historic hotel, established in 1856, is another throwback to gold rush times, with an adjacent restaurant and saloon that maintain the theme. You can really sink your teeth into the decor; it's almost as much of an attraction as the food. The fare on the plates remains fairly straightforward, with beef, fish, and chicken the main events; the desserts are homemade, and the wine list is good. Both Mark Twain and Ulysses S. Grant slept here and (presumably) broke bread here too.

## ANNUAL EVENTS

### FEBRUARY

**Amador Vintners' Barrel Tasting • P.O. Box 667 Plymouth 95669 • 209-245-6942, 209-245-6208, 800-649-4988**
A weekend of special events, dinners, and open houses, featuring the seventeen wineries in the Shenandoah Valley, Sutter Hill, and Jackson Valley areas. A ticket allows you to barrel taste at all the wineries, many also offering complimentary appetizers, music, demonstrations, and other activities.

### MARCH–APRIL

**Passport Weekend of the El Dorado Winery Association P.O. Box 1614 • Placerville 95667 • 916-446-6562, 800-306-3956**
Passport purchase entitles you to a weekend of wine tasting and other wine-related events, like barrel tastings, vertical tastings, and wine/food pairings at all the El Dorado wineries.

### MAY

**Sierra Showcase of Wines • 209-267-5978**
Annual tasting of Sierra Foothills wines at the Amador County fairgrounds in Plymouth to benefit local charities.

### JUNE

**Amador County Wine Festival • 209-245-6119**
Wine tasting festival, barbecue dinner, live music, and dancing at the Amador County fairgrounds in Plymouth.

## OCTOBER

**Amador Vintners' Harvest Festival • P.O. Box 667 • Plymouth 95669 • 800-649-4988**
Wine tastings and special winery open house events at all Amador County wineries.

**Calaveras Grape Stomp • P.O. Box 2492 • Murphys 95247 209-795-5000**
Part of Murphys gold rush days, the grape stomp contest is held at Murphys Park and includes wine tasting, food, musical entertainment, costume contest, waiter/waitress race, and silent auction.

## RESOURCES

### Amador County Chamber of Commerce
**P.O. Box 596 • Jackson 95642 • 209-223-0350, 800-649-4988**
Free full-color winery touring map; accommodations (including bed and breakfast listings) and dining guide. Seasonal events, recreations, and other activities.

### Bed and Breakfast Inns of Amador County
**P.O. Box 1347 • Sutter Creek 95685 • 800-726-INNS**
Brochure and availability of the region's twelve bed and breakfast inns.

### Calaveras Lodging and Visitors' Association
**P.O. Box 637 • Angels Camp 95222 • 209-736-0049, 800-225-3764**
Visitors' guide, including winery touring map, calendar of events, accommodations, restaurants, historical sites, recreations, and other activities.

## El Dorado County Chamber of Commerce
**542 Main St. • Placerville 95667 • 916-621-5885, 800-457-6279**
Accommodations, seasonal events, recreations, and other activities.

## El Dorado County Country Inns
**800-456-6279**
Free brochure describes the county's bed and breakfast inns (nine different properties).

## El Dorado Winery Association
**P.O. Box 1614 • Placerville 95667 • 916-446-6562, 800-306-3956**
Free full-color winery touring map, including a calendar of events. Accommodations and restaurant guide.

# BAY AREA:
# LIVERMORE,
# SAN JOSE,
# AND
# SOUTH SANTA CLARA

*N*apa and Sonoma are not the only wine areas within a short drive of San Francisco, though they seem the most prominent in visitors' minds. But east of the Bay and Oakland, the Livermore Valley was a large commercial grape-growing area in the late nineteenth century. South of the Bay, San Jose and surrounding Santa Clara County were home to the vine as early as 1780, courtesy of the good fathers at Mission Santa Clara. In fact, at the turn of the century this region had more wineries than the Napa Valley. In southern Santa Clara County, down by Morgan Hill and Gilroy, a number of old family wineries, principally begun by Italian immigrants, still retain some of the old charm of days gone by.

But over the last two decades, as the bedroom communities surrounding the Bay Area have expanded to house daily commuters, it has been at the expense of the vineyards. One of the largest producers in the country, J. Lohr, headquartered in San Jose, actually owns no vineyards in the county. Mirassou, now almost complete-

# Bay Area

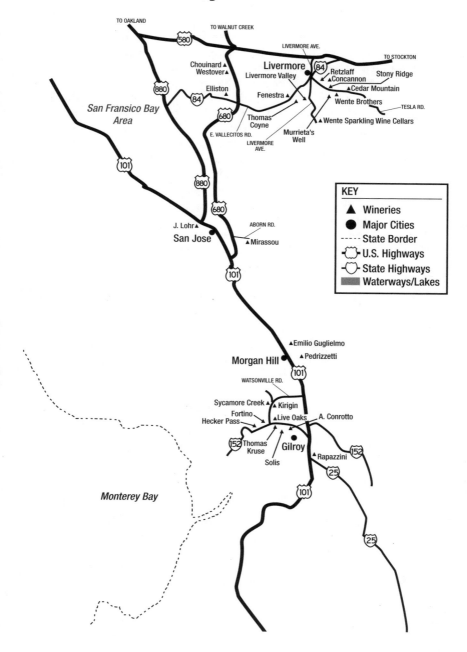

TO OAKLAND

TO WALNUT CREEK

580

LIVERMORE AVE.

TO STOCKTON

Chouinard ▲
Westover ▲

**Livermore**  84
Livermore Valley

Retzlaff
▲Concannon

Stony Ridge

880

Elliston
▲

Fenestra ▲

▲Cedar Mountain

Wente Brothers

*San Fransico Bay Area*

84
680

Thomas
Coyne

E. VALLECITOS RD.

TESLA RD.

▲Wente Sparkling Wine Cellars

Murrieta's
Well

LIVERMORE
AVE.

101

880

680

J. Lohr▲

**San Jose**

ABORN RD.

▲Mirassou

101

**KEY**

▲  Wineries
●  Major Cities
- - - -  State Border
U.S. Highways
State Highways
Waterways/Lakes

▲Emilio Guglielmo

▲ Pedrizzetti

**Morgan Hill**
101

WATSONVILLE RD.

Sycamore Creek ▲   ▲Kirigin

Fortino
Hecker Pass→   ▲Live Oaks    ▲ A. Conrotto

152 Thomas
Kruse   **Gilroy**

Solis

▲Rapazzini   152

25

*Monterey Bay*

101

25

ly surrounded by housing developments, sources the vast majority of its grapes from Monterey County.

Historically, Charles Wetmore was the seminal force in promoting the Livermore Valley as a grape-growing mecca, establishing Cresta Blanca Winery in 1882. James Concannon came a year later, an Irish immigrant whose business was to supply the Catholic Church with sacramental wine; it held him in good stead in the community and got him through Prohibition. Carl Wente came right on their heels and set up Wente Brothers, planting Sauvignon Blanc and Semillon as the principal varietals. Wente bottled the first varietally labeled Chardonnay in California in 1936, and many of the subsequent plantings of Chardonnay around the state are clones from this vineyard. The other wineries in the area are the products of the wine boom of the last two decades.

In San Jose, Mirassou claims to be the oldest continuous winemaking family in California, dating back to 1855, when Pierre Pellier brought grape cuttings back from France and planted a vineyard. The fifth generation of the Mirassou family finally brought the winery into the twentieth century, when they took over in 1966, attempting to improve all their varietal wines. J. Lohr began in 1975, but soon production climbed exponentially as the vineyard acreage under its control increased in other counties.

The southern Santa Clara wineries, on the other hand, are small mom and pop producers and consequently the tasting room host is likely to be an owner, relative, or friend who entertains visitors with the history of the establishment. The landscape is much more rural and, except for the huge outlet shopping mall in Gilroy, the pace of life slower.

## WINERIES

### LIVERMORE

*(listed clockwise)*

If you want to make the complete circuit of wineries, a long weekend is your best shot, since many of the smaller wineries are only open then. Coming from the Bay Area on Interstate 580, exit on Livermore Avenue, following it south a short distance until you see Retzlaff Vineyards. Continuing south, Livermore Avenue turns into Tesla Road and heads east; all the wineries here are easy to find. Make your way to Wente Champagne Cellars by taking Tesla Road back to make a left on Wente Street, which winds around to Marina Avenue, which ends up at Arroyo Road; a left on Arroyo leads you to the Wente complex. Go back to Arroyo and turn left on Wetmore Road to find Livermore Valley Cellars. Wetmore Road turns into Holmes Street, and then a left on E. Vallecitos Road (Highway 84) leads to both Thomas Coyne and Fenestra. Highway 84 runs through Sunol, where you'll find Elliston on Kilkare Road. Go back to Highway 84 and take it west for several miles until you hit Palomares Road. Here turn right and go up a winding road to Westover and Chouinard.

### Retzlaff Vineyards

**1356 S. Livermore Ave., Livermore 94550 • 510-447-8941**
**Weekdays 12–2, weekends 12–5 • Most varieties poured, no fee**
**Picnic area**

Truly a family-run operation, the compound of buildings off South Livermore Avenue often confuses first-time visitors. The owners, the Taylors, also make their home here, and the tasting room is unmarked. But once you drive down the gravel driveway past the farm machinery, you're committed; park anywhere and find the tasting room on the right.

Vintner Robert Taylor, a chemist at the Lawrence Livermore Lab, has fourteen acres of grapes and produces about 3,000 cases a year in what has become more than the original weekend diversion he anticipated. Riesling is still made here, along with Chardonnay, Sauvignon Blanc, Merlot, and an award-winning Cabernet.

### Concannon Vineyard

**4590 Tesla Rd., Livermore 94550 • 510-447-3760 • Weekdays**
**10–4:30, weekends 11–4:30 • Most varieties poured, no fee**
**Tours on weekends • Good gift selection • Picnic area**

Concannon has as long a history in the Livermore Valley as Wente does, which made them friendly competitors. So it's somewhat ironic that after Concannon changed ownership several times in the 1970s, a consortium led by Wente finally bought them out in 1992. After making it through Prohibition on its sales of sacramental wine, Concannon went on to make a reputation with Cabernet and the orphan grape, Petite Sirah. But by the time the wine boom rolled around, Concannon was not prepared, in a capital equipment and financial sense, to be a major participant. Wente has taken control, though as a separate and distinct entity, and for now all the traditional Concannon wines are being produced.

With encroaching suburbs in the visual background, the winery building still looks pretty much the same, with vineyards surrounding it. A picnic area with a gazebo under the shade trees makes the grounds a perfect respite for travelers. Vines cover the brick winery building, while the tasting room, with the entrance under a green awning, seems added on as a later extension. On a hot summer's day, though, it's cool, dark, and refreshing inside. Refreshing too are the Sauvignon Blanc and Chardonnay (Central Coast), as well as the Sauvignon Blanc–Semillon blend called Assemblage. Cabernet and Petite Sirah are old standbys. A rarely seen sweet wine fortified with Brandy, Muscat de Frontignan, makes a fine ending.

## Stony Ridge Winery

**4948 Tesla Rd., Livermore 94550 • 510-449-0660 • Daily 11–5**
**All varieties poured, no fee • Cafe on premises**

Stony Ridge Winery has been around for twenty years, but its last couple have been spent at this location on Tesla Road, sandwiched between Concannon and Wente. It seems perpetually busy during the day because locals congregate at the restaurant on the premises. Housed in a stucco building with a Spanish motif, the arched doorway on the patio leads to a small tasting area on the left. The rest of the space is taken up with restaurant business and display cases of takeout food.

Step up to the green-marble-topped tasting bar and enjoy a fine, buttery Chardonnay from Napa grapes or a Cabernet from El Dorado grapes. There's also Cabernet Franc, Sauvignon Blanc, Riesling, Merlot, and White Zinfandel. Malvasia Bianca is a well-balanced dessert wine; a good buy at only $6 per half bottle.

## Murrietta's Well

**3005 Mines Rd., Livermore 94550 • 510-449-9229**
**Weekends 11–4:30 • Most varieties poured, no fee**

Just off Tesla Road on a hillside beneath the sycamores, Murrietta's Well inhabits the historic nineteenth-century building that housed the original Mel Winery. Frenchman Louis Mel was one of the original champions of planting Sauvignon Blanc and Semillon, the traditional white wine grapes of his Bordeaux.

Today, the beautifully renovated winery, with barrel stacks out front, takes a different approach to Livermore Valley winemaking. One of the Wentes partnered with well-known local winemaker

Sergio Traverso to elevate the image of local wines by making the best possible white and red Bordeaux-style blends. Called Vendimia, the red is a traditional Cabernet-type blend, while the white combines Sauvignon Blanc and Semillon. Both are relatively expensive. Sometimes they also have an inky, monster Zinfandel available for tasting.

### Wente Brothers Winery

**5565 Tesla Rd., Livermore 94550 • 510-447-3603**
**Mon.–Sat. 10–4:30, Sun. 11–4:30 • Most varieties poured, no fee • Regular tours • Good gift selection • Picnic area**

Long the dominant winery in the area, Wente, nearly synonymous with winemaking in Livermore, is certainly the largest landholder and grape grower. This is the site of the original winery, which dates back to 1883; green and brown vines climbing to the roof soften its huge concrete-block industrial walls.

The tasting room, on the far end of the complex, is about thirty years old. Today it still seems uniquely modern, with its double octagonal brick rooms joined at the middle. Naturally, with the six-sided buildings, the Wentes put in a circular bar in the middle, allowing hosts to serve many tasters at once. And on summer weekends, the room definitely proves a popular spot. The Wentes really made their reputation on white wines, so don't miss the Chardonnays (sometimes three different kinds), Sauvignon Blanc, Semillon, or Riesling. Both the Merlot and Cabernet have gotten considerably better over the years. An excellent late-harvest Riesling provides the perfect ending.

### Cedar Mountain Winery

**7000 Tesla Rd., Livermore 94550 • 510-373-6636**
**Weekends 12–4 • Most varieties poured, no fee • Picnic area**

Producing about 1,000 cases a year, Cedar Mountain is probably the smallest winery in the valley, with an output that's just a drop in the bucket compared to Wente's, their closest winery neighbor. Owner Earl Ault, a physicist at the nearby Lawrence Livermore Lab—curiously there are a number of scientists/professors-turned-vintners in this valley—wanted to dabble in winemaking and set up shop in a barn further down Tesla Road near Greenfield Road.

His breakout vintage came in 1991, when his Cabernet got a rave review from *The Wine Enthusiast* magazine, a rarity for a small winery. A good Chardonnay is usually available for tasting.

## Wente Brothers Sparkling Wine Cellars

**5050 Arroyo Rd., Livermore 94550 • 510-447-3603**
**Mon.–Sat. 10–4:30, Sun. 11–4:30 • Most varieties poured,**
**no fee • Regular tours, usually on the hour**
**Restaurant adjacent • Excellent gift selection • No picnics**

In 1981 the Wentes purchased the long-abandoned Cresta Blanca Winery that Charles Wetmore founded in 1882. They planted the surrounding vineyards and restored the winery and sandstone aging caves. Spanish-themed whitewashed stucco buildings, with red tiled roofs and arched entryways, were constructed to serve as the hospitality center. Flora and fauna abound on the property; it's obvious that this is the Wentes' showpiece, where they hold all the special winery events and summer concerts.

The tasting room has the same clean, whitewashed look with a long blonde wooden bar and modern pin-point track lighting overhead. The tasting menu here is essentially identical to that of the original Wente winery, with the exception of the sparkling wines produced at this location. You'll find a very good Brut, along with a Blanc de Noir and a Blanc de Blanc. Two hundred yards across the way you'll see the Wente restaurant, great for a lunch meeting but also quite romantic in the evening.

## Livermore Valley Cellars

**1508 Wetmore Rd., Livermore 94550 • 510-447-1751**
**Daily 11:30–5 • All varieties poured, no fee • Picnic area**

This winery is small because, in some years, they don't make much wine! They have thirty-four acres of vines, planted in 1935, but the vineyard perennially produces a small crop. Follow a counry lane to find the cramped tasting room and winery building, along with the owner's personal residence. If you think there couldn't possibly be a winery here while driving up the gravel road, you're in the right place.

A large dog will greet you with a bark, not a bite. On a slow day, ring the buzzer, and one of the owners will saunter out to greet you. Since most of the small recent vintages sell out, you'll be poured odd but interesting wines, like an '84 Grey Riesling or an '86 Chardonnay reserve. The most recent wine still available for purchase is the '93 Old Vine Cuvee, a blend of Chardonnay, Riesling, Colombard, Golden Chasselas, and Lord knows what else. Actually, it's pretty tasty and a good buy at $7. Be sure and ask about the Rolls Royce of corks at this iconoclast winery.

## Thomas Coyne Winery

**51 E. Vallecitos Rd., Livermore 94550 • 510-373-6541**
**Weekends 12–5 • Most varieties poured, no fee • Picnic area**
After making wine for a number of years in an east bay warehouse, chemical engineer Tom Coyne moved his operation to Livermore Valley's oldest standing winery building, the historic 113-year-old Chateau Bellevue structure. Originally owned by Frenchman Alexander Duvall, Chateau Bellevue produced wines from 1881 to 1915, when the winery closed and the buildings were used for farm storage.

The renovated brick and stucco buildings house the new winery and tasting room, and while Coyne makes wines from Livermore Valley grapes, he also sources grapes from Napa and Sonoma too. Chardonnay, Cabernet, and Merlot are on the tasting list, but Coyne's curiosity shows up in other varietals, like Mourvedre, Petite Sirah, Zinfandel, and Port.

## Fenestra Winery

**83 E. Vallecitos Rd., Livermore 94550 • 510-862–2292**
**Weekends 12–5 • Most varieties poured, no fee • Picnic area**
Just up the road from Thomas Coyne, professor Lanny Replogle finally settled his Fenestra Winery in a weathered old barn that first served as a winery in 1889. For a number of years, his location was a moving target, until he finally decided to renovate the old True Winery. After retiring from teaching at San Jose State, he now devotes his full time to winemaking, having originally caught the wine bug as an amateur home winemaker.

White Zinfandel, Pinot Blanc, Chardonnay, Sauvignon Blanc, and Semillon are among the whites, while Cabernet, Merlot, Zinfandel, and Barbera are the reds. If the harvest conditions are right, you just might be offered some delicious late-harvest dessert wine. Prices are moderate, considering the quality.

## Elliston Vineyards

**463 Kilkare Rd., Sunol 94586 • 510-862-2377**
**Weekends 12–5 • Most varieties poured, no fee**
**Good gift selection**
The most famous thing about Elliston to this point in time is the fabulous old 1890 Victorian seventeen-room mansion that sits on the property. Used for business meetings, weddings, and private parties, it's been restored in loving detail. The tasting room, unfortunately, sits off to the side in a small cottage.

Sometime back, Dan Gehrs, formerly of Congress Springs and now at Zaca Mesa, served as consulting winemaker, and he put things on the right path at Elliston. Their strength lies in their white wines, including several Chardonnays, Pinot Blancs, and Pinot Gris, the latter two relatively rare in California. The Pinot Noir, Cabernet, and Bordeaux-style blends seem less interesting. A Malvasia Bianca provides a sweet finish.

## Westover Vineyards

**34932 Palomares Rd., Castro Valley 94546 • 510-537-3932**
**Weekends 12–5 • Most varieties poured, no fee • Picnic area**
This mom and pop winery lies further west, closer to Pleasanton than Livermore. The Spanish-style motif and the red tiled roofs identify the Westover compound. Inside, the tasting room seems like it might be a converted family room, with a pool table in the middle. Westover relies on purchased grapes for its wines but can be counted on for a thirst-quenching Chardonnay.

## Chouinard Vineyard

**33853 Palomares Rd., Castro Valley 94546 • 510-582-9900**
**Weekends 12–5 • Most varieties poured, no fee • Picnic area**
The Chouinard Vineyard supplements its couple of acres with purchased grapes to make a large number of varietals for such a small producer. Just a short distance from Westover, a red barn houses the winery with a picnic area nearby under sheltering shade trees. Hands-on winemakers, the Chouinards' attention to detail is reflected in fresh flavors of the wines. Zinfandel, Petite Sirah, and Cabernet are the reds, while Chardonnay, Riesling, and Semillon are the whites. Don't miss an unusual but tasty apple wine.

## SAN JOSE

*(listed from north to south)*

The two city wineries in San Jose open daily. For J. Lohr Winery, take U.S. 101 south to Interstate 880 south, exit Alameda, and go south about a mile to Lenzen Avenue. Backtrack to U.S. 101 and head south. Exit east on the Capitol Expressway to Aborn Road; turn right and head several miles up toward the hills to Mirassou.

## J. Lohr Winery

**1000 Lenzen Ave., San Jose 95126 • 408-288-5057**
**Daily 10–5 • Most varieties poured, no fee • Tours on weekends**
If you have notions about how rustic and romantic the wine-making business is, you can dissuade yourself by visiting J. Lohr

Winery, right in the heart of San Jose. Located in the old Fredericksburg Brewery, which dates back to 1869, this is urban, industrial winemaking at its highest level. J. Lohr sits across the street from the large Santa Clara health facility, so parking is at a premium, although you can usually squeeze into a spot on the west side of the winery's makeshift parking lot.

This has served as J. Lohr's main winery since 1974; several exist in other winemaking districts, though the only tasting room is here. In contrast to the exterior, the tasting room is subdued, quiet, and low key. Each varietal in the Cypress line costs less than $10 and is worthy of consideration; the line includes Chardonnay, Fume Blanc, Merlot, and Cabernet. However the two J. Lohr big sellers and perennial best buys on almost everybody's list are the Riverstone Chardonnay and Seven Oaks Cabernet; both have full, rich barrel-aged flavors but go down very easy.

## Mirassou Vineyards
**3000 Aborn Rd., San Jose 95135 • 408-274-4000**
**Daily 12–5 except Sun. 12–4 • Selected varieties poured,**
**no fee • Tours daily**

You'll have to wind your way through a shopping area and then several residential developments to see that civilization has pushed itself all the way to Mirassou's front door. The remaining vineyards marginally border the old stone winery buildings. Even the green hillsides to the south are becoming dotted with houses. In 1854, when Pierre Pellier planted Mirassou's first vineyards about one and one-half-miles northeast of the winery, this was considered way out in the country. Oh, what a difference 140 years makes! Decades ago, however, the Mirassou family foresaw the present condition and heavily invested in Monterey County vineyards to ensure the grape supply.

Look for the tasting room, covered with vines and perforated by an unusual glass wine-bottle window, right off the parking lot. During the week, two tasting bars stand ready right inside the door, and the knowledgeable staff will tell you as much as you want to know about the winery and the wines. Six specific selections, out of about two dozen, are usually available for tasting, and selections change monthly. On busy summer weekends, Mirassou opens the adjoining south hall, and the staff pours from long tables to make sure everyone gets to taste. The Mirassous have been most successful with the whites, particularly White Burgundy (a best buy), Pinot Blanc, Chardonnay, and Riesling. The reds have improved in recent years and exhibit more varietal character than in the past. Gamay, Petite Sirah, Zinfandel, Pinot Noir, Merlot, and Cabernet are the reds you may find on the tasting list.

## SOUTH SANTA CLARA

*(listed from east to west)*

Straight down U.S. 101 south, Gilroy is only about a half-hour from San Jose. First stop is technically in Morgan Hill, for Guglielmo and Pedrizzetti. For the former, take the Dunne Road exit, then go left on Condit Road and right on Main Street to the winery. Go back to Condit Road, continue south to San Pedro Street, and make a left to find Pedrizzetti. Get back on U.S. 101 and go all the way through Gilroy to the south end of town and Highway 25. Exit east and immediately take the frontage road back up to Rapazzini, by all the garlic shops. Now proceed north on U.S. 101 into Gilroy, and exit on Highway 152 west (Hecker Pass Highway). A half-dozen wineries, all clearly marked, are bunched along this road within several miles. After you've finished at Hecker Pass Winery at the far west end, backtrack on Highway 152, turning left at Watsonville Road; proceed several miles to Kirigin; then take Watsonville Road even further to Uvas Road to find Sycamore Creek.

### Emilio Guglielmo Winery
**1480 E. Main Ave., Morgan Hill 95037 • 408-779-2145**
**Daily 9–5 except Sun. 10–5 • Most varieties poured, no fee**
**Good gift selection • Picnic area**

Exiting U.S. 101, vineyards will come into view on East Main Street. Across from Live Oaks High School, you'll see several corrugated warehouse-style buildings. You might mistake a vine-covered rustic stone building for the tasting room, but it's actually straight back in the middle of the complex.

A third-generation member of the family will likely greet you inside the Old World tasting room, with its stucco walls, wood-beamed ceiling, and tiled floor. The wines, especially the reds, are still made in the rustic, gutsy Italian style begun by founder Emilio in 1925. The Italian Grignolino is a hearty red, as are the estate-bottled Cabernet, Zinfandel, Petite Sirah, and the blended Claret. White Zinfandel, Sauvignon Blanc, and Chardonnay are the whites to be sampled. Prices are reasonable, with nothing more than $12.

## Pedrizzetti Winery

**1645 San Pedro Ave., Morgan Hill 95037 • 408-779-7389**
**Daily 10–5 • All varieties poured, no fee • Picnic area hidden**
**in the back**

In 1945 John Pedrizzetti took over this small family winery established in 1913, with the idea of making drinkable, affordable everyday wines that reminded him of his Italian heritage. The old brick and stone slab winery has been expanded since then, with the tasting room in a separate building off to the side.

The tasting room, a small yellow cottage with blue trim and a red tiled roof, looks so cozy it seems like an extension of the Pedrizzettis' home. The white wines, Chardonnay, Riesling, and White Zinfandel, are OK, but the Pedrizzettis really shine with big reds like their Zinfandel, Petite Sirah, and Barbera. Chewy and teeth-staining, these are just the ticket with any tomato sauce and pasta dish. These wines don't have the most finesse, but by the same token, they are honest values, with no bottle more than $8.

## Rapazzini Winery

**4350 Monterey Rd., Gilroy 95037 • 408-842-5649 • Daily 9–6**
**Most varieties poured, no fee • Good gift selection**

Travelers know Rapazzini, destroyed by fire in 1980 and later rebuilt on this spot, because it sits right on the east side of U.S. 101, not far from all the garlic purveyors and fruit stands. The yellow corrugated warehouse building houses the winery operation, while the tasting room inhabits a rough-hewn stone building next to it. A large wine cask has been modified to create the double-doored entrance to the room, and a wonderful pounded copper-topped bar awaits tasters.

The tasting menu lists all the usual Cabernet and Chardonnay suspects and includes some oddballs, like honey wine, apricot wine, and cream marsala. But the main tasting event here has always been the famous Chateau de Garlic, which combines white wine with the essence of the stinking rose. It's the only garlic wine in the world, and they say it goes great with any Italian dish, especially one with garlic. An entire line of comestibles from Mama Rap's kitchen includes dressings, mustards, sauces, olives, olive oil, and almost anything that can be flavored with garlic. No breath mints though!

## A. Conrotto Winery
**1690 Hecker Pass Hwy., Gilroy 95020 • 408-842-3053**
**Sat.–Sun. 11–5; winter 11:30–5 • Most varieties poured, $1 fee**

If you blink, you'll miss this first winery west of Gilroy because it's on the left-hand side and not very well marked. Pull around back past the clapboard house until you see the sign Parking For Italians Only; All Others Will Be Towed. The winery operation doesn't even qualify as a barn; it's more like a shed, though the tasting room is right next to it.

In the early 1970s this winery made its wine in the basement of the house, but when it began to grow to around 5,000 cases, that proved impractical. The tasting room is in a small, dim utilitarian shack that was once the servants' quarters. The wines include Chardonnay, Sauvignon Blanc, Symphony, and a red wine blend of Petite Sirah, Cabernet, and Zinfandel. Sliding doors at the back open to a shaded wooden deck for leisurely sipping.

## Live Oaks Winery
**3875 Hecker Pass Hwy., Gilroy 95020 • 408-842-2401**
**Daily 10–5 • Selected varieties poured, no fee • Eclectic gift selection**

The Scagliotti family founded this winery in 1912, though a nurseryman has acquired it; you'll see a plethora of container plants for sale out front, bordering the highway. Turn in at the nursery and veer off down a gravel road past the barn until you come to an A-frame building that houses the combination winery and tasting room, burrowed into the hillside. Step down into a room that looks like a garage sale of knickknacks and walk all the way back to the tasting bar at the very end.

Your congenial host will likely be Al, who has presided over these premises longer than anyone can remember. He'll give has a low-key spiel as he pours the inexpensive Chenin Blanc, Riesling, Zinfandel, and Cabernet. More likely, the conversation will gravitate toward the thousands of celebrity pictures papered on every square inch of the tasting room. Al is a fountain of Hollywood trivia, and many of the public relations photos date back several decades. Young and old, living and dead; they're all enshrined in a winery tasting room that looks more like someone's basement.

## Solis Winery
**3920 Hecker Pass Hwy., Gilroy 95020 • 408-847-6306**
**Daily 11–5 except closed Mon. and Tues. in winter and spring**
**Most varieties poured, no fee • Picnic area**

Solis Winery dates back only to 1989, but—not surprising for this area—it too has an Italian heritage. The property is the site of the old Bertrero Winery that survived Prohibition but didn't make it to the wine boom of the 1980s. Later, it was called Summerhill until it came into the hands of the present owners, who wisely put University of California at Davis grad Corey Wilson in charge of the winemaking.

Directly across the road from Live Oaks, the tasting room has a wooden deck that fronts the perimeter and an ancient wine press out front. In the foyer, a rotating art show covers the walls; stepping down into the tasting room, you'll notice a half-moon tasting bar with brass footings and comfortable black arm rests. The big bay windows in back look out on the recently replanted vineyard and the winery, just down the lane. The Santa Clara Chardonnay and Riesling are good values under $8; the Seducente red blend falls into the same category. These are among the best wines from this area.

### Thomas Kruse Winery

**4390 Hecker Pass Hwy., Gilroy 95020 • 408-842-7016**
**Daily 12–5 • Most varieties poured, $1 fee applies to purchase**
Owner Thomas Kruse, a former professor, abandoned the academic life to become the iconoclast winemaker of southern Santa Clara County. You'll get some indication of this right away, as you note his hand-lettered cardboard sign of rules out front: No Ill-Behaved Children. No Bare Breasts. No Wine Snobs With Notebooks. No Large Groups of Republicans.

If you're not put off at that point, you'll have to knock around this complex of mishmashed buildings to stumble into the tasting area. Kruse isn't big on general tidyness, plus he obviously wants your visit to be an adventure. He revived an old Italian winery that lay dormant since the 1940s; he must have done some remodeling, though not so you'd notice. Viewing himself as the last outpost of prevailing winemaking tradition, he produces mostly red wines, like Grignolino, Carignane, Cabernet, Pinot Noir, and Zinfandel.

### Fortino Winery

**4525 Hecker Pass Hwy., Gilroy 95020 • 408-842-3305**
**Daily 9–6 • Most varieties poured, no fee • Excellent gift selection • Deli adjacent • Picnic area**
Fortino seems the most organized winery in the area, with a big parking lot the length of its white stucco California ranch-style building. A stained-glass window depicting ripe grapes decorates the double wooden-door entrance. Cool and dark inside, the tasting bar stretches fifty feet to handle the summer crowds. Large

wine casks loom high on both walls; some split wine casks on the floor serve as wine rack point-of-sale displays for the current offerings. The back half of the room is given over to wine-related and other gift items.

Ernie Fortino came here from Italy, bought and renamed this place after his family in 1970. He likes to make wines in the everyday-drinking Italian style, and that's what you'll find here. Skip the white wines; they're just window dressing. Fortino's real forte is big, mouth-filling red wines, like Cabernet, Zinfandel, and Pinot Noir. On a recent visit, Fortino was blowing out the '88 Petite Sirah for $54 a case, and the '89 Charbono was right behind it at $57. You can get already-aged Cabernets, starting with the '91 vintage and going all the way back to '75! In addition, two doors down in the same complex, an Italian-style deli awaits you, with cold pasta salads and full deli sandwiches costing around $5. A multitude of picnic tables rests under the shade trees just across the parking lot.

### Hecker Pass Winery

**4605 Hecker Pass Hwy., Gilroy 95020 • 408-842-8755**
**Daily summer 9–6, winter 10–5 • Most varieties poured, no fee**
**Picnic area**

Mario Fortino, Ernie's brother, decided he needed to open his own place in 1972, but he didn't go too far—just to the next turn in the road. In contrast to Ernie's place, Mario's tasting room is a dark rectangular building with red trim that's attached to his house and winery. He makes the wines in a similar vigorously flavored style, but to his own taste.

Only two white wines are on the tasting menu; skip those and go right to what Mario calls "medium dry red wines," meaning they have a touch of sweetness to them. Many people find they like this style and find Red Velvet and Hostess Burgundy delicious. In the bone-dry style, Zinfandel, Carignane, and Petite Sirah are the choices. Finish up with a medal-winning Cream Sherry or Port. Everything is less than $8.

### Kirigin Cellars

**11550 Watsonville Rd., Gilroy 95020 • 408-847-8827**
**Daily 10–5 • All varieties poured, no fee • Picnic area**

This winery sits off the main highway, on a back road between Gilroy and Morgan Hill; it's a little quieter and more rural. Signs on Watsonville Road direct you to Kirigin, and a circular drive takes you past a residence and around back to the winery and tasting room. Shrouded in vines and with a split barrel serving as a door, the tasting room has a no-nonsense linoleum floor and yellowing newspaper clippings about the winery on the walls.

If Nic Kirigin himself holds court in the tasting room, then you're in luck. Nic's a native of Croatia who retains his European accent; he came to California and worked for Peretti-Minelli and San Martin Winery before setting up shop here in the Uvas Valley in 1976. He basically doesn't believe in blending, so all his wines are one hundred percent varietal. He's happy to pour you a spot of all his wines, including Sauvignon Blanc, Chardonnay, Muscat, Pinot Noir, and Zinfandel. Some of his older Cabernets available are from the '84 and '85 vintages. He'll twist your arm to try his special dessert wine called Vino de Mocca, a blend of wine, orange, chocolate, and coffee. It may not sound attractive on paper, but it's a kick; seems like everyone who tastes it ends up buying a bottle. Everything costs less than $9.

### Sycamore Creek Vineyards

**12775 Uvas Rd., Morgan Hill 95037 • 408-779-4738**
**Sat.–Sun. 11:30–5 • Selected varieties poured, no fee**
**Picnic area**

Near the intersection of Uvas and Watsonville roads, you'll see a series of buildings that constitute Sycamore Creek Vineyards. Cross the narrow one-lane "bridge" over the dry creek bed, and park on the hillside across from the outdoor stainless steel fermenting tanks. Walk back toward the shaded gazebo, and you'll see a white barn, where the tasting room is located.

In 1975 a couple of schoolteachers began renovating the property, though it seems they didn't give too much thought to a visitors' center. The winery was sold in 1989 to a Japanese concern, which sent its own winemaker and increased the winery's production. The tasting room lies atop a flight of stairs in the barn, with rickety wooden floors and open-air windows. Here you'll get an example of rustic tasting room minimalism at its finest, though the unobstructed views of vineyards are pretty. But then, the wine's the reason for visiting, not the decor. The Sauvignon Blanc always sells out, and the Chardonnay is popular too. Among the reds, the Gamay is a quaffer, while the Cabernet is more serious. For dessert, try Romeo and Juliet, a late-harvest Riesling subtitled Lover's Nectar.

## RESTAURANTS

Since the wineries of Bay Area spread over a wide geographic area, it's difficult to recommend many specific restaurants. Certainly Livermore, Pleasanton, and San Jose have many restaurants where you can get a good meal. But if you're making day trips to these wineries out of San Francisco or Berkeley, then you'll have thousands of restaurant choices when you get back for dinner, obviously too numerous to mention here. Best tip: Wherever you stay, ask locals for their best recommendations. They won't be bashful about telling you.

### Stony Ridge Cafe
**4948 Tesla Rd., Livermore 94550 • 510-449-0660**
**Mon.–Sat. 11–5 • No reservations • Italian • Inexpensive**
How thoughtful it was for someone to put a deli-style place in the middle of Livermore Valley wine country. In fact, the same family that runs the Stony Ridge Winery takes care of the food side of things too. Now, the Carnegie Deli it ain't. Yes, the selection is limited, but you'll always find a couple of standard deli items on the menu, along with something in the way of creative pastas, salads, and sandwiches. It's primarily a lunch destination for the surrounding community, but Stony Ridge serves until 5 P.M., so you can get a substantial meal there anytime and enjoy it with a glass of wine on the sun-drenched patio.

### Wente Brothers Sparkling Wine Cellars Restaurant
**5050 Arroyo Rd., Livermore 94550 • 510-447-3696**
**Lunch and dinner daily; Sun. brunch • Reservations recommended • California/American • Moderate to expensive**
The Wentes wisely built a signature restaurant adjacent to their sparkling wine cellars and hospitality center in this semirural area. It's become a landmark destination for dinner in the east Bay Area. The spectacular vineyard setting makes you feel you've entered another world; the dining room is warm, moody, and intimate. Expect daily seasonal specials—chicken, duck, lamb—and, during the week, a wonderful *prix fixe* menu, a comparative bargain. Great award-winning wine list too.

### Harvest Time
**7397 Monterey Rd., Gilroy 95020 • 408-842-7575 • Lunch and dinner daily • Reservations recommended California/American • Moderate**
Okay, so not every dish comes with the local garlic, but plenty do. Beef, chicken, veal, and fresh seafood prepared in a variety of

ways, grace the menu, and the chef cooks up daily specials based on what fresh produce is in-season (he's big on mushrooms). The casual-yet-charming atmosphere of this neo-Victorian is nostalgically relaxing. A good list of local wines are featured.

### Station 55

**55 W. Fifth St. (downtown), Gilroy 95020 • 408-847-5555**
**Lunch and dinner daily • Reservations recommended**
**American • Moderate**

The old, brick fire station downtown has been artfully remodeled, but the fire house theme has been retained. Burgers are popular at lunch, while prime rib and barbecue ribs are the big draw at dinner. Shrimp, salmon, and chicken round things out, though you'll sometimes find an anomaly like bagna cauda or even a German dish sneaking onto the menu.

## ANNUAL EVENTS

### FEBRUARY

**Taste of the Valley • 510-462-3570**
Elegant food and wine tasting with the finest gourmet creations from local chefs and the best wines from Livermore Valley wineries. A fund-raiser for the Volunteer Center.

**Livermore Valley Barrel Tasting • 510-447-WINE**
Each winery in the valley offers tastings from the most recent vintage in barrels; many have special food, wine, and entertainment events at the individual wineries.

### APRIL

**Spring Wine Festival • P.O. Box 1192 • Morgan Hill 95037**
**408-779-2145**
Sponsored by the Santa Clara Valley Wine Growers' Association at Casa de Fruta Country Park. Outdoor wine festival featuring all the Santa Clara County wineries, plus food booths and live music.

### JULY

**Gilroy Garlic Festival • 408-842-1625**
The annual event, celebrating anything and everything about the stinking rose, is held on the grounds of Christmas Hill Park. Live

music, cooking demonstrations, garlic displays, arts and crafts booths, plus tons of garlic food, garlic wine, and garlic ice cream!

## SEPTEMBER

**Livermore Valley Harvest Festival • 510-447-WINE**
Celebration of harvest at all participating Livermore Valley wineries. Special food and wine events scheduled at each winery.

## OCTOBER

**Santa Clara Valley Fall Harvest Festival • P.O. Box 1192 Morgan Hill 95037 • 510-477-WINE, charge line 800-548-3813**
Wine, food, grape stomping, and live music at the annual harvest festival sponsored by the Santa Clara Valley Wine Growers' Association at Casa de Fruta Country Park.

## RESOURCES

**Gilroy Visitors' Bureau**
7780 Monterey Rd. • Gilroy 95020 • 408-842-6436
Restaurants, accommodations, and recreational activities.

**Livermore Chamber of Commerce**
2157 First St. • Livermore 94550 • 510-447-1606
Restaurants, accommodations, and recreational activities.

**Livermore Valley Wine Growers' Association**
P.O. Box 2052 • Livermore 94551 • 510-447-WINE
Full-color winery touring map.

**San Jose Convention and Visitors' Bureau**
333 W. San Carlos St. • San Jose 95110 • 408-998-7000
Restaurants, accommodations, and recreational activities.

**Santa Clara Valley Wine Growers**
P.O. Box 1192 • Morgan Hill 95037 • 408-779-2145
Full-color winery touring map with winery histories and descriptions.

# SANTA CRUZ

Quite a few small boutique-style wineries sit just outside San Jose on its western flank of ridges; many more are sprinkled throughout the mountains all the way down to the sea at Santa Cruz. Here you can find hobbyist winemakers, self-proclaimed family operators, and just folks fortunate enough to escape the nearby high-tech rat race of Silicon Valley. The majority of these wineries are not open to the public, even though you can easily find their wines in local shops and restaurants. Something about the idiosyncratic lifestyle of Santa Cruz coupled with the Jeremiah Johnson mountain man/winemaker image begs for privacy. But more and more wineries are opening their doors to visitors, albeit mainly on weekends.

Due to the very nature of the mountain geography, the Santa Cruz area will always provide a homestead for smaller, more eccentric wine producers. In the late nineteenth century, vineyards were planted around Bonny Doon, Woodside, and Los Gatos. The famous Montebello vineyard planted more than one hundred years ago still survives today, the source of Ridge's famous Cabernet. It was a burgeoning business for several decades, but few of the wineries survived Prohibition. Paul Masson's winery made it and was later purchased by the late Martin Ray, the most well-known promoter of wines in the area during the 1950s. David Bruce, a protégé of Ray's, went off to found his own winery, while a partnership established Ridge; thus a bit of a vineyard revival began.

In the last fifteen years, acreage planted to the vine has dramatically increased, as the area becomes known as a unique grape-growing region; still only a couple hundred acres of vines exist here.

# Santa Cruz

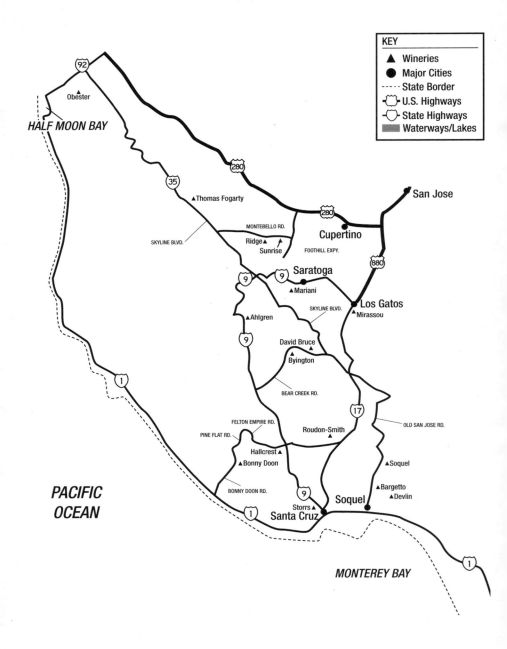

**KEY**

▲ Wineries
● Major Cities
---- State Border
〔〕 U.S. Highways
〔〕 State Highways
▓ Waterways/Lakes

92

▲ Obester

HALF MOON BAY

280

35

▲ Thomas Fogarty

280

San Jose

MONTEBELLO RD.
SKYLINE BLVD.
Ridge ▲
Sunrise ▲
Cupertino
FOOTHILL EXPY.

880

9    9    Saratoga
▲ Mariani

SKYLINE BLVD.
▲ Ahlgren
Los Gatos
▲ Mirassou

9
David Bruce
▲
Byington

1

BEAR CREEK RD.

17

FELTON EMPIRE RD.
PINE FLAT RD.
Roudon-Smith
▲
OLD SAN JOSE RD.

Hallcrest ▲
▲ Bonny Doon

▲ Soquel

PACIFIC
OCEAN

BONNY DOON RD.
9
Storrs ▲
Santa Cruz
Soquel
▲ Bargetto
▲ Devlin

1

MONTEREY BAY

1

Ridge is far and away the leading producer at 40,000 cases, a mere drop in the bucket to some of the larger Napa and Sonoma vintners. Some wineries produce as few as 1,000 cases, and you'll obviously have a hard time obtaining them outside the local area. Families own and operate almost all these wineries, so when you visit the tasting rooms, you may get a sense that you're talking to someone directly and enthusiastically involved in the winery's operations.

## WINERIES

Due to the geography of the Santa Cruz Mountains, the wineries spread wildly across the landscape. Many hide in areas reached by ridge routes or winding mountain roads. Don't expect an area like Napa Valley, where you can pick off wineries right and left. Certainly it takes several days to visit all the wineries, from the ridge-side communities of Cupertino, Saratoga, and Los Gatos all the way down to the ocean in Santa Cruz and beyond to Soquel. Keep in mind that many only open on weekends. I highly recommend using the free map provided by Santa Cruz Mountain Winegrowers' Association (see Resources at the end of this chapter). It makes the checkerboard area of winery roads much easier to comprehend.

Starting from the San Jose area, take Interstate 880 southwest to catch Interstate 280 north (from San Francisco, take I-280 south and reverse this order). Exit on Foothill Expressway and go left under the freeway. Foothill turns into Stevens Canyon Road; turn right when you come to Montebello Road and climb this winding road to Sunrise Winery and Ridge Vineyards.

Come back down off the ridge to Stevens Canyon Road and turn right; go several miles and fork to the left on Mount Eden Road, which turns into Pierce Road. Turn right at Congress Springs Road (Highway 9) to Mariani Winery. From Mariani, you can go two different ways. Reversing direction, go back to Highway 9, now Big Basin Way, and follow it past Saratoga and into Los Gatos, where you'll find Mirassou Champagne Cellars on College Avenue. Or if you continue on Highway 9 past Mariani, turn right on Skyline Boulevard and go several miles to Thomas Fogarty Winery; then if you're more interested in the scenery than wineries, travel all the way up Skyline Boulevard and go left on Highway 92, where shortly you'll come across Obester Winery, only several miles from the ocean in Half Moon Bay.

If you choose Half Moon Bay, you can travel south on Highway 1 and continue touring at Bonny Doon, four miles up Bonny Doon Road. If you're at Mirassou, return to Highway 9, and just past Skyline Boulevard is Ahlgren Vineyard. Follow Highway 9 and make a left at Bear Creek Road for Byington Winery and David Bruce Winery. Backtracking to Highway 9 again, go right on Felton Empire Road a short distance to Hallcrest Vineyards. Continue on Felton Empire Road as it becomes Ice Cream Grade, and turn left at Pine Flat Road, driving two miles to Bonny Doon Vineyard.

Follow Bonny Doon Road down to the ocean and Highway 1, turn left, and go about eight miles into Santa Cruz. Turn right on River Street (opposite Highway 9) and right again on Potrero Street for Storrs Winery. Go back to Highway 1, and turn right to go to Soquel and the Bargetto Winery; take the Porter Street exit and then make a quick right on Main Street, going through a residential area; for Soquel Vineyards, continue further on Main Street until it forks right to Glen Haven Road; the winery will be on your right. Continuing back down Highway 1 to the Park Avenue exit, go east. Follow the signs to the end of Park Avenue and up a hill to Devlin Wine Cellars.

If you're headed back up to San Jose, backtrack on Highway 1, go up Highway 17, and exit at the Mount Hermon Road turnoff, headed toward Felton; turn right at Scotts Valley Drive, and then a left turn comes up quickly at Bean Creek Road. Several twisty miles later you'll find Roudon-Smith Winery. To go to San Jose, get back to Highway 17 and head north; for Santa Cruz, take Highway 17 south.

### Sunrise Winery

**13100 Montebello Rd., Cupertino 95014 • 408-741-1310**
**Fri.–Sun. 11–3 • Most varieties poured, no fee • Hiking trail**
**Picnic area**

Located at the old Picchetti Ranch, Sunrise Winery traces its history back to the 1880s; the Zinfandel vines here are almost as old and, until recently, went into a distinctive bottling at nearby Ridge Vineyards. The entire area will now look the same to future generations because it has become part of the Montebello Open Space Preserve. The present owners of the winery, the husband and wife team of Ron and Rolayne Storz, have lovingly restored the property.

Winding up Montebello Road, several old barn structures come into view on the left; a large parking lot exists to accommodate not only winery visitors but hikers and naturalists who take advantage of the protected open space. Walking past the older buildings, a newer-looking red and white barn-style building, just a short hike up the hill, houses the tasting room. Sunrise makes wines in minuscule quantities, and Zinfandel is a definite must; also try Pinot Noir, Pinot Blanc, Cabernet, and Chardonnay.

### Ridge Vineyards

**17100 Montebello Rd., Cupertino 95015 • 408-867-3233**
**Sat.–Sun. 11–3 • Selected varieties poured, no fee**

If you make the incredibly winding drive up Montebello Road to find Ridge, you'll feel the winery should reward you with great wines. Most of the time, you won't be disappointed. Your reward will also include spectacular views of the valley below. But then you may wonder who would be crazy enough to plant vineyards at 2,600 feet and burrow a three-story winery into the mountainous hillside. Ridge began as a lark in 1959, started by a couple of engineers (obviously mad!) as a recreational activity, though the vineyard origins go back a hundred years.

From its small family origins, Ridge grew to become one of the largest quality producers in the area and was sold to Japanese interests some time back. However, Paul Draper, the twinkle-eyed winemaker/philosopher who came on board in 1969, still works his magic with the wines. Zinfandel, both the Lytton Springs and Geyserville, is great stuff; the Montebello Cabernet, a pricey monster, ranks with the best in California, while the Petite Sirah is a collector's item. The rustic tasting room isn't much to look at; on nice weekends, the tasting room moves to two tables set up outside so everyone can soak up the view along with the wine.

### Mariani Winery

**23600 Congress Springs Rd., Saratoga 95070 • 408-741-2930**
**Daily 11–5 • Selected varieties poured, no fee • Good gift selection • Picnic area**

The old Congress Springs Winery, where Dan Gehrs once held sway as winemaker, went through a change of ownership in the early 1990s. Now owned by two families, it's more or less on the same course, though wine quality may have slipped a notch or two since Gehrs's departure.

Barreling down Congress Springs Road, you'll likely miss the winery, situated on a curve and sheltered by the massive redwoods. The tasting room, separate from the winery on the property, is in a small rough-hewn wooden building that's more than eighty years old. Among the whites produced are Pinot Blanc, Sauvignon

Blanc, Riesling, Semillon, and multiple Chardonnays. The reds include Cabernet, Cabernet Franc, Merlot, and Zinfandel.

## Mirassou Champagne Cellars

**300 College Ave., Los Gatos 95032 • 408-395-3790**
**Wed.–Sun. 12–5 • Most varieties poured, no fee • Daily tours available • Small gift selection**

The brothers of the Novitiate began making wine here in the late nineteenth century. But the pressures of competing in the marketplace of the current wine boom convinced them to get out of the winemaking business altogether. While they still own this beautiful and historic property, the Mirassous took it over solely to produce their sparkling wines. Expansion was limited due to urban encroachment at their original facility in San Jose; they found this an adaptable and visitor-friendly site.

The Spanish mission-style winery and visitors' center is burrowed into the hillside, just above the town of Los Gatos. The sparklers produced are uniformly refreshing if not especially complex; they include the Brut, Blanc de Noir, and Au Naturel.

## Thomas Fogarty Winery

**19501 Skyline Blvd., Woodside 94062 • 415-851-6777**
**Thur.–Sun. 11–6, by appointment only • Most varieties poured, no fee**

Fogarty is one of many wineries located in a quasi-residential district in which local authorities may discourage wine-minded visitors by restricting advertised access. Read: Neighbors don't want to be disturbed by all the winery traffic, so you need to call ahead to make an appointment for tasting at the winery. But do call; it's worth it, if only for the majestic, panoramic view of the Bay Area, all the way from Mount Diablo to Mount Hamilton. Oh, and the wines are excellent too!

Slightly east and south of Stanford University, Fogarty produces the most award-winning Gewurztraminer in the state, one that is consistent from vintage to vintage. Chardonnay, Cabernet, and Pinot Noir are made with equal commitment and focus on quality and flavor complexity. It's a treat to taste in their glass-enclosed tasting room or adjacent wooden balcony, overlooking the vineyards.

## Obester Winery

**12341 San Mateo Rd. (Highway 92), Half Moon Bay 94019**
**415-726-9463 • Daily 10–5 • Selected varieties poured, no fee**

The Obesters started out as home winemakers, making batches of Zinfandel in their garage under the tutelage of Grandpa

Gemello, who had a long history of winemaking under the Gemello label. Of course, they got bitten by the winemaking bug and retrofitted an old hay barn in Half Moon Bay as their winemaking facility and tasting room.

Today, the old weathered barn looks like it was always meant to be a winery; it looks comfortable in its surroundings. People primarily know Obester for its white wines; Sauvignon Blanc, Riesling, and Chardonnay always seem fresh and fruity. Sangiovese and Cabernet might also be on the tasting menu, as well as special editions of Zinfandel, bottled under the Gemello label to commemorate Grandpa's contributions to the winery.

## Ahlgren Vineyard

**20320 Highway 9, Boulder Creek 95006 • 408-338-6071**
**Sat. only 12–4 • Selected varieties poured, no fee**
Dexter and Val Ahlgren have made small amounts of wine here for almost twenty years, after getting bitten by the bug while making wine in the garage of their Sunnyvale home. In 1972 they purchased this Santa Cruz Mountains property, which became the site for their vineyard, while the winery sits underneath their residence. Consequently, they open their home winery only on Saturdays. At this real mom and pop operation, you'll get the feeling they are properly proud of their wines and happy to talk about them.

Chardonnay and Cabernet are the main thing, but various vintages of Pinot Noir, Semillon, Sauvignon Blanc, and Chenin Blanc are often available. Production is limited, and distribution is not wide, so stock up if you like what you taste.

## Byington Winery

**21850 Bear Creek Rd., Los Gatos 95030 • 408-354-1111**
**Daily 11–5 • Most varieties poured, no fee • Small gift selection**
**Excellent picnic areas with views**
This winery looks like something out of a fairy tale, which probably explains why so many weddings occur on its Wedding Hill, which provides a clear view of redwood forests all the way to the Monterey Bay. It's the opposite of David Bruce (below). The gray stone building with the red tiled roof resembles a French chateau. The pinkish-orange tiles in the entryway lead to the tasting room, with a massive two-story wood-beamed ceiling and rough stone fireplace. The windows, near the tasting bar, look

directly into the winery's barrel room. The total impression is of a dignified, stately manor.

The white wines start with a popular Sauvignon Blanc (and a best buy), proceed to several Chardonnays, and end with a stylized Gewurztraminer. The reds include a Zinfandel, Merlot, and Cabernet. Gazebos shade many of the picnic areas, and a number have barbecue grills, making this an excellent place to stop for a picnic with a view.

### David Bruce Winery

**21439 Bear Creek Rd., Los Gatos 95030 • 408-354-4214, 800-397-9972 • Wed.–Sun. 12–5 • Selected varieties poured, no fee**

Dermatologist David Bruce blazed trails in this area since establishing his own winery in 1964. A disciple of Martin Ray, he was convinced grapes from the mountainous area could produce wine of world-class intensity and breeding. He carved a slice out of the hills on Bear Creek Road and began planting vines; today he is one of the largest producers in the area.

A cooling tank stands out front on the property, where a corrugated building has been added to the utilitarian stone-block winery. Park there, and then walk around the curve (past the double-wide trailer) and up the hill to the tasting room, which once functioned as the actual winery. It hasn't been gussied up since the old days, retaining the concrete floors and wood walls. Cases of wine are stacked around the perimeter, and a V-shaped bar beckons would-be tasters from one corner of the room. Several Chardonnays are available, but the big thing here is Pinot Noir. Bruce has been on a mission to make great Pinot Noir, and in some years, he has succeeded handily, particularly with the estate and reserve versions. Petite Sirah and Cabernet are of the big, brawny style. Many older vintages and special sampler cases come available at the winery only.

### Hallcrest Vineyards

**379 Felton Empire Rd., Felton 95018 • 408-335-4441, 800-699-9463 • Daily 11–5:30 • Selected varieties poured, no fee • Good gift selection • Picnic area**

Just off Highway 9 on a sunlit knoll, Hallcrest sits among the oaks and conifers. You can see a rolling, dry-farmed vineyard that tops the hill from the parking area; a short walk leads down to the redwood tasting room in what looks like an old schoolhouse or church, with a bell at the top. The shaded wooden patio provides plenty of room for picnicking, just outside the double doors of the tasting room.

Chafee Hall first established this historic wine site in 1941 (hence the name Hallcrest). About fifteen years ago, the Schumacher family took over the operation and moved toward producing wines from organically farmed grapes. They bottled those wines, produced without using chemicals or sulfites, under their Organic Wine Works label. Wines made from purchased grapes, with minimal handling, are bottled under the traditional Hallcrest label. Riesling is perhaps the house favorite, made from old vines surrounding the winery. Fume Blanc, Chardonnay, Petite Sirah, Zinfandel, Pinot Noir, Merlot, Barbera, and Cabernet may be open for tasting on a given day.

## Bonny Doon Vineyard

**10 Pine Flat Rd. (eight miles north of Santa Cruz), Bonny Doon 95060 • 408-425-3625 • Thurs.–Mon. 12–5 in winter; daily 12–5 except Tues. in summer • Selected varieties poured, no fee • Small gift selection • Picnic area nearby**

Winemaker Randall Grahm has taken over the local iconoclast mantle from pioneer Martin Ray, with his extensive philosophical rantings but with burgeoning curiosity about any and all of the wine grapes of the world. At one time or another, Grahm has explored traditional varieties, like Chardonnay and Pinot Noir, but he has also gotten knee-deep in French Rhone-style grapes and Italian varietals. And don't forget his fruit infusions (raspberry, blueberry, strawberry), his ice wines (dessert), and his grappas (a potent after-dinner drink).

The tasting room and winery are located in the hamlet of Bonny Doon—apparently the only things in Bonny Doon. Driving several miles down the hill from Hallcrest or four miles up from Highway 1 puts you at the tasting room, a spot once known to locals as The Lost Weekend Saloon. Bonny Doon has nearly achieved cult status among wine buffs, so expect a line at the V-shaped tasting bar. All the wines have funny names, including Le Cigare Volant, Old Telegram, and Clos de Gilroy, but all are tasty. Wines under the Ca del Solo label, like Big House Red, Il Pescatore, and Pacific Rim Riesling, are inexpensive and wonderfully drinkable.

## Storrs Winery

**303 Potrero St., No. 35, Old Sash Mill, Santa Cruz 95060 408-458-5030 • Fri.–Mon. 12–5 • Most varieties poured, no fee Small gift selection**

The husband-wife team of Stephan and Pamela Storrs took over the former Frick Winery site in the Old Sash Mill complex only a few blocks from the ocean in Santa Cruz. Both Storrses graduated from viticultural school, and both worked at the old Felton-Empire Winery (Hallcrest) before striking out on their own. They are strong proponents of Santa Cruz Mountains grapes and source their grapes from small microclimates within the region. Your tasting room host will likely be a member of the family and, given the slightest prompting, will happily point out the geography of the various vineyards on the large map that hangs opposite the tasting bar.

Single-vineyard Chardonnays are what Storrs does best. Each receives the full Burgundian treatment of barrel and malolactic fermentation, along with extended aging in French oak, which imparts rich, creamy, complex flavors. The reds, Merlot, Petite Sirah, and Zinfandel, are big, concentrated, and full bodied. Production is around 3,000 cases total—a look through the winery door indicates it's bursting at the seams with barrels stacked to the ceiling—and prices are moderate for such quality.

### Bargetto Winery

**3535 N. Main St., Soquel 95073 • 408-475-2258**
**Daily 9:30–5, except Sun. 11–5 • Most varieties poured, limited to four selections, no fee • Tours daily • Excellent gift selection**
**Picnic area**

The Bargetto family, now in its third generation, is one of the oldest and largest producers in the area, dating back to 1933. A more bucolic setting for a winery could not exist: right on Main Street, which is not a center of commerce but a tree-lined residential area off the main drag. A large parking lot in front is essential because ever-changing events occur here throughout the year, including art displays, craft shows, and the occasional Sunday brunch. The tasting room has a woodsy, homey feel, with dark wooden beams and a long bar at the back. Old portraits of the Bargettos along with ancient agricultural implements line the walls. The large windows and side patio overlook the gurgling Soquel Creek.

Except for the special Santa Cruz Mountains Cabernet and Chardonnay, the wines are inexpensively priced at $10 or less. A full range of selections include White Zin, Merlot, Chardonnay, Cabernet, Gewurztraminer, Sauvignon Blanc, and Moscato. Don't leave without trying one of the special sweet fruit wines released under the Chaucer's label. These dessert offerings include raspberry, olallieberry, apricot, and even mead.

## Soquel Vineyards

**7880 Glen Haven Rd., Soquel 95073 • 408-462-9045**
**Sat. only, April 4–Dec. 24 • Selected varieties poured, no fee**

The 2,000-case Soquel Vineyards was started in 1987 by Jon Morgan, Peter Bargetto, and Paul Bargetto, the latter two brothers from the clan of the famous and much larger winery down the road. They planned to produce limited quantities of outstanding wines from Santa Cruz Mountains grapes as well as from the Stag's Leap district in Napa. The winery is situated well back in a woodsy residential area; don't mistake the house with the pink flamingos for the tasting room. Look for the winery down the hill, past the curved wooden sign proclaiming Grover Gulch Winery—Est. 1979. More of an overgrown garage, you'll recognize it as the gray wood-sided building with the corrugated tin roof.

Tastings here are very informal, conducted on the small concrete crush pad outside the winery's front doors. Your host will likely pour Chardonnay unless it's sold out. A number of vintages of both Cabernet and Pinot Noir come from the famous Martin Ray estate vineyards, and occasionally Soquel offers a Zinfandel. Prices are in the high teens, but the wines present a good example of the old-fashioned, handcrafted way of doing things.

## Devlin Wine Cellars

**3801 Park Ave., Soquel 95073 • 408-476-7288**
**Weekends only 12–5; closed Superbowl Sunday**
**Selected varieties poured, no fee**

Take a drive through the backwoods to a hilltop vista and a building that looks suspiciously like a ranch-style private residence. The guard dog may actually manage to open his eyes and look up as you quizzically exit your car. Not to worry; this *is* the home of Chuck and Cheryl Devlin, who started the winery in this isolated spot in 1978. The tasting room lies to the left in what formerly must have been their recreation room; a full-size pool table sits in the middle of things, a holdover from their previous nonwinemaking lives. The actual winery is further back on the property.

The Devlins offer a wide range of wines which, depending on the vintage, may include White Zin, Sauvignon Blanc, Gamay, and Muscat. Chardonnay is particularly good, as well as the big, beefy reds: Merlot, Cabernet, and Zinfandel. Expect extremely moderate prices, and you won't see these wines much outside the area.

## Roudon-Smith Winery

**2364 Bean Creek Rd., Santa Cruz 95066 • 408-438-1244**
**Sat. 11–4:30 • Most varieties poured, no fee**
The Roudon and Smith families teamed up to make wine in 1972 and later moved to this property deep in the forest-laden Santa Cruz hills. Signage is minimal, so keep your eyes peeled; if you stumble onto an incredible mansion that seems incongruous here, that's not it, but you are within striking distance of the winery. Five acres of estate vines surround the winery, which is about as strictly functional as it can get. A simple weathered brown plywood building that has stood the test of time houses the winery. Walk around to the back and up the ramp into the bare bones tasting room, carved out of one corner of the warehouse-style winery.

The best (and most expensive) wines are the Pinot Noir and Chardonnay, both made from Santa Cruz grapes; the rest of the line, including Gewurztraminer, Zinfandel, and Petite Sirah go for around $10 or less. One of their specialties is an easy-drinking red, simply labeled Claret, which is a blend of different red wine varietals; it often sells for $50 a case and makes for a good everyday quaff.

## RESTAURANTS

## Cafe Sparrow

**8042 Soquel Dr., Aptos 95003 • 408-688-6238 • Lunch and dinner daily, Sun. brunch • Reservations recommended**
**French • Moderate to expensive**
Tucked away in Aptos, this charming little cafe might remind you of a quaint countryside bistro in France. Well-prepared salads and sandwiches are popular at lunchtime; in the evening, the menu might include a full-on caesar salad, rack of lamb or venison in dark cherry sauce, or Steak Diane. The wine list is a plus.

## Casablanca

**101 Main St. (corner of Beach St.), Santa Cruz 95060**
**408-426-9063 • Dinner daily, Sun. brunch**
**Reservations recommended • California/American cuisine**
**Moderate to expensive**
Locals and tourists alike have long made their way to this fantastic old estate cum restaurant that offers fine views of the Monterey Bay as well as imaginative food. Fresh fish, chops, steak, chicken,

and pastas loom large on the menu; the wine list wins awards. The Sunday Champagne brunch is wildly popular for good reason.

## Ciao Bella

**9217 Highway 9, Ben Lomond 95005 • 408-336-9221**
**Dinner daily, weekend brunch • Reservations recommended**
**Italian • Moderate**

Ciao Bella offers an oasis of good Italian food in the rural mountain community of Ben Lomond. The homey restaurant with the funky decor has a beautiful heated patio deck right in the middle of a grove of redwoods. A jovial unpretentious atmosphere prevails, and the friendly staff brings out plates of gnocchi, ravioli, and many other pasta selections. The flavorful entrees include scampi in garlic, butter, and lemon; and chicken with prosciutto, mozzarella, and fresh basil.

## Chez Renee

**9051 Soquel Dr., Aptos 95003 • 408-688-5566 • Lunch and**
**dinner Tues.–Sat. • Reservations recommended • French**
**Moderate to expensive**

Probably the most refined French cooking in the area is done by the mom and pop team of Jack and Renee Chyle at Chez Renee. Set among the redwoods, this romantic spot has wowed diners for more than ten years. Menu offerings change daily but might include things like eggplant terrine, several fresh pastas, halibut with wild mushrooms, duck with brandied cherries, and a panoply of desserts hand-made by Renee. A serious wine list for aficionados adds to the enjoyment.

## Front Street Pub/Santa Cruz Brewing Company

**516 Front St., Santa Cruz 95060 • 408-429-8838 • Lunch and**
**dinner daily • American/pub food • Inexpensive to moderate**

You can get your basic pub grub, hamburgers and such, here, but the real reason to visit is to sample the freshest ales, lagers, ambers, porters, and stouts. In other words, this is the place in Santa Cruz for a good microbrew; it's a real thirst-quenching stop, particularly after a hot summer day at the beach.

## Gayle's Bakery and Rosticceria

**504 Bay Ave., Capitola 95010 • 408-462-1200 • Breakfast,**
**lunch, and dinner daily • Bakery/Italian • Inexpensive to**
**moderate**

What started out as a small bakery has grown into a sort of Italian deli, modeled after a Tuscan-style rosticceria. It's all self-service, and in addition to the swell fresh-baked breads, you can go down the line of glass cases and see the various salads, cold pastas, casseroles, roasted chicken, and pork tenderloin. Stop in any time of the day for croissants, cookies, and pastries with a steaming espresso or cappuccino. A wine bar and pleasant patio add to the ambience.

### India Joze

**1001 Center St. (Santa Cruz Art Center), Santa Cruz 95060**
**408-427-3554 • Lunch and dinner daily, Sun. brunch**
**Reservations recommended • Pacific Rim/fusion cuisine**
**Moderate to expensive**

Fusion cuisine reaches a culinary high point at this near-legendary Santa Cruz dining spot. People drive from Monterey, San Jose, and even San Francisco for this exotic dining experience that melds Middle Eastern, Pacific Rim, and European culinary ideas into a vibrant, multicultural stew on their plates—sometimes quite literally. The menu changes often, but fresh fish always appears in some form. Go in the spirit of adventure to have yourself surprised and entertained. Good local wine list too.

### Memphis Minnie's

**1415 Pacific Ave., Santa Cruz 95060 • 408-429-6464**
**Dinner daily • No reservations • Cajun/Creole • Moderate**

If you're hankering for some New Orleans soul food, go to Memphis Minnie's. Gumbo, catfish, crawfish, black-eyed peas, and all the traditional staples crowd the menu, as well as some inventive vegetarian offerings. Local wines are featured.

### O'Mei

**2316 Mission St., Santa Cruz 95060 • 408-425-8458**
**Lunch (except weekends) and dinner daily**
**Reservations recommended • Chinese • Moderate**

The soothing, refined decor and the California chef-owner in the kitchen makes this Chinese restaurant not your typical Oriental eatery. Roger Grigsby, however, may cook even more traditionally than many Chinese; he's out to perfect the Szechuan style of cooking, not change or update it. As such, you'll find great spring rolls, hot and sour soups, sizzling rice dishes, and pan-fried noodle dishes; he prepares shrimp, chicken, pork, and beef, as well as vegetarian specialties, with the freshest ingredients in the seasonally changing menu. A good selection of wines by the glass too.

# Pearl Alley Bistro

110 Pearl Alley, Santa Cruz 95060 • 408-429-8070
Dinner daily • Reservations recommended • Eclectic/Pacific
Rim/California cuisine • Moderate to expensive

A hot spot in Santa Cruz for its lively bar, people-watching, and eclectic menu, this bistro shows international influences on the menu. The chef likes to spotlight a certain cuisine each month to match with wine, so you'll never know what you might find on the menu. Risotto, gnocchi, fresh oysters, Mongolian barbecue, lamb curry, and roquefort flan are just a smattering of things that show up from time to time. The wine list is as eclectic and as much fun as the menu. A dining adventure.

# ANNUAL EVENTS

## QUARTERLY

### Passport Saturdays • 408-479-WINE

Four times a year—in January, April, July, and November—the wineries of the Santa Cruz Mountains, including many not normally open to the public, open their doors with a purchase of a $10 passport. The wineries often offer tours, pour special wines, and even have a little food, among other events.

## JUNE

### Santa Cruz Mountain Vintners' Festival • 408-479-WINE

First two weekends in June. Wineries and restaurants—in Santa Clara and San Mateo counties one weekend and Santa Cruz County the other—offer special wines, food, music, and art shows at their individual wineries. Winemakers welcome you to their cellars to sample their finest wines. Purchasing a glass at any participating winery serves as a passport to all the other wineries in the area.

## FALL

### Wine and Roses Benefit Tasting • 408-724-3900

Annual wine and food tasting event to benefit Watsonville Community Hospital, including charity wine auction.

## RESOURCES

**Santa Cruz Mountains Winegrowers' Association**
**P.O. Box 3000 • Santa Cruz 95063 • 408-479-WINE**
   Full-color wine touring map (incredibly detailed and most helpful) and wine event information.

**Santa Cruz Visitors' Council**
**701 Front St. • Santa Cruz 95060 • 408-425-1234**
   Accommodations, restaurants, recreations, and other activities.

# MONTEREY

*P*eople think of Monterey County—home to Steinbeck's Cannery Row, Fisherman's Wharf, the Monterey Aquarium, Carmel, Pebble Beach, and Big Sur—more as a vacation mecca than as wine country. But directly east of these attractions is the interior Salinas Valley, long known as the salad bowl of the world, producing everything from lettuce to garlic to strawberries. The planting of vines, however, did not come until the early 1960s, as Wente, Mirassou, and Masson looked increasingly for additional sources of grapes. Those wineries, in the Santa Clara and Livermore valleys, found their local grape sources threatened by encroaching urbanization, and they took the grape-growing plunge in Monterey County in a big way.

Fueled by large investments and tax shelter money, vineyards were sometimes planted willy-nilly, without regard for soil, climate, geography, or grape varietal. Financial folks advised farmers to plant Cabernet, since that variety gave the highest return in dollars per ton. They were also encouraged to grow the grapes like tomato plants, to produce the largest yield per vine possible.

Unfortunately, this bumper crop mentality produced vegetal, diluted, washed-out wines. It took Monterey County wineries and grape growers more than a decade to recover from their poor reputation. In the meantime, they adjusted and grafted vineyards to the proper varietal on the proper site. Many of the smaller vintners in particular have been very successful planting specific areas in certain microclimates. The results, as evidenced by the wine in the bottles, have been well received. While the number of wineries has grown, so too has the number of vintners outside the county who

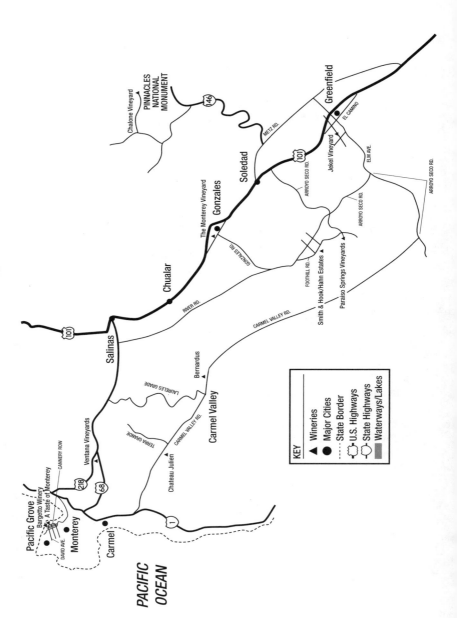

purchase Monterey grapes for their high quality. Today, the wines of Monterey County possess distinctive varietal flavors, reflecting the vintners' continuing adaption to the varied soils and climates of the region.

U.S. 101 traverses the floor of the Salinas Valley, where the majority of the vineyards lie. The northern part of the valley, near Gonzales, Soledad, and Greenfield, stays relatively cool, making it an ideal area for growing Pinot Noir, Pinot Blanc, Chardonnay, and Riesling. The valley acts like a funnel to bring in the cool air, wind, and fog from the nearby Pacific Ocean. Further south in King City and San Lucas, the climate is warmer and conducive to growing Cabernet and Merlot.

## WINERIES

*(listed from Monterey/Carmel and proceeding southeast)*

This easy day trip will put you back in Monterey/Carmel in time for dinner. Starting in Monterey, begin with the Cannery Row tasting rooms, A Taste of Monterey and Bargetto. Then head out Highway 68 to the Ventana Vineyards tasting room. If it's anywhere close to lunchtime, grab a patio table next door at Tarpy's Roadhouse for the fine sandwiches, salads, and pastas. Take Highway 68 into Salinas, and then go south on U.S. 101 to Gonzales, following the signs to The Monterey Vineyard (about a forty-five-minute drive from Monterey proper). Another ten minutes south on U.S. 101 takes you to Soledad; to get to Chalone, exit on Front Street in Soledad to East Street. Go east a few blocks to Metz Road, then south to Highway 146, and follow it about nine miles up toward the Pinnacles National Monument.

Back down on U.S. 101 briefly, exit at Arroyo Seco Road east, which turns into Paraiso Springs Road. You'll find the winery of the same name as it intersects Foothill Road. Several miles north on Foothill Drive is the well-marked entrance to Smith & Hook/ Hahn Estates. For the last winery in the Salinas Valley, Jekel, drive another ten minutes south to Greenfield. To get there, go back to U.S. 101, south to the Walnut Road exit, and proceed west until you see the vineyards; or drive down Arroyo Seco Road south to Elm Avenue and take it into Greenfield, turning north at Fourteenth Street and then traveling up to Walnut Road.

If you're making this a day trip and are not pressed for time, make your way back to Carmel/Monterey by backtracking on Elm

Avenue to Arroyo Seco Road west (head west, not back toward Paraiso Springs Winery); eventually it runs into Carmel Valley Road. This nice, soothing one-hour drive in the countryside, full of beautiful scenery, will take you to two Carmel Valley tasting rooms: Bernardus, hidden in a Carmel Valley Village office building, and Chateau Julien, with architecture that dominates the landscape. From there, it's only about five miles back to Highway 1 and Carmel/Monterey.

If you don't want to do the entire circuit, an easy half-day trip (or less) starts with A Taste of Monterey and Bargetto on Cannery Row and, a short drive from Highway 1 down Carmel Valley Road, ends with Chateau Julien and Bernardus.

## A Taste of Monterey

**700 Cannery Row, Monterey 93940 • 408-646-5446**
**Daily 11–6 • Selected varieties poured, $3 fee • Multimedia wine and food exhibits • Good gift selection • Appetizers available**

The former Paul Masson tasting room has recently been turned into a celebration of Monterey's bounty of wine and food. Located down the street from the Monterey Bay Aquarium in the heart of historic Cannery Row, the upstairs room at the very end of the complex affords a luxurious view of the Monterey Bay from its windows.

For a small fee you can choose to sample wines from more than twenty local wineries, several not open to the public for tasting. A great rest stop from shopping, A Taste of Monterey also offers wines by the glass, as well as a variety of Monterey County produce plates and appetizers. A Monterey County mural graces one wall, and several entertaining wine and food exhibits are artfully done. In addition, you may purchase items from an extensive line of local comestibles and accessories. This is a one-stop wine center for information about Monterey County's wineries; if you visit only one place, A Taste of Monterey will give you sample tastings and a great overview. If on the other hand you plan to visit area wineries, it's a great place to start.

## Bargetto Winery Tasting Room

**700 Cannery Row, Monterey 93940 • 408-373-4053**
**Daily 10–5 • Most varieties poured, no fee • Extensive gift selection**

Bargetto is located in the same 700 complex as A Taste of Monterey, right on Cannery Row. The Bargetto Winery actually calls Santa Cruz home, but having a tasting room in the Monterey/Carmel tourist mecca gives Bargetto a lot more visibility and foot traffic. Even though their Monterey store is a huge converted warehouse, they've tried to make it look like an old-time general store, with a homey but oversized stone fireplace and two huge tasting bars (you'll have to brave the crowds on weekends).

The wines range from Chardonnay and Cabernet to fruit and mead wines, sweet and dry ones as well as everything in between, so there's something for everybody. Every form of food and wine accessories and tons of comestibles jam the display areas. If you're planning a winery touring picnic later in the day, Bargetto has everything you'll need.

### Ventana Vineyards

**2999 Monterey-Salinas Hwy. (two and one-half-miles east of Highway 1), Monterey 93940 • 408-372-7415 • Weekdays 9–5, Sat.–Sun. 11–5 • Most varieties poured, no fee**

On the road out of Monterey, if you blink you'll miss this unpretentious place. The most recognizable landmark also serves as the hottest restaurant in the area, Tarpy's Roadhouse, which overshadows the old stone building. At the junction of Highways 68 and 218, this was the site of the Monterey Peninsula Winery for many years. In those days, it was actually used as a winery; you might have stepped over barrels of fermenting wine to get to the tasting bar.

Today, Ventana Vineyards has cleaned up the place considerably, probably because no wine is actually made here anymore; it functions only as a tasting room for Ventana, whose vineyard is much further south in the county near the Arroyo Seco River. Owner Doug Meador has always been a grape grower at heart, selling his award-winning grapes to other wineries, but he manages to produce a number of good wines under his Ventana label. Chardonnay, Sauvignon Blanc, and Riesling lead the way for the whites, while Cabernet, Pinot Noir, Syrah, and Merlot are the reds.

### The Monterey Vineyard

**800 S. Alta St., Gonzales 93926 • 408-675-2316 • Daily 10–5 Selected varieties poured, no fee • Regular tours, exhibition gallery • Good gift selection • Picnic area**

Look for a pebble-stone slab-sided winery building, which hides the stainless steel fermentation tank farm of The Monterey Vineyard, as a visual landmark on a flat, unremarkable stretch of U.S. 101. A large parking lot in front of the beige stucco mission-style tasting room indicates the winery is geared toward visitors. Established in 1973, this winery is one of the oldest and largest producers in Monterey County. A horseshoe-shaped bar takes up half the large tasting room, and various wine- and food-related gifts, the other half.

The eminently affordable flagship wines bear the Classic designation, including Classic Red and Classic White, as well as White Zinfandel, Chardonnay, Merlot, and Cabernet. The best lots are designated as limited releases, and many of these Cabernets, Chardonnays, and Pinot Noirs are only available at the winery, albeit at a price premium to the Classic wines. An art exhibit in an adjacent room features Depression Era photographs by Walker Evans and Dorthea Lange, while near the parking lot entrance, a wonderful shaded picnic area overlooks a duck pond.

### Chalone Vineyard

**Stonewall Canyon Rd. (Highway 146), Soledad 93960**
**408-678-1717 • Sat.–Sun. 11:30–4; call for weekday**
**appointment • Selected varieties poured, no fee**

If you know about Chalone and make the trek high into the Gabilan Mountains on the east side of the Salinas Valley, the tasting room staff believes you should be rewarded for your perseverance. High up off the valley floor in the shadow of the Pinnacles National Monument, through hairpin turns, switchbacks, and a road that narrows to one lane at times, you'll find Chalone Vineyards tucked into a hillside. A beige stucco building juts out from the precipice, but half the facility is ingeniously hidden in underground caves.

Chalone has some of the oldest vines in the county, planted to Burgundian varietals of Chardonnay and Pinot Noir, along with a smattering of Pinot Blanc and Chenin Blanc. In the white-washed second-floor tasting room, with dark wood trim and a marble-topped bar, you can taste an assortment of varietals and vintages on any given day. The tasting room host sometimes will open older bottles, depending on her whim, and will sometimes entertain your requests from the printed list. If time permits, especially during the week, she will personally tour you through the underground cellars and allow you to taste the latest vintage right out of the barrel! Tasting these fine wines is a great treat, but be sure and call ahead on weekdays (an hour or two before) to make sure someone is there that day. Or ask the neighborly folks at one of the other tasting rooms, like Paraiso Springs or Jekel, to call for you.

# Paraiso Springs Vineyards

**38060 Paraiso Springs Rd., Soledad 93960 • 408-678-0300**
**Weekdays 12–4, Sat.–Sun. 11–5 • Most varieties poured, no fee**
**Small gift selection • Picnic area**

Rich and Claudia Smith, proprietors of Paraiso Springs, have more than twenty years of experience growing grapes in the area. Rich helped found the Monterey organization devoted to promoting the region's wines; then in 1988, he decided to put up a few buildings and make a little wine under his own label. With their children helping in the operation, Paraiso Springs has now grown to 5,000 cases a year.

The winery complex sits on a knoll, off the main road but among the vineyards. The corrugated, metal-sided winery is utilitarian in nature, but the visitors' center, directly across from it, looks homey and inviting. A small tasting bar sits just inside the front door, and some folksy homemade gift items decorate the room. A wooden patio deck connected to the tasting area invites you to sit and sip; umbrella-shaded tables and a wooden seating bench run the entire perimeter of the deck, with Pinot Noir vines growing right up to the edge. The white wines are big here, with Pinot Blanc leading the way, followed by nice versions of Chardonnay, Gewurztraminer (dry), and Riesling (both sweet and late-harvest dessert styles).

## Smith & Hook Winery/Hahn Estates

**37700 Foothill Rd., Soledad 93960 • 408-678-2132**
**Daily 11–4 • Most varieties poured, no fee • Hiking and**
**biking trails • Small gift selection • Picnic area**

Removed from U.S. 101 and the valley floor, you'll drive two miles on an uphill gravel road from the entrance at the well-marked sign on Foothill Road to Smith & Hook Winery. An incredible, breathtaking view of the valley below will reward your effort. The winery buildings and offices are spread out ranch-style, with the Santa Lucia foothills in the background. The tasting room is on your far left, unmistakable once you realize this 420-gallon redwood vat contains not wine but the entire tasting room! Even more clever, the winery has installed a skylight in the top of the cask to allow the natural sunlight to filter in.

The Smith & Hook wines are the mainstay, but the Hahn Estates wines, which debuted in 1991, are also available for tasting. The newer Hahn wines came about after proprietor Nicky Hahn purchased additional acreage in the area and bottled the wines under his own name. The only white wine here is the Hahn Estates Chardonnay; the others in the line are Merlot, Cabernet, and Cabernet Franc, all excellent values around $10. Cabernet and Merlot are also bottled under the Smith & Hook label; these have considerably more depth because of the longer time spent aging in barrel and bottle; recent pours in the tasting room included a trio of Cabs from the '88, '89, and '90 vintages.

### Jekel Vineyard

**40155 Walnut Ave., Greenfield 93927 • 408-674-5522**
**Daily 10–4 • Most varieties poured, no fee • Picnic area**
Although grapes grow further south in the county than this, Jekel is the southernmost winery open to the public. It's a little stretch off the highway, but you'll recognize the compound by the old windmill. The red barn winery soon comes into view, and the reddish-brown clapboard tasting room is in front. Through the double window-paneled doors, a cozy tasting space with a small, blonde wood bar awaits. To one side is a vine-covered gazebo, while a large window on the back bar gives a view into the winery.

Bill Jekel was a pioneer in the area (1978), and he established his reputation with cool-climate Riesling, still inexpensively priced as is the Gravelstone Chardonnay. The Jekel family has since sold the winery to Brown Forman, who also owns Fetzer in Mendocino, but the pursuit of quality continues. It's particularly notable in their recent red wine releases, which include Cabernet, Cabernet Franc, Merlot, Pinot Noir, and a blended Meritage.

### Bernardus

**5 W. Carmel Valley Rd. (fourteen miles east of Highway 1),**
**Carmel Valley 93924 • 800-223-2533, 408-626-1900**
**Wed.–Sun. 11–5 • Most varieties poured, no fee**
International investor Bernard Pons decided to start a winery the old-fashioned way: to build it from the ground up. As the newest winery in the county, Bernardus focuses on making rich, full-bodied dry wines from ripe grapes, with the full French oak barrel treatment. Knowledgeable winemaker Don Blackburn turns out stellar and stylish wines to fine reviews.

The actual winery is not open to the public, but if you look for an ancient wine press out front of an office building in Carmel Valley Village, you'll find the corporate headquarters and tasting room. It's easy to miss the low-slung facility on Carmel Valley Road, because of all the shade trees. Turn into the parking lot, and you'll see the big redwood double doors that lead to this airy, contemporary tasting room. Chardonnay, Sauvignon Blanc, and Pinot Noir here are among the best in the county.

## Chateau Julien

**8940 Carmel Valley Rd. (five miles east of Highway 1), Carmel Valley 93922 • 408-624-2600 • Weekdays 8:30–5, Sat.–Sun. 11–5 • Most varieties poured, no fee • Good gift selection • Excellent picnic area**

Most Carmel tourists never venture much out of the quaint village that seems like it's from another century. But just minutes outside town, Carmel Valley Road leads to wide open greenbelts, vineyards, and several wineries. Chateau Julien is hard to miss: With its thatched roof, imposing turrets, and stained-glass windows, it looks more like a fairy tale castle right out of Hans Christian Andersen's imagination. The beige stone walls with the brown trim and roof reinforce the fantasy that this might be some medieval fortress. The interior of the tasting room looks authoritatively baronial, with a massive fireplace and circular tasting bar.

The winery produces under the Garland Ranch and Emerald Bay labels, but its flagship Chateau Julien wines have the biggest flavors and get the most attention. Chardonnay, Sauvignon Blanc, Cabernet, and Merlot are the pricey mainstays, though Riesling, Gewurztraminer, and Sherry are sometimes offered. Out back, against a background of green-jacketed steel fermentation tanks and lush canyon hillsides, lies the perfect picnic spot. Surrounded by lovely gardens and embellished with old wine barrels and winery paraphernalia, graceful conifer pines shade the picnic tables.

## RESTAURANTS

### Domenico's

**50 Fisherman's Wharf, Monterey 93940 • 408-372-3655 Lunch and dinner daily • Reservations recommended Seafood • Moderate to expensive**

This restaurant has stood the test of time on Monterey's Fisherman's Wharf, where establishments come and go according to the whim of tourists. Combining a fine view of the yacht harbor and good seafood, Domenico's has attracted both locals and tourists for more than ten years. Shrimp, crab, scallops, calamari, and gargantuan lobsters grace the menu, as well as mesquite-broiled catch of the day. Non-fish eaters can dive into steaks, chicken, lamb, and a variety of pastas.

## Fandango

**223 Seventeenth St., Pacific Grove 93950 • 408-372-3456**
**Lunch and dinner daily; Sun. brunch**
**Reservations recommended • European • Expensive**
It's Italian, it's French, it's . . . well, European might best describe the menu, as well as the staff's sensibility. Start your international meal with tapas, melon and prosciutto, or pate and move on to paella, veal, sweetbreads, couscous, and a half-dozen familiar but well-turned-out pastas.

## Fresh Cream

**99 Pacific St., 100 C Heritage Harbor, Monterey 93940**
**408-375-9798 • Dinner daily • Reservations recommended**
**French • Expensive**
Expect classic French fare with a California flair at Fresh Cream. Intimate ambience with a harbor view will compete with the artistic plate presentations of rack of lamb dijonnaise and roast duckling with black currant sauce. The desserts are made in-house and include homemade vanilla ice cream as well as Grand Marnier soufle. A good, if expensive, wine list too.

## From Scratch and La Pergola

**3626 The Barnyard, Carmel 93923 • 408-625-2448**
**Breakfast, lunch, and dinner daily • American/Italian**
**Moderate**
*The* place for breakfast in the area. Corralito's smoked bacon and Wolferman's muffins are two "imported" items that let you know this kitchen pays attention to quality. Eggs many different ways, as well as granola, fresh fruit, and freshly roasted and brewed coffee make up the menu; creative specials are offered daily. At lunch and dinner, the space turns into the Italian-influenced La Pergola, featuring salads, pannini, pastas, and grilled meats. Dine indoors or on the patio.

## Melac's

**663 Lighthouse Ave., Pacific Grove 93950 • 408-375-1743**
**Lunch and dinner daily except Mon. • Reservations**
**recommended • French • Moderate to expensive**
Here's a little place that serves country-style French food, the kind you always wished you had in your neighborhood. Janet, a Cordon Bleu trained chef, and her husband, Jacques, operate their restaurant

with style and panache but with no haute French stuffiness. The menu changes daily to ensure the freshest produce; salads and soups can taste especially good. Country pate and moules marinieres (mussels) are a treat, as well as fresh seafood, duck, lamb, and veal. It's French bistro cooking but even better; locals like to keep this place to themselves because it's so charming and comfortable.

### Old Bath House

**620 Ocean View Blvd., Pacific Grove 93950 • 408-375-5195**
**Dinner daily • Reservations recommended • French/European**
**Expensive**

Overlooking the scenic Lover's Point Cove in Pacific Grove, the Old Bath House—occupying the site of a former 1880s bathhouse—offers its Victorian charm along with a menu of fresh seafood, duck, chicken, prime beef, wild game (in season), and the freshest regional produce. Mesquite-grilled prawns with wild boar sausage might be the featured appetizer, while a beef tenderloin in a puff pastry napped with Cabernet sauce might be the main course. As the Lover's Point location suggests, this place has a lot of romantic ambience.

### Pacific's Edge/California Market At the Highlands Inn

**One and four-tenths miles south of Carmel • 408-624-3801**
**Lunch and dinner daily; Sun. brunch • Reservations**
**recommended • California cuisine • Expensive**

The theory behind Pacific's Edge is California perfection: the perfect view of the Pacific, the perfect California cuisine, and the perfect wine list. And Pacific's Edge has come as close to those standards as any place in the state. Fresh oysters, carpaccio of local salmon, and seared ahi tuna with greens and toasted sesame vinaigrette are just a sliver of the inventive menu. Typical entrees include roasted Monterey salmon with saffron noodles in a pesto broth and mahimahi on curried eggplant caviar with couscous. Pacific's Edge offers a *prix fixe* seasonal menu nightly and an incredible wine list. California Market provides a similar experience with simpler but tasty preparations, albeit casual and about half the cost of Pacific's Edge.

### Rio Grill

**Highway 1 at Rio Rd., Carmel 93923 • 408-625-5436**
**Lunch and dinner daily; Sun. brunch • Reservations**
**recommended • California/American grill • Moderate**

Still a favorite after the newness of its California grill menu wore off, Rio Grill reinvents itself with a fresh and seasonal changing menu. Fresh artichokes, fire roasted with sun-dried-tomato aioli, and roasted garlic to spread on the fresh bread make fine appetizers. Entrees sound familiar but have enough flavor oomph to make them interesting. Baby back ribs, smoked and barbecued until the meat falls off the bone, and a roasted half chicken with smoked chile butter and new potatoes taste great. Salads, grilled fish, and pastas are always on tap, and about a half-dozen specials show up on the blackboard menu of the day. A reasonably priced but fantastic California wine list and a great selection of wines by the glass make for a total experience. Rio Grill is a bargain for the quality. Don't let the casualness of the place fool you; they make seriously flavorful food here!

### Sardine Factory
**701 Wave St., Monterey 93940 • 408-373-3775 • Dinner daily Reservations recommended • Seafood • Expensive**
Long before rehabilitated Cannery Row attracted the thousands of visitors it does today, the Sardine Factory, atop Wave Street overlooking the abandoned fishery warehouses, almost single-handedly kept interest in the area alive. The restaurant itself reflects the past, with its Barbary Coast setting and paintings of sea captains on the walls. Each dining room has a different mood, though many prefer the airy, patiolike conservatory room, surrounded by a private garden and covered by a glass dome. Seafood and prime steaks reign here, and large portions are the order of the day. You'll also see pizza and pastas on the menu, but more as an afterthought. Dine here for the crab cakes, bay prawns, rack of lamb, lobster tails, cioppino, and abalone. The wine list is incredibly broad and comprehensive, with many older vintages.

### Tarpy's Roadhouse
**Highway 68 and Canyon Del Rey, Monterey 93940 408-647-1444 • Lunch and dinner daily • California/American grill • Moderate**
This is still the hottest restaurant in town . . . or out of town, since it's just a short drive down Highway 68 from Monterey, thus the roadhouse moniker. The folks responsible for the Rio Grill wanted to bring back good, old-fashioned, hearty American fare, infused with a 1990s California cuisine sensibility. Taking over an old stone structure, they renovated and transformed the front into an inviting patio, a favorite lunch spot. Look for inventive entrees,

like citrus and pecan-barbecued duck, molasses-bourbon pork chops with braised red cabbage, and venison with green peppercorn sauce and wild rice pilaf. Super wine list too.

## The Tinnery

**631 Ocean View Blvd., Pacific Grove 93950 • 408-646-1040**
**Breakfast, lunch, and dinner daily • American • Moderate**
This casual, moderately priced eatery serves just about anything you want, from early morning to late at night. Breakfasts are hearty, with eggs, pancakes, waffles, and blintzes; lunch features salads, pizza, pasta, and sandwiches (how about a calamari burger?); dinner gets serious, with the fresh seafood of the day, prime meats, and chicken. Kids are also welcome at this restaurant with the postcard view of the bay.

## Ventana Inn

**Twenty-eight miles south of Carmel on Highway 1, Big Sur**
**93920 • 408-667-2331, 408-624-4812 • Reservations**
**recommended • California cuisine • Expensive**
Long known as one of the bastions of California cuisine on the coast, the drive to this out-of-town destination spot is worth it (great ocean views from the highway). Fresh pastas and inventive salads are always on the menu. Fresh fish and shellfish are prominently featured, as well as veal, poultry, and in-season game. Great for that romantic get-away-from-it-all dinner. Eclectic wine list too.

## Whaling Station Inn

**763 Wave St., Monterey 93940 • 408-373-3778 • Dinner daily**
**Reservations recommended • Seafood • Moderate to expensive**
Proprietor John Pisto has done more to promote interest in dining on the Monterey Peninsula than just about anybody. His flagship restaurant (he has several) is the Whaling Station Inn, down the road from his friendly competitor, the Sardine Factory. Step back in time as you enter the old-fashioned dining room, with its Victorian stained-glass windows and crystal chandelier. Again, fresh seafood is the highlight, with three-pound lobsters, Monterey Bay prawns, salmon, scallops, and abalone. On the meaty side of the menu, there is the thirty-two-ounce porterhouse steak, filet mignon, rack of lamb, and the three-pound prime rib. Come hungry, because it's virtually guaranteed you won't leave that way. Good wine list.

## ANNUAL EVENTS

### MARCH

**The Masters of Food and Wine • 408-624-3801**
This week-long festival is always one of the greatest gatherings of the world's finest chefs and winemakers from both the United States and Europe. In the setting of the beautiful Highlands Inn overlooking the Pacific Ocean, the event offers a great range of culinary programs, ranging from lunch and dinners jointly planned by chefs and vintners to cooking demonstrations, wine tastings, wine and food pairings, and educational seminars. This is as epicurean as it gets. Program packages are available, or events may be attended individually.

**The Monterey Wine Festival • P.O. Box 1793
Monterey 93942-1793 • 408-656-WINE**
The largest festival spotlighting only California wines: more than 200 wineries and more than 800 wines at one place at one time. Three-day event includes seminars, cooking demonstrations, nightly grand tastings, auction, and dining out in the Monterey area.

### MAY

**The Great Monterey Squid Festival • 2600 Garden Rd.,
No. 208 • Monterey 93940 • 408-649-6547**
Held Memorial Day weekend (last weekend in May), this festival celebrates the indigenous squid (calamari, as it's sometimes called) with cooking demonstrations, marine displays, exhibits, and of course tasting all manner of squid preparations. At the Monterey County fairgrounds.

## RESOURCES

### Monterey Peninsula Visitors' and Convention Bureau
**P.O. Box 1770 • Monterey 93942 • 408-649-1770**
Restaurants, accommodations, and recreational activities.

### Monterey Wine Country Associates
**P.O. Box 1793 • Monterey 93942-1793 • 408-375-9400**
Full-color wine touring map and information.

# CENTRAL COAST

*Y*ou wouldn't know it from driving the main freeway (U.S. 101) north of Santa Maria out of Santa Barbara County, but if you turn onto the backroads between Arroyo Grande and San Luis Obispo, you'll stumble across some extinct volcanic peaks, along with the small hills and canyons of Arroyo Grande and Edna valleys. These inland valleys only stand about fifteen miles, as the crow flies, from the cooling influence of the ocean, making this one of the coolest coastal regions for grape growing. Chardonnay, Sauvignon Blanc, and Pinot Noir grapes grow well in this environment.

Grapes were first planted here in the late eighteenth century at the nearby Mission San Luis Obispo. Commercial grapevines did not come to the area for another hundred years, when viticultural success at what is now Saucelito Canyon Vineyard spawned several other nearby vineyards, primarily of Zinfandel and Muscat. Wine production was minimal though. In Edna Valley, no renewed interest surfaced until the early 1970s, when the Niven family took the plunge with Paragon Vineyard (they jointly own Edna Valley Vineyard with Chalone) and the MacGregors planted their eponymous vineyard. Their successes drew other grape growers and vintners to the area.

San Luis Obispo, a hip college town, is just north of this small enclave of vineyards. Traveling north over the Cuesta Grade, you won't see grapevines until you reach the Templeton/Paso Robles area, the northernmost and warmest part of San Luis Obispo County. Temperatures here can reach more than 100°F on a sum-

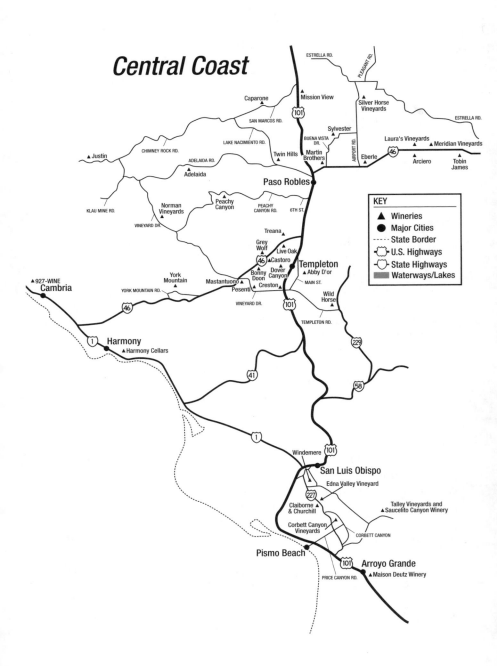

# Central Coast

ESTRELLA RD.

PLEASANT RD.

Caparone ▲

▲ Mission View

Silver Horse ▲
Vineyards

101

ESTRELLA RD.

SAN MARCOS RD.

Sylvester ▲

LAKE NACIMIENTO RD.

BUENA VISTA
DR.

Laura's Vineyards ▲
▲ Meridian Vineyards

AIRPORT RD.

CHIMNEY ROCK RD.

Twin Hills ▲

Martin ▲
Brothers

Eberle ▲

46

▲ Justin

ADELAIDA RD.

Arciero ▲

Tobin
James

Adelaida ▲

Paso Robles ●

KEY

KLAU MINE RD.

Norman ▲
Vineyards

Peachy ▲
Canyon

PEACHY
CANYON RD.

6TH ST.

▲ Wineries

VINEYARD DR.

Treana ▲

● Major Cities

----- State Border

Grey ▲
Wolf

Live Oak ▲

🛡 U.S. Highways

46

▲ Castoro

Templeton

🛡 State Highways

▲ 927-WINE
Cambria

York
Mountain ▲

Mastantuono ▲

Bonny ▲
Doon

Dover ▲
Canyon

▲ Abby D'or

Waterways/Lakes

YORK MOUNTAIN RD.

Pesenti ▲

▲ Creston

MAIN ST.

VINEYARD DR.

101

Wild ▲
Horse

46

TEMPLETON RD.

229

Harmony

▲ Harmony Cellars

41

58

1

Windemere ▲

101

San Luis Obispo

Edna Valley Vineyard ▲

227

Claiborne ▲
& Churchill

Talley Vineyards and
▲ Saucelito Canyon Winery

Corbett Canyon ▲
Vineyards

CORBETT CANYON

Pismo Beach

101

Arroyo Grande

▲ Maison Deutz Winery

PRICE CANYON RD.

mer day, but when the sun goes down, they can plummet 40 degrees due to the on-shore coastal breezes.

Again, no doubt grapes first came here with the Franciscan fathers from Mission San Miguel. The oldest continuing winery, dating from 1882, is York Mountain Winery; although located on a rarely traveled winding country road, it's well worth a visit as a piece of preserved history. Famed pianist and composer Ignace Paderewski, who later briefly served as the president of Poland, visited Paso Robles for mineral water springs (long since closed) and then decided to stay. He planted Zinfandel, vinified for him at York Mountain. Pesenti Winery began right after Prohibition, so this area has plenty of precedent for planting grapes.

However, there was not a renewed interest in the region until the late 1960s and early 1970s. Dr. Stanley Hoffman came from Los Angeles to plant the HMR Vineyard; Estrella River planted acre upon acre and encouraged other growers. Meridian, a Johnny-come-lately in 1989, took over the old Estrella River facility and is now the largest producer, turning out about one million cases of quality wine a year. These successes have really helped the reputation of the Paso Robles area; it's likely to be enhanced even further when the vineyards of the Perrin family of Chateau de Beaucastel in France come into fruition by the end of the decade.

It's unfortunate, then, that many people zoom up and down the freeway on their ways to San Francisco and Los Angeles without stopping to observe the agricultural way of life preserved here. Most folks who make their livings here know grape growing is not cold tabletop nuclear fission. They're dirt farmers but darn good ones, and they take pride in that without pretension. And as more visitors each year discover this region as a major up-and-coming producer of fine wine, the locals hope to maintain that rural feeling. It's a lot like the Napa Valley of twenty-five years ago.

## WINERIES

### EDNA VALLEY/ARROYO GRANDE VALLEY

*(listed from south to north)*

Although Maison Deutz is worth searching out, you won't have to because it's right on U.S. 101, set on a hill just before you get to Arroyo Grande. In Arroyo Grande, take Grand Avenue east, following the Lopez Lake signs for about seven miles to Talley and Saucelito Canyon. Backtrack a bit and turn right (north) on Orcutt Road, then left on Tiffany Ranch Road, and finally right onto Corbett Canyon Road, where you'll shortly see the entrance to Corbett Canyon Winery. Proceeding north up Corbett Canyon Road, you'll be on Highway 227 and find Claiborne & Churchill first on the left and then Edna Valley Vineyard off to the right. Continue on Highway 227 north, and you'll begin to find civilization and the suburbs of San Luis Obispo. Not far from the airport and Tank Farm Road, a small industrial complex houses Windemere.

## Maison Deutz

**453 Deutz Dr., Arroyo Grande 93420 • Three miles south of Arroyo Grande on U.S. 101 • 805-481-1763 • Daily 11–5, except Tues. • $4–$5 charge for sparkling wine tasting plus light appetizer**

Cruising up U.S. 101, it's easy to miss the turn to an attractive winery building that seems out of place on this rural hillside. Maison Deutz is so named because it is the California outpost of the 160-year-old Champagne house of Deutz. And, as is normal for the French, they have built a stylish, top-of-the-line facility, including a super visitors' center. Stools gather around the roomy tasting bar, with individual tables scattered throughout the high-ceilinged sunlit room.

Sparkling wine is the main product, and hosts usually pour the Brut and Blanc de Noir versions for tasting. Sometimes vintage-dated sparklers or special cuvees are also open, depending on availability. Recently, still wines—Chardonnay, Pinot Noir, and Pinot Blanc—have been added to the tasting menu. Along with a glass of wine, you'll receive an appetizer plate of cheese or pate spread, fruit, or nuts. The whole ambience of the place lends itself to a civilized, sit-down, relaxing type of tasting experience. Afterward, take a look at the magnanimous four-ton traditional Champagne basket press in the crush room, and then meander over to the aging cellar, where a peek through the window reveals thousands of sleeping bottles on their way to becoming bubbly.

## Talley Vineyards

**3031 Lopez Dr., Arroyo Grande 93420 • Five miles east of Arroyo Grande • 805-489-0446 • Daily 10:30–4:30; Thurs.–Mon. in winter • Most varieties poured, no fee Small gift selection • Picnic area in rear**

The Talleys have been lifelong farmers in this part of the country (mostly peppers), and the vegetable sheds you see on Lopez Drive probably belong to them. A few years back, they thought they'd try their green thumbs at grape growing, at first selling the harvest to other local vintners. It turned out so well they decided to go into the winemaking business themselves. They set about restoring the 1863 Rincon Adobe left over from a Spanish land grant to use as their hospitality center and tasting room. They then built the modern, functional winery several hundred yards to the rear.

The adobe sits under sheltering palms, framed by a gazebo on one side and hills on the other. The front room is decorated and maintained the way it might have looked in the old days. You'll find the small tasting room with a bar in the rear. Talley specializes in the two cool-climate varieties that grow best in this area: Chardonnay and Pinot Noir. A limited amount of Sauvignon Blanc and late-harvest Riesling is also made, though usually only available at the winery or local restaurants. Prices are moderate, but the quality is excellent.

### Saucelito Canyon Vineyards

**3031 Lopez Dr. (five miles east of Arroyo Grande), Arroyo Grande 93420 • 805-489-0446 • Daily 10:30–4:30, Thurs.–Mon. in winter • All varieties poured, no fee Picnic area in rear**

The Saucelito Canyon winery rests a ways past Talley, back up in the hills. The hundred-year-old head-pruned, dry-farmed Zinfandel vines yield small amounts but produce a heady, rich high-alcohol red wine. To make the wines accessible, Saucelito Canyon pours in a room adjacent to Talley in the Rincon Adobe. Red Zinfandel is the mainstay, and several vintages may likely be open for tasting. On occasions, a real taste treat is available: a late-harvest dessert wine made from overripe Zinfandel.

### Corbett Canyon Vineyards

**2195 Corbett Canyon Rd., Arroyo Grande 93420 805-544-5800 • Mon.–Fri. 10–4:30, Sat.–Sun 10–5 All varieties poured, no fee • Tours on weekends at 11, 1, 3 Good gift selection • Picnic area**

This attractive mission-style winery, named for a blacksmith who settled in these parts, sits on a hill in the middle of nothing but rural countryside. Formerly the Lawrence Winery, it changed ownership a number of times, most recently to The Wine Group (Franzia) in 1988. It is without a doubt the largest winery in the valley but also the most visitor-friendly winery in terms of creature comforts.

You'll pass through an archway to the large, spacious tasting room with its cooling stucco walls. You can view the winery, or at least the huge barrel aging part of it, through the floor-to-ceiling glass at the rear of the room. The friendly staff pours anything and everything, though they suggest six samples is sufficient. Two lines of wines exist here: the larger-volume Coastal Classic line and the special reserve designations. Actually the best deals are the Coastal Classic Chardonnay, Merlot, Cabernet, and Sauvignon Blanc (packaged in larger one-liter bottles rather than the usual 750-milliliter). The reserve wines, which also include a Pinot Noir, can be uneven depending on the vintage.

### Claiborne & Churchill

**2649 Carpenter Canyon Rd. (Highway 227), San Luis Obispo 93401 • 805-544-4066 • Daily 10–4 • All varieties poured, no fee**
The last time I visited the husband and wife team of Claiborne Thompson and Fredericka Churchill, the winery was located in an industrial park next to gear grinders and auto wreckers, just south of San Luis Obispo. Recently though, the two were crazy enough to take the big plunge and built a real winery in the valley. The unique yellow barn-style building is totally insulated with straw bales as interior walls.

Former teachers, they were bitten by the wine bug, but instead of trying to compete with every California winery, they decided to specialize in *dry* Riesling and Gewurztraminer, and they have succeeded quite admirably in making refreshing white wines. In addition, small lots of both Chardonnay and Pinot Noir are also produced.

### Edna Valley Vineyard

**2585 Biddle Ranch Rd. (between Highway 227 and Orcutt Rd.), San Luis Obispo 93401 • 805-544-9594 • Daily 10–5 All varieties poured, no fee • Regular tours • Picnic area**
Paragon Vineyards, which jointly owns this winery with the Chalone Group, pioneered grape growing in this area in 1973. In the early days, Chalone bought grapes from Paragon, but the fruit proved to be such high quality that they formed a joint operation to build a winery at the vineyard site, naming it Edna Valley Vineyard. From day one, it was to be a Burgundian-style winery specializing in Chardonnay and Pinot Noir; it has remained true to its vision, though Edna Valley makes ten times more Chardonnay than Pinot.

Not a showplace winery by any means, everything here is geared to be the most utilitarian method for processing the harvest and then fermenting and aging (all in barrels) the wine. Stick your head in the underground wine cellars and you will find triple stacks of barrel rows as far as the eye can see. The tasting room, also purely functional, lies around the corner from the parking lot, just inside one of the winery buildings. From behind the small bar, hosts usually pour Chardonnay from several vintages; you may taste Pinot Noir if any of the current vintage remains. Older bottlings of Cabernet (now discontinued) and other special winery-only lots sometimes come available.

**Windemere**

**3482 Sacramento Dr., Ste. E, San Luis Obispo 93401**
**805-542-0133 • Thurs.–Sun. 11:30–4 • Most varieties**
**poured, $2 fee**

At this small producer's winery, as you might imagine by looking at it, the tasting room can be a couple of upturned empty barrels at the front of the building. The owner-winemaker, Cathy MacGregor, comes by her profession naturally: Her father, Andy, owns and operates the highly respected MacGregor Vineyards in Edna Valley. Nepotism is not the key here though, because Cathy graduated from the University of California at Davis wine program and worked at several Napa and Sonoma wineries before coming back home.

No one's saying if she gets the best grapes from her dad's vineyard, but her signature wine is a toasty Chardonnay from the MacGregor Vineyard. She uses her north coast contacts to secure Napa Valley Cabernet and also buys grapes for Paso Robles Zinfandel. Other small lots of winery-only releases may disappear quickly, so always stop to see what Cathy has been up to.

**TEMPLETON**

Exit on the appropriately named Vineyard Drive from U.S. 101; go east to Main Street for Abbey D'or, or go to Templeton Road, turn right, and travel two miles to Wild Horse. Go back to Vineyard Drive and cross the freeway to the Creston tasting room. Further down Vineyard Drive are Pesenti and Mastantuono. Finding yourself at Highway 46 west, you have two choices. If you want to go to the coast, proceed east to York Mountain Winery, then to Harmony Cellars and 927-WINE, quite some distance away in Harmony and Cambria, respectively. If you intend to stay in town, several more wineries lie only minutes away. East on Highway 46 west leading back to U.S. 101, you'll find Bonny Doon, Grey Wolf, Live Oak, Castoro, Dover Canyon, and Treana.

## Abbey D'or

**590 Main St., Templeton 93465 • 805-434-3257 • Daily 12–5**
**Most varieties poured, $2 fee includes logo glass**

The Farleys produce wines from grapes they grow themselves and named the winery in honor of their ancestral village home in Ireland. The winery itself is located back in the hills on Hog Canyon Road, but this former storefront tasting room on the main drag in Templeton was vacated recently, and Abbey D'or snapped it up to introduce its wines to a wider audience.

Although small, Abbey D'or makes a lot of different wines. Chardonnay, Cabernet, and Zinfandel lead the list, but a Chenin Blanc is interesting as is an inexpensive, everyday workhorse wine simply labeled Red Table Wine.

## Wild Horse Winery

**1437 Wild Horse Winery Ct. (go right off Vineyard Dr. exit, over the bridge, and right on Templeton Rd. about two miles), Templeton 93465 • 805-434-2541 • Daily 11–5 • Most varieties poured, no fee • Small gift selection • Picnic area**

Picturesque Wild Horse, one of the more modern wineries in the area, sits near the east side of the Salinas River, away from the cluster of wineries around Vineyard Drive and Bethel Road. It's certainly worth the small effort to find. Vintner Ken Volk started making wine in his garage in 1978, and eventually his hobby blossomed into a full-time pursuit in 1981, when he purchased this property and finally built the winery in 1987. One of the largest in the area, the winery produces about 30,000 cases now. The original French country-style building sits in the middle of sixty-four acres of vineyards; due to growth, Volk added a 10,000-square-foot warehouse for case goods and barrel aging.

The bright, sunny whitewashed tasting room usually offers the winery's major varietals, like Chardonnay, Merlot, and Cabernet. But Volk is always up to something new or different, so you might also find hosts pouring Cabernet Franc, Gewurztraminer, Zinfandel, and Malvasia Bianca too. Many of the latter are produced in small lots and sometimes available only at the winery.

# Creston Vineyards

**U.S. 101 and Vineyard Dr., Templeton 93465 • 805-434-1399**
**Daily 10–5 • Most varieties poured, no fee • Good gift selection**
**Picnic area**

Creston's vineyards and winery are actually south of the area and require traversing interior, remote back roads. It's easier and much more convenient to just find their tasting room directly adjacent to U.S. 101. Shade trees shelter a white clapboard house, like your Grandma used to have, and a grape arbor houses a shady picnic area.

The tasting room seems small only because it's filled to the gills with books, gourmet items, and wine accessories. At the front bar, you'll find that knowledgeable hosts who know the wines talk about them in plain English. Creston makes a wide range of wines from pink to white to red and from dry to sweet; your hosts will happily help navigate your palate through the various wines. Perennial favorites are Zinfandel, Pinot Noir, and in good vintages, a very accessible Cabernet. Prices seem very fair for the quality. Game show host Alex Trebek of *Jeopardy!* fame is a partner in the operation.

# Pesenti Winery

**2900 Vineyard Dr., Templeton 93465 • 805-434-1030**
**Mon.–Sat. 8–5:30, Sun. 9–5:30 • Most varieties poured, no fee**
**Small gift selection**

You'll recognize Pesenti almost immediately, surrounded by ancient, gnarled Zinfandel vines that look like bonsai trees on steroids. The old brick and adobe structures on the property also have the requisite patina of age, some dating back to the winery's founding in 1934. The wood-paneled tasting room, converted from part of the storage warehouse, looks like a basement recreation room from the 1950s. Hi-tech this place is not.

Pesenti is the remaining vestige of how things were in the old days, when a person brought his empty gallon jug to the winery and had them "fill 'er up" right from the cask. The present-day wines haven't changed all that much, with heavy-duty Zinfandel and Cabernet leading the charge, followed by a number of other lesser offerings. The reds, made in the old Italian style, can charitably be called rustic. It's a fun place to visit, and if you taste through enough, you might stumble across a real inexpensive find, which is half the fun of touring.

## Mastantuono Winery

**100 Oak View Rd., Templeton 93465 • 805-238-0676**
**Daily 10–6 in summer; 10–5 in winter • Most varieties poured,**
**no fee • Good gift selection, comestibles, and deli food**
**Picnic area with gazebo**

In direct antithesis to the physical trappings of Pesenti, Mastantuono looks like a miniature castle growing out of the landscape. The faux chateau houses a beautifully big and comfortable tasting room with a high-beamed ceiling. The V-shaped wooden bar has enough room so it doesn't seem crowded, even on a summer weekend. A large selection of Italian pastas, sauces, and oils—many with the Mastantuono private label—makes up a display area in the rear. Perusing the wall-mounted corkscrew collection will fascinate you between sips of wine.

Pasquale Mastantuono (everyone calls him Pat) retired to make wine in the 1970s, which makes this one of the older wineries in the area. While he made his reputation on big reds, like Cabernet and Zinfandel, the most interesting wines are the ones made from little-known grapes. Aleatico (an Italian variety), Carminello (a red hybrid grape), and Muscat (a dessert wine) are the kind of oddball wines you don't see too often.

## York Mountain Winery

**York Mountain Rd. (off Highway 46 west), Rt. 2, Templeton**
**93465 • 805-238-3925 • Daily 10–5 • Most varieties poured,**
**no fee; small charge for older reserve wines • Good gift selection**
**Picnic area**

A winding country road, sometimes reduced to one lane, leads back up in the hills to York Mountain Winery. The place looks small and primitive, but that's because they haven't seen the need to change much of the traditional winemaking that has gone on here since 1882. History imbues the tasting room itself, made from kiln-dried, hand-formed bricks; wagons brought the timber from the Cayucos pier, while the two huge fireplaces were solidly built to provide real heat, not to serve as mere ornamentation. In the 1930s, Ignace Paderewski, composer, pianist, and first premier of Poland, brought grapes from his nearby vineyard ranch to be vinified here. Certainly this is one of the funkiest wineries to visit in the area.

Hosts often pour Chardonnay, but the mainstays are the reds, like Cabernet, Zinfandel, and Pinot Noir (the latter tasted more like Zinfandel to me). Sparkling wine and Sherry are often available for tasting too, along with simple red and white table wines. Prices are very reasonable, except for the bottle-aged older reds. On the patio deck out front, you'll often find winery cats doing what they do best: sunning themselves.

## Harmony Cellars

**Harmony Valley Rd. (between Morro Bay and Cambria, just off Highway 1), Harmony 93435 • 805-927-1625 • Daily 10–5**
**Most varieties poured, no fee • Small gift selection; some food items • Picnic area**

The town of Harmony, located off a lonesome stretch of Highway 1, was once promoted as the smallest town in California. And indeed it may still be, with a couple shacks, an old post office, and a creamery building still standing but adapted to present-day tourist commerce. Vintner Chuck Mulligan thought it would be fun to make wine here and, for a number of years, operated the tasting room in the old town. He has since moved it up the hill, where the actual winemaking takes place.

Harmony offers quite a variety of wines, including Chardonnay, Riesling, and Cabernet. The Pinot Noir can often be very flavorful and a bargain to boot. An unusual wine you'll not encounter elsewhere is Zinjolais, a contraction (and blend) of Zinfandel and Gamay Beaujolais; it's priced right and goes down easy.

## 927-WINE

**788 Main St., Cambria 93428 • 805-927-WINE, 800-927-WINE • Daily 10:30–6 and Sun. 10:30–5 in winter; summer hours longer • Selected varieties poured, $1 fee; usually about a dozen wines including Port, Sherry, and Champagne**
**Good selection of comestibles • Restaurant on premises**
**Special events include quarterly wine tasting dinners**

Calvin Wilkes, longtime member of the wine trade on the Central Coast, closed his International Wine Center tasting room in Moonstone Gardens and teamed up with Christine Quinn to open a wine tasting bar cum bistro in downtown Cambria. Located across the street from a soldier factory and next to an olive store, the tasting room offers a wide range of not only local but international wines for tasting.

The ever-changing list of locals includes Le Cuvier, Wild Horse, Eberle, and Lockwood, but many bottles come from Oregon, Washington, Australia, Chile, Spain, France, Italy, and South Africa. The on-premises wine bistro offers lunch daily (except

Tuesday) and dinner Wednesday through Saturday. A good cheese selection and fresh baked bread is available, making this a great stop for picnickers too.

### Bonny Doon Vineyard Tasting Room at Sycamore Farms

**2485 Highway 46 west (three miles west of U.S. 101), Paso Robles 93446 • 805-239-5614, 800-576-5288**
**Daily 10:30–5 • Selected varieties poured, $2 fee includes logo glass • Excellent selection of comestibles, cookbooks, kitchen equipment, and decor items; fresh or potted herbs available from adjacent herb farm**

Here's a beautiful countrified setting right off the highway that has something to entertain everyone. Even before you get to the wooden building housing the tasting room, you can amuse yourself by taking a self-guided tour of the herb and flower plantings and even buy fresh or potted herbs to take with you. And the kids can be introduced to real free-range chickens, as well as the resident tabbies.

Walking into the gift shop cum tasting room, the amount of colorful decor items crammed into this space may overwhelm you. The tasting bar, though, is apparent as you enter and is now home to the wines of Bonny Doon, whose eclectic winemaker, Randall Grahm, is always in this area buying grapes for his winery in Santa Cruz. A blackboard usually lists the Bonny Doon wines being poured (Grahm makes twenty or thirty different wines!); just about anything he makes tastes interesting if not downright flavorful. The dessert-style ice wines (made from frozen grapes) and fruit infusions (made with ripe blueberries, etc.) are great fun.

### Grey Wolf Cellars

**2174 Highway 46 west, Paso Robles 93446 • 805-237-0771**
**Daily 11–5:30 • Most varieties poured, no fee • Picnic area**

A partnership recently took over the former Baron Vineyards, originally established as Baron and Kolb in 1976 by a Los Angeles fireman, and renamed it Grey Wolf Cellars. Formerly located south of Highway 46 on Penman Springs Road, the winery moved to this renovated fifty-year-old farmhouse west of U.S. 101, amid the other popular winery stops on Highway 46 west.

The fifteen acres of estate vines yield Fume Blanc, Muscat Canelli, and Cabernet, augmented by locally purchased Chardonnay. Also available are limited quantities of Zinfandel and Merlot. The production is very small and sometimes available locally, but most is sold out of the tasting room.

# Live Oak Vineyards

**1480 N. Bethel Rd. (one and one-quarter miles west of U.S. 101), Templeton 93465 • 805-227-4766 • Daily 10–6**
**Most varieties poured, $2 fee • Small gift selection • Picnic area**

The homey, old former schoolhouse circa 1880 that once housed Castoro Cellars' tasting room is the new home of Live Oak Vineyards. This great piece of history has been preserved by the Alberts, who wisely have not fiddled with success. Antiques still abound in the front room of the white clapboard schoolhouse, and on blustery winter afternoons, the glow from the fireplace warms up the room.

White Zinfandel, Chardonnay, and Sauvignon Blanc are the whites, while the traditional Paso Robles trio of Cabernet, Zinfandel, and Merlot compose the reds, though the latter two tend to be on the soft, drink-me-now side. Moderate prices.

# Castoro Cellars

**1315 N. Bethel Rd., Templeton 93465 • 805-238-0725**
**Daily 11–5:30 • All varieties poured, $2 fee includes logo glass**
**Good gift and comestible selection • Picnic area**

For years, visitors made the trek to the old schoolhouse now occupied by Live Oak Vineyards. But in 1994, Castoro moved across the road to the old El Paso de Robles Winery. Word had gotten around about the great quality of wine at low prices so much that Castoro needed some room for expansion. The new place is all Spanish mission-style with a grand tasting room—as different from the old tasting room as day is from night.

But the wines remain the same, offering a continuing bargain. Many proudly serve them as house wines at local restaurants and bed and breakfast inns. The Chardonnay is exemplary in every way, the Cabernet is delightfully drinkable, and even the White Zinfandel is refreshing and well balanced. It's hard to go wrong here, considering the quality and the moderate prices.

# Dover Canyon Winery

**Bethel Rd., Templeton 93465 • 805-434-0319 • Daily 11–5:30**
**All varieties poured, no fee • Good gift and comestibles selection**
**Picnic area**

Situated on a hilltop off the main road on the former JanKris property, Dover Canyon sells bottles from a tasting room out of its hundred-year-old Victorian farmhouse. The new regime, headed by a former assistant winemaker from nearby Eberle Winery, took over in early 1997. A homey front porch is perfect for savoring the wines, and a glassed-in garden gazebo beckons you to have a leisurely picnic.

The signature reds, Cabernet, Zinfandel, and Merlot are formidable. The white wine focus is changing to spotlight unusual Rhone varieties, like Roussanne and Marsanne. Only 1,200 cases are produced, so buy here if you like what you taste.

### Treana Winery

**2175 Arbor Rd. at Highway 46 west (one mile west of U.S. 101), Paso Robles 93446 • 805-238-6979 • Daily 10–5 All varieties poured, no fee • Deli and comestible selection Picnic area**

This tasting room doesn't look like any make-do adjunct to a winery. The white clapboard Victorian-style building with the green-shingled top and large, fully paved parking lot contrasts some of the funkier wineries in the area. Inside, the cool (temperature-wise) tasting room looks elaborate, with busy wallpaper, fine draperies, and even carpeting. Samples of the comestibles are often offered gratis.

While the small tasting bar only has room for about ten people at a time, the wines are worth a little wait. Zinfandel and Cabernet are really the featured varietals, though the Sauvignon Blanc, Chardonnay, and Viognier are coming on too. Muscat Canelli, in the sweet dessert style, is a real crowd pleaser. Prices are relatively modest, in the $6–$13 range.

### WESTSIDE PASO ROBLES

U.S. 101 conveniently divides the west side of Paso Robles from the east side. If you've just tasted at Mastantuono and are ready for a scenic country ride, then go across Highway 46 and continue on Vineyard Drive, turning right on Peachy Canyon Road to Peachy Canyon Winery. If you're starting your day in downtown Paso Robles, head out Sixth Street west, which will also eventually put you on Peachy Canyon Road. In either event, then go to Vineyard Drive and turn right (north) to Norman Vineyards. Further north, go right on Adelaida Road to Adelaida Cellars. Backtrack on Adelaida Road, take a brief jog on Klau Mine Road, and then a left on Chimney Rock Road to Justin. Take Chimney Rock Road back east to the San Marcos Road fork, where Caparone is located, or the Lake Nacimiento Road fork, where Twin Hills sits. Both roads eventually lead back to U.S. 101.

# Peachy Canyon Winery

**4045 Peachy Canyon Rd. (five and one-half-miles west of Paso Robles), Paso Robles 93446 • 805-237-1577, 800-315-7908 Sat., Sun., and holidays only, 11–5 • All varieties poured, no fee Picnic area**

Doug Beckett, owner-vintner of Peachy Canyon, has not exactly been in the area a long time. A former schoolteacher, he apprenticed at a winery in the area and then decided to make a go of it on this property due west of Paso Robles in 1987. A two-story Colonial-style house will first hint you're in the right place, and the barking of the family dogs will clue you next. Go around back to the tasting room, and a member of the Beckett family will undoubtedly greet you and might just regale you with local historical facts and myths.

Red wine is king here, and Zinfandel sits on the throne. Their Westside-designated Zin, indicating all its grapes come from vineyards west of Paso Robles, provides a reliable barometer of California Zinfandel. Cabernet can be equally interesting.

# Norman Vineyards

**7450 Vineyard Dr. (five miles northwest of Highway 46 west), Paso Robles 93446 • 805-237-0138 • Sat., Sun., and holidays only, 11–5:30 • All varieties poured, no fee • Picnic area**

Art and Lei Norman finally completed their winery building just a few years ago, but these longtime residents began planting vineyards here back in 1971. Old-timers in this area can put up any kind of winery they want . . . and the Normans did. Driving down rural Vineyard Drive, you almost do a double take at the imposing mission-revival-style building that seemingly extends into the hillside. Even if it were not a winery, you would want to stop and look at, if not admire, the construction of the masonry-reinforced stucco building that's become a local landmark. The Normans are not just a pretty face though; they've learned their grape growing well, utilizing erosion control, minimal pesticides, and little irrigation.

A long outside stairway leads into a hacienda-style tasting room, with tiles on the floor and ceiling fans whirling overhead. People usually taste on the far end of the room at the tables by the kitchen. Scattered around the rest of the room, overstuffed chairs and divans beckon to you to dally and relax. Out back, a splendid patio, also convenient for relaxing, overlooks the vineyards. The Normans do produce Chardonnay, but that's just a warm-up for their intense reds, like Cabernet, Zinfandel, Merlot, and Barbera.

## Adelaida Cellars

**5805 Adelaida Rd. (four and one-half-miles east of Vineyard Dr.), Paso Robles 93446 • 805-239-8980, 800-676-1232**
**Daily 10–5 • Most varieties poured, $2 fee**

John Munch is the vintner here, so does that make this Munchkinland? Actually Munch looks like a roly-poly elf from some monastic order, but he offers much more than sacramental wine here. Munch grew up in South America, and his wife in Europe, which explains the hybridization of winemaking styles and techniques here.

Adelaida has been a moving target for some time, making wine in spaces leased to Munch by other wineries, until he landed in his own facility in 1991. The tasting room, sandwiched in one end of the winery, usually is a pretty casual affair. Chardonnay is poured, but that's not the reason to visit; Cabernet and Zinfandel are. Adelaida recently got access to Pinot Noir from the old HMR ranch nearby, so look for it to show up in the tasting room.

## Justin Winery

**11680 Chimney Rock Rd., Paso Robles 93446 • 805-237-4150, 800-726-0049 • Daily 10–5 • Most varieties poured, no fee**
**Picnic area**

This winery lies the furthest out of all the "far-out wineries of Paso Robles," as a promotional brochure explains. But driving west down a winding country road, it may shock you to come upon an entire compound of buildings, most of them painted a bright mustard yellow. An oddly formal English garden and gazebo are equally surprising. Set amid the rolling hills of vineyards, former Los Angeles investment banker Justin Baldwin and his family decided to relocate here. Sixty-five acres have been planted to vineyards on the ranch, and there is even an elaborate bed and breakfast called The Just Inn (two suites only and reservations a must!). With so much going on here and with the increasing popularity of the wines themselves, Baldwin is constructing a new winery.

The reception foyer and tasting room, gracious and elaborate, may remind you of someone's home. A toasty barrel-fermented Chardonnay is offered, but Baldwin has more interest in red wine, particularly following the Bordeaux model. To that end, he spotlights Cabernet, Merlot, and Cab Franc, as well as Justin's exclusive Bordeaux combination of these grapes, called Isosceles.

## Caparone Winery

**2280 San Marcos Rd., Paso Robles 93446 • 805-467-3827**
**Daily 11–5 • All varieties poured, no fee**

Dave Caparone doesn't stand on ceremony or pretension, and his winery, looking like a prefab Butler building, may not visually entice you. But Caparone wants to make red wine, and that's just what he's done here since 1979.

In the tasting room, a few steps inside the winery building, scores of barrels of aging red wine are stacked. Big, thick, heady red wines are the ticket here, and the Cabernet, Merlot, and Zinfandel tend to bowl you over with their big, ripe flavors. Lately the winery has also turned its attention to red Italian-style wines, like Brunello, Sangiovese, and Nebbiolo.

## Twin Hills Winery

**2025 Nacimiento Lake Dr., Paso Robles 93446 • 805-238-9148**
**Daily 11–5 • All varieties poured, no fee • Small gift selection**
**Picnic area**

The name comes from the two rolling hills near the winery. Country French in style, with adorned arbors, gardens, and plenty of shaded picnic tables, the winery has a homey, comfortable tasting room. Established in the early 1980s, a Bay Area couple purchased the winery in 1992 and revamped the style of wines made through their own personal involvement.

Twin Hills draws on forty acres of vines to make a wide variety of wines to please every palate. White Zinfandel, Chardonnay, and Riesling represent the lighter side, while Cabernet and Zinfandel are gutsy and robust. A rare and unusual solera-style Sherry and Zinfandel Port, both sweet dessert wines, round out the list.

## EASTSIDE PASO ROBLES

Look for most of the eastside wineries on both sides of Highway 46 east. The exception is Mission View Estate, with its tasting room just north of Highway 46 on U.S. 101. Otherwise, swing onto Highway 46 east to Martin Brothers, follow Buena Vista Drive around to Sylvester, then turn left on Airport Road and right on Estrella Road to Pleasant Road, where you'll find Silver Horse. Retrace your route back to Highway 46 east and turn left (east) for a straight shot to Eberle, Arciero, Laura's, Meridian, and Tobin James.

## Mission View Estate

**Wellsona Rd. at U.S. 101 (three miles north of Paso Robles), Paso Robles 93447 • 805-467-3104 • Daily 10–5 • All varieties poured, no fee • Small gift selection**

Mission View's winery actually sits back up the road on a hillside, but leasing a former restaurant right on U.S. 101 encourages travelers to discover these wines. Mission View relies on its forty-six acres of estate-grown grapes, as well as purchased grapes, to make the wide variety of wines.

White Zinfandel along with oaky Chardonnay and Sauvignon Blanc lead the way for the whites, while the reds consist of Zinfandel, Cabernet, and Merlot. An added attraction here is the antique doll museum and shop right next door; nearby, the often overlooked Mission San Michael Archangel has one of the best-preserved interiors of any mission, as well as an interesting cactus garden and a cemetery.

## Martin Brothers

**Highway 46 east at Buena Vista Dr. (one mile east of Paso Robles), Paso Robles 93447 • 805-238-2520 • Daily 10–6, Winter 10–5 • Most varieties poured, no fee • Good gift selection, including cookbooks, comestibles, and picnic items Picnic area**

This white sunwashed tasting room is about a mile south of the winery on Highway 46, taking a high-profile position as the first winery you'll come to as you head east out of town. The Irish Martins, aware that Ireland has little history with the vine, decided Italian wines were the most interesting at a time when all other wineries patterned themselves after the French model. And while they make the normal varietals, like Cabernet and Zinfandel, the Martins were among the first to bottle a Nebbiolo (1981), long before the recent spate of California wineries rushed to get their hands on traditional Italian-style grapes.

Indeed friendly, the tasting room staff will happily explain some of the unique Italian-style offerings, many with oddball labels and unusual bottle shapes. Instead of just one Nebbiolo, they also offer a gutsy Nebbiolo Vecchio, which spends more time in the barrel. The Sangiovese is called Il Palio, while the super Tuscan-style Cabernet blend is called Cabernet Etrusco. The Chardonnay *in Botti* is fermented and aged in Italian chestnut barrels, which impart an interesting flavor to the wine. Truly an eye-opening, educational experience for those who like trying something different.

## Sylvester Winery

**5115 Buena Vista Dr., Paso Robles 93446 • 805-227-4000**
**Daily 11–5 • Most varieties poured, no fee • Picnic area**
Named after its European industrialist founder, Sylvester is the newest operation in the area. Presently, the wines are made at space leased from Castoro Cellars, but the owner plans an elaborate winery on this ninety-acre vineyard site.

The labels are a classic black-and-white traditional Bordeaux style, and the first releases were very well received, boding well for the winery's future. The Chardonnay is of the heavily toasted, oak variety, while the Cabernet was soft enough to drink on release. In addition, the wines are fairly priced.

## Silver Horse Vineyards

**2995 Pleasant Rd., Paso Robles 93447 • 805-467-WINE**
**Fri., Sat., Sun. 11–5 • Most varieties poured; no fee**
**Picnic area**
Appropriately named, this area comprises a combination horse ranch and vineyard. The Simons family invites you to one of the few places where you can watch the thoroughbreds run through their paces as you taste wine. Located off Highway 46 and down Airport Road, the winery and tasting room are as straightforward as they come in these parts. White Zinfandel and Chardonnay lead the list, but muscular red wines, like Zinfandel and Cabernet, are the house favorites at this small winery.

## Eberle Winery

**Highway 46 east (four miles east of U.S. 101), Paso Robles 93447 • 805-238-9607 • Daily 10–5, summer 10–6**
**All varieties poured, no fee • Tours daily • Good gift selection**
**Picnic area**
Winemaker Gary Eberle, former Penn State lineman, helped pioneer this grape-growing area, tirelessly flying his plane to tastings around the country, proclaiming the quality the region offers—not the least of which are his own wines. Eberle began his career at the old Estrella River Winery and then started his own place down the road.

The dramatic winery has a lovely tasting room that looks down into the winery itself at one end and has French doors that lead to a shaded patio on the other end. In between, a long tasting bar and spacious area allows for uncrowded, unhurried tasting. The latest attraction is a tour of the winery's aging caves. Eberle is phasing out Chardonnay, but Viognier and Muscat Canelli are among the whites to taste. Red wines, like Cabernet, Zinfandel, and Syrah, are big and bold.

## Arciero Winery

**Highway 46 east at Jardine Rd. (six miles east of U.S. 101),
Paso Robles 93447 • 805-239-2562 • Daily 10–5, summer
weekends 10–6 • Most varieties poured, no fee • Excellent gift
selection, including books, comestibles, and deli foods
Picnic area**

As southern California developers and builders, the Arciero brothers knew exactly what they wanted to do when they constructed this winery in 1984. The ornate Mediterranean style of the winery and its huge visitors' center reflects their Italian heritage. From the landscaped drive to the shaded picnic areas and right down to the cavernous tasting room, everything about this place welcomes visitors.

A self-guided tour allows you to enjoy the faux Italian villa architecture, as well as peer into the working parts of the winery. The Arcieros are also auto-racing enthusiasts, so you may see a Grand Prix or Indy car on the premises. As for the wines, they serve up a wide variety, including Chenin Blanc, Sauvignon Blanc, Chardonnay, Zinfandel, Cabernet, Petite Sirah, and the Italian-influenced Nebbiolo; all are modestly priced.

## Laura's Vineyard

**5620 Highway 46 east (six miles east of U.S. 101),
Paso Robles 93447 • 805-238-6300 • Daily 10–6
All varieties poured, no fee • Good gift selection • Picnic area**

Cliff Giacobine, one of the original principals in the Estrella River Winery, has since struck out on his own, much like his half brother, Gary Eberle, did. His place, right across the road from Arciero, is not as elaborate; once a functional trailer, he remodeled it into a small cottage to serve as a tasting room. The wines are made elsewhere.

The moderately priced offerings poured include a supple Cabernet, as well as Chardonnay, Cabernet Franc, Riesling, Syrah, and White Zinfandel. They are not widely available, since production is only around 3,000 cases; if you like what you taste, buy the wines at the source.

## Meridian Vineyards

**7000 Highway 46 east (seven miles east of U.S. 101),
Paso Robles 93447 • 805-237-6000 • Daily 10–5
Most varieties poured, no fee • Small gift selection • Picnic area**

The Meridian tasting room faces a pleasant, manicured courtyard, the perfect place for lounging in the mid-afternoon sun. Inside, a long narrow space provides an expansive view into the aging cellar, with barrels stacked high and tight. Cleverly, the winery has been constructed so the landscaping and architecture of the building hide the huge rotary fermenters and other mechanics of winemaking. Don't be fooled, though, by Meridian's modest facade; this is the largest winery on the Central Coast.

But at least in this case, quantity is synonymous with quality. Winemaker Chuck Ortman came down from Napa Valley and applied his twenty years of experience to making the best wines he possibly could, on a large scale. Coupled with an infusion of cash for capital equipment from former owner Nestle, Meridian has become wildly successful. The Santa Barbara County Chardonnay leads the way with many gold medals and is often cited as the best Chardonnay in the country for less than $10. Sauvignon Blanc, Pinot Noir, Cabernet, and Syrah are all winners and very reasonably priced, considering the quality.

## Tobin James

**8950 Union Rd., Paso Robles 93446 • 805-239-2204**
**Daily 10–6 • Most varieties poured, no fee • Picnic area**

Toby, as winemaker Tobin James Shumrick is called, first came to prominence as the assistant winemaker at Eberle, where he schlepped hoses and did the grunt work of winemaking, but also honed his winemaking skills while paying his dues. When he opened his own place, he decided the whole wine business was a bit too serious, and he intended to inject a little levity into it.

Certainly his funky tasting room has no pretensions. A great bar with oodles of character forms the centerpiece; various references to outlaw Jesse James reinforce the western atmosphere. No stuffed shirts need apply for tasting here. Be sure to bring your sense of humor and whimsy though, because Toby obviously stays up nights thinking up names for each of his wines, like the James Gang Zinfandel. The other Zins, as well as Cabernets, sport funny monikers, but the wines themselves are big and powerful, indicating some serious stuff is in the bottle.

## RESTAURANTS

## Giuseppe's

**891 Price St., Pismo Beach 93449 • 805-773-2870**
**Lunch Mon.–Fri.; dinner nightly • No reservations**
**Southern Italian • Moderate**

This old-style southern Italian eatery emphasizes pastas and pizzas, but nothing here comes out of a can. You can smell the freshness of olive oil, garlic, sauces, and herbs as soon as you walk in the door. Meals are bountiful in the traditional Italian style, with no nouvelle California touches. Fresh fish of the day is always available, as well as assorted chicken, veal, scampi, and lamb specials. You can mitigate your wait for a table by indulging in local wines by the glass from the hidden bar in back.

### F. McLintock's

**750 Mattie Rd., Shell Beach 93449 • 805-773-1892**
**Lunch and dinner daily • No reservations • American**
**Moderate**

McLintock's is as cowboy as eating comes in these parts. A cowboy saloon and roadhouse, with an ocean view, is just the ticket for serious beef eaters, whether you prefer the two-pound steak or the oversized rack of ribs. Chicken and seafood seem like afterthoughts. Just follow the crowds and the pickup trucks to one of the top-grossing restaurants in America. There must be a reason McLintock's has so much success, though the long wait on weekends can't be it.

### Gardens of Avila (at Sycamore Springs)

**1215 Avila Beach Dr., Avila Beach 93424 • 805-595-7365**
**Lunch Tues.–Sat., dinner Tues.–Sun.; Sun. brunch**
**Reservations recommended • California cuisine**
**Moderate to expensive**

The restaurant is located in the heart of the Sycamore Mineral Springs complex, where folks come to enjoy the sulfured waters in hillside hot tubs. But since chef Michael Albright set up shop here a couple years ago, it's also rapidly become a dining destination on the Central Coast. A flavorful eclectic California menu shows a Pacific Rim influence in a dish like chicken pot stickers in a coconut and red curry sauce, and it shows a Provencal style in mussels with leeks, pancetta, tomatoes, garlic, and white wine. The signature offering is surely the halibut encrusted with pesto and bread crumbs and baked with lemon, sun-dried tomatoes, and white beans. Vegetarian dishes show up regularly, and locals flood the wine list.

### Olde Port Inn

**Port San Luis, Pier 3, Avila Beach 93424 • 805-595-2515**
**Lunch and dinner daily • Reservations recommended**
**Fresh seafood • Moderate to expensive**

Fish doesn't get any fresher than direct from the fishing day boats to the end of the pier, where the Olde Port Inn awaits. You may think you've lost your way as you dead-end at a weathered sea shanty of a restaurant amid all sorts of working and fishing equipment and regalia. Large bay windows yield excellent ocean views, while the recently remodeled downstairs dining room provides an unusual viewing vista—through the floor! The cioppino, their version of Italian fisherman's stew, is extremely popular on cold nights. The stuffed shrimp as well as the catches of the day are also favorites. Ask for the Four Corners wines, the first to come in attractively embossed square-sided bottles.

## Apple Farm

**2015 Monterey St., San Luis Obispo 93401 • 805-544-6100**
**Breakfast, lunch, and dinner daily • No reservations**
**American • Inexpensive**

The just-a-little-too-cutesy, days-gone-by theme of the Apple Farm seems a bit much for this glorified coffee shop. But maybe that's part of its attraction. Breakfast is your best bet; try the justly famous, huge plates of apple pancakes and waffles. Lunch and dinner feature the kind of homey food you might expect from a place that looks like this. Soup or salad complement a traditional American menu of fresh catfish, burgers, chicken pot pie, ribs, and meatloaf. All in all, not a bad deal and a particularly good place to take small children.

## Buono Tavola

**1037 Monterey St., San Luis Obispo 93401 • 805-545-8000**
**Lunch and dinner daily except Sun.**
**Reservations recommended • Italian • Moderate**

When Hemingway wrote about "a clean, well-lighted place," he could have been talking about Buono Tavola. The storefront location presents an image, through the large plate glass window, that exudes a cool, soothing vibe. The house salad of arugula, radicchio, and mushrooms is classic, and the various pastas are exemplary. Entrees include a finely marbled steak seasoned with garlic, thyme, and rosemary; and chicken breasts in a mustard and garlic sauce.

## Cafe Roma

**1819 Osos St., San Luis Obispo 93401 • 805-541-6800**
**Lunch Mon.–Fri., dinner Mon.–Sat.**
**Reservations recommended • Italian • Moderate to expensive**

The Rizzo family labored long to establish Cafe Roma as one of the top casual-but-food-serious trattorias on the Central Coast. Located a little off the beaten path in the former Reidy Hotel, Cafe Roma maintains its prominence with dishes like osso bucco on a bed of tasty risotto or roasted Tuscan-style chicken massaged with garlic and herbs. A side of pasta is almost obligatory. The well-chosen wine list splits between top Italian offerings and the best from local wineries.

## SLO Brewing Company

**1119 Garden St., San Luis Obispo 93401 • 805-543-1843**
**Lunch and dinner daily • No reservations • American**
**Inexpensive to moderate**

The first brew-pub on the Central Coast has become wildly popular with the students from nearby California Polytechnic Institute; in fact, on the weekends SLO features live music and gets practically mobbed. Go early if you want to avoid the din. Fresh beer is the main reason to stop in, though they do a creditable job with burgers, chicken wings, nachos, and other munchies. Upstairs in this historic building in old downtown, the main hub of activity features barkeeps pulling pints of Brickhouse Ale and Cole Porter. Downstairs in an old-time pool hall, you can contemplate the bank shots of the pool sharks from the small bar or the scattering of tables.

## Hoppe's at Marina Square

**699 Embarcadero, Morro Bay 93442 • 805-772-9012**
**Lunch Fri.–Sun., dinner Wed.–Mon.; Sun. brunch**
**Reservations recommended • California cuisine**
**Moderate to expensive**

This is the best restaurant on the Central Coast, bar none. The setting, right on the embarcadero with a bigger-than-life view of Morro Rock jutting out from the ocean, looks inviting. But the food matches the view, as imaginative as what you'll find in San Francisco or Los Angeles. A signature appetizer is a conceit called tiramisu, a mousse of smoked salmon between ladyfingers and topped with a piece of fresh lobster. Hoppe's changes its menu seasonally, but recent entrees included sea bass in a black pepper and peanut sauce, duck with a red onion compote, and chile-and-pepper-rubbed ribeye steak for two. The daily *prix fixe* menu of four courses is a bargain, considering the quality.

## Dorn's

**801 Market St., Morro Bay 93442 • 805-772-4415**
**Breakfast, lunch, and dinner daily • Dinner reservations**
**recommended • American • Inexpensive to moderate**

Dorn's has always been *the* place to go for breakfast in Morro Bay. Set on a hill above the waterfront embarcadero, it has an exemplary view of the volcanic Morro Rock from its bay windows. At breakfast (served until early afternoon), choose from any number of specials: eggs, bacon, sausages, blueberry pancakes, fruit waffles, french toast, and the homey pigs-in-a-blanket. At lunch and dinner, Dorn's has pastas and salads, though the order of the day seems to be the fish chowder and fresh seafood.

### Inn at Morro Bay

**19 Country Club Rd., Morro Bay 93442 • 805-772-5651**
**Breakfast, lunch, and dinner daily; Sun. brunch**
**Reservations recommended • French/Californian**
**Moderate to expensive**

Located inside Morro Bay State Park, the Inn looks charmingly upscale rustic in the same way Carmel does. A number of fine chefs have presided over the kitchen here before moving on. Rest assured though, there will usually be salads with warm goat cheese combined creatively with local produce. Grilled New York steak in a pool of red wine sauce and roasted duckling in a piquant cream sauce represent some of the more sophisticated types of entrees. Soothing views of the bay reinforce the romantic, charming atmosphere.

### Old Harmony Pasta Factory

**2 Old Creamery Rd. and Highway 1, Harmony 93435**
**805-927-5882 • Lunch and dinner daily; Sun. brunch**
**Reservations recommended • Italian • Moderate**

A restaurant that actually seemed to begin life as a gimmick ("Come dine in the smallest town in California") has not only survived but also advanced by offering good, hearty fare at reasonable prices. Only a short drive from Cambria and Hearst Castle, it's fun to dine in an old creamery building, artfully renovated. Pasta is the big deal here, served up a dozen different ways, but you can also order chicken, pork, and shrimp, all done in a decidedly Italian way. For sunny days, a great outdoor garden patio beckons, and Sunday brunch draws crowds.

### Ian's

**2150 Center St., Cambria 93428 • 805-927-8649**
**Lunch Fri. and Sat., dinner nightly; Sun. brunch**
**Reservations recommended • California cuisine • Moderate**

Though Ian McPhee, the restaurant's namesake chef, has long since departed, some locals claim the food now is just as good or better than the old days. The modern, airy dining room drips with burnished wood and sophisticated lighting, making it a great place for small talk over a romantic dinner. Among the first in the area to demand top-quality meat and fish, the staff continues to embellish that with fresh seasonal greens and vegetables. Fresh fish—anything with shrimp—is always a good choice, as well as perfectly done grilled meats in a variety of creative sauces, accompanied by unique vegetable presentations. The wine list is the pick of the Central Coast wineries.

### Berardi's

**1202 Pine St., Paso Robles 93446 • 805-238-1330 • Lunch and dinner daily • Reservations recommended • Italian • Moderate**

Paso Robles has not yet become a dining mecca, even with all the success of the surrounding wineries; it's still mainly a town that centers on agriculture and the simpler things on the plate. Berardi's has stood the test of time as the old-style Italian dinner house that locals return to again and again. Trendy it's not, but bountiful are the servings. Expect garlic bread, antipasto, soup, and salad, along with hearty red-sauced pastas and grilled meats and fish.

### McPhee's Grill

**416 Main St., Templeton 93465 • 805-434-3204 • Lunch Tues.–Fri., dinner Tues.–Sun. • Reservations recommended California cuisine • Moderate to expensive**

Chef Ian McPhee, formerly of Ian's in Cambria, left his namesake restaurant to move a bit eastward to Templeton, where the great need for food matched the quality of the local wines. Since its opening, it has become a haven for vintners and locals alike who want something creative and a bit more sophisticated on their plates. The menu is as diverse as the chef's culinary interests. Pacific Rim influence can be seen in shrimp tempura, pot stickers, or pheasant with ginger. You can order prime beef, chops, and fresh fish as well, albeit with the chef's own idiosyncratic style, which draws on the best aspects of California cuisine fused with classical cooking techniques.

## ANNUAL EVENTS

### MARCH

**Ignace Paderewski Festival Featuring A Celebration of Zinfandel 805-239-8463**

Seminars, winemaker dinners, grand Zinfandel tasting and auction, barrel tastings, and special winery events over a three-day weekend.

## MAY

**Paso Robles Wine Festival Weekend • 805-239-8463**
Grand outdoor wine tasting in City Park on Saturday, followed by winemaker dinners, concerts, winery open houses, and special events all weekend.

## JULY

**KCBX Central Coast Wine Classic and Auction • 4100 Vachell Ln. • San Luis Obispo 93401 • 805-546-WINE**
A four-day extravaganza in Avila Beach featuring barrel tastings, winery dinners, auction, Champagne reception and award dinner, and grand tasting finale.

## SEPTEMBER

**Central Coast Wine Festival • 800-634-1414**
On Labor Day weekend, annual tasting of county wines, held outdoors in downtown San Luis Obispo.

## OCTOBER

**Paso Robles Harvest Wine Fair • 805-239-8463**
Local wine and local food to celebrate the bounty of the harvest. More than forty producers—herbs, apples, nuts, produce, baked foods, and condiments—are offered with the wines.

## NOVEMBER

**Edna Valley/Arroyo Grande Valley Vintners' Association Harvest Celebration • 805-541-5868**
Held on the first Saturday of the month, an outdoor tasting featuring all the wineries in the two valleys; on the following Sunday, special events and open houses, including several wineries not usually open to the public.

## DECEMBER

**Holiday open houses at the wineries for gift shopping 805-239-8463**
Evening celebration, with hayride, horse-drawn trolley, and parade of Paso Robles' historic Victorian homes.

## RESOURCES

### Edna Valley/Arroyo Grande Valley Vintners' Association

**2195 Corbett Canyon Rd. • Arroyo Grande 93420**
**805-541-5868**
Free wine touring map/brochure available.

### Paso Robles Chamber of Commerce

**1113 Spring St. • Paso Robles 93446 • 805-238-0506,**
**800-406-4040**
List of accommodations, restaurants, recreations, and other activities.

### Paso Robles Vintners and Growers

**1225 Park St. • Paso Robles 93446 • 805-239-8463,**
**800-549-WINE**
Call for recorded information and a free wine touring map/brochure.

### San Luis Obispo County Visitor and Conference Bureau

**1041 Chorro St., Ste. E • San Luis Obispo 93401**
**800-634-1414, 805-541-8000**
Bounty of the County Food and Wine Tour brochure free; list of accommodations, restaurants, recreations, and other activities.

# SANTA BARBARA COUNTY

*H*undreds of people weekly visit the quaint town of
Solvang, the self-proclaimed Danish capital of
America, to sample the local pastries, sausages, and
aebleskiver, as well as to admire the gingerbread Danish architecture and windmills. More recent visitors have been attracted by the
growing number of factory outlet stores. Many are unaware they
are in the heart of Santa Barbara County wine country; that would
not have seemed unusual twenty-five years ago because little culti-
vation of grapevines existed. The most visible industries were—and
still are—ranching, farming, and horse breeding. People still treasure the quiet, unhurried life in this largely rural area on the northern edge of the county, just thirty-five miles up the coast from
Santa Barbara and a short two-and-one-half-hour drive north of
Los Angeles.

The Franciscan fathers planted grapes in the county 200 years
ago to provide sacramental wine for the nearby missions in Solvang
and Lompoc. But serious commercial vineyard plantings began
only a quarter century ago. Local growers noticed their longer,
cooler growing season resulted in richer, more flavorful fruit.
Utilizing their vineyards, they started their own wineries, proudly
proclaiming the local appellation.

When Firestone Winery made a major financial commitment to
planting vineyards and building a modern winery in 1972, it vali-
dated Santa Barbara County's vineyard viability. Other wineries

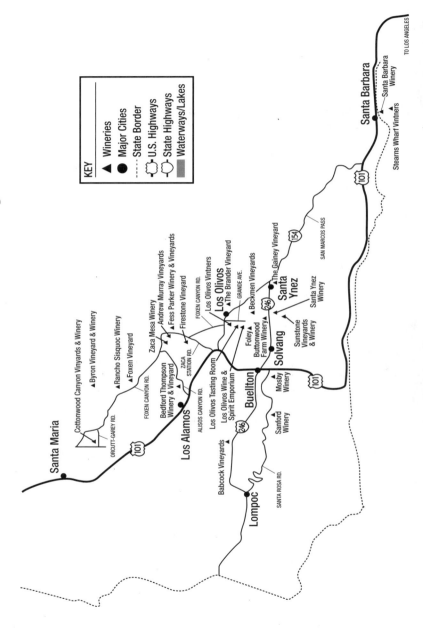

Santa Barbara County

KEY
- ▲ Wineries
- ● Major Cities
- State Border
- U.S. Highways
- State Highways
- Waterways/Lakes

TO LOS ANGELES

Santa Barbara

Santa Barbara Winery

Stearns Wharf Vintners

SAN MARCOS PASS

The Gainey Vineyard

Santa Ynez

Santa Ynez Winery

Beckmen Vineyards

Los Olivos Vintners

The Brander Vineyard

GRANDE AVE.

Los Olivos

Andrew Murray Vineyards

Fess Parker Winery & Vineyards

Firestone Vineyard

FOXEN CANYON RD.

Zaca Mesa Winery

Foley

Buttonwood Farm Winery

Solvang

Sunstone Vineyards & Winery

Mosby Winery

Bedford Thompson Winery & Vineyard

ZACA STATION RD.

Buellton

FOXEN CANYON RD.

Cottonwood Canyon Vinyards & Winery

▲ Byron Vineyard & Winery

▲ Rancho Sisquoc Winery

▲ Foxen Vineyard

ORCUTT-GAREY RD.

Santa Maria

ALISOS CANYON RD.

Los Olivos Wine & Spirit Emporium

Los Olivos Tasting Room

Los Alamos

Sanford Winery

Babcock Vineyards ▲

SANTA ROSA RD.

Lompoc

soon began to establish themselves. Now more than two dozen wineries span a thirty-mile radius; many sit out in the country, where the only sound is the rustling of wind through the vines and the plaintive call of cattle. It's a perfect setting for picnics and quiet talks while tasting the fruit of the vine. An easy day trip from Santa Barbara or Los Angeles, the back country roads also lend themselves to extended stays and exploration.

Because Santa Barbara County is so far south of other premium wine-producing regions in California, people often think it too warm for grape growing. However, most of the vineyards are among the coolest in the state, comparable to Carneros in southern Napa and Sonoma counties. This is due to the unique geography of the county. Unlike the north-south mountain ranges of Napa and Sonoma, the Santa Ynez Mountains run east to west, forming a valley open to the ocean, allowing the direct flow of fog and on-shore breezes. The coastal geography coupled with the mountain topography make it susceptible to convection fog, which develops during the early evening hours and blankets the county. This marine influence, along with the bright sunny days, allows for a long, cool growing season that brings the grapes to full, mature ripeness.

In the last ten years, large north coast wineries, like Robert Mondavi, Beringer, and Kendall-Jackson, have purchased large amounts of vineyard acreage in the county, proving what the locals knew all along: Santa Barbara County produces quality wines on a par with any region in California.

Ironically, touring the wineries can begin at two tasting rooms right in the city of Santa Barbara. But the vineyards and most of the wineries lie about thirty-five miles north of the city on both sides of U.S. 101, close by the cities of Buellton, Solvang, Santa Ynez, Los Olivos, and not too distant Santa Maria.

## WINERIES

*(listed from south to north, with U.S. 101 as the main route)*

### SANTA BARBARA

Start your wine tasting near the beach in Santa Barbara proper: Visit Santa Barbara Winery for the wines and Stearns Wharf for the view and surroundings.

## Santa Barbara Winery

**202 Anacapa St., Santa Barbara 93101 • 805-963-3633, 800-225-3633 • Daily 10–5 • Most varieties poured, no fee Regular tours • Good gift selection • Small picnic area**

French Canadian Pierre LaFond started the winery at this location just two blocks from the beach in 1965, after he ran out of room in his garage. At first, the winery focused on fruit wine, then jug wines, and now, under winemaker Bruce McGuire's guiding hand, premium varietal wines.

With vineyard fruit from the winery's own vineyard (first planted in 1972) near Buellton on the Santa Ynez River, McGuire produces a wide-ranging menu of wines. Perhaps best known for the Chardonnay and Pinot Noir, the winery also offers old vine Zinfandel and even a fresh and fruity *nouveau-beaujolais*-style Zin. Don't miss the sweet, late-harvest Sauvignon Blanc, a terrific dessert wine at a bargain price!

## Stearns Wharf Vintners

**217 G Stearns Wharf, Santa Barbara 93101 • 805-966-6624 Daily 9–9 • Most varieties poured, no fee • Good gift selection Picnic area with ocean view**

While Santa Barbara Winery is only two blocks east of the beach, Stearns Wharf Vintners is two blocks the other way, out over the ocean on the restored Santa Barbara wharf. With its vast ocean vistas, it may be an understatement to declare this the California tasting room with the most spectacular view.

In 1981 Doug and Candy Scott established the Stearns Wharf label, utilizing grapes grown in nearby Santa Ynez Valley. The unique setting, with a long bar and big bay windows, encourages visitors to relax and sample the long list of available wines, including those from Santa Ynez Winery, which the Scotts also own. Along with the wines, you may purchase a variety of cheeses, meats, and breads, which can be enjoyed on the open-air balcony overlooking the panoramic blue Pacific. Obviously this makes a good lunchtime stop or before dinner for a light snack with a glass of wine. Chardonnay, Muscat Canelli, Riesling, and Pinot Noir are among the favorites poured daily.

## BUELLTON

You can see the red carriage house of Mosby Winery on Santa Rosa Road from U.S. 101 as you pull into Buellton; further along a few miles down Santa Rosa Road is Sanford. Back in town, you'll go west on Highway 246 toward Lompoc and the ocean to Babcock.

## Mosby Winery

**9496 Santa Rosa Rd., Buellton 93427 • 805-688-2415**
**Mon.–Fri. 10–4, Sat.–Sun. 10–5 • Most varieties poured,**
**$2 fee includes logo glass • Small gift selection • Picnic area**

After doing some home winemaking in the early 1960s, Bill Mosby, a dentist in nearby Lompoc, and his wife, Jeri, decided to take the plunge professionally when they bought some acreage in the Santa Ynez Valley. The Mosbys acquired land from the old Rancho de la Vega land grant, along U.S. 101 just south of Buellton, and planted vineyards in 1976. They restored the old, red nineteenth-century carriage house and converted it into a winery facility and tasting room. Across the parking area, Jeri often cooks and hosts winemaker dinners in the historic old adobe.

Originally called Vega Vineyards in honor of the land grant, the name changed to Mosby in 1989, and the winery got a striking new label. The Mosby red barn, clearly visible from the highway, is the northbound traveler's first introduction to Santa Barbara County vineyards. The tasting room, appended to the west side of the winery, was remodeled a few years back and now has a light, airy feeling, with windows looking out on the vineyard. Mosby produces a lean, sleek Chardonnay but is also one of the few in the area to concentrate on Italian varieties like Sangiovese, Nebbiolo, and Pinot Grigio. Very rare are the Grappa di Traminer and a distillate of Wild Plum.

## Sanford Winery

**7250 Santa Rosa Rd., Buellton 93427 • 805-688-3300**
**Daily 11–4 • Most varieties poured, no fee • Picnic area**

Nearly five miles west of Mosby on Santa Rosa Road lies the Sanford Winery. Originally, vintner Richard Sanford became involved in winemaking with partner Michael Benedict by planting a vineyard in the mid-1970s and releasing wine under the Sanford and Benedict label. By 1981, Sanford went his own way on a property down the road from the old vineyard.

Set back from the road, the rustic tasting room nestles amid the hills of Sanford's Rancho El Jabali; dappled natural light spills in from the open-air windows of this southwestern adobe-style building that seems to fit naturally into the surrounding landscape.

Sanford focuses on Sauvignon Blanc, Chardonnay, and Pinot Noir, believing it's best to concentrate on only varieties that grow well and produce the best wines in the county. An added plus: Each vintage of each varietal features a new full-color illustration of a California wildflower by well-known artist Sebastian Titus. Thus Sanford's beautiful labels reflect the quality of wine in the bottle.

### Babcock Vineyard
**5175 Highway 246, Lompoc 93436 • 805-736-1455**
Sat.–Sun. only, 10:30–4 • Most varieties poured, no fee
Picnic area

The Babcock family owns several restaurants in southern California and consequently already had an interest in fine wines. In 1978 they bought the 110-acre Santa Rita Ranch, about nine miles west of Buellton on Highway 246, and eventually planted fifty acres and a winery building.

Son Bryan had studied enology at the University of California at Davis and quickly stepped in to make the wines, with help and advice from local winemakers. Bryan has a progressive and experimental mind, so besides the usual Chardonnay, Pinot Noir, and Sauvignon Blanc, he also produces Syrah, Riesling, Gewurztraminer, and Sangiovese. The tasting room, a short ride up a dirt road off the highway, is a cozy adjunct to the winery proper, where picnic tables line the perimeter. The regular bottlings are moderately priced, while the single-vineyard wines can be outstanding but expensive.

## SOLVANG/SANTA YNEZ/LOS OLIVOS

The largest cluster of wineries and tasting rooms lie within a five-mile radius of Solvang, the Danish capital of America, aptly named after its early settlers and lingering architecture. It's the most central location to make accommodations for winery touring day trips. A short triangular route allows you to sample at ten different places. Driving east on Highway 246 out of Solvang brings you to Santa Ynez Winery, Sunstone, and Gainey; going left at Highways 246 and 154 takes you to Brander; another left on Grand Avenue, the main drag of Los Olivos, gives you Los Olivos Vintners, Los Olivos Tasting Room, and Los Olivos Wine and Spirits Emporium. Jog off Grand to Ontiveros, and follow the signs to Beckmen; driving back to Grand and then over to Alamo Pintado Road brings you to Foley and Buttonwood; traveling shortly back to Highway 246 and Solvang completes the circuit.

## Santa Ynez Winery

**343 N. Refugio Rd., Santa Ynez 93460 • 805-688-8381**
**Daily 10–5 • All varieties poured, $2.50 fee • Regular tours**
**Small gift selection • Picnic area**

The old Bettencourt dairy ranch dates back to 1923, although grapes were only planted as recently as 1968, with a wide variety of test plots. By 1976 the winery hired Fred Brander, who would later start his own winery across the highway, to make the wine in a converted dairy shed. In 1988 the Scott family, which also owns Stearns Wharf Vintners, took over ownership and has continued to build on the past reputation.

Santa Ynez Winery is south of the corner of Highway 246 and Refugio Road (former president and first lady Ronald and Nancy Reagan live about six miles up in the hills), a few minutes east of Solvang. From the road, you can see acres of rolling vineyards next to the barn. The pleasant tasting room offers a wide variety of Santa Ynez's wines, including Cabernet, Chardonnay, Sauvignon Blanc, Riesling, and Pinot Noir. A number of special wines are only available at the winery. Concerts, winemaker dinners, open houses, and harvest parties occur throughout the year. On a busy weekend, tasters often spill out onto the front redwood deck, a fine spot for a picnic.

## Sunstone Vineyards and Winery

**125 N. Refugio Rd., Santa Ynez 93460 • 805-688-WINE,**
**800-313-WINE • Daily 10–4 • All varieties poured, $2 fee**
**includes logo glass • Picnic area**

Right down the road from Santa Ynez Winery is the entrance to Sunstone, one of the newer wineries in the valley. Owned by a family in the construction business, family members did an impressive job of making this brand-new winery look like an Old World building, right down to the faux cracks in the walls. A French/Italian country atmosphere prevails, with a European-style courtyard and tasting room overlooking the usually dry Santa Ynez River. A front porch provides a fine spot to wile away the time with the tables set up with board games; the river overlook has a number of picnic tables.

Inside, you'll get a warm country inn type feeling; a full kitchen, utilized for winery events and open houses, is off to the right, while a stone cave for aging the wines is bored into the hillside. Top favorites are Cabernet, Merlot, and Chardonnay, with limited production of Rhone-style varietals Syrah and Viognier.

## Gainey Vineyard

**3950 E. Highway 246, Santa Ynez 93460 • 805-688-0558**
**Daily 10–5 • All varieties poured, $2.50–$3.50 fee**
**includes logo glass • Regular tours • Good gift selection**
**Shaded picnic area**

Part of an 1,800-acre diversified ranching complex, the Gainey family established this ranch in 1962, and it has become well known for breeding Arabian horses. The Gaineys took notice in the late 1960s, when people began planting new vineyards in the area, but they didn't take the plunge until 1982, planting fifty-four acres. Two years later, they built a beautiful winery and visitors' center on the northern edge of the ranch, right off Highway 246.

The Spanish-style winery, with its long bar and oversized fireplace, resembles a woodsy but upscale hunting lodge. The twenty-minute tour is among the best in the area, presenting a close-up look at the whole winemaking process, from the individual display row of vines to the fermentation room and barrel-aging cellars. The tour concludes in the tasting room, where the host offers Sauvignon Blanc, Riesling, Chardonnay, Pinot Noir, Merlot, and Cabernet. Steps away, plenty of picnic tables lounge in the shaded vineyard garden. Gainey is well known for its annual concert series at the winery, with major music acts, as well as educational cooking demonstrations and seminars.

## Brander Vineyard

**2401 Refugio Rd. (Highway 154 at Roblar Ave.),**
**Los Olivos 93441 • 805-688-2455 • Daily 10–5**
**All varieties poured, $2 fee includes logo glass**
**Small gift selection • Picnic area**

You'll easily recognize the tasting room at Brander from Highway 154: It's the only pink chateau around. Inside, it's all polished wood and glass, with colorful banners hung from the high wood-beamed ceiling. Vineyards border the winery; in fact, you can see Brander's new high-density vineyard plantings in front of the old barn that serves as the winery. Also, shaded picnic areas abound on the grounds.

Although Brander produces Chardonnay, the winery is one of the few in the area that emphasizes Bordeaux varietals: Sauvignon Blanc, Merlot, and a proprietary wine called Bouchet, a blend of Cabernet Franc and Merlot that's akin to a French St. Emilion. Two limited-release refreshing white wines you shouldn't miss are Cuvee Nicholas and Cuvee Natalie, sumptuously flavorful blends.

## Los Olivos Vintners

**2923 Grand Ave., Los Olivos 93441 • 805-688-9665,
800-824-8584 • Daily 11–6 • All varieties poured, no fee
Good gift selection**

In downtown Los Olivos, Tony Austin, the winemaker who put Firestone on the map many years ago, and his partners have changed their winery's name from Austin Cellars to Los Olivos Vintners. Austin started the winery in 1983 and then opened the tasting room in the middle of art-gallery-laden Los Olivos. The tasting room has recently been remodeled to offer ever-changing gallery shows, as well as purvey wines.

The winery gained a reputation for Pinot Noir and late-harvest Riesling but lately has focused on Cabernet Franc and the Bordeaux-style blends. Recent tastings included Pinot Noir and Chardonnay under the Austin Cellars label and Riesling and Cabernet under the Los Olivos Vintners label, earmarked for the reserve wines.

## Los Olivos Tasting Room and Wine Shop

**2905 Grand Ave., Los Olivos 93441 • 805-688-7406
Daily 11–6 • Usually ten different wines poured, $3 fee**

This tasting room, next to Los Olivos Vintners (look for the flagpole in the middle of the intersection), is one of the oldest buildings in the valley, dating back to 1887, when it was the town's general store. Today it's a wine store and tasting room devoted to quality Central Coast wineries that are not open to the public for tasting or touring. For the modest tasting fee, you can taste the selections of the day from small producers, like Hitching Post, Au Bon Climat, Qupé, Ojai, Pagor, Daniel Gehrs, and Lane Tanner.

## Los Olivos Wine and Spirits Emporium

**2531 Grand Ave., Los Olivos 93441 • 805-688-4409
Daily 11–6 • Usually ten to fourteen different wines poured,
$4 fee**

Located in the historic Los Olivos Market, about a half-mile south of town, this commercial tasting room features a variety of local wines not widely available for tasting or sale. Alban, Chimere, Fiddlehead, Jaffurs, Qupé, and Whitcraft are some labels usually open for tasting here. You may also buy small-batch Bourbons, Tequila, and other selected grappas, Brandies, and fruit infusions.

## Beckmen Vineyards

**2670 Ontiveros Rd., Los Olivos 93441 • 805-688-8664**
**Daily 10–4 • All varieties poured, no fee • Picnic area**

The Beckmen family recently purchased the former Houtz Vineyards and are enthusiastic about the new wines they produce from sixteen acres of vineyards planted in 1982. Traverse through several horse-breeding farms to a small country road that takes you through a gate, past a pond, and deposits you at a California-style redwood barn that serves as the winery.

Winemaking is no mystery here, as the tasting room sits off to one side of the winery; you can observe the barrel, tank, and other paraphernalia as you sip. Picnic in the gazebo by the pond or under the oaks near the rose garden, and enjoy the bucolic surroundings. Mainstays are Cabernet, Chardonnay, and Sauvignon Blanc, while future plans include Merlot, Syrah, and Muscat.

## Foley Estate

**1711 Alamo Pintado Rd., Solvang 93463 • 805-688-8554**
**Daily 10–4, Sat.–Sun. 10–5 in summer • All varieties poured,**
**no fee • Small gift selection • Picnic area**

A trio of Carey family physicians who joined forces to renovate an old dairy barn on the property in time for the 1978 harvest founded Carey Cellars. In 1987 Kate Firestone bought the winery as her own personal project but kept it separate and distinct from the large Firestone Vineyards over the hill. Kate immediately set out to improve the production facility and fine-tune the wines. Renaming the winery Curtis, she recently hired winemaking guru John Kerr to take the wines to the next level of quality. Recently, the Foleys, from Santa Barbara, purchased the winery.

Foley is the prototypical idea of what city folks think a winery should look like: off the beaten path and rustically housed in a weathered red barn, surrounded by rows of symmetrical vineyards. The tasting room is across from the winery in a circa 1926 clapboard house like your grandmother might have lived in. It's a charming and intimate environment for sampling the range of wines that include Sauvignon Blanc, Orange Muscat, Chardonnay, Pinot Noir, Rose, Cabernet, and Merlot.

## Buttonwood Farm Winery

**1500 Alamo Pintado Rd., Solvang 93464 • 805-688-3032**
**Daily 11–5 • All varieties poured, $2.50 fee includes logo glass**

This winery began life as one of the many vegetable-fruit farms in the area but also began to plant vineyards. For many years, Buttonwood sold its grapes to other wineries, until 1989, when the owners decided to try their hands at the winemaking end of things too. They brought on Aussie native Mike Brown, who had made wines in the area for more than a decade, as winemaker. Buttonwood has been on a roll ever since.

The tasting room looks more like a renovated, enclosed produce stand, because that's still a big part of what they do here. The wines come from estate-grown grapes and include Cabernet, Cabernet Franc, Merlot, Sauvignon Blanc, and Marsanne, all reasonably priced for such quality. In spring and summer, hosts often pour the wines outside on the back patio.

## FOXEN CANYON

For this circuit, you need plenty of time to explore the country back roads because these wineries are spaced quite a bit further apart. Coming from U.S. 101, go east on Zaca Station Road, which turns into Foxen Canyon Road; if you're extending your triangular tour from Los Olivos, Foxen Canyon is the first northbound road off Highway 154 after Grand Avenue. Proceed up and down the hills until you reach a T intersection. Firestone is a left turn and close to U.S. 101; a right sends you east on Foxen Canyon Road, where Fess Parker, Andrew Murray, and Zaca Mesa come into view; a detour on Alisos Canyon Road takes you to Bedford Thompson. Back on Foxen Canyon, you'll pass Foxen and Rancho Sisquoc. A right turn onto Tepusquet will take you over a dry riverbed and up to Byron; then go back to Foxen Canyon and continue up the road for several miles, making a left at Orcutt-Garey Road and then a right at Old Dominion Road to Cottonwood Canyon.

## Firestone Vineyard

**5017 Zaca Station Rd., Los Olivos 93441 • 805-688-3940**
**Daily 10–4 • All varieties poured, no fee • Regular tours**
**Good gift selection • Picnic area**

With the vines first planted in 1972 and the sleek, low-slung winery completed in 1975, Firestone was one of the pioneers in the area and the first to make a major investment on a large scale. Brooks Firestone (yes, that Firestone of the tire and rubber fortune), with the backing of his father and Suntory Limited, eventually planted 540 acres of estate grapes. Last year, Firestone bought out the Japanese interest and now solely owns the winery.

Still the largest winery in the valley, consider it a must if you are interested in a winery tour that takes you through some inside details of winemaking. Besides the informative tour, the winery itself is spectacular; its four-level structure features redwood, stained glass, miles of red tile, and even a pleasant cobblestoned courtyard with a gurgling fountain. Even the wines—Riesling, Chardonnay, Sauvignon Blanc, Merlot, and Cabernet—seem to taste even better in the cool tasting room that offers a great view of the surrounding vineyards.

## Fess Parker Winery

**6200 Foxen Canyon Rd., Los Olivos 93441 • 805-688-1545**
**Daily 10–5 • All varieties poured, $2 fee includes logo glass**
**Tours • Picnic area**

Fess Parker, of Daniel Boone and Davy Crockett television fame, is no Johnny-come-lately to the real estate or hospitality business: He owns the Red Lion Inn on the beach in Santa Barbara. But he is a newcomer to the wine business. After a slow start, the beautiful new winery building has been completed, and the wines have greatly improved from the first releases. Son Eli has got a handle on making the wines, with help from seasoned consultants.

They draw on sixty recently planted acres surrounding the winery as well as eighty acres of the esteemed Sierra Madre Vineyard. They've decided to concentrate on Riesling, Muscat, Chardonnay, Pinot Noir, Syrah, and Merlot. You may see Fess himself in the tasting room on weekends, autographing wine purchases for his visitors. And yes, he'll even sell you a coonskin cap!

## Andrew Murray Vineyards

**6701 Foxen Canyon Rd., Los Olivos 93441 • 805-686-9604**
**Daily by appointment only**

Founded in 1990, a family owns Andrew Murray and has dedicated it to producing Rhone-style wines from its thirty acres of hillside vines,

1,400 feet off the canyon floor. The winery is excavated into the hill for natural insulation and fashioned after a French country manor, complete with aromatic gardens. The initial Rhone varietals released are Rose of Syrah, Syrah, Viognier, and Roussanne. A call in advance is necessary (because of the small staff) to reserve a private tasting and tour.

## Zaca Mesa Winery

**6905 Foxen Canyon Rd., Los Olivos 93441 • 805-688-9339**
**Daily 10–4 • All varieties poured, no fee • Regular tours**
**Good gift selection • Picnic area**

Recognizable by its weathered wood exterior that blends in with the natural surroundings, Zaca Mesa Winery itself has weathered ups and downs in its winemaking and varietal focus over the years. This older, established winery has graduated a number of winemakers— Ken Brown, Jim Clendenen, Bob Lindquist, and Lane Tanner—who have gone on to start their own wineries. In 1993, Zaca Mesa hired Dan Gehrs as winemaker, designed a new label, and focused on the wines it makes best—to renewed critical acclaim. The '93 Syrah has been honored as one of the best ever made in California.

The tasting room remains the same: a timeless, majestic space with a cathedral ceiling. The tours are well done. Drawing on the elevated mesa vineyard nearby, the well-made wines include Chardonnay, Syrah, Viognier, Pinot Noir, and the special Z Cuvee, a delicious blend of Rhone grapes in a Chateauneuf-du-Pape-style blend. Some of the smaller wine lots are only available at the winery; be sure to ask about them.

## Bedford Thompson Winery and Vineyard

**9303 Alisos Canyon Rd., Los Alamos 93440 • 805-344-2107**
**Sat.–Sun. 10–5 or by appointment • Picnic area**

Established in 1993 by winemaker Stephan Bedford and viticulturalist David Thompson, the winery produces wine from twenty-five acres of steep, hillside vineyards located in the surrounding Los Alamos Valley, augmented by purchased grapes. Riesling, Pinot Blanc, and Chardonnay are the first releases, followed by Pinot Noir, Cabernet Franc, and Syrah.

## Foxen Vineyard

**7200 Foxen Canyon Rd., Santa Maria 93454 • 805-937-4251**
**Sat.–Sun. 12–4, when wines are available • Most varieties poured, no fee**

The Foxen boys, Dick Dore and Bill Wathen, handcraft wines from their own Tinaquiac Vineyard, as well as other quality vineyards in the county. The surroundings are decidedly low-tech, with the winery in an old barn and the tasting room in a small shack just steps away, right on Foxen Canyon Road. If you're speeding though the back roads, you'll probably whiz by it without even knowing.

Foxen produces only a few thousand cases a year, so the winery only opens on the weekends, when one of the vintners will likely serve you. Chardonnay and Pinot Noir are produced, and their Cabernet is generally acknowledged as one of the best in the valley. Don't pass up sampling the Chenin Blanc, an overlooked variety that the Foxen boys have taken a liking to and vinified in a full, rich style.

### Rancho Sisquoc Winery

**6600 Foxen Canyon Rd., Santa Maria 93454 • 805-934-4332**
**Daily 10–4 • All varieties poured, no fee • Tours • Picnic area**

Further down Foxen Canyon Road, the white San Ramon Chapel (built in 1875 by Benjamin Foxen, namesake of the Foxen Vineyards) sitting high on the hill, gives you a visual sign to turn right to Rancho Sisquoc Winery. This 37,000-acre cattle and fruit ranch also houses a small 5,000-case winery. Expect a step back in time, as you pass farming fields, pastures, and orchards: symbols of a more rustic time that still exists here.

Rancho Sisquoc is the second-oldest vineyard in the county, planted in 1968. Its owners sold their grapes at first, so the winery wasn't established until 1977. They still sell most of the grapes from their 220 vineyard acres but reserve the best for themselves. You won't often see the label outside the Central Coast, and much of the wine is sold through its mailing list. Chardonnay, Cabernet, and Merlot are all made in small lots and aged in a combination of American and French oak. One of the last plots of Sylvaner, some-times called Franken Riesling, is planted here, and it produces a spirited, refreshing white wine. A new tasting room will soon replace the old, rustic one, but the setting still exudes Old World charm, with plenty of room for a wine country picnic.

### Byron Vineyard and Winery

**5230 Tepusquet Rd., Santa Maria 93454 • 805-937-7288**
**Daily 10–5 (winter 10–4) • All varieties poured, no fee**
**Small gift selection • Picnic area**

An alumnus of Zaca Mesa, winemaker Byron "Ken" Brown left in 1984 to start Byron and hasn't looked back since. The winery has been so successful that the Robert Mondavi Winery bought it a few years back, but it continues to operate locally. So far, the Mondavi influence has been an infusion of capital to plant more vineyards and a new gravity-flow winery that sits on the river bench.

The old ranch-style winery, state-of-the-art in its time, was not large enough for the future. But visitors are still welcomed in the small tasting room on the east side of the old winery. In the back, a shaded gazebo with picnic tables overlooks rustling Tepusquet Creek. Byron is particularly proud of the many medals its Sauvignon Blanc, Chardonnay, and Pinot Noir have won over the years. Both Pinot Blanc and Pinot Gris, interesting alternatives to Chardonnay, are produced in limited quantities.

## Cottonwood Canyon Vineyard

**3940 Old Dominion Rd., Santa Maria 93454 • 805-937-9063**
**Daily 10:30–5:30, winter Fri.–Sun. 10:30–5 • All varieties**
**poured, no fee • Picnic area**

The Beko family, a newcomer to the wine scene, began producing premium, estate-grown Pinot Noir and Chardonnay in 1987. Cottonwood has two tasting rooms, this one among the vineyards, amid the back-road lettuce, onion, and strawberry fields of Santa Maria.

Cottonwood claims to embrace the traditional Burgundian wine-making methods for both these classical varietals. The winery makes several different versions of Chardonnay: One is the Bistro Classic, primarily for the restaurant trade, while a full-blown Chardonnay and a reserve are also offered. The Pinots get some extra bottle aging here; it's not unusual to find a five-year-old vintage available for tasting and sales. The newest additions to the line are the premium reserve versions of Cabernet and Merlot.

## RESTAURANTS

## The Wine Cask

**813 Anacapa St., Santa Barbara 93101 • 805-966-9463**
**Lunch and dinner daily; breakfast on weekends • Reservations**
**recommended • Regional California cuisine • Moderate to expensive**

If you're day tripping to the wine country from a base in Santa Barbara, The Wine Cask is the No. 1 place for wine and food aficionados to dine in this area. Not only do the beautiful room and patio with a gurgling fountain convey the essence of Santa Barbara style, but the food equals the surroundings. In addition, the best wine shop in town is next door; as a bonus, you can buy any wine and have it served at dinner for only $10 corkage. The Wine Cask features Santa Barbara spot prawns, Sonoma foie gras, organic produce, and a variety of ever-changing preparations of fish, lamb, game, and beef.

## Blue Shark Bistro

**21 W. Victoria St., Santa Barbara 93101 • 805-564-7100**
**Serving from 11:30 daily except Mon. • California bistro cuisine**
**Inexpensive to moderate**

Bistros, where you can eat and drink with friends in a casual atmosphere, are back, and Blue Shark Bistro epitomizes value. The menu does double duty; if you want an omelette for dinner, so be it; or filet mignon for lunch, then full speed ahead. Only a couple selections cost more than $10, and more than half the bottles (featuring local wineries) cost less than $20. Start with spicy onion soup or the salad special of the day. Look for entrees like salmon in red wine sauce with potato pancakes, pork tenderloin in garlic sauce with fried noodles, or the signature dish: grilled shark in five peppercorn sauce with an array of tender squash.

## Downey's

**1305 State St., Santa Barbara 93101 • 805-966-5006**
**Dinner daily except Mon. • Reservations imperative**
**Regional California cuisine • Expensive**

Those who are willing to pay for the ultimate dining experience in Santa Barbara should seek out chef John Downey's place. He gained his legendary reputation as a master of California cuisine by continually reinventing the menu on a daily basis, depending on the best available produce, fish, and meats in the marketplace. If it doesn't meet his standards, it won't be on the menu that night—and his standards are very high. Mussels, prepared any number of ways, are a favorite, as well as foie gras. Local spot prawns, scallops, grilled ahi, and salmon make regular appearances too. He also prepares duck, lamb, and beef inventively, with excellent accompaniments.

## The Hitching Post

**406 E. Highway 246, Buellton 93427 • 805-688-0676**
**Dinner nightly • Reservations recommended • American**
**Moderate**

Santa Maria-style barbecue—beef cooked over a live oakwood fire—doesn't get any better than this. You can watch the proprietor-winemaker, Frank Ostini, cook up a storm behind the glassed-in grill in the dining room. Corn-fed prime beef from the

Midwest is king here, where the preferred cuts are filet mignon, New York strip, and top sirloin. Specials of the day might include salmon, ahi, smoked duck, turkey, and wild game in season. Don't miss the seasoned, grilled artichokes and the best-ever french fries. All dinners come complete with an old-fashioned relish tray, shrimp cocktail, salad, choice of potato or rice, and garlic bread (whew!). Save room for fine desserts. Great local wine list too, including the chef's own Pinots.

### Cold Spring Tavern

**5995 Stagecoach Rd., San Marcos Pass, Santa Barbara 93105 805-967-0066 • Lunch and dinner daily; breakfast Sat.–Sun Reservations recommended • American • Moderate**

Halfway between Santa Barbara and Solvang, down a gorge off the San Marcos Pass, you'll find a real dining oddity: a hundred-year-old stagecoach stop that still looks like it did back then. Cold Spring Tavern couldn't get funkier even if Hollywood set designers tried to recreate the Old West. Don't let looks or the legions of Harleys parked out front fool you though; the food has kept up with the times. Cold Spring features fresh fish from nearby Santa Barbara waters, along with venison, ribs, chicken, and even a burger or two.

### Cafe Angelica

**490 First St., Solvang 93463 • 805-686-9970 • Lunch and dinner daily • Reservations recommended • Italian/Tex-Mex Moderate**

A bright spot in the Danish dining firmament of Solvang, this cafe serves up great salads, spicy crab cakes, and whole trout stuffed with shrimp and crab, as well as a half-dozen pastas. A local wine list and a patio for people-watching provide an added plus.

### Cafe Chardonnay

**2436 Baseline Rd., Ballard 93463 • 800-638-2466 Dinner Wed.–Sun. • Reservations imperative • California cuisine Moderate**

Located inside the Victorian-style Ballard (bed and breakfast) Inn, this cozy dining room offers fresh organic greens, soups, pastas, and grilled meats. The menu often features leg of lamb, pork chops, and roasted chicken, along with the chef's specials of the day. The wine list is ninety-nine percent local at fair prices.

## Mattei's Tavern

**Highway 154 at Main St., Los Olivos 93441 • 805-688-4820**
**Lunch Thurs.–Sun., dinner nightly • Reservations recommended**
**American • Moderate**

Mattei's began life as a stagecoach stop in 1886 and later was the end of the line for the old Pacific Coast railroad. Felix Mattei built a hotel where travelers could also refresh themselves with food and drink. The hotel is long gone, but the weathered saloon and restaurant remain, serving up steak, prime rib, chicken, and fish, all with salads and hot bread.

## Cuvee

**26 W. Anapamu St., Santa Barbara 93101 • 805-730-1766**
**Lunch and dinner daily • Reservations reommended • California cuisine/eclectic • Moderate to expensive**

As one of the most exciting new restaurants in Santa Barbara, Cuvee is sophisticated yet casual. California cuisine meets its ethnic match in starters like duck shui mai set atop a spicy Hunan salad or local rock shrimp sautéed in cilantro-sage butter, served on handmade corn tortillas with avocado salsa. Expect entrees like pan-roasted filet in red wine-huckleberry sauce or grilled salmon with eggplant-artichoke hash along with a sauté of spinach, basil, and shiitake mushrooms. Desserts are to die for (Death By Chocolate), and the wine list is seriously eclectic. Separate cigar bar downstairs with live entertainment on weekends.

## Chef Rick's Ultimately Fine Foods

**4869 S. Bradley Rd., Santa Maria 93454 • 805-966-9676**
**Dinner daily except Sun. • No reservations**
**American/Southwest/Cajun • Inexpensive to moderate**

It's just a storefront in a shopping plaza, but Chef Rick's dishes up splendid entrees, like New Mexican grilled garlic chicken with black bean chili, and shrimp and chicken etouffee with green rice. Order off the blackboard menu at the counter, and then wait to be served and smothered in waves of spicy and herbal flavors. Prices are low for such quality; the same can be said of the great local wine selection. Located at the southern end of Santa Maria, it's not that far from the wineries.

## ANNUAL EVENTS

### FEBRUARY

**The International Festival of Methode Champenoise**
**P.O. Box 790 • Avila Beach 93424 • 805-544-1285**

Weekend celebration in Santa Barbara, featuring seminars and tastings of both sparkling wine and Champagne. Lifestyle and sparkling wine auction, along with luncheon, food and wine pairings, dinner dance, and Champagne brunch.

## APRIL

**Santa Barbara County Vintners' Festival • P.O. Box 1558 Santa Ynez 93460 • 805-688-0881, 800-218-0881.**
In Buellton/Solvang, the Vintners' Association's outdoor wine and food festival, with all county wineries pouring and participating; tickets limited to 1,500 each day. In addition, many winemaker dinners, winery open houses, and special events are scheduled.

## OCTOBER

**Celebration of Harvest • P.O. Box 1558 • Santa Ynez 93460 805-688-0881, 800-218-0881**
In Buellton/Solvang, this is the Vintners' Association's other annual event, celebrating the end of harvest. Outdoor wine and food festival with all county wineries involved, as well as food purveyors, ag exhibits, silent auction, etc. Many winery open houses and special events scheduled.

## RESOURCES

### Santa Barbara Convention and Visitors' Bureau

**510 State St., Ste. A • Santa Barbara 93101 • 805-966-9222, 800-676-1266, 800-927-4688**
Accommodations, restaurants, recreations, and other activities.

### Santa Barbara County Vintners' Association

**P.O. Box 1558 • Santa Ynez 93460 • 805-688-0881, 800-218-0881**
Full-color touring map available, as well as information about the Vintners' and Harvest festivals.

### Solvang Chamber of Commerce

**P.O. Box 70 • Solvang 93463 • 805-688-0701, 800-468-6765**
Accommodations, restaurants, recreations, and other activities.

# TEMECULA

*I*n the late eighteenth century, when Father Junipero Serra came northward through old California establishing the missions, he also planted vineyards. Two centuries later, little vestige of those vineyards remains, thanks to vast urban developments in what are now San Diego and Los Angeles. Frenchman and pioneer viticulturalist Jean Louis Vignes (appropriately, his last name translates as "vines") established the then-largest California vineyard east of the dusty pueblo of Los Angeles in the early 1800s. Today, only a smattering of old vines remain in Fontana and Rancho Cucamonga, sandwiched between factories and housing developments.

Temecula, located not quite midway between San Diego and Los Angeles, was literally a cowtown that serviced local ranchers until the early 1960s, when Kaiser bought a big chunk of land with thoughts of turning it into a planned development community. So the gentrification began in earnest, with chain restaurants, motels, and tracts of model homes.

In 1967 the first vineyards were planted in a seemingly desert region. The area's secret, however, is the Rainbow Gap, an opening in the hills providing a direct passageway to the cooling air of the Pacific Ocean, only thirteen miles west. The gap acts as a conduit, covering the valley with early morning fog that usually burns off to bright sun. Then almost every afternoon, a cooling breeze blows through. Warm days and cool nights make this a good spot for grapevines in parched southern California.

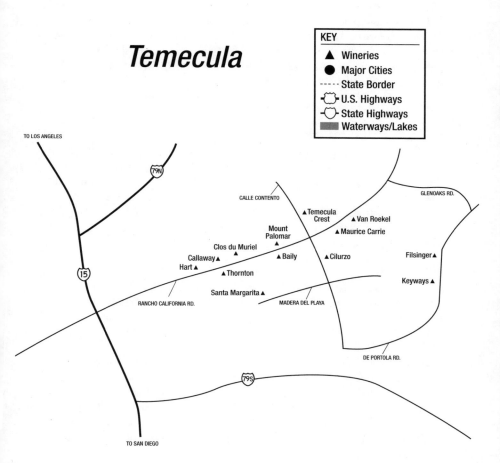

## Temecula

KEY
▲ Wineries
● Major Cities
----- State Border
U.S. Highways
State Highways
Waterways/Lakes

TO LOS ANGELES

79N

CALLE CONTENTO

GLENOAKS RD.

▲ Temecula
Crest

▲ Van Roekel

Mount
Palomar ▲

▲ Maurice Carrie

Clos du Muriel
▲

Callaway ▲

▲ Baily

▲ Cilurzo

Filsinger ▲

Hart ▲

15

▲ Thornton

Keyways ▲

Santa Margarita ▲

RANCHO CALIFORNIA RD.

MADERA DEL PLAYA

DE PORTOLA RD.

79S

TO SAN DIEGO

Callaway was the first winery to set up shop in 1974, and since then the area's winery population has mushroomed to more than a dozen. Shopping centers sprung up to serve the fast-growing local population, as well as day tripping and weekend tourists who come for wine tasting and hot-air ballooning. It may seem incongruous to pass a housing subdivision labeled Chardonnay Hills, but so far, the developments and vineyards have coexisted, the latter now protected by agricultural preserve laws.

## WINERIES

Whether coming from San Diego or Los Angeles, exit Interstate 15 at Rancho California Road, heading east through town. Most of the wineries are either visible from the street or lie on adjacent side roads with directional signage. Van Roekel is the last winery on Rancho California Road, but follow it a short distance and turn right on Glen Oaks Road and then right again on De Portola Road to find both Filsinger and Keyways.

### Hart Winery

**41300 Avenida Biona (at Rancho California Rd.), Temecula 92593 • 909-676-6300 • Daily 9–4:30 • All varieties poured, $2 fee includes logo glass**

Joe Hart started out planting vineyards as a weekend pursuit, back in the early 1970s. But soon the winemaking bug bit him, and a few years later he built a utilitarian barn of a winery. There's nothing fancy about the place; it's a crazy quilt of various barrels, pallets, cardboard boxes, and bottles, seemingly randomly stacked on each other. The tasting room consists of a small area in the front, cleared of winemaking debris. If more than a dozen people show up at the same time, it might seem slightly claustrophobic, though there's plenty of room on the front porch.

No Sweet Wines reads the sign near the front door of the winery. He also could have posted Not Many White Wines, as Hart specializes in traditional, flavorful red wines. For something cold and off-dry though, the Grenache Rose pleases the masses. The best reds—Grenache, Mourvedre, Merlot, and Syrah—are all soft, fruity, and very drinkable, without necessarily any need of further aging. The newest blend of Rhone varietals, called Cuvee du Sud, is a tasty bargain at $12. Price range, $8–$20.

# Callaway Vineyard & Winery

**32720 Rancho California Rd., Temecula 92589**
**909-676-4001 • Daily 10:30–4:45 • All varieties poured, $3 fee**
**includes logo glass • Tours Mon.–Fri. 11, 1, 3, weekends 11–4**
**hourly • Wines by the glass and appetizers available at the**
**Vineyard Terrace overlooking the vines • Good gift selection**

Ely Callaway helped pioneer grape growing in this formerly over-looked region. When he retired from Burlington Industries, he rolled the dice and hired the best vineyard and winemaking talent money could buy. When the vines had sufficiently matured, he threw up a simple Butler-style building and started making wines in 1974. Ely later sold the winery to Hiram Walker and now makes the wildly successful line of Big Bertha golf clubs.

Callaway caters to visitors, from its smiling, knowledegable tour guides to its gift and tasting room staff. If you only take one tour in Temecula, this should be it; you'll get the best overview of modern winemaking equipment and methodology, explained without unnecessary wine jargon. Afterward, enjoy tasting the wines. You can also taste these wines without a tour at the long bar in the large sun-dappled, whitewashed hospitality room.

In the early years, Callaway experimented with a lot of different grapes; eventually they came to the conclusion that white wine varieties worked best for them. The most popular wine is the Calla-Lees Chardonnay, so called because the wine ages on the lees (spent yeast cells), which gives it a richer, creamier taste that complements the citric fruit and vanilla flavors. The tasting menu includes Fume Blanc, Sauvignon Blanc, dry Chenin Blanc, and the sweeter White Riesling, and Muscat Canelli; Cabernet is the sole red wine. A limited amount of Viognier and Pinot Gris is available for purchase. Wine prices, $6–$10.

# Thornton Winery

**32575 Rancho California Rd., Temecula 92589**
**909-699-0099 • Daily 11–5 • Most varieties (sparkling wines**
**and Brindiamo still wines) poured, $6 fee includes logo glass**
**Tours every half-hour on weekends • Cafe California adjacent**
**with indoor and patio dining, 909-699-0088**
**Extensive gift selection**

Thornton is perhaps the most sophisticated and relaxing winery experience in the valley. The massive stone-cut buildings that make up the compound remind one of French chateaus. Centered around a cobblestoned courtyard with a gurgling fountain are the winery, tasting room, and the much-praised Cafe Champagne, all surrounded by vineyards.

With the recent change in ownership, the winery has taken on a dual personality. Originally named Culbertson, it produced only sparkling wines, but now it also offers an interesting number of premium still wines under the Brindiamo label. Most people come to be tickled by the bubbles in the sparkling wines, made in the traditional French *methode champenoise*, which means the wine undergoes the secondary fermentation, where it acquires its bubbles, right in the bottle.

The two favorites and multiple gold medal winners are the Brut, a blend of different varietals, and the Blanc de Noir, which gets its wonderful salmon color primarily from Pinot Noir. A Brut reserve, which spends several years aging in the cellars, has more complexity and depth. In addition, a limited amount of Cuvee Rouge and Cuvee de Frontignan are usually released around the holidays. The still wines under the Brindiamo label include Chardonnay and Pinot Noir, as well as the popular Rhone-style blend, Rosso Vecchio.

## Clos du Muriel

**33410 Rancho California Rd., Temecula 92589**
**909-676-5400 • Daily 10–5 • All varieties poured, $4 fee**
**includes logo glass • Small gift selection**

The former Picone Winery is now Clos du Muriel, which moved from larger digs, east down the road. Built in 1982, the whitewashed adobe-and-wood-framed building shys away from the road on a modest ridge with a valley view. The open second-story tasting room overlooks the winery below, with its stainless steel tanks and oak barrels. You can conduct your own informal tour of the working winery in its naked glory by following the tasting room railing.

An anomaly in Temecula, the winery imports many of its grapes from both Napa and Sonoma, including Chardonnay, Sauvignon Blanc, Merlot, and Cabernet. The easily likeable White Riesling and Vin Blanc are vinified from local grapes.

## Mount Palomar Winery

**33820 Rancho California Rd., Temecula 92591**
**909-676-5047 • Daily 9–5 • Most varieties poured, $2 fee**
**includes logo glass • Tours Mon.–Fri. 1:30 & 3:30, weekends**
**11:30, 1:30, 3:30 • Good gift selection and gourmet deli**
**Extensively landscaped picnic grounds**

One of the older wineries in the area, Mount Palomar hides from view off Rancho California Road; a winding driveway leads to a well-devised parking area and the hacienda-style winery. The tasting room, all in adobe and dark woods, has a double-sided tasting bar, surrounded by attractive displays of wine and related paraphernalia. On the premises, a full Mediterranean-style deli and snack shop is available for picnickers. The grounds have beautiful landscaping with a shaded gazebo, while hidden on the far side of the parking lot, an even larger picnic area sits amid desert flora and fauna. An added plus for fussy travelers: the most convenient and well-maintained restroom facilites in the valley.

Sweetish White Zin and Riesling are popular, along with dry Chardonnay, Sauvignon Blanc, and Cabernet. Syrah and Sangiovese are among the up and comers. Rhythm is the name given to the interesting red wine blend. Many visitors come just to taste the sweeter-style late-harvest dessert wines, Cream Sherry, and Port.

## Baily Vineyard & Winery

**33833 Rancho California Rd., Temecula 92592
909-676-1895 • Daily 10–5 • Most varieties poured
(five wines), $2.25 fee includes logo glass • Small gift selection
Picnic area**

The Baily tasting room was once located at the winery, tucked in the valley off De Portola Road. But it was a far piece for most to travel, so they conveniently moved it to the heart of Winery Row, Rancho California Road. Still you'll have to jaunt off the highway down a short but narrow, winding road to reach the new tasting room, on a bluff. While the exterior looks nondescript, the interior is functionally cozy, with a fireplace opposite the tasting bar.

The slightly sweet Cabernet Blanc is a real crowd pleaser with the locals, followed by the similarly styled White Riesling. The TV Red (Cabernet) and TV White (Chardonnay–White Riesling blend) are also extremely popular due to their high quality and inexpensive price tag. Cabernet tends toward the herbaceous side. The Muscat Blanc and White Riesling dessert wines round out the selections.

## Temecula Crest Winery

**40620 Calle Contento (quarter mile north of Rancho California
Road), Temecula 92591 • 909-676-8231 • Daily 10–5
Most varieties poured (five wines), $2.25 fee includes logo glass
Shaded picnic area**

Formerly Britton Cellars and then Clos du Muriel, the Bailys and a group of investors took over the property and rechristened it Temecula Crest. Clearly visible from Rancho California Road, the winery sits amid the vines on a hilltop. Built to resemble a large redwood barn, prepare yourself for one of the most striking interiors in the valley. The front tasting room is completely open to the winery proper, with its long rows of oak barrels; it has an almost magisterial feeling. The sense of openness extends to the tasting room; it has a long bar with old barrels scattered about, utilized as displays for wine-related merchandise. The sweeter wines lead the pack, including White Zin, Cabernet Blanc, and White Riesling. Chardonnay, Sauvignon Blanc, and Cabernet represent works in progress. The dessert wine is a rich late-harvest Sauvignon Blanc.

### Cilurzo Vineyard and Winery

**41220 Calle Contento (quarter-mile south of Rancho California Road), Temecula 92592 • 909-676-5250**
**Daily 9:30–5 • Most varieties poured (five wines), $1 fee applies to purchase • Small gift selection • Picnic area on the lake**

Now going on its twenty-seventh year, the Cilurzo winery has probably changed very little since Vince Cilurzo, a Hollywood cameraman who thought winemaking would be a pleasant diversion, founded it. Quite the antithesis to the open-armed Maurice Carrie Winery down the road, the clapboard, wooden-sided winery building looks more functional than visitor friendly. Once you find the front door to the tasting room though, you will enter a land that time forgot (with apologies to Disney).

This tasting room has not been gussied up to appeal to the modern-day traveler, but instead retains the quaint charm of the little old winemaker of bygone years. It's funky all right, with cards, signs, posters, menu clippings, and yes, autographed pictures of Hollywood stars, lining almost every inch of the walls. Accolades, press clippings, and winery awards accumulated over the years bear the yellowed patina of age. The tasting space, a no-nonsense area against the west wall, has rows of folding metal chairs. No fancy rough-hewn wooden bars and no standing on ceremony here!

You can taste more than a dozen wines on the list, including White Zin, Chenin Blanc, Sauvignon Blanc, Chardonnay, Merlot, and Cabernet. The red wines, like Zinfandel and Mourvedre, are big and gutsy, while Petite Sirah is Cilurzo's crowning glory. The inexpensive prices (less than $10 a bottle) befit the low-tech, traditional surroundings.

## Santa Margarita Winery

33490 Madera de Playa (one and one-quarter miles southwest
of Rancho California Road), Temecula 92592 • 909-676-4431
Weekends only 11–4:30 • Most varieties poured, no fee

Further down the gravel road than Cilurzo and then west back
toward town, Santa Margarita, housed in a small barn, specializes
in aged Cabernet Sauvignon; this mom and pop operation opens its
modest digs only on weekends. Originally hobbyists, Barrett and
Margaret Bird began making wine in 1985 and began selling it
commercially in 1991. But you won't find these wines in any
stores, because the production is small and very limited; presently
the Cabernets available are '86, '87, and '89. Chardonnay, Sauvignon Blanc, and Rose of Cabernet are sometimes poured too (if
they're not sold out).

## Maurice Carrie Winery

34225 Rancho California Rd., Temecula 92592
909-676-1711 • Daily 10–5 • Most varieties poured, no fee
Limited deli items • Extensive gift selection • Picnic area

Blooming roses line both sides of the walkway to Maurice
Carrie's rambling, visitor-friendly tasting center. While the large
tasting room cum gift center provides the main focus, the winery
hides in back, with private meeting and party rooms on the side.
On a busy day, hang out on the front running porch; there is also
a large, shaded gazebo set in a rose garden. Two dozen picnic
tables dot the premises. An old barn and windmill provide the
ambience of a once rural area; nearby, a modern play area beckons
to children.

For the blush and white wines, the tasting list indicates the level
of residual sugar in the wine, a great help in steering tasters to their
preferred level of dryness/sweetness; among the sweeter are White
Zin, Sara Bella (White Cab), soft Chenin Blanc, Riesling, and
Muscat Canelli, while the Chardonnay and Sauvignon Blanc are
dry. The reds, Cabernet, Pinot Noir, Merlot, Syrah, and Nebbiolo,
are all dry, full-bodied wines. The lone exception, Cody's Crush, is
a blended red that's like a light Beaujolais, with a slight sweetness
that lends itself to chilling before serving. Prices are reasonable,
with many bottles less than $10.

## Van Roekel Vineyards

**34567 Rancho California Rd., Temecula 92581**
**909-699-6961 • Daily 10–5 • Most varieties poured, no fee**
**Extensive gift selection of wine-themed items, deli items**
**Picnic area**

If Maurice Carrie Winery didn't wow you, then Van Roekel Vineyards, just up the hill, will. In fact, after Bud and Maurice Carrie Van Roekel established Maurice Carrie Winery, they decided to do something even more elaborate, and Van Roekel resulted. They turned the site of the abandoned Mesa Verde Winery into a Dutch village, complete with a quaint little windmill out front. Set on a cul-de-sac, the six buildings model a post-modern Dutch dairy barn style, complete with flowering tulips on the perimeter. Plenty of picnic tables await visitors, as well as an oversized kid's sandbox.

The tasting room, at the top of the hill, is large and airy. A long, blonde wood tasting bar sits in the far corner, while the front features an extensive selection of gifts, including some exquisite wine-themed jewelry. A cold deli case and an entire wall of refrigerated cold drinks (both wines and soft drinks) complete the picture.

The difference between the Carrie line and the Van Roekel line is the latter offers more upscale, premium wines, based on a single grape variety. Chardonnay, Fume Blanc, Gewurztraminer, and Muscat Canelli lead the whites; Cabernet and Merlot lead the red wine parade, with spicy and distinct Syrah and Mourvedre bringing up the rear. Chardonnay *a boire*, which tastes fruity and has a touch of residual sugar, resembles the popular Kendall-Jackson style. Pinot Blanc, not much seen in these parts, is a real winner. For these premium wines, prices are not much more than at Carrie, with many bottles less than $10.

### Filsinger Vineyards and Winery

**39050 De Portola Rd., Temecula 92592 • 909-676-4594**
**Weekends only 10:30–5 • Most varieties poured, no fee**
**Regular tours • Good gift selection • Picnic area**

Those adventuresome souls who like to explore back roads will enjoy a visit to Filsinger. When you run out of wineries on Rancho California Road, go just a bit further and make a right on Glen Oaks Road and another right on De Portola Road; you'll soon see Filsinger, hard by the futuristic buildings of a religious retreat. Filsinger wines are a handcrafted labor of love, as is the winery, constructed over the years mostly by family members. The old-style white stucco California hacienda building with a tile roof has a timeless look. The cool interior has tile floors and an ornate tasting bar. Vineyards surround a partly shaded gazebo and a half-dozen picnic tables. The ubiquitous White Zin is a bit tastier than most. The whites include Chardonnay, Chenin Blanc, Fume Blanc, and—reflecting the Filsingers' German heritage—a fine Gewurztraminer. Cabernet is American oak aged, while sparkling wines are made in the traditional *methode champenoise* style.

## Keyways Vineyard and Winery

**37338 De Portola Rd. (at Vineyard Ln.), Temecula 92592**
**909-676-2152 • Daily 10–5 • Most varieties poured, $1 fee**
**Antiques display • Good gift selection • Picnic area**

Several miles beyond Filsinger, you'll come upon what appears to be a desert outpost; but in fact, vines do grow quite well on proprietor Carl Key's land. A mission-style rancho, with the traditional tile roof, houses the tasting room. The interior acts as a veritable museum to the proprietor's collecting interests: There are miniature kerosene lamps, as well as full-sized ones, ancient clocks and radios, colorful sombreros, and so much bric-a-brac that you don't know where to look next. The topper, literally, is the G-scale L-G-B model railroad that runs overhead. Then there's Carl, quite a character himself, who's in his second or third "retirement."

The white wines, Chardonnay and Riesling, are soft and fruity, while the reds, Cabernet and Zinfandel, are properly big and bold. White Zin is made in the ready-to-go, quaffing style. Prices are reasonable, and if the wines are not enough reason to visit, the pastiche of collectibles are.

## RESTAURANTS

### Baily Wine Country Cafe

**27844 Ynez Rd., Temecula 92591 • 909-676-9567 • Lunch and dinner daily • Reservations recommended • California cuisine**
**Moderate**

The Baily family is an enterprising lot; they not only run their eponymous winery and have an interest in Temecula Crest Winery, but when they decided Temecula needed a restaurant to match the area's wines, they established their own restaurant. Set back off Rancho California Road, in the main shopping center off Interstate 15, the cafe rapidly became a destination for wine and food lovers. Light and airy with floor-to-ceiling glass walls, the restaurant features fresh, flavorful California cuisine. The wine selection befits the Bailys' regional chauvinism, with the widest selection of Temecula wines in the area (including their own, of course). Dinner entrees range from $10–$20.

## Cafe Champagne

**32575 Rancho California Rd., Temecula 92591**
**909-699-0088 • Lunch and dinner daily except Mon.;**
**Sun. brunch • Champagne happy hour with half-priced**
**appetizers and wines by the glass every Thurs. and Fri.**
**Reservations recommended • California cuisine • Expensive**

Cafe Champagne has the longest tenure and highest reputation among locals; the dining experience here is almost universally recommended. The seasonally changing menu features contemporary California cuisine paired with their wines. Dinner prices are $10–$23.

## Fish Exchange

**24910 Washington Ave., Murietta 92564 • 909-677-9449**
**Lunch and dinner daily • Reservations helpful • American**
**Moderate**

For the best fish in the area, make the short ten-minute drive from Temecula to nearby Murietta. Start with a glass of wine and munch on sourdough bread as you peruse the menu of the freshest seafood available. Mesquite grilling is the way to go here, with thick filets, like halibut and swordfish, but prime steaks also get the same treatment. Pastas available.

## Temecula Pizza Company

**Interstate 15 at Highway 79 south, Temecula 92591**
**909-694-9463 • Lunch and dinner daily except Mon. lunch**
**Pizza • Moderate**

All manner of California pizzas are offered here, from the hearty to the sublime, including some odd but tasty ones, like fresh pears with gorgonzola and pine nuts. All the salads feature the freshest ingredients. Choose to dine inside or on the wonderful patio. Moderate prices.

## Hungry Hunter

**27600 Jefferson Ave., Temecula 92590 • 909-694-1475**
**Lunch Mon.–Fri., dinner daily • Reservations helpful**
**American • Moderate**

As the name implies, a healthy appetite will be well satisfied at the Hungry Hunter. The wide and varied menu features steak and prime rib served without a lot of embellishment. Straight-ahead preparations and large portions are the rule here. No one goes away hungry.

### Tony Roma's

**27464 Jefferson Ave., Temecula 92590 • 909-676-7662**
**Lunch and dinner daily • Reservations helpful • American**
**Moderate**

The Temecula outpost of this nationwide chain conveniently sits right off Interstate 15 and Rancho California Road. Expect the usual ribs and chicken, along with the brick of onion rings. If you have a diverse group of eaters, this place can cover all the bases, though fans of real slow-smoked barbecue will be disappointed. But as a quick and easy fill-up, Tony Roma's is up to the task.

### Swing Inn

**Corner of Third and Main sts. (Old Town), Temecula**
**909-676-2321 • Breakfast, lunch, and dinner daily • American**
**Inexpensive**

Located in the historic Old Town district, this cafe with a view of Boot Hill serves up heaps of American-style food. Here's the best place in town for breakfast, but it dishes up a good lunch and dinner too. You could eat at any of those nameless, faceless coffee shops, or you could eat at a place with history and character where folks are friendly.

## ANNUAL EVENTS

### FEBRUARY

**Barrel Tasting • 909-699-3626**

On the first weekend in February, sample wines not yet bottled or released to the public directly from barrels and tanks. Enjoy food and talking with the winemaker at each winery.

### MAY

**Balloon and Wine Festival • 909-676-4713**

On the first weekend in May, watch the mass launching of gigantic hot-air balloons over the valley; enjoy the "glow" at twilight. Complimentary wine and food tasting, along with the cool sounds of live jazz.

## JUNE

### Taste of the Valley • 909-699-9177

One-day outdoor event, featuring many of the area's fine restaurants and wineries. Also art show and entertainment.

## JULY

### Toast to the Winemakers • 909-699-3626

This mid-July weekend celebration of winemaking honors the creativity of the area's winemakers and their contributions to winemaking.

## NOVEMBER

### Nouveau Wine and Food Tasting • 909-699-3626

On the third weekend in November, sample the newest wines from the just-completed harvest, and taste an eclectic assortment of food while visiting the wineries.

## RESOURCES

### Temecula Valley Chamber of Commerce

**27450 Ynez Rd., Ste. 104 • Temecula 92591 • 909-676-5090**
**In the Town Center Shopping Center • Open Mon.–Fri. 9–5**

Listings and information about all restaurants and accommodations. Guide to Old Town and wineries. Current calendar of events.

### Temecula Valley Vintners' Association

**P.O. Box 1601 • Temecula 92593 • 909-699-3626**

Winery touring map, wine festival information, and current calendar of events at each of the wineries.

# WINE VARIETALS

**Cabernet Sauvignon (Cabernet)**

Cabernet is the king of red wines in California. Wineries in the Napa Valley established Cabernet's reputation, though other regions have varying measures of success with it. While sometimes harsh and tannic in its youth, Cabernet has the ability to mature into a rich, full-bodied wine, much like the great reds of Bordeaux. Serve Cabernet with grilled or roasted meats, perhaps something as simple as a filet mignon from a live-oak fired grill or something more intense like oven-roasted breast of duck in cherry sauce.

**Merlot**

This variety was once relegated to blending in with other lots of red wine, like Cabernet. But in the last two decades, Merlot began to establish its own identity; then, in the last five years, its popularity soared off the sales charts. Wineries suddenly can't make enough Merlot. The wine has berry and herbal flavors, similar to Cabernet, but Merlot also has a smooth, supple character in the mouth without the accompanying astringency. The popularity of Merlot can be directly attributed to its easygoing flavors and its drinkability at a young age. It matches up with the same types of foods as Cabernet does, albeit less distinctly.

## Pinot Noir

This wine has the potential to be the most seductive, supple, user-friendly wine in existence. Unfortunately, in the past consumers have found Pinot Noir thin and watery. But the bad old days of Pinot Noir ended in the mid-1980s; in the last ten years, this wine has shown the greatest increase in quality of any varietal. Lighter than Cabernet, Pinot Noirs have a richness and intensity of fruitiness coupled with elements of dark spices unmatched by any other wine type. Good with meats, the wine can also pair up with chicken, rabbit, and salmon. The best areas for producing Pinot Noir are both the Napa and Sonoma sides of Carneros, Sonoma's Russian River Valley, Mendocino's Anderson Valley, and Santa Barbara County.

## Syrah

The great grape of France's Rhone Valley is successfully being rendered in California; in the last fifteen years, the production of Syrah has exploded as more people discover it. The trademarks of Syrah include its aromatic nose and spicy, smokey, berry-type flavors. It pairs with traditional meat dishes, but shines with lamb, duck, venison, and all manner of wild game. The Syrah grape tolerates a wide variety of climates and soils and grows in such diverse regions as Napa, Sonoma, the Sierra Foothills, the Central Coast, and Santa Barbara.

## Zinfandel

Zin, for short, has always been considered California's true grape, one that did not have its origins in Europe. It remains a mystery where the grape came from, though recent signs point to Italy or Yugoslavia. In any event, no other country makes Zinfandel. Peppery, briary, brawny, and chewy describe this often tannic but mouth-filling wine. It seems to have a real penchant for matching up with tomato-based sauces and other herb-infused meat and vegetable dishes. Vintners in Napa, Sonoma, the Sierra Foothills, and the Central Coast seem to do the best job with it.

## Other Reds

This section names the also-ran grapes, those grapes cultivated in certain regions that have not yet achieved mainstream status. They are not second class, however, when it comes to flavor. When handled well in the winery, they can taste delicious. Barbera, Sangiovese, and Nebbiolo are Italian grapes moving to the forefront, while Grenache and Mourvedre are the prominent Rhone grapes.

## WHITE WINE VARIETALS

### Chardonnay

This wine has become the 1990s euphemism for a glass of white wine. It's far and away the most popular varietal for a reason: It's cold, fruity, and easy to drink. The seductive use of barrel fermentation and aging adds another layer of toasty vanilla flavors on top of the mineral, citrus, and tropical fruit flavors. Chardonnay works perfectly well as an aperitif and can carry over to the dinner table with roasted chicken, grilled fish, and sauce or cheese influenced dishes. Every region feels an obligation to turn out a Chardonnay, but the best may hail from Sonoma, Napa's Carneros, Santa Barbara, and Monterey.

### Gewurztraminer

This aromatic-styled varietal is making a small comeback in California. *Gewurz* translates as "spice," and that's exactly what you smell when you pour it into a glass. Gewurztraminer flavors echo the fragrant and flowery nose, while providing additional oomph with the piquant, spicy flavors. This wine works well as an aperitif, and its residual sweetness makes it a good counterpoint to spicy Chinese or Thai dishes. The best examples grow in Mendocino, Sonoma, and Santa Barbara County.

### Riesling

Another of the aromatic varietals finding a home in California, Riesling offers a particularly refreshing alternative to the Chardonnay syndrome. Less flowery than Gewurztraminer, it also has less spice, instead relying on delicate aromas and subtle flavors for its power. With its slight sweetness, it pairs well with lighter dishes. Generally the cooler regions produce the better-quality examples.

### Sauvignon Blanc

Some people think of Sauvignon Blanc as a diminutive form of Chardonnay, which it is not, either by grape type or by taste. One of its most attractive qualities is it usually costs half as much as Chardonnay. Generally, the winery or vineyard neuters the grassy and herbaceous flavors, and it ends up tasting like generic white wine. However, more and more wineries choose to make Sauvignon Blanc with character, including barrel fermentation and oak aging. The best taste very different from Chardonnay.

Sauvignon Blanc does service at the table when paired with strong, forceful herbal flavors like goat cheese and radicchio salad or roasted garlic-rosemary chicken. Just about every region produces a passable Sauvignon Blanc, though the northern coastal region from Napa and Sonoma to Mendocino, particularly Lake County, seems to do the best job.

### Other Whites

A host of other white wine grapes grow throughout California. The interesting French varieties include Chenin Blanc, Pinot Blanc, and Pinot Gris. Also French but with a much different flavor profile are the new Rhone grapes, like Marsanne, Roussanne, and Viognier, all perfumed and flowery. Muscat Canelli often serves as a dessert wine, as do late-harvest versions of Riesling, Gewurztraminer, and Sauvignon Blanc.

# GLOSSARY OF TASTING TERMS

**ACIDITY:** A principal component of wine that shows up as tartness, giving wine freshness and snap.

**AROMA:** The smell the wine acquires from the grapes and the fermentation process.

**ASTRINGENCY:** The mouth-puckering quality found in many young wines.

**AUSTERE:** Indicates a one-dimensional wine, usually lacking roundness or fullness.

**BALANCED:** When all the elements of the wine contribute to a harmonious whole; no individual component of the wine stands out.

**BERRY:** Taste characteristic found in many red wines; may resemble the flavors of strawberry, blackberry, blueberry, or cherry.

**BODY:** The weight of the wine in the mouth; usually manifested by a richness, fullness, or viscosity.

**BOUQUET:** The smell the wine develops from the process of aging in the bottle.

**BUTTERY:** A descriptor usually applied to white wines; a feeling of richness and roundness that resembles the taste of butter.

**CHEWY:** Denotes a wine that has a richness with big body; usually applied to reds that seem to have several levels of flavor.

**CLARITY:** Refers to the appearance of a wine; a young wine should be clear not cloudy.

**COMPLEX:** A wine that displays many levels of flavor, from both winemaking technique and time spent aging in the barrel and bottle.

**DRY:** A wine with no apparent sweetness (residual sugar). In fermentation terms, the yeast totally consumes all the grape sugars and converts them into alcohol.

**EARTHY:** Positive characteristics of loamy topsoil, mushrooms, or truffles sometimes found in red wines, particularly Pinot Noir.

**FAT:** A big wine with big flavors, good fullness, and good length in the mouth, though it may lack finesse.

**FLORAL:** Flowery aromas and tastes, usually associated with white wines.

**FRUITY:** The taste of the grapes themselves, often manifested as other comparative flavors like apple, strawberries, or black currants.

**GRASSY:** An aroma and flavor often found in Sauvignon Blanc, akin to freshly mowed hay; negative if extreme.

**HARD:** A wine that does not have open or generous flavors; particularly applied to young, tannic red wines.

**HERBACEOUS:** Aromas and flavors displaying various types of herbs; negative when extreme.

**HOT:** A high level of alcohol in a wine that throws the other elements out of balance.

**INTENSE:** Powerful, rich, and concentrated in flavor.

**JAMMY:** In red wines, concentrated berrylike flavors, almost like jam.

**NOSE:** All the elements detected by the sense of smell, encompassing the aroma and bouquet.

**OAKY:** Toasty, woody vanillalike aromas and tastes in the wine as a result of barrel fermentation and/or aging.

**SMOKY:** A roasted or charred wood spice aroma arising from the use of toasted barrels for fermentation and/or aging.

**SPICY:** General terms for many spice flavors found in wine, such as pepper, cardamom, clove, and cinnamon.

**SUPPLE:** A wine with no hard edges; soft, smooth, and easy to drink.

**TANNIC:** A mouth-puckering astringency often found in young red wines.

**VEGETAL:** Unattractive component in wines, often resembling bell peppers, celery, cabbage, or asparagus.

# INDEX

Page numbers in bold type indicate main entries.